A

D. H. LAWRENCE

MISCELLANY

*

HARRY T. MOORE is a Professor of English at Southern Illinois University. In addition to his work on D. H. Lawrence, he is the author of a book on John Steinbeck, co-editor of a volume of selections from Lewis Mumford's writings, and a reviewer of twentieth-century literature for the *New York Times, Saturday Review* and other periodicals. His best known works on Lawrence include *The Life and Works of D. H. Lawrence* and *The Intelligent Heart: The Story of D. H. Lawrence.* He is now at work on a new edition of Lawrence's *Letters,* which will be published in 1960, and is also preparing an edition of Rainer Maria Rilke's letters.

A
D. H. LAWRENCE
MISCELLANY

EDITED BY *Harry T.* *Thornton* *Moore*

Southern Illinois University Press

CARBONDALE, 1959

© 1959, by Southern Illinois University Press
Library of Congress Catalog Card Number 59-11268
Printed in the United States of America by   4-19-60
the Vail-Ballou Press, Inc., Binghamton, N. Y.
Designed by Andor Braun

ACKNOWLEDGMENTS

IN ADDITION to the copyright notices accompanying some of the essays in this volume, special acknowledgment must be made to The Viking Press, Inc., to Alfred A. Knopf, Inc., and to William Heinemann, Ltd., for quotations throughout the volume from Lawrence's work. The Viking Press publishes the following Lawrence titles: *Aaron's Rod; Amores; Apocalypse; The Boy in the Bush; The Captain's Doll; Collected Poems; England, My England; Etruscan Places; Fantasia of the Unconscious; Kangaroo; Last Poems; The Letters of D. H. Lawrence; Look! We Have Come Through!; The Lost Girl; Love Among the Haystacks; The Lovely Lady; A Modern Lover; New Poems; Phoenix; The Prussian Officer; Psychoanalysis of the Unconscious; The Rainbow; Sea and Sardinia; Sons and Lovers; Studies in Classic American Literature; Touch and Go; Twilight in Italy; The Widowing of Mrs. Holroyd; Women in Love.* Alfred A. Knopf publishes: *Assorted Articles; David; The Man Who Died* (actually, *The Escaped Cock*); *Mornings in Mexico; The Plumed Serpent; Pornography and Obscenity; St. Mawr; The Woman Who Rode Away; The Virgin and the Gipsy.* In England, all these Lawrence titles are the property of William Heinemann, Ltd. The Viking Press, Inc., William Heinemann, Ltd., and the D. H. Lawrence Estate (represented by Laurence Pollinger, Ltd.) have permitted publication of the manuscript of the early version of "The Fox" (from the Viking volume, *The Captain's Doll,* and the Heinemann volume, *The Ladybird*). Alfred A. Knopf, Inc., William Heinemann, Ltd., and the D. H. Lawrence Estate have permitted publication of the music from Lawrence's play *David* in manuscript form; the firms of Knopf and Heinemann publish this play in the United States and the United Kingdom, respectively. Heinemann and, in the United States, Viking, are holders of publication rights in Lawrence's letters, and any letters quoted in this volume are quoted by permission of these publishers and the Lawrence Estate.

CONTENTS

LIST OF ILLUSTRATIONS

INTRODUCTION

D. H. Lawrence has been the most controversial figure in English literature in the twentieth century. But, since the end of the Second World War, there has emerged a growing concensus of opinion that he is the most significant writer of his time. Controversy continues about him; but in the main it is about which of the two conspicuous elements in him is the more important—the artist or the prophet. His significance itself is no longer in debate. Yet as poet and novelist he has no imitators; as prophet no successors. And that also is significant.

THESE meaningful sentences by the late John Middleton Murry, written early in 1956, about a year before his death, raise the curtain on this book, here and in the first essay in this collection.

There is one correction that might be made, however, since John Murry wrote his essay, in which he further said that Lawrence's poetry was "now the most neglected" aspect of his achievement. The *now* was 1956; by the time of our later *now,* Lawrence's poetry is being rediscovered, perhaps actually for the first time discovered, as the last four essays in this book show. Otherwise, Murry's article is a timely introduction to Lawrence by one who knew his writings almost from the first and changed his perspective on them several times before finally seeing what had helped to create a revival of interest in them in the 1950's: "Lawrence was alone in the depth of his prescience of the crisis of humanity which has developed since his death." In making these statements, Murry was not unaware of Lawrence's powers of expression, pointing out that "as a poet . . . he displays, at his best, a marvelous power of exploring the instant moment of emotion or perception; as a novelist he used this gift of sensational immediacy to make vivid 'a life-and-thought adventure' (as he called it) which is unique in our literature."

We need this stress on the power of Lawrence's expression, too often neglected by those who concentrate exclusively on his ideas or his personality. Murry himself needed to be reminded of this after he had written *Son of Woman* in 1931, a book which Aldous Huxley (in his Introduction to Lawrence's *Letters* in 1932) said was "about a Lawrence whom you would never suspect, from the curious essay in destructive hagiography, of being an artist." The title of *D. H. Lawrence: Novelist* (1955), by F. R. Leavis, suggests that, in this most exciting of critiques yet written of Lawrence, Mr. Leavis was dealing with him first of all as an artist, though he didn't neglect Lawrence's prophetic side. The biggest absurdity is the kind of book that abstracts Lawrence's ideas and tries to make him into an original philosopher, which he decidedly was not; his vision was deep and compelling, but his originality lay in the power of his utterance.

That Lawrence was a prophetic writer cannot be denied. As Stuart Sherman once said, "His novels do not leave you where they found you. They have designs upon you." But when, in Lawrence's work, the preacher runs away with the artist, the results are often lamentable, as in *The Plumed Serpent*. Despite occasionally magnificent passages in that book, its ideas about the need for a primitivistic revival of "leadership" are often preposterous—though for a different opinion, see Jascha Kessler's essay "Descent in Darkness" in this book. It is when the prophetic side of Lawrence is best realized in the expressional, as in *The Rainbow* and *Women in Love,* that his work is most successful. In *D. H. Lawrence: Prophet of the Midlands* (1951), Vivian de Sola Pinto finds that Lawrence was not the kind of prophet "who foretells what will happen in the future, though he may do that incidentally, but one who *tells forth* (the literal meaning of the Greek word) great living truths which come from the depths of his being." Professor Pinto believes that "the best parts of Lawrence's writings," both in poetry and prose, are in the great English tradition of Langland, More, Latimer, Bunyan, Blake, Ruskin, and Morris.

Mr. Leavis places Lawrence in another "great tradition," that of Jane Austen, George Eliot, Henry James, and Joseph Conrad, the only "novelists in English worth reading" for other than historical purposes. This judgment has been often challenged since it was first announced in 1948 (in *The Great Tradition*) but it has also been rather widely accepted, and it is in keeping with the general estimate of Lawrence held today.

LAWRENCE'S REPUTATION

When Lawrence was alive, his reputation as a writer was never very high. In the English novel it was the age of Galsworthy, whose fame has now collapsed; and the other huge names of the time have faded—Bennett and Wells. Lawrence's refusal to truckle to conventional ideas, and to the editors who purveyed them to the public, and above all his independence of the Bloomsbury Group and other cliques that dominated the politics of criticism—all this didn't help. Neither did his troubles with the police during the first world war, when he was suspected of being a spy (one of the nonsensical notions people acquire in times of panic), nor the suppression of his writings and the seizure of his paintings by what he called "the censor-morons."

Yet he made his living as a writer and, except for restrictions on his movements during that first war, he went where he pleased and met whom he pleased or displeased. There was an intelligent minority of readers that responded to Lawrence, that bought enough of his books to keep him alive, and a few people in the literary world had the courage to speak well of him. When he died in 1930, some of the obituaries were poisonous with hatred, but friends of Lawrence—such as Richard Aldington, Catherine Carswell, Murry, and Lady Ottoline Morrell—came staunchly to his defense. So did Rebecca West, who barely knew him; and E. M. Forster, in contradiction of the ungraceful statements by his fellow-Bloomsburies, called Lawrence "the greatest imaginative novelist of our generation," a remark of the kind which Arnold Bennett had once or twice made earlier.

In the next few years Lawrence's reputation as a writer sank beneath the weight of the reminiscences which so many of those who had known him now rushed into print. Even the friendlier books, such as Catherine Carswell's *The Savage Pilgrimage* (1932) and Dorothy Brett's *Lawrence and Brett* (1933), somehow helped to make him look foolish. Murry had published *Son of Woman* in 1931, a book summarized by Aldous Huxley in a sentence already quoted here. Perhaps the most damaging memoir was Mabel Dodge Luhan's *Lorenzo in Taos* (1932), which made readers wonder whether a man who would associate with the cast of characters of that book could write anything worth reading. By this time the Depression was on, and soon wars began to shake the earth; readers turned to writers dealing with what seemed to be more topical themes, missing the very point that Murry made so tellingly in the passage already quoted from his 1956 essay: "Lawrence was alone in the depth of his prescience of the crisis of humanity which has developed since his death."

After the second world war, there was a renascence of interest in Lawrence, in England and in various European and Asiatic countries; it was somewhat slower in coming to America. In 1953, *The Achievement of D. H. Lawrence,* edited by Frederick J. Hoffman and Harry T. Moore, collected some of the finest essays up to that time on Lawrence's writing, essays by Huxley, Sigrid Undset, Father William Tiverton (Martin Jarrett-Kerr), Edmund Wilson, William York Tindall, T. S. Eliot, Horace Gregory, and F. R. Leavis (along with James Thurber's extremely funny parody on the biographies), as well as perceptive new essays by Mark Schorer, Richard Ellmann, and others. Since then, numerous articles and books have marked the continuing interest in Lawrence.

LAWRENCE AND THE CRITICS

The Achievement of D. H. Lawrence contained a 42-page Introduction by the editors which surveyed Lawrence's critical reputation up to 1953. There is not room enough, here, to bring this to the present moment, though the principal books on Lawrence which have appeared since 1953 will be either mentioned or discussed.

In 1953, Eliot Fay's *Lorenzo in Search of the Sun* appeared, a mild biography with no new material. The Introduction to Harry T. Moore's edition of Lawrence's *Essays on Sex, Literature and Censorship* (1953) was a history of Lawrence's struggles against censorship; this volume was reprinted in England in 1955 with additional material, including some of the Lawrence paintings as color illustrations and an essay by H. F. Rubinstein on legal aspects of obscenity. This edition was published in Japan in 1956.

The preceding year, F. R. Leavis' *D. H. Lawrence: Novelist*

(1955) had appeared in both London and New York. This book boldly said that Lawrence was not only the greatest imaginative writer of the century, but also that he deserved to be ranked among the great novelists of the past. Mr. Leavis' book carried a vigorous attack against T. S. Eliot for not being sufficiently enthusiastic about Lawrence, but it took up most of its space in close readings of Lawrencean texts. Mr. Leavis usually dealt with only certain phases of the stories he was examining, but he examined these phases deeply, in a way which has made his book the most controversial critical study of Lawrence.

That same year a book by a younger man, Mark Spilka, *The Love Ethic of D. H. Lawrence* (1955), made a contribution of a different kind in its attempt to trace a theme through Lawrence's major novels. Mr. Spilka tended to oversimplify here and there, but brought some important insights to the subject. A book published only in England, Leone Vivante's *A Philosophy of Potentiality* (1955), contains a long and important chapter, "Reflections on Lawrence's Insight Into the Concept of Potentiality"—the most significant of all essays on the "philosophic" aspects of Lawrence's vision.

In 1955, the fullest Lawrence biography to date appeared: Harry T. Moore's *The Intelligent Heart* (copyright 1954, but published in 1955). This was followed in 1956 by Moore's *Post Restante: A Lawrence Travel Calendar,* whose Introduction by Mark Schorer, "Lawrence and the Spirit of Place," is reprinted in the present volume. Graham Hough's *The Dark Sun* (1956) was a critical study of greater thoroughness than Leavis', but far less exciting; Mr. Hough's finest chapter, "The Doctrine," was a notable attempt to sum up Lawrence's thought in terms of his work. Mr. Hough's book was a milestone in that it was in many ways a summary of all previous criticism of Lawrence.

The first volume of Edward Nehls's *D. H. Lawrence: A Composite Biography* (1957) was a book that could only be called monumental (and it was frequently called just that). It assembled many documents—bits of memoir, autobiographical statements by Lawrence, and some of his letters (a number of them published for the first time)—and brought Lawrence's life up to 1919. The succeeding volumes (1958 and 1959) dealt respectively with the years 1919–25 and 1925–30, again reflecting Lawrence's life from many angles. The final volume may be a bit overstuffed with unnecessary material, but altogether the three books represent one of the great accomplishments of our time in biography, not only for the expertness and accuracy of the editing of such a massive amount of material, but above all for the way form is achieved out of its fullness.

Comparative studies showing Lawrence in relation to other writers have for years appeared as separate articles: Lawrence and Sherwood Anderson, Lawrence and Nietzsche, and so on— and at last this kind of treatment began to appear in books. John Middleton Murry's *Love, Freedom and Society* (1957) was essentially a comparison between Lawrence and Albert Schweitzer; Sir Richard Rees's *Brave Men* juxtaposed Lawrence and Simone Weil. J. M. Murry's posthumous volume, something of an irritant to the Schweitzerites, expresses respect for both men, but suggests that in the collapse of Christian civilization each of them failed—Lawrence by putting his faith in "blood" thinking, Schweitzer by putting his in rationalism—and did not find the true way which, Murry believed, was through Murry's concept of love. Rees's book, whose title comes from Lawrence's assertion that we need more brave men, reconciles those apparently opposite figures, Lawrence and Simone Weil, in a reverence for life such as no one else in our time has known.

The Lawrence number of *Modern Fiction Studies* (Spring 1959) has the force of a book; it is a collection of generally excellent critical essays, of which Kingsley Widmer's "Lawrence and the Fall of Modern Woman" is by far the best. The editor of this journal, Maurice Beebe, collaborated with Anthony Tommasi to compile an extremely useful checklist of Lawrence criticism.

As the present volume goes to press, F. Warren Roberts of the University of Texas is completing his long-awaited bibliography of Lawrence, and Harry T. Moore is preparing a comprehensive edition of Lawrence's *Letters,* to be published in 1960. In May 1959, Grove Press, New York, published the first American edition, unbowdlerized, of *Lady Chatterley's Lover,* with an Introduction by Mark Schorer. At this writing (summer 1959), the novel is near the top of the best-seller lists. It has been helped to that position by the Postmaster General's refusal to let the book go through the mails; this ban was upset by Judge Bryan's enlightened opinion, a decision which is being protested by the Postmaster General. Ultimately the matter may go to the

Supreme Court. Fortunately, Mark Schorer's Introduction contains an explanation, at once sensible and brilliant, of what Lawrence was trying to do. Lawrence's own explanations are available in his essays "Pornography and Obscenity" and "À Propos of *Lady Chatterley's Lover*," which appear in *Sex, Literature and Censorship* (reprinted, 1959). As to the future of *Lady Chatterley's Lover,* this cannot be foretold now; so this discussion cannot end on a note of finality, but then Lawrence is always dynamic and never "set."

THE PRESENT COLLECTION

The idea for this Lawrence *Miscellany* was suggested by Mr. Vernon Sternberg, Director of the Southern Illinois University Press, soon after he had accepted for publication *A James Joyce Miscellany: Second Series.*

These books are, as their names indicate, miscellanies—a combination of critical, scholarly, and biographical items. The Joyce collection consists entirely of previously unpublished articles; in the case of the Lawrence volume, the editor has made every effort to have as much new material as possible. In several instances he requested reprint rights of published essays, none earlier than Murry's 1956 article; but most of the items have not been published before. They were either commissioned or sent in as a result of notices in the (London) *Times Literary Supplement* and the *New York Times Book Review,* in which contributions were invited. Some published essays, such as Eliseo Vivas' 45-page study of *Women in Love* (*Sewanee Review,* Fall 1958), were too long even to be considered for the present collection. Several critics who were asked to write essays for this book unfortunately could not prepare them within the time limit. The editor regrets that Alfred Kazin's "Lady Chatterley in America" (*Atlantic,* July 1959) appeared too late to be included in the present collection.

Before we look at the essays that appear in this volume, let us consider some of the illustrations (saving until later a discussion of the manuscript reproduction of "The Fox"). The four pages of music, scored in Lawrence's hand, were written to accompany his play *David.* This music is particularly interesting because of Lawrence's lifelong fascination with hymns and because we here find Lawrence writing tunes for Psalms and for other passages of his play, largely adapted from the Bible. The music, too, is derivative: Lawrence had no pretensions as a composer. In a holograph manuscript of the play, Lawrence noted, in connection with the music for Scene XI, "tune the church-bell tune of the Indians"; and in an unpublished letter to S. S. Koteliansky (October 17, 1926), Lawrence wondered if in the music he would "recognize the prophets singing Ranané Sadíkim," a reference to a Hebrew chant of Koteliansky's after which Lawrence named the Utopian colony he wanted to establish, Rananim. The letter accompanying the music is addressed to the former Old Vic director, Robert Atkins, producer of *David* for the Stage Society in London in 1926.

The illustrative feature "The Road to Villa Mirenda" is based on a map Lawrence made showing a friend how to get to his Italian residence (1926–28) from Vingone, at the end of the tramcar line from Florence. The inset photographs were taken by the editor of the present volume in 1957.

Two of the essays in this book go back to 1956. John Middleton Murry's "D. H. Lawrence: Creative Iconoclast," which had appeared only in the (London) *Times Educational Supplement,* seemed to be designed for the introductory essay to such a volume as this. Mark Schorer, busy with his study of Sinclair Lewis and unable to prepare a new critique on some phase of Lawrence, suggested his favorite among all his writings on the subject so far, his Introduction to *Poste Restante* (1956). One section of the present book dates from late 1957—Karl Shapiro's dialogue, "The Unemployed Magician," which appeared in *Poetry* at the very end of that year (the December issue). Everything else is from 1958 and 1959, representing the latest material available on Lawrence.

Regrettably, Leone Vivante's chapter from *A Philosophy of Potentiality* goes back to 1955, and is in any event too long for the present volume; besides, it needs, for fullest understanding, the two preceding parts of Signor Vivante's book, which should be read by everyone considering Lawrence deeply. It explores Lawrence's experience-as-knowledge theories, his sense of the "quick," and his opposition of "creative spontaneity" to "mechanical-material activity," as no other book has done.

Back to the present volume: Wright Morris' "Lawrence and

the Immediate Present" helps to place Lawrence. Taken from Mr. Morris' book on American literature, *The Territory Ahead,* this chapter shows Lawrence in relation to other leading authors of his time, such as Joyce and Eliot, and it further indicates how highly American writers such as Mr. Morris esteem Lawrence when they look over both the American literary situation and the state of writing in today's world. Kingsley Widmer's previously unpublished essay sets Lawrence inside still another tradition, the demonic. Mr. Widmer is a new commentator on Lawrence. His essays which have recently appeared in various journals are noted here because readers may wish to consult them (they would all have been reprinted here if space had permitted): "Birds of Passion and Birds of Marriage in D. H. Lawrence" (*University of Kansas City Review,* Autumn 1958); "D. H. Lawrence and the Art of Nihilism" (*Kenyon Review,* Autumn 1959); "The Primitive Aesthetic: D. H. Lawrence" (*Journal of Aesthetics and Art Criticism,* Spring 1959); "Lawrence and the Fall of Modern Woman" (*Modern Fiction Studies,* Spring 1959).

The manuscript of the early version of Lawrence's "The Fox" is reproduced in this book, along with a transcription, through the kindness of the owner of the manuscript, Mr. George Lazarus. This represents the story as it stood when it was first written, apparently in December, 1919, when Lawrence was living above the snowfields at Mountain Cottage, Middleton-by-Wirkswirth, Derbyshire. The setting invokes the atmosphere of Hermitage, Berkshire, where Lawrence and his wife had stayed intermittently during the preceding two years. In 1921 Lawrence noted in his diary, "16 Nov: Finish Fox." In a letter of the same day, he told Earl Brewster that he had "put a long tail to 'The Fox,' which was a bobbed short story." On December 7 he sent the revised manuscript, among others, to his agent, Curtis Brown, pointing out that "the first part of 'The Fox' was published in *Nash's Magazine.*"

For many reasons, the manuscript facsimiled here is of great interest. It shows Lawrence's own corrections and, when compared with the final version of the story as first printed in the volume called *The Ladybird* in England and *The Captain's Doll* in the United States, it further shows how Lawrence developed his original idea and his first statement of it.

Note that he changed little in the opening sections; but as the story developed, and the relationships became more complicated, Lawrence deepened the psychological situation and made it more intricate. In the earlier draft, the marriage is accomplished rather suddenly and easily; in the later published version, the wedding takes place after tense oppositions and difficulties, and it virtually needs a murder to make it possible. Even then, the situation is not altogether resolved, for again Lawrence gives the story one of his effectively indefinite endings, with a human relationship held in suspension.

The psychological aspects of "The Fox" are commented upon here by a professional, Edmund Bergler, M.D., who shows the relation of the story to the psychoanalytical theory on Lesbianism. (Dr. Bergler's study is of course based on the final, published version of "The Fox.")

This discussion is followed by a critical consideration of what is generally believed to be Lawrence's finest work, his related novels *The Rainbow* and *Women in Love.* The first is treated by Marvin Mudrick in terms of its originality and its setting in the history of the English novel; in the course of the discussion, the author provides one of the finest explications of *The Rainbow,* fit to stand beside F. R. Leavis'. Likewise, Angelo Bertocci, in discussing *Women in Love* as a *symboliste* novel, gives us one of the best commentaries on that book, one worthy of place in the tradition of the essays by Martin Jarrett-Kerr, F. R. Leavis, and Mark Schorer.

When we turn to the biographical aspect of Lawrence, we find this has been treated with such thoroughness in Edward Nehls's *Composite Biography* that it might not seem possible for anything new to be found on the subject of Lawrence's life; yet memoirs, commentaries, and related matters are still turning up. And a *Miscellany* must take such material into account.

One of Lawrence's most significant autobiographical sketches is "Hymns in a Man's Life," discussed here with an examination of an earlier draft of the essay as published in *Assorted Articles* (and in *The Later D. H. Lawrence*). Vivian de Sola Pinto, head of the English Department at Lawrence's own university (Nottingham), describes and comments upon the manuscript, now the property of that university.

Stressing the biographical as an approach to the thematic,

Diana Trilling's letter to Norman Podhoretz places Lawrence between the somewhat older generation of readers who have known his work for some years, with varying responses to it, and a younger generation, as represented by Mr. Podhoretz, a critic who was born in 1930, the year of Lawrence's death. Mrs. Trilling's letter is part of her Introduction (as originally published in *Partisan Review*) to *The Selected Letters of D. H. Lawrence*. The informality of the letter form permits Mrs. Trilling to make a good many statements which could not have been made with such ease in a formal essay and to present her insights with a particular forcefulness.

The next item is a vivid letter from Katherine Mansfield, of which only a snippet has been published before. Its view of Lawrence and his wife Frieda in 1916 is hardly a flattering one, yet the quarrel described here was made public, in detail, as long ago as 1936, in the "Higher Tregerthen" chapter (XXVII) of John Middleton Murry's autobiography, *Between Two Worlds*. What Katherine Mansfield wrote to S. S. Koteliansky in this letter corroborates Murry's account, probably based on a passage in his journal. Murry's later reflection, in *Between Two Worlds*, was, "I have lived to learn that there is a truly fearful power of exasperation in a woman, and even to understand that the consequent explosion in a man of a frenzy which seems, and may actually be, murderous, is an elemental happening, really quite outside the scope of a moral judgment, or any judgment at all." Frieda said, after Lawrence's death, that living with a man of genius was more than compensation for all such quarrels. This particular one came at perhaps the lowest ebb of the Lawrences' fortunes, the Cornwall period, when they were suspected of being German spies—a time when Lawrence, because of the suppression of *The Rainbow*, found it almost impossible to publish anything. But whatever the background, Katherine Mansfield's letter is an important document, not only in the Lawrence history but also in her own, as an important self-revelation.

Some gentler memoirs follow, by Derek and Brigit Patmore and by Elizabeth Mayer. In London in 1958, the editor of the present volume read parts of Mr. Patmore's forthcoming autobiography and asked for use of the passages about Lawrence; also, upon learning that Mr. Patmore's mother had written an essay on Frieda not included in her fine reminiscence of Lawrence (printed in the *London Magazine* and subsequently in Nehls's *Composite Biography*), he asked for that, too; as far as his recollection goes, this is the first memoir devoted entirely to Lawrence's wife. In New York City, shortly after leaving London, the editor discovered that Elizabeth Mayer, well known for her translations, had met Lawrence toward the end of his life, and Mrs. Mayer (who had found him bright and genial, as so many people did) was thereupon requested to write the memoir which appears in this book.

Martin Green's reflections on the Nehls volumes are not directly biographical, yet they concern—often piquantly—Lawrence's life as seen by the people Mr. Nehls incorporated into his *Composite* series. Likewise, Richard Aldington's Introduction to the third volume of that series is a commentary on Lawrence's life as well as on Mr. Nehls's books; and Mr. Aldington, who knew Lawrence well across the years, makes some important observations about him as well as placing him in perspective in the grand literary tradition. James L. Jarrett's essay on Lawrence and Bertrand Russell is primarily a study of the ideas of the two men, but it also deals with their personalities. Yet, because it is essentially concerned with what the two men wrote, it takes us back out of the realm of biography.

Six of the seven studies which follow are by younger writers. Working with them, meeting some of them personally, has been one of the editor's great pleasures in putting this book together. For the most part, these six essays are representative of current work on Lawrence being done in graduate schools or by young teachers; one of these contributions was written by an undergraduate.

Robert E. Gajdusek's "A Reading of *The White Peacock*" is the fullest study yet made of Lawrence's first novel. Both this and the following essay, "D. H. Lawrence's Singing Birds," by Patricia Abel and Robert Hogan, represent the kind of scholarly research that will be increasingly applied to Lawrence. The essay on his story "The Blind Man" was written by Nancy Abolin while she was a Wellesley undergraduate in 1959, and S. Ronald Weiner's study of "Irony and Symbolism in 'The Princess' " was written while the author was teaching and doing graduate work at Harvard. Jascha Kessler's investigation of *The Plumed Serpent* leads us to a deeper understanding of that book. The editor's

review of the new edition of *Lady Chatterley's Lover,* written at
the time the present volume was going to press, comes next.
Frederick R. Karl's view of "The Man Who Loved Islands" (as
"The Crusoe Who Failed") shows a somewhat neglected story
of Lawrence's in a fresh light.

We now go from islands to Lawrence's sense of "place": Mark
Schorer's essay on "Lawrence and the Spirit of Place" has already
been mentioned as his own favorite among the essays he has
written on Lawrence; and since Mark Schorer is one of the
finest of all writers on various aspects of that author, his essay
is particularly welcome here. So is that of Raymond Williams,
whose comparison of Lawrence and Carlyle may flutter some of
the Lawrenceans—it is, however, an inevitable comparison, and
in many other ways this essay opens entirely new vistas of Lawrence study. In the next piece, "Criticism as Rage," Richard
Foster emphasizes the moral element that is so emphatically
present in Lawrence's critical judgments.

We conclude with five essays that consider a side of Lawrence too often neglected (except in such excellent studies as
Horace Gregory's *Pilgrim of the Apocalypse,* 1933): Lawrence
the poet. Herbert Lindenberger puts the novels in the Romantic
tradition; A. Alvarez, finding Lawrence "the foremost emotional
realist of this century," boldly says that the originality of his
poetry makes it as important as any of our time—and shows
why; Harold Bloom defends Lawrence against R. P. Blackmur
and T. S. Eliot and goes on to make some important positive
statements about him, while Christopher Hassall gives us a fresh
view of Lawrence's poetics and some new perceptions of the
origins of Lawrence's poems. Karl Shapiro's dialogue is not concerned exclusively with Lawrence but, as the reader will see, it
places Lawrence in the center of modern poetry—and this seems
an excellent piece with which to end the book.

WORDS OF THANKS

Some special acknowledgments should be made here, in addition to the formal acknowledgments and the copyright notices
that appear at the bottom of the first page of several of the
essays. Mr. Laurence Pollinger, of Laurence Pollinger, Ltd.,
London, representing the D. H. Lawrence Estate, deserves spe-

cial thanks for co-operation in many matters which made the publication of this book possible.

Personal acknowledgments are also due to all who sent in manuscripts, whether or not these were accepted—with special thanks to these writers for their patience and good humor. Among publishers, Mr. Marshall Best and Miss Marjorie Griesser of The Viking Press, Inc., and Mr. William A. Koshland of Alfred A. Knopf, Inc., have been particularly helpful. Gratitude must also be expressed for the kind and expert assistance of Mr. Alan Cohn, Humanities Librarian of Southern Illinois University, to his assistant, Mr. Earl Tannenbaum, and to another librarian, Mr. Marcus A. McCorison, Chief, Rare Books Department, Baker Library, Dartmouth College, owner of the *David* music and the letter accompanying it. Not least, the editor's thanks also go out to Messrs. George A. Lazarus and Bertram Rota. Mr. Lazarus, an English collector of distinction, kindly permitted use of his manuscript of the early version of "The Fox"; Mr. Rota, that rarest of rare-book dealers, went to special trouble to have the manuscript reproduced for its appearance here. The wife of the present editor once again deserves full thanks for practical help and patient understanding.

So, as this book goes to press, thanks to them all. If the volume justifies itself, there will be further editions of *A D. H. Lawrence Miscellany*.

August 16, 1959   Harry T. Moore
Boulder, Colorado

A

D . H . LAWRENCE
MISCELLANY

John Middleton Murry

D. H. LAWRENCE: CREATIVE ICONOCLAST

D. H. LAWRENCE has been the most controversial figure
in English literature in the twentieth century. But, since the end
of the Second World War, there has emerged a growing consensus
of opinion that he is the most significant writer of his time. Controversy continues about him; but it is in the main about which
of the two conspicuous elements in him is the more important—
the artist or the prophet. His significance itself is no longer in
debate. Yet as poet and novelist he has no imitators; as prophet
no successors. And that also is significant. Perhaps the best
brief explanation of the latter fact is in the words of a recent
reviewer in *The Times Literary Supplement:*

> Lawrence, in his life and works, touched the deepest misgiv-
> ings of mankind. He was the most formidable and searching
> critic of materialistic civilization [to which all willy-nilly are
> committed] that is likely to be encountered on the way to
> universal Cockaigne or universal oblivion.

The operative words are those in brackets. Lawrence's despair
over the future of the machine society grew steadily and was at
the last unmitigated. Rightly or wrongly he saw it as doomed,
through its suppression of the natural urges of man. But we

John Middleton Murry (1889–1957) was a leading English critic and
editor whose stormy friendship with Lawrence is reflected in the
critical biography *Son of Woman* (1931); Murry was author of many
other books, including *The Problem of Style* (1921), *Keats and Shakespeare* (1925), *Studies in Keats* (1930), *William Blake* (1933), *Jonathan
Swift* (1954), and *Love, Freedom and Society* (1957). His present essay
was published previously in the (London) *Times Educational Supplement* of June 15, 1956, and is reprinted here by permission of the *Times*
editors.

3

cannot come out of it, as he demanded. It is a destiny which we must undergo.

For a different reason Lawrence's art is inimitable. As a poet —his poetry is now the most neglected of his achievement—he displays, at his best, a marvelous power of exploring the instant moment of emotion or perception; as a novelist, he used this gift of sensational immediacy to make vivid "a life-and-thought adventure" (as he called it) which is unique in our literature. While working on *The Rainbow,* in April, 1914, he wrote to Edward Garnett: "Primarily, I am a passionately religious man, and my novels must be written from the depths of my religious experience." He said that at the moment when he had become fully conscious of his powers and his purpose. And it is the essential truth about him. Therefore his works have been called a continuous spiritual autobiography. More exactly, they are the record, in an imaginative drama, of an unremitting exploration of life by a man with not only a genius for vivid utterance but a rare power of penetrating behind the conventions of thought and stereotypes of experience. This iconoclasm, which outraged many, was in origin entirely natural to him. An element of deliberate provocation did enter into his later work; but that was only after he had suffered the bitter experience of having the first serious work of his maturity publicly condemned.

The figure whom he chiefly calls to my mind is Rousseau, but whereas Rousseau opened an epoch, Lawrence seems to have closed one; as it were a Rousseau with two centuries of Rousseauism to fight his way out of. Others have compared him to Rozanov, the Russian, who combined a veneration of the sexual mystery with a return to the Orthodox Church, and who, for his magic of style, has been pronounced the greatest of Russian prose-writers. Unfortunately, only two books of Rozanov have been translated; Lawrence reviewed them both, and recognized the affinity.

> Rozanov [he wrote] is modern, terribly modern. And if he does not put the fear of God into us, he puts a real fear of destiny, or of doom; and of "civilization" which does not come from within, but which is poured over the mind by "education."

Education, here, does not primarily mean, though it includes, what is done in schools and colleges. Concerning that, Lawrence was what is called a reactionary. He held that most children should not be exposed even to the rudiments of it. But chiefly the false education which had produced a false civilization was for him that of prevalent social and religious ideals which he ascribed to Christian influence. Those he particularly incriminated were the political ideal of equality, and the ideal in personal relations of spiritual love. He often lumped them together as "the love ideal," which he held to be based on a fatal abstraction from the reality of man. It had infected the instinctive and emotional being with the "faked love" which, he said, "has rotted our marrow"; and, above all, it had vitiated the primary sexual relation, which had ceased to be truly religious. This it could only be when it was based equally in a reverence for the profound otherness of man and woman and for the mystery of their sexual union. As for society, the only mode of organization that was in accord with human reality was theocratic; the few who possessed true life-wisdom must take responsibility for the many who were incapable of it. And one of their tasks would be if not entirely to abolish, at least drastically to control, the machine.

Such a literal summary of Lawrence's chief doctrines is, inevitably, a caricature. For not only did he present them with a wonderful richness of concrete embodiment; but he held them with only half his being. Though he did not go to the Russian extreme of Rozanov, Lawrence's violent repudiation of Christian influence was itself repudiated by the manifest impossibility of eradicating it from himself. What he was struggling to achieve —at the cost of long inward conflict—was a rebirth of the religious consciousness in which the lost insights of Paganism and the true insights of Christianity should be reconciled. This was necessary because he was deeply convinced that the civilization of industrialism and materialism and democracy had become fundamentally irreligious and unnatural, therefore productive, in the suppressed and maddened psyche, of terrible outbursts of massive self-destruction. This conviction was planted in him by his experience of the First World War, which produced in him a spiritual convulsion from which, some have said, he never recovered. But, in fact, it is Lawrence's supreme justification that he could not recover from it, for it was to him the unmistakable warning of the dissolution of Christian civilization. This reaction was complicated by the simultaneous condemnation of

The Rainbow, which he felt to be a rejection of his innermost truth. It envenomed the deep psychical wound he received from the war.

Thenceforward, his novels became autobiographical in a unique sense. A figure, recognizably himself, was the protagonist in them. They are not mere chronicles of his experiences; but a peculiar blend of fact and imaginative dialectic, whereby he projected himself into situations which revealed to him what was annihilable (to use Blake's phrase) in the essential being of himself. From all the inevitable inward contradictions with which he struggled there emerges a vivid and unforgettable figure, isolated, pathetic, heroic, and prophetic. For Lawrence was alone in the depth of his prescience of the crisis of humanity which has developed since his death. He had this in common with the general conviction of these post-Christian times; that he believed man must find his fulfillment in this life or not at all; but in him this belief was transformed by an incessant awareness of the immensities before birth and after death, and of the mystery that surrounds the life between.

Wright Morris

LAWRENCE AND THE IMMEDIATE PRESENT

LITERATURE, as distinct from life, finds it easier to come to terms with such a puzzle as *Finnegans Wake* than with the fact that the author exchanged so much of his life to accomplish it. Joyce took this risk with his eyes open, and accepted the consequences. But we are men as well as artists, and if art is to remain a permissible illusion there must continue to be room in it for life, the very life that is so conspicuously absent from *Finnegans Wake*. Those faded ghosts of Villiers de L'Isle-Adam who let their servants do their living for them are not the answer, on the evidence, to either life or art.

The dilemma is an old one: the relationship between literature and life. In American terms the problem has been academic— life has usually overwhelmed literature, and the artist, haunted by a sense of failure, has been partially consoled by his grip on life. Men seem to be driven into one or the other extremity. On the one hand we have the master craftsman Joyce armed with nothing but silence, exile, and cunning. On the other we have such a figure as D. H. Lawrence, a man of genius, a novelist, and a poet, whose primary concern was not art, but *life,* a man who believed, with a devotion and example equal to that of Joyce, that if life itself could be led to the full, art would grow out of it. The purpose of art was to make such life possible. To give

Wright Morris, American novelist, who has three times been a Guggenheim Fellow, attended Pomona College. He has lectured at Sarah Lawrence, Swarthmore, Haverford, and the University of Utah. His books include *The Deep Sleep* (1953), *Love Among the Cannibals* (1957), and *The Field of Vision*, which won the National Book Award for 1956. His essay is from *The Territory Ahead*, copyrighted, 1957, 1958, by Wright Morris, and is reprinted by permission of Harcourt, Brace and Company, Inc.

up living *for art* would have struck him as a form of madness: one of those tragic delusions, fostered by cant and sophistication, which led men to choose the death in life rather than the life in it. To free men from this deception, to give them life rather than art, made him a poet and a novelist. The gods of Joyce would have struck him as both strange and false.

With characteristic perception, T. S. Eliot was the first to recognize this polarity. In *After Strange Gods* he summed it up in this fashion:

> We are not concerned with the author's *beliefs,* but with the orthodoxy of sensibility and with the sense of tradition, our degree of approaching "that region where dwell the vast hosts of the dead." And Lawrence is for my purposes an almost perfect example of the heretic. And the most ethically orthodox of the more eminent writers of my time is Mr. Joyce.

This statement exhibits Mr. Eliot's talent for coining the rules, as well as the terms, of the game that he chooses to play. That we are *not* concerned with the author's *beliefs,* but only with the orthodoxy of his sensibility, is an observation, to speak charitably, that throws light only on the man who made it. But the distinction he draws, if not the terms, is central to our discussion. Some writers appear to be orthodox, others heretics. Mr. Eliot's purpose, however, is not merely to throw light on this schism, but by this light to read the heretic out of the church. Lawrence is not merely unorthodox, he is dangerous.

In an essay published more than thirty years ago, entitled "The Shame of the Person," Laura Riding lucidly anticipated Mr. Eliot's position, and the new criticism:

> There results what has come to be called criticism. . . . In the end the literary sense comes to be an authority to write which the poet is supposed to receive, through criticism, from the age that he lives in. . . . More and more the poet has been made to conform to literature instead of literature to the poet—literature being the name given by criticism to works inspired or obedient to criticism. Less and less is the poet permitted to rely on personal authority. The very word genius, formerly used to denote the power to intensify a sense of life into a sense of literature, has been boycotted by criticism; not so much because it has become gross and meaning-

less through sentimentality as because professional literature develops a shame of the person, a snobbism against the personal self-reliance which is the nature of genius.

We can see, in Mr. Eliot's attack on Lawrence, how profoundly she grasped the critical trend, whose tone was established, naturally, by Mr. Eliot. In "Tradition and the Individual Talent," the latitude that exists in theory is singularly circumscribed in practice—by talent Mr. Eliot does not mean *genius,* if genius does *not* choose to knuckle under. Mr. Eliot allows that Lawrence had *genius,* but since his talent was unorthodox, his genius was little more than a critical embarrassment. The shame of Lawrence's *person*—the very substance of his genius—could hardly be better expressed. Lawrence also suffered, Mr. Eliot informs us, from "a lack not so much of information as of the critical faculties which education should give, and an incapacity for what we ordinarily call thinking."

At another time, and in another place, this statement might have served Mr. Eliot as a definition of genius. But Lawrence *suffers* from it. An incapacity for what is ordinarily called thinking did not destroy him, but made him *suspect.* Mr. Eliot's talent for the destructive comment—I mean the lethal, irrelevant comment—is here displayed at its most masterly. It is the donnish form of "A Genius, but—" of Richard Aldington. At the thought of Lawrence a kind of panic seems to rock Mr. Eliot's mind. What begins as criticism slips imperceptibly into abuse:

The point is that Lawrence started life wholly free from any restriction of tradition or institution, that he had no guidance except the Inner Light, the most untrustworthy and deceitful guide that ever offered itself to wandering humanity. It was peculiarly so of Lawrence, who does not appear to have been gifted with the faculty of self-criticism, except in flashes, even to the extent of worldly shrewdness.

If we look for the source of what is unreasonable in Mr. Eliot's treatment of Lawrence, we shall find it in a review of *Ulysses,* written at the time of its publication:

In using the myth, in manipulating a continuous parallel between contemporaneity and antiquity, Mr. Joyce is pursuing a method which others must pursue after him. . . . It is simply a way of controlling, of ordering, of giving a shape and a significance to the immense panorama of futility and anarchy which is contemporary history. . . . It is, I seriously believe, a step toward making the modern world possible in art.

This is both analysis and prophecy, since Mr. Eliot, as a poet, has continued to give a shape to the immense panorama of futility by manipulating parallels. Both Joyce and Eliot are masters of the collage. The works of both men sometimes contain more of the past than they do of the present—a relevant fact, since it is *in* the past that both men have lived.

But to make the modern world possible in art is not the same, as Lawrence would have insisted, as making life possible in the modern world. The myths that Mr. Eliot is at such pains to parallel are, almost without exception, not acceptable to Lawrence. They were, indeed, the very things that made living his life all but impossible. He chose, both as an artist and as a man, not to manipulate myths but life itself. It is this that stigmatizes him as a dangerous heretic. He was, in fact, anarchy compounded, which may explain, if not justify, the element of panic in Mr. Eliot's attack that leads him into such unwarranted abuse. Lawrence is the pagan bull run amok in the critics' orderly arrangement of myths.

There is no need to let Lawrence speak for himself, since Mr. Eliot's attack has the merit of doing that for him. It is Lawrence's *defects,* indeed, that make him important to us. In this world— the one in which we must live—the strange gods of D. H. Lawrence appear to be less strange than those of Mr. Eliot. It is why—as the critic describes them—these defects have the ring of familiar virtues. Lawrence speaks as a *man,* that is, a living man, a fearless and independent man, who attempted to live very much as he wrote. His independence, his stubborn self-reliance, his passionate distaste for cant and humbug are not merely in the vein but in the very grain of the American mind. It is this grain that shows in the mind and prose of Thoreau:

Be it life or death, we crave only reality. If we are really dying, let us hear the rattle in our throat and feel the cold in the extremities; if we are alive, let us go about our business.

This might have served as an epitaph for Lawrence. It brings us face to face with the paradox that it is Lawrence, the Englishman in exile, who speaks for the brave new world, and Eliot, the American in exile, who speaks for the old. It has been the purpose of this inquiry to explain this paradox, not merely how it came to pass, but that it was inevitable. In the poet from St. Louis we have the classic example, carried to its ultimate conclusion, of the American artist's tendency to withdraw into the past, to withdraw, that is, from America. His knowledge of the past being what it is, Mr. Eliot has been able to withdraw into it deeper than any of his forerunners or contemporaries. Insofar as such a past is useful to us, he speaks for it.

Lawrence speaks—whenever he speaks—with a different voice:

> For man, the vast marvel is to be alive. For man, as for flower and beast and bird, the supreme triumph is to be most vividly alive. Whatever the unborn and the dead may know, they cannot know the beauty, the marvel of being alive in the flesh. The dead may look after the afterwards. But the magnificent here and now of life in the flesh is ours, and ours alone, and ours only for a time.

That is a voice in the present. It is the speech of a man alive. It is this voice that recommends his wayward genius to us. It is this man of whom we can say—as Picasso said of Matisse— that he has a sun in his belly. The sun in the belly of Mr. Eliot is a mythic sun. It is a clinker to manipulate: the fire has gone out of it. The man alive in the present is that patient etherized on the table, awaiting burial.

In a statement on the importance of the novel, Lawrence observed that "it can inform and lead into new places the flow of our sympathetic consciousness, and it can lead our sympathy away in recoil from things that are dead."

In this, Henry James, the master of consciousness, would have concurred. It is a question of the death in life, or the life in it. We must deal with both. But we must also exercise a preference. Mr. Eliot speaks for the past—that region where dwell the vast hosts of the dead; Lawrence speaks for the present— that region where dwell the rest of us. In these two men, representative men, irreconcilable attitudes toward life and literature come face to face. Each man, in his fashion, seeks to give a form, a shape of significance, to the immense panorama of futility in which we live. Allowing for the truth in each persuasion, it is Eliot who speaks for what lies behind us, and Lawrence, the heretic, who speaks for the territory ahead.

In his essay on Philip Massinger, T. S. Eliot observes:

> He is not, however, the only man of letters who, at the moment when a new view of life is wanted, has looked at life through the eyes of his predecessors, and only at manners through his own.

This seems to me a just and penetrating estimate of Mr. Eliot's role in modern life and letters. It does nothing to diminish his importance, but explains the nature of his persuasion. He speaks for the past, and it is the past that speaks to most of us. The present is a sight on which we turn our backs, and lid our eyes. It will not change its nature through a manipulation of parallels. In the sense that Mr. Eliot is important, D. H. Lawrence is indispensable.

Kingsley Widmer

OUR DEMONIC HERITAGE: D. H. LAWRENCE

The devil and anathema of our forefathers hides the Godhead which we seek.[1]

D. H. Lawrence

THE demonic has not received its due. Arguments for the nature and significance of our major cultural, moral, and religious traditions frequently show a benign selectivity. Religious esthetes who delight in finding Christ-heroes in the incidental symbolism of literature ignore an even larger number of exalted devil-heroes; and sly dogmatists dig out the verbal residue of broken values instead of the rocks that have smashed them. Thus earnest pietists sketch not only an unlived and unlivable past, but blandly recommend for our enlightenment and succor orthodoxies whose very demise has been the result of negations and heterodoxies of which they appear to be unaware. Then more secular moralists of literature construct a "great tradition" of delicate academic sensibility which lacks most of the heroic excess, passion, and peculiarity which are major qualities of both continuity and greatness.

Or, if we need to put the issue in terms of archetypal and poetic sensitivity, let us turn to a major source of our tropes: Satanism. Though the frequently obsessive identification of our nineteenth-century literary ancestors with the devil and his powers and problems appears to many contemporary critics as "minor pathology" or "embarrassing" gaucherie, Satanism forms a large part of our imaginative reach. In French literature, which has keyed so much of modern literary sensibility, the positive treat-

Kingsley Widmer, who describes himself as "educated at diverse labors and Universities of Wisconsin, Minnesota, and Washington (Ph.D.)," has taught at Reed College, is now at San Diego State College, and is the author of literary essays on varied subjects; the present article is part of a longer study now in preparation, "The Art of Perversity."

ment of orthodox Christian evil and the wisdom of the demon ascends to Heaven (Hugo), descends to Hell (Rimbaud), or simply lurks at one's shoulder (Gide). And the Satanist variations of Musset, Vigny, Baudelaire, Verlaine, Nerval, Huysmans, France, Valéry, Breton, and Sartre, among others, provide a distinguished century of demonic insights. Nor is the tradition simply French, as we know from Lermontov and Artzybashev and Goethe and Mann; or, in Anglo-American literature, from glorifications of the devil and demonic in Blake, Burns, Byron, Shelley, Melville, Swinburne, Shaw, Santayana, and in rather more indirect forms such as surrealism and hipsterism.

Archetypal and symbolist critics should be able to enlarge the list from the variations of the demonic antitype ranging from the Romantics Cain and Prometheus to recent versions of Sisyphyus and the transcendental "outsider." The Romantic and post-Romantic devil-heroes, whether exalted *Übermensch* or degraded bohemian, with the inevitable narcotic or sexual derangement of the senses and worship of amoral vitality, draw upon our most ancient heresies of knowledge, as moralists since Plato have been uncomfortably aware. The quest for the dark powers of death, rebellion, and forbidden desires by primitive shaman-artists, by Dionysian and other erotic mystery religions, by many of the medieval heresies, and by the major cult movements connected with the love-romance, are part of a tradition of extreme awareness far older than the Romantics and Symbolists and their twentieth-century issue. The insights and feelings which will not fit into our standard humanistic, scientific, and religious traditions are indeed vast.

Like the rest of history, literary tradition reveals as much eccentricity as decorum and as much extremity as morality. Must we not, then, assume yet another tradition—another point of critical departure and literary awareness—a sustained and rich demonic heritage which has been, and still is, antithetical to official cults, which seek to obscure it, and the institutional moralities, which seek to repress it? Certainly some of the most interesting literature, especially that marked by the distinctive tensions and explorations of Western culture, cannot be fully understood without an awareness of the demonic—and in a quite serious and nonmoralistic sense. A principled perversity may well be an inadequately acknowledged part of our sensibility.[2]

ii

Now part of the manifold and perplexing art of D. H. Lawrence would seem to be illuminated when seen in the demonic perspective: there is a recognizable wisdom in Lawrence's waywardness. Neither simple praise nor blame, nor the much more vitiating moral-sentimental piety that characterizes the cultural institutionalization of a controversial figure (a method for neutralizing the authentic qualities), would be appropriate. Lawrence's "dark god," for example, was not born of personal pathology nor twentieth-century ideology, nor even from some peculiar sexual or mystical technique. The dark god, the "demon of life" out of the "blackness," like Lorca's *"duende,"* [3] was generated by a harsh vitality, itself the product of rebellion, negation, and defiance.

Like Blake and Baudelaire, Lawrence declared that Satan was the hero of *Paradise Lost*.[4] His own version of the demon as hero, and the lines of the downward path to wisdom, can perhaps best be seen in the shorter fictions. And early as well as late, for the demon lover and the infernal tropes, the moral inversions and the choices beyond good-and-evil, are not a post-realism acquisition of a newly deracinated, invertedly messianic Lawrence-out-of-England. He was born that way. In one of his earliest stories, "A Fragment of Stained Glass," the awkwardly Gothic narrative centers on a violently rebellious medieval serf who becomes the "fiend." Fleeing to the outlaws from avenging authority with his redheaded girl ("the fox"—one of Lawrence's recurrent animal tropes linked with demonic passion), the serf makes a "jump at God" when he sees in the night the stained-glass window of the Crucifixion in a lighted chapel. When the demon lover breaks the glass, his bloody and flame-lighted face appears to be that of the devil to the pious worshippers below. For surrendering a piece of the sacred glass—the broken religious image is itself consubstantial with the lover: "my life-stone," my "bloodstone"—to his girl, she surrenders to him. The scene of violence and extremity, the rebellious devil-hero rending both the social order and the Christian forms, the totemic animals of passion (horse and fox), the imagery of fire, blood, and darkness, and the concluding deathly sexual consummation become substantial and recurrent elements in Lawrence's art. So, too, does the avowed purpose of this Satanic fairy tale—"A Bible of the English people—the Bible of their hearts." [5]

Even in Lawrence's most characteristically "English" fictions —that is, those with a confinement to the domestic milieu, a technique of social-psychological analysis, and an ostensible culmination of erotic violence in the moral order of marriage—the lovers are demonic figures. Whether it be in the simple fulfillment of the rural Cain-brother and the outcast woman in the early novella "Love Among the Haystacks," or in the sophisticated comedy about the nihilistic gentleman in the later novella "The Captain's Doll," alienation and violence and perversity and denial are central.

Or if we take a representative short story on Lawrence's major theme of the power of fate in unrecognized erotic contact, "You Touched Me," we see that the English hero is but a lightly disguised amoral and alien rebel in a scornful assault on the middle-class moral order. Here the mocking orphan-emigré appears to his virginal and genteel stepsisters as "dangerous," "malevolent," "a thing of evil," and a "sliving demon"; even to the narrator-author, Hadrian's virtues are linked with the malign: he has the slyness, tenacity, courage, and "underground quality of the rat." With the aid of covert physical need and the "unscrupulous" use of his stepfather's mysogony, the demonic hero makes a semi-incestuous marriage with one of the resisting stepsisters.

A related novella, "The Fox," is dominated by the sly animal totem that is consubstantial with the hero. The fiendish fox, both part of the literal narrative and a recurrent figure of sexual anxiety in the heroine's dreams, draws upon the usual tropes ("demon," "serpent," and "devil"). His predatory qualities foreshadow the necessities for the consummation of love. Nor is this just symbolic, for the hero's climactic act of love-assertion consists of murdering the genteel Lesbian who stands in the way of his erotic "destiny." Here, as elsewhere, Lawrence adapts his vibrant animism to one of the most drastic versions of the Western love-and-death destiny which transcends the social and moral order.

Both of these last heroes are orphans and emigrés, rebels against the usual ethos, committed to a passional fulfillment which sanctions moral violations. The demonic rhetoric from

Satanist and animistic traditions (fused in Christian thought) identifying the demon lovers is only part of the basic pattern of inversion. In most of these fictions, Lawrence also insistently—sometimes to the point of rasping stylistic repetition—reverses the traditional valuational metaphors of light and dark. As in "The Blind Man," it is the "positive darkness" and the thorough shattering of almost all "light" values of reason and benevolence that provide the affirmation of the irrational and negative sources of strength. From the hard and defiant matings of the early mining stories through the sardonic studies of upper-bohemian civilized malaise of desire to the final parables of the beyond-good-and-evil world sundering regenerative moments of eros, all depends on the demonic inversion of ordinary values.

The true Lawrencean lover finds his *amor fati* by the nihilism of the demonic dialectic. Like the hero of "The Border Line," he holds that "only the cold strength of a man, accepting the destiny of destruction, could see the human flow through the chaos and beyond to a new outlet. But the chaos first and the long rage of destruction." [6] In "The Border Line," one of Lawrence's supernatural tales, the negative way to affirmation follows the heroine's journey through chaos and the destruction of ordinary reality. Traveling across the borderline of war and normal consciousness, she achieves, ironically, the demonic awareness when looking at a Gothic church in the twilight. She sees a "Thing" that is "looking down with vast, demonish menace," and recognizes a "demonish heathen" force of "implacable blood" and "mystery . . . blotting out the cross it was supposed to exalt." [7] Lawrence's lengthy apocalyptic rhetoric about the dark and phallic demon, as in analogous passages in Yeats and Faulkner, provides an extremity of dark awareness as the locus of passionate knowledge.

In "The Border Line," the heroine's demonic "vision" is replaced by its persona, the demon lover. This time it is the ghost of her dead first husband who appears as a "duskily ruddy" figure come "from the halls of death to her." The concluding consummation of the ghostly demon lover and the wife takes place, a harsh scene, adjacent to the corpse of the woman's morally decent and intelligent second husband who is the Lawrencean villain. While there may well be some *roman à clef* malice here as well as some other implications about the World

War I scene, the biographical and political interpretations of the story quite miss those ever reappearing demonic motifs and tropes of Lawrence's work, as well as the demonic "vision" that is the heart of the story.

Certainly in some of Lawrence's fictions the more destructive aspects of the demon lover—such as murdering the moral side of the double female image, killing off the decent husband—are subordinated to time and place; yet perhaps the most distinctive aspect of Lawrence as a fictionist is his ability to fuse his inverted religious dialectic with the very substance of ordinary characters, scenes, and society itself. Readers with an arithmetical cast of mind might count up the characters whose essential identity develops with the demonic metaphors. The pattern, of course, does not deny Lawrence's variety. In some stories ("Jimmy and the Desperate Woman" or the weak sketch "The Last Laugh") the demonic or "Mephistophelian" figure is employed for satiric point. But far more to the point are Lawrence's dark and death-ridden lovers, such as Romero in Lawrence's American story "The Princess." This ambiguous cicerone-lover is a superlatively "proud," "dark," virile, "sinister," uniquely "different" and alien "gentleman" dressed "all in black." This rapist, finally brought to self-destruction by the frigid American woman, attracts because he is a "death worshipper" and a "fine demon."

The detailed genesis of Lawrence's obsession with the dark hero and his destructive-erotic fire of passion—in romantic Satanism, in a self-conscious but also guilty attack on Christian good-and-evil, in a narcissistic hyperbole aimed at revitalizing the effete modern Anglo-Saxon, in vitalistic and nihilistic philosophy—need concern us less than what Lawrence does with the demon lover. Most of the tales discussed so far are, I think, relatively successful, if viewed from the proper—demonic—perspective. But the demonic has distinct limits of authenticity, and overreaching Lawrence went beyond them. Thus he sometimes attempted to turn the demonic into a dogma, instead of a rebellion against one, and then wrote badly. In a novella such as "The Ladybird" ("Glad Ghosts" is another) the demonic aim turns a fiction starting in social realism into a ponderous mythology riddled with tawdry poeticization (the heroine has a "pearl-like beauty," is a "hot-house flower," etc.). The sexual ambivalence of our usual *ménage à trois* love-plot is wedded to synthetic allusive patterns: the Daphne legend (with Dionysius replacing Apollo), the Tristan-Iseult pattern with its strange wound, alien hero, divided fealty, unresolvable adultery, and death as consummation of passion. Dionys, the hero, a wounded officer and Bohemian aristocrat, is not only Dionysius and Tristan; he is also a primitive animist, an ancient Mediterranean death-cult figure and the post-Crucifixion Christ; and he is a hero of darkness and fire, a spokesman for the "under-conscious," "King of Hades," "risen death," and the arch rebel. But this demon lover of a bored upper-class English nymph (wife of a villainously idealistic English officer and gentleman) also stands for social-moral order with his aristocratic ethic of "obedience, submission, faith, belief, responsibility, power." [8]

The weakness is not just in the portentous plenitude linked to the demonic. Can the demon be a figure of social order and authority? Not, surely, and retain his distinctive vitality: his powers of perversity, passion, alienation, rebellion, seduction, death-knowledge, defiance, and uniqueness. The artistic failure evident in the pastiche of hortatory social morality and poetic fragments would seem to be based on a larger incoherence—the moral apotheosizing of the demonic. The falsity comes from the failure of the demonic hero, Dionys and Lawrence, to maintain fully his authentic role, and pay the lonely price. Demonic insight may provide knowledge of what has been hidden in the depths by the prevailing order—passion, courage, unique being—and demonic defiance may even lead beyond insight to vitality and change, but it is diabolic to claim the demonic itself as order.

While even the weakest of Lawrence's fictions stop short of full diabolism because of the characteristic pyrrhic ambiguity which lets through the underlying hard awareness, even the best of the fictions are also marred by momentary claims of the demonic awareness to power, order, and finality. And Lawrence knew it. In a prose partly marred by desperate insistence, and in idyllic scenes strangely undershot with destructiveness, Lawrence in his final novellas rejected social and moral authority for the demon lover. The anonymous seducers and outcasts of "The Virgin and the Gipsy" and "The Escaped Cock" clearly become seasonal heroes, pagan hypostatizations of the Satanic, whose defiance of social and moral values results neither in love, marriage, social power, nor even in doctrine. Their regenerative moments of "intense immediate life" produce heightened awareness and integral being, but provide no "excessive salvation" for these wanderers who, like his Christ joying in his rejection of *agape* for *eros,* can say, "I inherit the earth, since I lay no claim to it." [9] In a world he never made, and in a society to which his only obligations are individuality and defiance, it is (to quote the next to the last line of "The Escaped Cock") "the gold and flowing serpent" that maintains his intense demon. But, as with most twentieth-century dreams of the absolute adventure and the regenerative cosmic cycle, these are forlorn demons.

iii

Behind the demon lover lies a demonic cosmos—an exhilarating nothingness. The pervasiveness of the demonic develops in two opposed directions in what is perhaps Lawrence's most crucial work, the long novella "St. Mawr." In this, one of Lawrence's harshest efforts to bring salvation to the frigid upper-middle-class Anglo-Saxon woman, the demonic tends to diffuse itself through everything. The antihero, a covertly homosexual artist-poseur, is the usual outsider and "a trifle Mephistophelian"; his "malevolent" mother-in-law is the comically willful American matriarch, and a "witch" of destructiveness; the rather autobiographical animist barely disguised as a Welsh groom "answered evasively" when asked if he believed in the devil. Even one of the author's minor choral figures is emphatically presented as Pan, predecessor (according to Lawrence) of the Christian devil; [10] he of course defends the potent sacredness of the dark and defiant mystery. And again the central totemic figure, the stallion St. Mawr, is pure demon: he "glowed red with power," this "god out of the darkness" and "Master of Doom" who always raised "the demonish question"; the stallion is a dangerous, vindictive, fascinating, passionate, rebellious, defiant menace (Lawrence's words) from "another world, an older heavily potent world"; and those who could truly see, saw "demons upon demons in the chaos of his horrid eyes," and were glad. The decisive action takes place at a cleft called "the Devil's chair," and this gives the nihilistic heroine the opportunity to identify with and praise "the old fighting stock that worshipped devils," and to contrast them to the modern decent people who don't really "exist." There are more of these demonic flourishes, but both the dialectic and the artistic difficulty should already be evident. That the hero, the heroine, the mother-in-law, the servant, the visitor, the horse, the place, all belong to the infernal lets recurrent imagery—in contrast to the non-recurrent life imagery so essential to fictional prose that seeks to present a time and a place—undermine dramatic distinctions. It would seem to be Lawrence's perception that the demonic qualities provide the premoral and prerational vitality wherever they appear. But when all is demonic, nothing quite is.

Yet despite such overreaching, much art of both scenic delight and demonic subtlety remains. The crux of the early action comes when the demonic horse injures the effete husband and the heroine moves outside moral choice to that of a kind of transcendental sodomy (the stallion) in preference to social convention (the husband). In the process the heroine has a "vision of evil," and Lawrence has another of his long, characteristically personal and apocalyptic passages on his *bête noir,* idealism. A rather diverse range of viciousness "masquerading as the ideal" is fused together: the denuding of the natural world, Communism, Fascism, modern production, social success, gentility, the ideology of comfort and convenience and, most important, the imperative of contemporary civilization to "multiply itself million on million . . . until the accumulation of mere existence is swollen to a horror." [11]

In Lawrence's dialectic, this "positive evil" can be overcome only by the demonic denial. With a subtlety characteristic of romantic thought, and antithetical to more dominant moralities and religions, evil and the demonic are *not* equated and, indeed, become the ultimate choices. Such a transvaluation tends to break out of the fictional form as choice must leave the socially possible (horse over husband; wilds over civilization), and psychological insight is replaced by gnomic utterance ("Retreat to the desert, and fight"; "Try to hold fast to the living thing, which destroys as it goes, but remains sweet").

Rather than exercise judgments on the provocative bastard forms that result when "vision" and aphorism undercut the social milieu and the psychology of character, and which suggest some inherent incompatibility of the transcendental quest and the traditional fictional forms, we may look at the final extension of the demonic. In "St. Mawr" the visualization of the demonic is appropriately transferred from the totem (the malevolent stallion) to the cosmos (the "malevolence that was in the spirit of the place") [12] as the action moves from society to the desert. And in an allegorical tale within the tale, the history of the mountain ranch-refuge in the American Southwest, we see that the demonic results from no simple perversity of yearning but from the defining condition of life.

With fulsome lyric exaltation, Lawrence elaborates the savage frenzy of the natural scene. Even the inverted "sex-passion" of the hard-working puritan pioneer to overcome nature was defeated by the beautiful but destructive *"absolute"* of the amoral cosmos. The seething disintegration at all levels—weeds, pack rats, lightning, human despair—comes from the nature of existence. The *"ne plus ultra"* allows no phallic salvation, for the very tree of life is a "demonish guardian," a nonphallic column of "blind will" representing the "raging, seething conflict" basic to all. With fantastic impartiality, Lawrence finds that "sordidness" is equally inevitable in primitive and civilized life. The demonic awareness thus demands a hardness of spirit, a "cleaner energy" than ideal goodness, to match destruction with life. So *"Jesus and a God of Love,"* all "universal Love," are *"nonsense."* [13]

Cause for despair? Apparently for Lawrence and his heroines, the knowledge of the nihilistic cosmos leads to "life, intense bristling life." And to the demonic assertion of defiance: *"This is more awful and more splendid. I like it better."* Lawrence's heightened descriptions, apocalyptic rhetoric (and italics), and fabulistic pattern insist that the absolute knowledge gained from the affirmation of denial is the source of all vitality, though his sensitive demonics sometimes come dangerously close to imitating the nihilistic cosmos in their effort to step into intense immediate life and purpose by perversely planting one foot on the reality of nothingness.

iv

Satanism, it is sometimes suggested, went under with the nineteenth-century moral deity—presumably about the time Nietzsche announced that God was dead. Lawrence's demon lovers, Christly serpents, and exhilarating cosmic nihilism, then, would be historical post-mortem effects—or, at least in the more erotic works, some sort of late-Victorian phallic baroque. While it is true that Lawrence's "Godhead" hidden in the "devil and anathema of our forefathers" has an erotic emphasis as inversely defined by the nineteenth century (just as his literary technique draws upon late Romanticism), there is much more. A principled perversity remains the serious center of Lawrence's work, and this major demonic emphasis in Western culture is more than historical and literary revolt. We suffer from bland liberalism's foreshortening of history if we assume that traditional forms of the demonic (any more than institutional pieties and dogmas) disappear. The amorality and extremity, the intensification of alienated subjectivity, and the erotic heightening of the imme-diate, the nihilistic affirmations and the demon of denial, are es-sentially the traditional anathema. Though some twentieth-century demonics have a protective secular coloration, Law-rence still had the traditional rhetoric. He, too, combined the existential skepticism ("Anything that *triumphs,* perishes") [14] with the extreme faith that on the other side of denial is a new-valued richness of life.

"No, no, my boy, don't be on the side of the angels, it's too lowering," [15] Lawrence once wrote a successful friend. And whether in personal wryness or in psychic melodrama, his demon was usually present to warn him away from accepting the valua-tions that are. Including his own. For Lawrence, after announc-ing (with the usual incantatory repetition), "The Almighty has vacated, abdicated, climbed down," [16] then proceeded to find some "dark" way to raise up new "unknown gods." But these, too, fell out of the vibrantly negative cosmos. The gods—vari-ously animistic, sexual, theocratic, utopian, Protestant-pagan, or sun-cult—were themselves heterodox revolts from the Western dynamism toward social, moral, and sentimental homogeneity.

The proliferation of heterodoxies as well as of demonic nega-tions (they go together) probably constitutes just as important a function of our literary traditions as do the maintenance of orthodoxies and the exploration of morals and manners. The relevant criticism is not the literary moralist's distaste for violence, extremity, and perversity. The demonic has its own limits, such as diabolism, when falsely extended. And, as in Lawrence's longer works, demonic art tends to violate any esthetic mode with the same denial that applies to every created pattern of values. The tender, organic Lawrencean moments, never long sustained, are the cathartic result of the extremity that dominates much of the shorter fictions, the polemics and crucial parts of every novel. The strategy of excess produces a markedly brilliant but necessarily idiosyncratic and irregular literature. Without the demonic heritage, much of the perplexity of our art would be gone, and so would much else, including the impassioned disenchantment and the reaching for the boundaries of awareness, which renews individual identity.

NOTES

[1] Edward D. McDonald, ed., *Phoenix: The Posthumous Papers of D. H. Lawrence* (New York, 1936), p. 90. In context, the statement refers to "the black demon of savage America." Lawrence is equating the primitive and the demonic (rather than viewing the primitive as utopian, idyllic, barbaric, etc.). I find the demonic, not the primitive, the primary category here, as elsewhere in Lawrence. For another aspect of this problem, see my "The Primitivistic Aesthetic: D. H. Lawrence," *Journal of Aesthetics and Art Criticism* (Spring 1959). For other aspects of Lawrence's shorter fictions, which relate to the view presented in this essay, see also my "D. H. Lawrence and the Art of Nihilism," *The Kenyon Review* (Autumn 1958); "Birds of Passion and Birds of Marriage," *University of Kansas City Review* (October 1958); and "Lawrence and the Fall of Modern Woman," *Modern Fiction Studies* (Spring 1959).

[2] While there are a number of studies of the devil in terms of demonology, dogmatics, iconography, literary history, and pathology, most of them notably lack both subtlety and relevance to modern literature. An unanalytic but useful historical compilation is M. J. Rudwin, *The Devil in Legend and Literature* (Chicago, 1931); less naïve, but also less useful, is Mario Praz, *The Romantic Agony* (New York, 1955), an erudite technical study of the pathology of some demonic motifs severed from the works. A catalogue of *some* of the works in which the devil has a major role is Watson Kirkconnell, *The Celestial Cycle, The Theme of Paradise Lost in World Literature* . . . (Toronto, 1952). Of the studies of the devil and related materials in English Romanticism, E. Railo, *The Haunted Castle: A Study of the Elements of English Romanticism* (New York, 1937), provides some of the Gothic background. But far more important here are individual studies of nineteenth-

century demonics: Blake, Rimbaud, etc. For more general views of the problems raised by the devil, see Paul Carus, *The History of the Devil and the Idea of Evil* (Chicago, 1900), a rationalist approach; Edward Langton, *Satan, A Portrait* (London, [1945]), a moderate Protestant approach; Denis de Rougement, *The Devil's Share* (New York, 1956), an urbane but unperceptive moralist's attempt to revivify the devil; *Satan. Collection de Psychologie Religieuse Études Carmelitaines* (New York, 1952), a varied collection of Catholic studies, of which three essays inaccurately discuss the demonic (Paul Zunthor, "The Turning-Point of Romanticism"; Claude-Edmonde Magny, "The Devil in Contemporary Literature"; and, best of the lot, Paulus Lenz-Medoc, "The Death of God"). There appears to be very little critical but nonmoralistic and nondoctrinaire discussion of the devil and the demonic, though some of the same issues are met in discussions of other forms of literary extremity, such as Norman Mailer, "The White Negro" in *The Beat Generation and The Angry Young Men,* ed. G. Feldman and M. Gartenberg (New York, 1958).

[3] See Federico García Lorca, "The Duende," Appendix V, *Poet in New York,* Ben Belitt trans. (New York, 1955). For the most part, only polemics *against* Lawrence emphasize his demonic qualities. A few examples from various points of view: in an amusingly bad early argument, Harvey Wickham finds Lawrence's work to be "Satanism, pure and simple," *The Impuritans* (New York, 1929), p. 268. Apparently not having read any literature from Catholic countries, he can explain Lawrence and all modern "Satanism" as a personal revolt against Protestantism. The same argument has been made many times. T. S. Eliot some time before this insisted that Lawrence was a *"démoniaque, un démoniaque simple et naturel muni d'un évangile."* "Le Roman Anglais Contemporain," *La Nouvelle Revue Française* (Mai, 1927), p. 671. He has also said that Lawrence's works have "demonic powers," *After Strange Gods* (New York, 1934), p. 65. The Eliot statement is also quoted by F. R. Leavis, *D. H. Lawrence, Novelist* (London, 1955), p. 23, but Leavis, with a moralistic righteousness about Lawrence which is simply an inversion of Eliot's, totally ignores such aspects of Lawrence. From the different vantage of a (then) political-literary critic, we find the condemnation of Lawrence for turning "nihilism" to "diabolism," in Eric Bentley, *A Century of Hero-Worship* (New York, 1947), p. 241. In the many (at least seven from 1931 to 1957) biographical-religious attacks on Lawrence of J. Middleton Murry (which are well known) the "demonic" is one of Lawrence's horrifying sins. Even the devilish literary *blaguer* Henry Miller, however, tends to condemn Lawrence (in contrast to Giono) for using "hymns of hate" to proclaim "the life abundant," part of Lawrence's "romantic, demonic, confessional, subjective" emphasis, *The Books in My Life* (New York, 1952), pp. 113 and 202. While the demonic condemnation did not disappear, it was briefly submerged by a spate of academic moralists: Leavis, *op. cit.;* Mark Spilka, *The Love-Ethic of D. H. Lawrence* (Bloomington, 1955); Ralph Maud, "D. H. Lawrence . . . ," *Western Humanities Review* (Summer 1955), who carried ponderous moral positiveness to its logical absurdity by equating Lawrence with Irving Babbitt. There is considerably less moralistic misreading of the works when a more complex, and frequently negative, quality in Lawrence is allowed, as in the critical biography of Harry T. Moore, *The Intelligent Heart* (New York, 1955), or

in the interpretive study of Graham Hough, *The Dark Sun* (London, 1956), though neither has anything to say about the demonic. But we may suspect, still, an only slightly disguised moral repulsion to the demonic in the flat rejection of Lawrence's "ideas" by literary-liberal moralists, as in Jacques Barzun, "Lawrence in Life and Letters," *Griffin* (February 1958), pp. 4–11, who is echoing Diana Trilling, "A Letter of Introduction to Lawrence," *Partisan Review* (Winter 1958), p. 32. Some emphasis, after all, should be put on the Lawrence who is totally beyond both the stock responses of Christian morality and the "liberal imagination," the Lawrence who as a youth so insistently said, "With *should* and *ought* I have nothing to do." Quoted by Helen Corke, *D. H. Lawrence's "Princess": A Memory of Jessie Chambers* (Thames Ditton, Surrey, 1951), p. 41. It is the same Lawrence who, three decades later, approvingly quotes the nihilistic Rozanov's "profound" aphorism, "I am not such a scoundrel yet as to think about morals," *Phoenix*, p. 368. (The few times Lawrence uses the word "morality" in a positive sense, as in "Art and Morality" and "Morality and the Novel," *Phoenix*, pp. 521–32, the context clearly shows it as a synonym for "vital.") It is of course a long-term irony that much of our serious art is a product of transcendent amoralists, while most of those who write about it are genteel idealists, Lawrence's very *bête noir*. Not that everything in Lawrence is clearly demonic—with some works we have to apply Lawrence's own critical principle and "look through the surface . . . and see the inner diabolism," *Studies in Classic American Literature* (New York, 1953), p. 93.

⁴ *Phoenix*, p. 559.

⁵ *The Complete Short Stories of D. H. Lawrence* (3 vols., London, 1955), I, p. 188. For convenience of reference, all quotations are from this edition, though several novellas and stories are mentioned which are not collected here. Citations are not given for single words and brief phrases quoted from this source.

⁶ A major Lawrencean point: "All we have to do is accept the true chaos that we are. . . ." *Phoenix*, p. 262. The "blarney about pure constructive activity is all poppycock—nine-tenths at least must be smash-smash!—or else *all* your constructivity turns out feebly destructive." *The Letters of D. H. Lawrence*, ed. Aldous Huxley (New York, 1932), p. 777. Or, in Lawrence's most affirmative way of putting it: "Man fights for a new conception of life and God, as he fights to plant seeds in the spring. . . . To plant seed you've got to kill a great deal of weeds and break much ground." *Assorted Articles* (New York, 1930), p. 258. And "once we are driven on to nihilism we may find a way through."

⁷ *Complete Short Stories*, III, p. 802. *Demon* is a recurrent *positive* word in Lawrence's work, as are most of its contingent qualities. In his metapsychological speculations, the reason is suggested: the passionate man appears to others as a "demon," and we have the "primary or bodily self—appearing often like a black demon." *Assorted Articles*, p. 233. The affirmation of "darkness" undoubtedly has some connection with Lawrence's obsessive concern with death, which itself is the basis for his insistence that (what he says Rozanov was the first to see), "immortality is in the vividness of life." *Phoenix*, p. 369.

⁸ *The Tales of D. H. Lawrence* (London, 1934), p. 398. The discussion of the novella is necessarily abbreviated. Some insight into the story, which I do not recall having seen mentioned before, can be gained by

comparing "The Ladybird" with an earlier version of the same material, the weak and inconclusive story "The Thimble." *The Seven Arts* (March, 1917), pp. 435–48. Lawrence's additions especially center on the demonic "outsider" (Lawrence's word, long before its current fashion), his traditional compact with death (as in *Isaiah*, xxviii, 15: "We have made a covenant with death and with hell are we at agreement. . . .") and the romantic adultery pattern—for this see Denis de Rougement, *Passion and Society* (London, 1956), pp. 15–169. Incidentally, de Rougement's gross moralizing about Lawrence, whom he links to Erskine Caldwell and Fascism (pp. 236–37), is based only on the expository writings (and probably one essay). For some of Lawrence's ecstatic statements about death and the "darkness of power," see *Reflections on the Death of a Porcupine* (London, 1934), p. 25, and *Phoenix*, pp. 680–87. A fuller discussion of the demonic leader would include the "Lord of Death" motif in *The Boy in The Bush* and the dark religious leaders of *The Plumed Serpent*.

[9] *Tales*, p. 1114. Anti-Lawrencean critics frequently fail to note the demonic intention; but, then, so have many pro-Lawrencean critics, who take the figure as a re-done saviour instead of the anonymous demon lover, the endless enemy of all social order, etc.

[10] See "Pan in America," *Phoenix*, pp. 22–31. Knut Hamsun, Michael Arlen, and others, were also resurrecting Pan at the time Lawrence was writing.

[11] *Tales*, p. 614. The aphorisms quoted below are from the same page.

[12] *Tales*, p. 676.

[13] *Tales*, p. 680. The next quotations are from the same page.

[14] *Reflections on the Death of a Porcupine*, p. 17.

[15] *Letters*, p. 703. Or as Lawrence wrote elsewhere: "No more uplift." "Brethern, let us go down." *Fantasia of the Unconscious* (London, 1933), p. 15. There is of course a less wry side to all this: "Don't tell me there is no Devil; there is a Prince of Darkness. Sometimes I wish I could let go and be really wicked—kill and murder—but kill chiefly. I do want to kill. But I want to select whom I shall kill [in contrast to modern mass warfare]. . . . It is this black desire that I have become conscious of." *Letters*, p. 241. While contemporary theologians tend to tell us that goodness is divine, evil human (no devil), modern literature (Baudelaire, Corbière, Conrad, Lawrence, etc.) tends to find goodness tangible and human, and evil transcendent.

[16] *Phoenix*, p. 726. This key to modern existential revolt is itself religious, as are most of our patterns of rebellion. The very manners of bohemianism—such as the current "cool" mode of black-dressed witch girls, jazz-and-narcotic ecstasy and moral inversions in flight and violence —obviously belong to the tradition of the Black Mass and the Feast of Fools. As with Lawrence, such strategies of extremity *aim* at embracing the religious absolute of "Life as it is!" *Reflections on the Death of a Porcupine*, p. 109.

D. H. Lawrence

THE FOX

THE two girls were usually known by their sur-names, Banford and March. They had taken the farm together, intending to work it all by themselves: that is they were going to rear chickens, making a living by poultry, and add to this by keeping a cow, and raising one or two young beast[s]. Unfortunately things did not turn out well.

Banford was a small, thin, delicate thing with spectacles. She, however, was the principal investor, for March had little or no money. Banford's father, who was a tradesman in Islington, gave his daughter the start, for her health's sake, and because he loved her, and because it did not look as if she would marry. March was more robust. She had learned carpentry and joinering at the evening classes in Islington. She would be the man about the place. They had, moreover, Banford's old grandfather living with them at the start. He had been a farmer. But unfortunately the old man died after he had been at Bailey Farm for a year. Then the two girls were left alone.

They were neither of them young: that is, they were over thirty. But they certainly were not old. They set out quite gallantly with their enterprise. They had numbers of chickens, black leghorns and white leghorns, Plymouths and Wyandots: also some ducks: also two heifers in the field. One heifer, however, refused absolutely to stay in the Bailey Farm closes. No

This is a first version of "The Fox," probably written late in 1919 at Middleton-By-Wirkswirth, Derbyshire. The type transcription given here has been made by the editor from photostats of the manuscript, now the property of George L. Lazarus. A facsimile reproduction of the manuscript itself, an excellent example of Lawrence's working methods, may be found in the illustrations section of this volume.

matter how March made up the fences, the heifer was out, wild in the woods, or trespassing on the neighbouring pasture, and March and Bancroft [Banford] were away, flying after her, with more haste than success. So this heifer they sold in despair. Then, just before the other young beast was expecting her first calf, the old man died, and the girls, afraid of the coming event, sold her in a panic, and limited their attention to fowls and ducks.

In spite of a little chagrin, it was a relief to have no more cattle on hand. Life was not made merely to be slaved away. Both girls agreed in this. The fowls were quite enough trouble. March had set up her carpenter's bench at the end of the open shed. Here she worked, making coops and doors and other appurtenances. The fowls were housed in the bigger building, which had served as barn and cowshed in old days. They had a beautiful home, and should have been perfectly content. Indeed, they looked well enough. But the girls were disgusted at their tendency to strange illnesses, at their exacting way of life, and at their refusal, obstinate refusal, to lay eggs.

March did most of the outdoor work. When she was out and about, in her puttees and breeches, her belted coat and her loose cap, she looked almost like some graceful, loose-balanced young man, for her shoulders were straight, and her movements easy and confident, even tinged with a little indifference, or irony. But her face was not a man's face, ever. The wisps of her crisp dark hair blew about her as she stooped, her eyes were big and wide and dark, when she looked up again, strange, startled, shy and sardonic at once. Her mouth, too, was almost pinched as if in pain and irony. There was something odd and unexplained about her. She would stand balanced on one hip, looking at the fowls pattering about in the obnoxious fine mud of the sloping yard, and calling to her favourite white hen, which came in answer to her name. But there was an almost satirical flicker in March's big, dark eyes as she looked at her three-toed flock, pottering about under her gaze, and the same slight dangerous satire in her voice as she spoke to the favoured Patty, who pecked at March's boot by way of friendly demonstration.

Fowls did not flourish at Bailey Farm, in spite of all that March did for them. When she provided hot food for them, in the morning, according to rule, she noticed that it made them heavy and dozy for hours. She expected to see them lean against the pillars of the shed, in their languid processes of digestion. And she knew quite well that they ought to be busily scratching and foraging about, if they were to come to any good. So she decided to give them their hot food at night, and let them sleep on it. Which she did. But it made no difference.

War conditions, again, were very unfavourable to poultry keeping. Food was scarce and bad. And when the Daylight Saving Bill was passed, the fowls obstinately refused to go to bed as usual, about nine oclock in the summer time. That was late enough, indeed, for there was no peace till they were shut up and asleep. Now they cheerfully walked around, without so much as glancing at the barn, until ten oclock or later. Both Banford and March disbelieved in living for work alone. They wanted to read or take a cycle-ride in the evening: or perhaps Banford wished to paint curvilinear swans on porcelain, with green background, or else make a marvellous fire-screen by processes of elaborate cabinet-work. For she was a creature of odd whims and unsatisfied tendencies. But from all these things she was prevented by the stupid fowls.

One evil there was greater than any other. Bailey Farm was a little homestead, about a hundred and fifty years old, lying just one field removed from the edge of the wood. Since the war the fox was a demon. He carried off the hens under the very noses of March and Banford. Banford would start and stare through her big spectacles with all her eyes, as another squawk and flutter took place at her heels. Too late! Another white leghorn gone. It was disheartening.

They did what they could to remedy it. When it became permitted to shoot foxes, they stood sentinel with their guns, the two of them, at the favoured hours. But it was no good. The fox was too quick for them. So another year passed, and another, and they were living on their losses, as Banford said. They let their farm-house one summer, and retired to live in a railway-carriage that was deposited as a sort of out-house in a corner of the field. This amused them, and helped their finances. None the less, things looked dark.

Although they were usually the best of friends, because Banford, though nervous and delicate, was a warm, generous soul, and March, though so odd and absent in herself, had a strange magnanimity, yet, in the long solitude, they were apt to become a little irritable with one another, tired of one another. March had four-fifths of the work to do, and though she did not mind, there seemed no relief, and it made her eyes flash curiously sometimes. Then Banford, feeling more nerve-worn than ever, would become despondent, and March would speak sharply to her. They seemed to be losing ground, somehow, losing hope as the months went by. There alone in the fields by the wood, with the wide country stretching hollow and dim to the round hills of the White Horse, in the far distance, they seemed to have to live too much off themselves. There was nothing to keep them up—and no hope.

The fox really exasperated them both. As soon as they had let the fowls out, in the early summer mornings, they had to take their guns and keep guard: and then again, as soon as evening began to mellow, they must go once more. And he was so sly. He slid along in the deep grass, he was difficult as a serpent to see. And he seemed to circumvent the girls deliberately. Once or twice March had caught sight of the white tip of his brush, or the ruddy shadow of him in the deep grass, and she had let fire at him. But he made no account of this.

One evening March was standing with her back to the sunset, her gun under her arm, her hair pushed under her cap. She was half watching, half musing. It was her constant state. Her eyes were keen and observant, but her inner mind took no notice of what she saw. She was always lapsing into this odd, rapt state, her mouth rather screwed up. It was a question, whether she was there, actually consciously present, or not.

The trees on the wood-edge were a darkish, brownish green in the full light—for it was the end of August. Beyond, the naked, copper-like shafts and limbs of the pine-trees shone in the air. Nearer, the rough grass, with its long brownish stalks all agleam, was full of light. The fowls were round about—the ducks were still swimming on the pond under the pine trees. March looked at it all, saw it all, and did not see it. She heard Banford speaking to the fowls, in the distance—and she did not hear. What was she thinking about? Heaven knows. Her consciousness was, as it were, held back.

She lowered her eyes and, suddenly, saw the fox. He was looking up at her. His chin was pressed down, and his eyes were looking up. They met her eyes. And he knew her. She was spell-bound. She knew he knew her. So he looked into her eyes, and her soul failed her. He knew her, he was not daunted.

She struggled, confusedly she came to herself, and saw him making off, with slow leaps leaping over some fallen boughs, slow, impudent jumps. Then he glanced over his shoulder, and ran smoothly away. She saw his brush held smooth like a feather, she saw his white buttocks twinkle. And he was gone, softly, soft as the wind.

She put her gun to her shoulder, but even then pursed her mouth, knowing it was nonsense to pretend to fire. So she began to walk slowly after him, in the direction he had gone, slowly, pertinaciously. She expected to find him. In her heart she was determined to find him. What she would do when she saw him again she did not consider. But she was determined to find him. So she walked abstractedly about on the edge of the wood, with wide, vivid dark eyes, and a faint flush in her cheeks. She did not think. In strange mindlessness she walked hither and thither.

At last she became aware that Banford was calling her. She made an effort of attention, turned, and gave some sort of screaming call in answer. Then again she was striding off towards the homestead. The red sun was setting, the fowls were retiring towards their roost. She watched them, white creatures, black creatures, gathering to the barn. She watched them spell-bound, without seeing them. But her automatic intelligence told her when it was time to shut the door.

She went indoors to supper, which Banford had set on the table. Banford chatted easily. March seemed to listen, in her distant, manly way. She answered a brief word now and then. But all the time she was as if spell-bound. And as soon as supper was over, she rose again to go out, without saying why.

She took her gun again and went to look for the fox. For he had lifted his eyes upon her, and his knowing look seemed to have entered her brain. She did not so much think of him: she was possessed by him. She saw his dark, shrewd, unabashed eye looking into her, knowing her. She felt him invisibly master her psyche. She knew the way he lowered his chin as he looked up, she knew his muzzle, the golden brown, and the greyish white. And again, she saw him glance over his shoulder at her, half inviting, half contemptuous and cunning. So she went, with her great startled eyes glowing, her gun under her arm, along the wood edge. Meanwhile the night fell, and a great moon rose above the pine trees. And again, Banford was calling.

So she went indoors. She was silent and busy. She examined her gun, and cleaned it, musing abstractedly by the lamp-light. Then she went out again, under the great moon, to see if everything was right. When she saw the dark crests of the pine-trees against the blond sky, again her heart beat to the fox, the fox. She wanted to follow him, with her gun.

It was some days before she mentioned the affair to Banford. Then suddenly, one evening, she said:

"The fox was right at my feet on Saturday night."

"Where?" said Banford, her eyes opening behind her spectacles[.]

"When I stood just above the pond."

"Did you fire?" cried Banford.

"No, I didn't."

"Why not?"

"Why, I was too much surprised, I suppose." It was the same old, slow, laconic way of speech March always had. Banford stared at her friend for a few moments.

"You saw him?" she cried.

"Oh yes! He was looking up at me, cool as anything."

"I tell you," cried Banford—"the cheek!—They're not afraid of us, March."

"Oh no," said March.

"Pity you didn't get a shot at him," said Banford.

"Isn't it a pity! I've been looking for him ever since. But I don't suppose he'll come so near again."

"I don't suppose he will," said Banford.

And she proceeded to forget about it: except that she was more indignant than ever at the impudence of the beggars. March also was not conscious that she thought of the fox. But whenever she fell into her odd half-muses, when she was half rapt, and half intelligently aware of what passed under her vision, then it was the fox which somehow dominated her unconsciousness, possessed the blank half of her musing. And so it was for weeks, and months. No matter whether she had been climbing the trees for the apples, or beating down the last of the damsons, or whether she had been digging out the ditch from the duck-pond, or clearing out the barn, when she had finished, or when she straightened herself, and pushed the wisps of hair away again from her forehead, and pursed up her mouth again in an odd, screwed fashion, much too old for her years, then was sure to come over her mind the old spell of the fox, as it came when he was looking at her. It was as if she could smell him, at these times. And it always recurred, at unexpected moments, just as she was going to sleep at night, or just as she was pouring the water into the teapot, to make tea—there it was, the fox, it came over her like a spell.

So the months passed. She still looked for him unconsciously, whenever she went towards the wood. He had become a settled effect in her psyche, a state permanently established, not continuous, but always recurring. She did not know what she felt or thought: only the state came over her, as when he looked at her.

The months passed, the dark evenings came, heavy, dark November, when March went about in high boots, ankle deep in mud, when the night began to fall at four oclock, and the day never properly dawned. Both girls dreaded these times. They dreaded the almost continuous darkness that enveloped them on their desolate little farm near the wood. Banford was physically afraid. She was afraid of tramps, afraid lest someone should come prowling round. March was not so much afraid, as uncomfortable and disturbed. She felt discomfort and gloom in all her physique.

Usually, the two girls had tea in the sitting room. March lighted a fire at dusk, and put on the wood she had chopped and sawed during the day. Then the long evening was in front, dark, sodden, black outside, lonely and rather oppressive inside, a little dismal. March was content not to talk, but Banford could not keep still. Merely listening to the wind in the pines outside, or the drip of water, was too much for her.

One evening the girls had washed up the tea-things in the kitchen, and March had put on her house-shoes, and taken up a roll of crochet-work, which she worked at slowly from time to time. So she lapsed into silence. Banford stared at the red fire, which, being of wood, needed constant attention. She was afraid to begin to read too early, because her eyes would

not bear any strain. So she sat staring at the fire, listening to
the distant sounds, sound of cattle lowing, of a dull, heavy,
moist wind, of the rattle of the evening train on the little railway
not far off. She was almost fascinated by the red glow of the
fire.

Suddenly both girls started, and lifted their heads. They
heard a footstep—distinctly a footstep. Banford recoiled in
fear. March stood listening. Then rapidly she approached the
door that led into the kitchen. At the same time they heard
the footsteps approach the back door. They waited a second.
The back door opened softly. Banford gave a loud cry. A man's
voice said softly:

"Hello!"

March recoiled, and took a gun from a corner.

"What do you want?" she cried, in a sharp voice.

Again the soft, softly-vibrating man's voice said:

"Hello! What's wrong?"

"I shall shoot!" cried March. "What do you want?"

"Why, what's wrong? What's wrong?" came the soft, wondering, rather scared voice: and a young soldier, with his heavy kit
on his back, advanced into the dim light. "Why," he said, "who
lives here then?"

"We live here," said March. "What do you want?"

"Oh!" came the long, melodious wonder-note from the
young soldier. "Doesn't William Grenfel live here then?"

"No—you know he doesn't."

"Do I?—Do I?—I don't, you see.—He *did* live here, because
he was my father, and I lived here myself five years ago.—
What's become of him then?"

The young man—or youth, for he would not be more than
twenty, now advanced and stood in the inner doorway. March,
already under the influence of his strange, soft, modulated voice,
stared at him spell-bound. He had a ruddy, roundish face, with
fairish hair, rather long, flattened to his forehead with sweat.
His eyes were blue, and very bright and sharp. On his cheeks,
on the fresh ruddy skin were fine, fair hairs, like a down, but
sharper. It gave him a slightly glistening look. Having his heavy
sack on his shoulders, he stooped, thrusting his head forward.
His hat was loose in one hand. He stared brightly, very keenly
from girl to girl, particularly at March, who stood pale, with

great dilated eyes, in her belted coat and puttees, her hair knotted in a big crisp knot behind. She still had the gun in her hand. Behind her, Banford, clinging to the sofa-arm, was shrinking away, with half-averted head.

"I thought my father still lived here?—I wonder if he's dead."

"We've been here for three years," said Banford, who was beginning to recover her wits, seeing something boyish in the round head with its rather long, sweaty hair [.]

"Three years! You don't say so!—And you don't know who was here before you?"

"I know it was an old man, who lived by himself."

"Ay!—Yes, that's him!—And what became of him then?"

"He died.—I know he died——"

"Ay! He's dead then!"

The youth stared at them without changing colour or expression. If he had any expression, beside a slight baffled look of wonder, it was one of sharp curiosity concerning the two girls, sharp, impersonal curiosity, the curiosity of that round young head.

But to March he was the fox. Whether it was the thrusting forward of the head, or the glisten of fine whitish hairs on the ruddy cheek-bones, or the bright, keen eyes, that can never be said: but the boy was to her the fox, and she could not see him otherwise.

"How is it you didn't know if your father was alive or dead?" asked Banford, recovering her natural sharpness.

"Ay, that's it," replied the softly-breathing youth. "You see I joined up in Canada, and I hadn't heard for three or four years.—I ran away to Canada."

"And now have you just come from France?"

"Well—from Salonika really."

"So you've nowhere to go now."

"Oh, I know some people in the village. Anyhow, I can go to the Swan."

"You came on the train, I suppose.—Would you like to sit down a bit?"

"Well—I don't mind."

He gave an odd little groan as he swung off his kit. Banford looked at March.

"Put the gun down," she said. "We'll make a cup of tea."

"Ay," said the youth. "We've seen enough of rifles." He sat down rather tired, on the sofa, leaning forward.

March recovered her presence of mind, and went into the kitchen. There she heard the soft young voice musing:

"Well, to think I should come back and find it like this!" He did not seem sad, not at all—only rather interestedly surprised.

"And what a difference in the place, eh?" he continued, looking round the room.

"You see a difference, do you?" said Banford.

"Yes—don't I?" His eyes were almost unnaturally clear and bright, though it was the brightness of abundant health.

March was busy in the kitchen preparing another meal. It was about seven oclock. All the time, while she was active, she was attending to the youth in the sitting-room, not so much listening to what he said, as feeling the soft run of his voice. She primmed up her mouth tighter and tighter, puckering it as if it was sewed, in her effort to keep her will uppermost. Yet her large eyes dilated and glowed in spite of her, she lost herself. Rapidly and carelessly she prepared the meal, cutting large chunks of bread and margarine—for there was no butter. She racked her brain to think of something else to put on the tray —she had only bread, margarine, and jam, and the larder was bare. Unable to conjure anything up, she went in to the sitting room with her tray.

She did not want to be noticed. Above all, she did not want him to look at her. But when she came in, and was busy setting the table just behind him, he pulled himself up from his sprawling, and turned to look over his shoulder. She became pale and wan.

The youth watched her as she bent over the table, looked at her slim, well-shapen legs, at the belted coat dropping around her thighs, at the knot of dark hair, and his curiosity, vivid and widely alert, was again arrested by her.

She turned round, but kept her eyes sideways, dropping and lifting her dark lashes. Her mouth unpuckered, as she said to Banford:

"Will you pour out?"

Then she went into the kitchen again.

"Have your tea where you are, will you?" said Banford to the youth—"unless you'd rather come to the table."

"Well," said he, "I'm nice and comfortable here, aren't I? I will have it here, if you don't mind."

"There's nothing but bread and jam," she said. And she put his plate on a stool by him. She was very happy now, waiting on him. For she loved company. And now she was no more afraid of him than if he were her own younger brother. He was such a boy.

"Nellie," she called. "I've poured you a cup out."

March appeared in the doorway, took her cup, and sat down in a corner, as far from the light as possible. She was very sensitive in her knees. Having no skirts to cover them, and being forced to sit with them boldly exposed, she suffered. She shrank and shrank, trying not to be seen. And the youth, sprawling low on the couch, glanced up at her, with long, steady, penetrating looks, till she was almost ready to disappear. Yet she held her cup balanced, she drank her tea, screwed up her mouth and held her head averted. Her desire to be invisible was so strong that it quite baffled the youth. He felt he could not see her distinctly. And ever his eyes came back to her, searching, unremitting, with unconscious fixed attention.

Meanwhile he was talking softly and smoothly to Banford, who loved nothing so much as gossip, and who was full of perky interest, like a bird. Also he ate largely and quickly and voraciously, so that March had to cut more hunks of bread and margarine, for the roughness of which Banford apologised.

"Oh well," said March, suddenly speaking, "if there's no butter to put on it, it's no good trying to make dainty pieces."

Again the youth watched her, and he laughed, with a sudden, quick laugh, showing his teeth and wrinkling his nose.

"It isn't, is it," he answered, in his soft, near voice.

It appeared he was Cornish by birth and upbringing. When he was twelve years old he had come to Bailey Farm with his father, with whom he had never agreed very well. So he had run away to Canada, and worked far away in the West. Now he was here—and that was the end of it.

He was very curious about the girls, to find out exactly what they were doing. His questions were those of a peasant: acute, practical, a little mocking. He was very much amused by their attitude to their losses: for they were amusing on the score of heifers and fowls.

"Oh well," broke in March, "we don't believe in living for nothing but work."

"Don't you?" he answered. And again the quick young laugh came over his face. He kept his eyes steadily on the obscure woman in the corner.

"But what will you do when you've used up all your capital?" he said.

"Oh, I don't know," answered March laconically. "Hire ourselves out for land[-]workers, I suppose."

"Yes, but there won't be any demand for women land-workers, now the war's over," said the youth.

"Oh, we'll see. We shall hold on a bit longer yet," said March, with a plangent, half sad, half ironical indifference.

"There wants a man about the place," said the youth softly. Banford burst out laughing.

"Take care what you say," she interrupted. "We consider ourselves quite efficient."

"Oh," came March's slow, plangent voice, "it isn't a case of efficiency, I'm afraid. If you're going to do farming you must be at it from morning till night, and you might as well be a beast yourself."

"Yes, that's it," said the youth. "You aren't willing to put yourselves into it."

"We aren't," said March, "and we know it."

"We want some of our time for ourselves," said Banford.

The youth threw himself back on the sofa, his face tight with laughter, and laughed silently but thoroughly. The calm scorn of the girls tickled him tremendously.

"Yes," he said, "but why did you begin then?"

"Oh," said March, "we had a better opinion of the nature of fowls then, than we have now."

Again the face of the youth tightened with delighted laughter.

"You haven't a very high opinion of fowls now, then," he said.

"Oh no—quite a low one," said March.

He laughed out.

"Neither fowls nor heifers," said Banford.

The youth broke into a sharp clap of laughter, delighted. The girls began to laugh too, March turning aside her face and wrinkling her mouth in amusement.

"Oh well," said Banford, "we don't mind, do we[,] Nellie?"

"No," said March, "we don't mind."

The youth was very pleased. He had eaten and drunk his fill. Banford began to question him. His name was Henry Grenfel—no, he was not called Harry, always Henry. He continued to answer with courteous simplicity, grave and charming. March, who was now not included, cast long, slow glances at him from her recess, as he sat there on the sofa, his hands clasping his knees, his face, bright and alert, turned to Banford. She became almost peaceful, at last. He was identified with the fox—and he was here in full presence. She need not go after him any more. There in the shadow of her corner she gave herself up to a warm, relaxed peace, almost like sleep, accepting the spell that was on her. But she wished to remain hidden. She was only fully at peace whilst he forgot her, talking with Banford. Hidden in the shadow of her corner, she need not any more be divided in herself, trying to keep up two planes of consciousness. She could at last lapse into the odour of the fox.

For the youth, sitting before the fire in his uniform, sent a faint but distinct odour into the room, indefinable, but something like a wild creature. March no longer tried to reserve herself from it. She was still and soft in her corner like a passive creature in its cave.

At last the talk dwindled. The youth relaxed his clasp of his knees, pulled himself together a little, and looked round. Again he became aware of the silent, half-invisible woman in the corner.

"Well," he said, unwillingly, "I suppose I'd better be going, or they'll be in bed at the Swan."

"I'm afraid they're in bed anyhow," said Banford. "They've all got this influenza."

"Have they!" he exclaimed. And he pondered. "Well," he continued, "I shall find a place somewhere."

"I'd say you could stay here, only——" Banford began. He turned and watched her, holding his head forward.

"What——?" he asked.

"Oh well," she said, "propriety, I suppose——." She was rather confused.

"It wouldn't be improper, would it?" he said, gently surprised.

"Not as far as we're concerned," said Banford.

"And not as far as *I'm* concerned," he said, with grave naïeveté [naïveté]. "After all, it's my own home, in a way."

Banford smiled at this.

"It's what the village will have to say," she said.

"I see," he answered. And he looked from one to another.

"What do you say, Nellie?" asked Banford.

"I don't mind," said March, in her distinct tone. "The village doesn't matter to me, anyhow."

"No," said the youth, quick and soft. "Why should it?—I mean, what should they say?"

"Oh well," came March's plangent, laconic voice, "they'll easily find something to say. But it makes no difference, what they say. We can look after ourselves."

"Of course we can," said the youth.

"Well then, stop if you like," said Banford. "The spare room is quite ready."

His face shone with pleasure.

"If you're quite sure it isn't troubling you too much," he said, with that soft courtesy which distinguished him.

"Oh, it's no trouble," they both said.

He looked, smiling with delight, from one to another.

"It's awfully nice not to have to turn out again, isn't it?" he said gratefully.

"I suppose it is," said Banford.

March disappeared to attend to the room. Banford was as pleased and thoughtful as if she had her own young brother home from France. It gave her just the same kind of gratification to attend on him, to get out the bath for him, and everything. Her natural warmth and kindliness had now an outlet. And the youth luxuriated in her sisterly attention. But it puzzled him slightly to know that March was silently working for him too. Still, it seemed, he had not really seen her. He felt he should not know her if he met her in the road.

That night March dreamed vividly. She dreamed she heard a singing outside, which she could not understand, a singing that roamed round the house, in the fields and in the darkness. It moved her so, that she felt she must weep. She went out, and suddenly she knew it was the fox singing. He was very yellow and bright, like corn. She went nearer to him, but he ran away, and ceased singing. He seemed near, and she wanted to touch him. She stretched out her hand, but suddenly he bit her wrist, and at the same instant, as she drew back, turning round to bound away, he whisked his brush across her face, and it seemed his brush was on fire, for it seared and burned her mouth with a great pain. She awoke with the pain of it, and lay trembling as if she were really seared.

In the morning, however, she only remembered it as a distant memory. She arose and was busy preparing the house and attending to the fowls. Their guest came downstairs in his shirt-sleeves. He was young and fresh, but he walked with his head thrust forward, so that his shoulders seemed raised and rounded, as if he had a slight curvature of the spine. It must have been only a manner of bearing himself, for he was young and vigorous. He washed himself and went outside, whilst the women were preparing breakfast.

He saw everything, and examined everything. His curiosity was quick and insatiable. He compared the state of things with that which he remembered before, and cast over in his mind the effect of the changes. He watched the fowls and the ducks, to see their condition, he noticed the flight of wood-pigeons overhead: they were very numerous; he saw the few apples high up, which March had not been able to reach; he remarked that they had borrowed a draw-pump, presumably to empty the big soft-water cistern which was on the north side of the house.

"It's a funny, delapidated little place," he said to the girls, as he sat at breakfast.

His eyes were wide and childish, with thinking about things. He did not say much, but ate largely. March kept her face averted. She, too, in the early morning, could not be aware of him, though something about the glint of his khaki reminded her of the brilliance of her dream-fox.

During the day the girls went about their business. In the morning, he attended to the guns, shot a rabbit and a wild duck that was flying high, towards the woods. In the afternoon, he went to the village. He came back at tea-time. He had the same alert, forward-reaching look on his roundish face. He hung his hat on a peg with a little swinging gesture. He was thinking about something.

"Well," he said to the girls, as he sat at table. "What am I going to do?"

"What do you mean, what are you going to do?" said Banford.

"Where am I going to stay?" he said.

"I don't know," said Banford. "Where do you think of staying?"

"Well——" he hesitated—"I should like to stay here, if you could do with me, and if you'd charge me the same as they would at the Swan.—That's what I should *like*——"

He put the matter to them. He was rather confused. March sat, with her elbows on the table, her two hands supporting her chin, looking at him unconsciously. Suddenly he lifted his clouded blue eyes, and instantaneously looked straight into March's eyes. He was [startled] as well as she. He too recoiled a little. March felt the same knowing, domineering spark leap out of his eyes and take possession of her psyche. She shut her eyes.

"Well, I don't know——" Banford was saying. She seemed reluctant, as if she were afraid of being imposed upon. She looked at March. But, with her weak, troubled sight, she only saw the usual semi-abstraction on her friend's face. "Why don't you speak, Nellie?" she said.

But March was wide-eyed and silent, and the youth, as if fascinated, was watching her without moving his eyes.

"Go on—answer something," said Banford. And March turned her head slightly aside, as if coming to consciousness, or trying to come to consciousness.

"What do you expect me to say?" she asked automatically.

"Say what you think," said Banford.

"It's all the same to me," said March. And again there was silence. A pointed light seemed to be on the boy's eyes, penetrating like a needle.

"So it is to me," said Banford. But he had dropped his head, and was oblivious of what she was saying.

"Well, I suppose you can please yourself, Henry," Banford concluded.

Still he did not reply, but lifting his head, with a strange, cunning look, watched March, only watched her. She sat with face slightly averted, and mouth suffering, quite dim in her consciousness. Banford became a little puzzled. Even she perceived the steady concentration of the youth's eyes, their fixed, knowing, unabashed attention, as he looked at March, whose mouth quivered a little, not with tears—indescribably.

"Cut a bit more bread, Nellie," said Banford uneasily.

And March automatically reached for the knife. The boy dropped his head again, so that they only saw its shapely round dome.

One or two days went by, and the boy stayed on. Banford was quite charmed by him. He was so soft and courteous in speech, not wanting to say much himself, preferring to hear what she had to say, and to laugh in his quick, half-mocking way. He helped a little with the work—but not too much. He loved to be out alone with the gun in his hands, to watch, to see. For his sharp-eyed, impersonal curiosity was insatiable, and he was most free when he was quite alone, half-hidden, watching.

Particularly he watched March. She was a strange character to him. Her figure, like a graceful young man's, piqued him. Her dark eyes made something rise in his soul, with a curious elate triumph, when he looked into them, a triumph he was afraid to let be seen, it was so keen and secret. And then her odd, shrewd speech made him laugh outright. He felt he must go further, he was inevitably impelled.—But he put away the thought of her, and went off towards the wood's edge with the gun.

The dusk was falling as he came home, and with the dusk, a fine late-November rain. He saw the fire-light leaping in the window of the sitting-room, a leaping light in the little cluster of dark buildings. And suddenly, he wanted to stay here permanently, to have this place for his own. And then the thought entered him like a bullet: why not marry March? He stood still in the middle of the field for some moments, the dead rabbit hanging still in his hand, arrested by this thought. His mind opened in amazement—then his soul gave an odd little laugh, and something in him began to burn. He wanted to marry her. Even a sense of ridicule hardly affected him. Secretly, he was keen, subtly and secretly keen, to have her.

He scarcely thought of his intention openly to himself. Yet in his mind he began to scheme, to scheme endlessly: what it would be like; what she would probably say to him; could he stay on the farm when he had got his ticket. He would like to be on a little place of his own, to do as he liked. For of all things, he hated most a master. The quick scheming of his mind soon resolved itself. The sense of ridicule was the strongest deterrent: there was something ridiculous in the idea, to him. And he was very much afraid that she might reject him. But when he thought of the actual proposal something beat up with keen and secret desire in him. He knew he could *make* her obey his will. And again he burned.

He went about just the same for two more days. Only it was evident he had something on his mind. But his nature was secretive, it would be impossible to speak to him, or even to surmise about him. He seemed to draw a cloak of invisibleness about him.—At the end of the second day however he determined to speak. The great nerves in his thighs and at the base of his spine seemed to burn like live wire.

He had been sawing logs for the fire, in the afternoon. Darkness came very early: it was still a cold, raw mist. It was getting almost too dark to see. A pile of short sawed logs lay beside the trestle. March came to carry them indoors, or into the shed, as he was busy sawing the last log. He was working in his shirt sleeves, and did not notice her approach[.] She came unwilling, as if shy. He saw her stooping to the bright-ended logs, and he stopped sawing. A fire like lightning flew down his legs, in the nerves.

"March?" he said, in his quiet young voice.

She looked up from the logs she was piling.

"Yes?" she said.

He looked down on her in the dusk. He could see her not too distinctly.

"I wanted to ask you something," he said.

"Did you? What was it?" she said.

"Why——" his voice seemed to draw out soft and subtle, it penetrated her nerves—"why, what do you think it is?"

She stood up, placed her hands on her hips, and stood look-ing at him transfixed, without answering. Again he burned with a sudden power[.]

"Well," he said, and his voice was so soft it seemed rather like a subtle touch, like the merest touch of a cat's paw, a feeling rather than a sound. "Well—I wanted to ask you to marry me."

March felt him rather than heard him. She was trying in vain to turn aside her face. A great relaxation seemed to have come over her. She stood silent, her head slightly on one side. He seemed to be bending towards her, invisibly smiling. It seemed to her fine sparks came out of him.

Then very suddenly, she said:

"What do you mean? I'm old enough to be your mother."

"I know how old you are," came his soft voice, as it were imperceptibly stroking her. "You're thirty-three—and I'm nearly twenty-one. That's not old enough to be my mother.—I knew you'd say that.—What difference does it make?"

She could hardly attend to the words, the sound of his voice had such effect on her, taking away all her power, loosing her into a strange relaxation. She struggled somewhere for her own power. But she knew she was lost—lost—lost. The word seemed to rock in her as if in a narcotic dream. Suddenly again she spoke.

"You don't know what you're talking about," she said, in a brief and transient stroke of scorn.

"Ha!—don't I? Don't I though! Yes I do. Yes I do," he said softly, as if he produced his voice in her blood. "Yes I do know what I'm talking about. I ask you to marry me, because—I want you—you see——"

The swoon passed over he[r] as he slowly concluded. She felt she had been born too late, and must give up. She could not help herself—she gave up in a deathly darkness, through which his voice came, resonant in her as if she were its medium.

"I want you—you see—that's why——" he proceeded, soft and slow. He had achieved his work. Her eyelids were dropped, her face half-averted and unconscious. She was in his power. He stepped forward and put his arm round her.

"Say then," he said. "Say then you'll marry me. Say—say?" He was softly insistent.

"What?" she asked, faint, from a distance, like one in pain. His voice was now unthinkably near and soft.

"Say yes."

"Yes—yes," she murmured slowly, half articulate, as if semi-conscious, and as if in pain, like one who dies.

He held her, and he seemed to glisten above her. He was so young—and so old. This also seemed to occupy her consciousness: he was so young—and so old—so old. She was in his power.

He did not kiss her or caress her. Suddenly he pressed her hard, and brought her to herself.

"We'll carry in these logs," he said. "We'd better tell Banford." Without knowing, she obeyed him.

It was he who told Banford.

"Well," he said, "What do you think?" And his face glistened like a were-wolf at poor Banford. He had that power for strangely smiling without altering a muscle of his face, exultantly, domineeringly smiling.

"What?" said Banford.

"March and I are going to get married."

"Don't be silly," said Banford.

"No silliness. It's quite right—isn't it March?"

And March, with her wide, dark, lost eyes, and her inscrutable pale face, glanced at him and answered "Yes."

Banford was utterly overcome. Her eyes nearly fell out of her head. She laughed, and she was angry. But the boy sat there in his shirt-sleeves, like a man, and both women were at his mercy. All the time there was this indescribable shining on his face, a sort of whitish gleam, which Banford could have vouched for, and which repelled her. But he made her discuss all arrangements with him. They decided the marriage should take place by special licence, in a few days time.

Somewhere, Banford now disliked him intensely, almost mystically. But she did what he wanted. She was quite helpless. And the sight of the wide-eyed, lost March angered her and almost broke her heart. But she was powerless as if enmeshed in fine electric cobwebs.

He was very jaunty in his silence as he took all the necessary measures, very jaunty and self-satisfied, very cocky in his quiet way. The women were at his mercy. He did not make love to March. He did not even want to be with her very much. He almost kept her at a distance. But he held her completely, none the less.

One day she said to him, as they happened to be busy together.

"You remind me so much of the fox." She put aside her strands of hair mistily. His face turned suddenly on her, with its gleam.

"Which fox?" he said, laughing.

"The one that fetched the fowls."

"Do I remind you of *that?*" he said, laughing strangely, and putting his hand on her arm. She almost winced. But she watched him fixedly. "Do you think I've come for your fowls?" he continued, still laughing invisibly. He put his hand behind her neck and drew her head towards him. He kissed her for the first time, on the mouth. Then he laughed aloud. "Well," he said, "tomorrow we shall be married."

And on the morrow they were married, although to Banford it seemed utterly impossible. Yet it was so. And he seemed so cocky, in his quiet, secret way. And Banford was so curiously powerless against him, and March was so curiously happy. This also angered Banford. She could not bear to see the secret, half-dreamy, half knowing look of happiness on March's face. It seemed wicked. March seemed to her to have a secret wickedness, gentle, receptive wickedness, like a dream.

In March, the dream-consciousness now predominated. She lived in another world, the world of the fox. When she dreamed, the fox and the boy were somehow indistinguishable. And all through the day, she lived in this world, the world of the fox and the boy, or the fox and the old man, she never knew which. Her ready superficial consciousness carried her through the world's business all right. But people said she was odd. And she talked so little to her husband.

He had to go away in ten days['] time after the marriage. She suffered when he was gone, and he suffered in going. But he went in the inevitable decision to come back, and his decisions fulfilled themselves almost like fate, unnoticeably. He would come home by instinct.

Edmund Bergler M.D.

D. H. LAWRENCE'S *THE FOX* AND THE PSYCHOANALYTIC THEORY ON LESBIANISM

In his comparatively obscure novelette called "The Fox," D. H. Lawrence told the story of two half-intellectual Lesbians living on a farm in England at the end of World War I. They are trying, unsuccessfully, to raise chickens; their main obstacles are a fox which repeatedly raids the barnyard, a number of strange illnesses, and their flock's "obstinate refusal to lay eggs." The fox gradually becomes the most serious of their problems. The women plan to shoot him, but he is too elusive for them. At length one of the women, March, comes face to face with the fox:

> She lowered her eyes and suddenly saw the fox. He was look-ing up at her. His chin was pressed down, and his eyes were looking up. They met her eyes. And he knew her. She was spell-bound—she knew he knew her. So he looked into her eyes, and her soul failed her. He knew her, he was not daunted. . . . She struggled, confusedly she came to herself, and saw him making off, with slow leaps over some fallen boughs, slow, impudent jumps . . . [Later] she took her gun again and went to look for the fox. For he had lifted his eyes upon her, and his knowing look seemed to have entered her brain. She did not so much think of him: she was possessed by him.

Edmund Bergler, M.D., a graduate of the Medical School of the University of Vienna and a psychoanalytic psychiatrist there and in New York since 1927, has written 255 scientific studies, in twelve countries, on the theory and therapy of neurosis, and is the author of nineteen books, among them *Kinsey's Myth of Female Sexuality* (1954), *Homosexuality: Disease or Way of Life?* (1956), and *Counterfeit-Sex* (2nd, enlarged edition, 1958). His essay is printed here with the consent of the editors of the *Journal of Nervous and Mental Disease* (Baltimore, Maryland), where it was first published in 1958.

She saw his dark, shrewd, unabashed eye looking into her, knowing her. She felt him invisibly master her spirit . . . And again, she saw him glance over his shoulder at her, half-inviting, half-contemptuous and cunning. . . .

The fox invades March's reveries:

March also was not conscious that she thought of the fox. But whenever she fell into her half-musing, when she was half-rapt and half-intelligently aware of what passed under her vision, then it was the fox which somehow dominated her unconscious, possessed the blank half of her musing. And so it was for weeks, and months.

A young soldier then comes to the farm. The two women find out that he is the grandson of the previous owner, and had not known of his grandfather's death; he had enlisted in Canada. Lawrence describes March's reaction to the stranger in these terms:

The young man—or youth, for he would not be more than twenty—now advanced and stood in the inner doorway. March, already under the influence of his strange, soft, modulated voice, stared at him spell-bound. He had a ruddy, roundish face, with fairish hair, rather long, flattened to his forehead with sweat. His eyes were blue, and very bright and sharp. On his cheeks, on the fresh ruddy skin, were fine, fair hairs, like a down, but sharper. It gave him a slightly glistening look. . . . But for March he was the fox. Whether it was the thrusting forward of his head, or the glisten of fine whitish hair on the ruddy cheek-bones, or the bright, keen eyes, that can never be said: but the boy was to her the fox, and she could not see him otherwise.

The young man spends his leave at the farm, and falls in love with March. For some time, he cannot make out the relationship of the two young women: March acts the "man," and Banford, her companion, the "wife." Confronted with the boy's advances, March is quite helpless and evasively confused. Then the young man shoots the fox:

The first thing that both she and Banford did in the morning
was to go out to see the [dead] fox. It was a lovely dog-fox
in his prime, with a handsome thick winter coat: a lovely
golden-rod colour, with grey as it passed to the belly, and
belly all white, and a great full brush with a delicate black and
grey and pure white tip. . . . "He's a beauty, isn't he?" said
Henry, standing by.—"Oh, yes, he's a fine big fox. I wonder
how many chickens he's responsible for," she replied. . . .
"Are you going to skin him?" she asked.—"Yes, when I've
had breakfast and got a board to peg him on." . . . "My
word, what a strong smell he's got! Pooo! It'll take some
washing off one's hands. I don't know why I was so silly as
to handle him."—And she looked at her right hand, that had
passed down his belly and along his tail, and had even got a
tiny streak of blood from one dark place in his fur.—"Have
you seen the chickens when they smell him, how frightened
they are?" he said.—"Yes, aren't they!" Later in the day
she saw the fox's skin nailed flat on a board, as if crucified. It
gave her an uneasy feeling.

At last March consents to marry Henry, but subsequently
changes her mind again and again. Severe conflicts with Banford,
her Lesbian friend, follow. Here is one scene involving the
women:

He heard Banford's fretful: "Why don't you let me help you
with the parcel?" She had a queer plaintive hitch in her voice.
Then came March's robust and reckless: "Oh, I can manage.
Don't you bother about me. You've all you can do to get yourself over."—"Yes, that's all very well," said Banford fret-
fully. "You say 'Don't bother about me' and then all the while
you feel injured because nobody thinks of you." . . . "When
do I feel injured?" said March.—"Always. You always feel
injured. Now you're feeling injured because I won't have that
boy to come and live on the farm."—"I'm not feeling injured
at all," said March.—"I know you are. When he's gone you'll
sulk over it. . . ."

In addition to "feeling injured," March enjoys the conflict between Banford and the young man:

March seemed to flourish in this atmosphere. She seemed to sit between the two antagonists with a little wicked smile on her face, enjoying herself. There was even a sort of complacency in the way she laboriously crocheted, this evening.

The end of the story is that the young man "inadvertently" kills his Lesbian competitor while felling a tree ("No one saw what was happening besides himself"); March marries the young man, although the marriage does not seem to work out sexually because March still cannot accept her new passive role.

"The Fox" contains a series of observations and between-the-lines allusions which are clinically correct. Mingled with these are inaccuracies, but the clinically correct observations predominate.

1. Lawrence describes the typical husband-wife camouflage of Lesbians, and at the same time stresses the psychic-masochistic substructure of the camouflage. March places her masochism in fantasies, remains helpless against the "mocking" fox although she has a shotgun in her hands, is equally masochistic in her relationship with the young man after he has shot the fox.

2. Lawrence correctly describes March's constant "injustice collecting," hence her hidden psychic masochism. Banford's specific reference to this, "You always feel injured," is quoted above.

3. Lawrence accurately depicts the two sets of identification in March: the "leading" masochistic identification with the victim, and the "misleading" masculine identification, deposited in the Oedipal camouflage of her relationship with Banford.

4. Lawrence ingeniously hints that the fox, the devourer of chickens, symbolizes the "devouring" mother; we know that the fear of being devoured has priority in the "septet of baby fears."

5. With a combination of naïveté (on a conscious level) and good intuition (on the unconscious level), Lawrence describes the unvarying inner defense of his masochistic heroine: the search for love, which these sick women can find neither in the Lesbian nor in the connubial bed since "injustice collecting" is the real aim.

6. Finally, Lawrence presents with clinical correctness the defensive pseudo-aggression so predominant in Lesbians. March

speaks harshly to Banford, enjoys the conflict between Banford and her male competitor, and even marries the man who has been directly or indirectly responsible for Banford's death. Moreover, in some "tender" manner, she is glad of the fox's death.

Lawrence's accurate observations outweigh in importance his cherished mystical ideas on sex-predominance, which are brought in at the end of the story when he explains March's frigidity in terms of the superficial defensive masculine camouflage. Lawrence also misunderstands March's reason for turning to the young man: he declares that March identified the fox with the young man ("The boy was to her the fox"), and claims that March had been helpless against the fox. Putting the two statements together, one sees that March lands exactly at the point she tried desperately to escape—the point of masochistic passivity on the part of the victim (the devoured "chicken").

The initial analytic theory on Lesbianism assumed that a specific elaboration of an Oedipal situation was involved. In 1927, Ernest Jones suggested that Lesbianism could be traced to two factors: "an unusually intensive oral eroticism and an unusually strong sadism." In 1931, in his study "On Female Sexuality," Freud described the pre-Oedipal phase of the girl. Freud assumed that basically this attachment is shattered through ambivalence and hate. In application of these ideas, H. Deutsch reported in 1932, in her study "On Female Homosexuality," that her Lesbian patients repeated the child-mother and not the Oedipal fixation in their perversion: should the hatred for the pre-Oedipal mother be too pronounced, the reactive feeling of guilt gives rise to an attempt to deny its contents, according to the formula: "I'm not the refused and rejected child; I'm a child loved and nourished by you."

In a series of papers on Lesbianism, summarized in my books, *Neurotic Counterfeit-Sex* (1951), *Kinsey's Myth of Female Sexuality* (in collaboration with W. Kroger, 1954), and *Homosexuality: Disease or Way of Life?* (1956), I have pointed out that the oral-masochistic (not sadistic, hate-filled) basis of Lesbianism works on a five-layer structure:

1. Stabilization on the oral-masochistic, hence pre-Oedipal, level;

2. First superego veto, objecting to the "pleasure-in-displeasure" pattern;

3. First defense of pseudo-aggression;
4. Second superego veto, objecting to this "hatred";
5. Second defense of pseudo-love, with Oedipal camouflage.

(It should be understood that this last defense, which reaches the surface as the husband-wife relationship, does not represent a re-enactment of the roles of good mother and beloved child, as alleged, but an unconscious—and wholly concealed—dramatization of the fantasy of the masochistically mistreated child and cruel, denying mother.)

The five-layer basis of Lesbianism explains a number of phenomenologically observable facts.

First, the typical high tension of the Lesbian relationship as well as the pathological jealousy. This jealousy, in inner reality, merely provides a point of departure for masochistic injustice-collecting.

Second, the abundance of ever-ready hatred in Lesbian relationships, which becomes evident at the least excuse and often is expressed in physical attacks. The pseudo-love which is the final defense of the Lesbian is easily penetrated to reveal the pseudo-aggression beneath.

Third, the husband-wife drama enacted as Oedipal camouflage is merely an admission of the lesser intrapsychic crime, devised as a screen for the more guilt-laden masochistic mother-child relationship, which dates back to pre-Oedipal conflicts.

Fourth, the inevitable failure of a relationship established within the framework of Lesbianism. A person unconsciously seeking constant psychic masochistic satisfaction is incapable of conscious happiness.

Fifth, the central point of the homosexual's "solution" consists of a specific elaboration of psychic masochistic vicissitudes stemming from the first months of life. It is necessary to distinguish between the genetic and clinical pictures in psychic masochism. The genetic picture, worked out by Freud though little utilized by him, begins with infantile aggression. This aggression recoils because of guilt, and the guilt is secondarily libidinized.

The clinical picture, comprising the phenomena actually observable in the adult neurotic, begins here. It appears in response to the veto pronounced by the inner conscience (superego). The superego objects to any pleasure, including of course the pleasure of psychic masochism. The clinical picture, worked out more than two decades ago by myself, is connected with the earliest (oral) level of regression. Its pattern is that of the "mechanism of orality": construction of external defeats; simulated struggles against these defeats; masochistic whimpering, and self-pity.

Consciously, neurotics controlled by the mechanism of orality are aware only of the "righteous indignation" with which they attempt to fight against their self-constructed defeats, and which leads to self-pity. They remain consciously oblivious to their initial provocation, and to the masochistic pleasure derived from contemplating their humiliation or failure. Since both these vital points remain completely repressed, the illusion of "aggression" can be successfully maintained. The dynamically decisive masochistic substructure does not become conscious.

The outcome is injustice-collecting, practiced without letup. The individual's conscious desire for success is invariably canceled by his unconscious desire for refusal, rejection, or denial. The unconscious aim is the more powerful; it molds the neurotic into an unconscious glutton for punishment.

The effectiveness of "The Fox" derives from Lawrence's predominantly correct—and obviously intuitive—observations of a series of clinically verifiable facts on Lesbianism.

Marvin Mudrick

THE ORIGINALITY OF *THE RAINBOW*

MANNERS and morals: they are, critics agree, what novels properly concern themselves with; and the specialist in the English novel can readily demonstrate the English novelist's expert attention to both from *Moll Flanders* to the latest thriller by Graham Greene. Certainly, fiction is of all literary genres the most intractable to description or definition, and we are grateful for any indices to its nature. We are also proud of our language and literature; and the novel in English has an illustrious history, no doubt about it. So the manners and morals, and the fiction, we are specially interested in are English and American. It may not, then, seem chauvinistic to us when Caroline Gordon (in *How to Read a Novel,* Viking, 1957) discovers the world history of the novel to be a triumphant progress toward apotheosis in the work of the Anglo-American Henry James, who was obliging enough to scrutinize, with the tact of an exquisite sensibility, Anglo-Saxon manners and morals—of only a few social groups, to be sure—on *both* sides of the Atlantic. Even Dr. Leavis, who demotes or dismisses Richardson, Fielding, Sterne, Smollett, Dickens, Thackeray, Hardy, and Joyce, expresses much admiration for Hawthorne, and finds a great tradition in Jane Austen, George Eliot, James, Conrad, and Lawrence, in whose work, as it seems to him, manners are so chosen and placed as to reflect on their particular surfaces the image of that sober absolute morality, essentially secular and embat-

Marvin Mudrick (Ph.D., California), a critic of fiction who writes for the *Hudson Review, Kenyon Review,* and other journals, teaches English at the University of Santa Barbara (Goleta); he is a Guggenheim Fellow working in Paris on a study of Colette. His essay is taken from a paper read at the M.L.A. meetings in December 1958, and printed in *Spectrum,* Winter 1959.

tled, which for two centuries has been the strength of England if not of the entire civilized world.

It is just here, regarding the rest of the world, that a doubt arises. Compare, for instance, George Eliot and Tolstoy, or Conrad and Dostoievsky—comparisons that Dr. Leavis, at any rate, ought to accept as fair, since one great tradition ought to be able to stand up against another, and since George Eliot and Tolstoy share a preoccupation with the social and ordinary as Conrad and Dostoievsky share a preoccupation with the psychological and extraordinary. Or compare Stendhal and Jane Austen, or Turgenev and James, or almost any nineteenth-century French or Russian novelist and Hawthorne.

Fiction, and a tradition of fiction, may be genuine without being great. Greatness is, after all, relative, and when we compare George Eliot and Tolstoy we are aware of such differences in magnitude that to describe the two of them by the same honorific epithet is to do no service to either. Nor is George Eliot a feeble representative of the tradition Dr. Leavis singles out. *Middlemarch,* at least, is a very impressive novel; with a breadth of intelligent sympathy it fixes for all time the manners and morals of its own place and time, and it is perhaps the only English novel that sensitively registers something like a whole society. Yet it is, as the author notes, "A Study of Provincial Life." There is, in fact, no English novel that registers a whole society; and, in the balance with Continental fiction, there is almost no English novel that cannot fairly be described as provincial.

It is not, of course, merely a question of subject: a novelist may be as cosmopolitan as he pleases in treating provincial life —Flaubert or Galdós, for example. The point is that for the English novelist a provincialism of temperament is likely to go along with his provincialism of subject. Mme. Bovary, not to mention Bouvard and Pécuchet, has written some of the better-known English novels, and the sturdy pragmatism of the English petty bourgeoisie has penetrated and sustained English fiction since those redoubtable self-made innovators and moral men of practical affairs, Defoe and Richardson. The English novel has characteristically been partisan, either protective or rebellious; and the standard of conduct—of manners and morals —which it lavishly illustrates, and by which it measures itself, is the middle-class standard. *Wuthering Heights* and *Tristram*

Shandy are as pertinent to the case as *Pamela,* and together they exemplify the three major modes of English fiction: romance as protest, satire as protest, and sentiment as affirmation. Perhaps Dr. Leavis recoils with such a spasm of distaste from Sterne because *Tristram Shandy* is the most subversive protest in English fiction against the bourgeois imperatives that Dr. Leavis, by implication, finds so congenial to the flowering of a great artistic tradition.

These imperatives are, of course, overwhelmingly materialistic. Tom Jones in the hay (sowing his wild oats) with a pretty chambermaid, Scrooge converted to the obsession of giving rather than withholding smiles and crowns and guineas, Pamela indignantly rejecting premarital advances for the sake of wealth and rank later—all of them are enjoying the satisfactions of a morality that ultimately, despite its solemn façade, repays its adherents and sinks human problems in cash and Christmas pudding, a morality of trivial appetites. Whether the English novelist is examining, with intelligence or sentimentality or cynicism, the manners and squeamishness of the cultivated provinces, or the local color of urban and rural low life, or the sinister fascinations of the *haut monde,* or the convulsive freakishness of grand supersexual and asexual passions, or the palpitating idealism of young women who—not having been told what they can importantly do—are looking for something important to do: whatever the English novelist tries, the manners and morals of the earliest and most oppressively successful middle class in history are breathing down his neck and directing his pen into the official view of a life that is in any case considerably less exhilarating than the life visible to the great Continental novelists. Or, for that matter, to Chaucer and Shakespeare.

We must come to it at last, the bourgeois imperative which has defended the materialist order against its gravest threat, and which Anglo-Saxon fiction had perforce to accept for two centuries: the imperative against human normality. You may, the imperative declares, transcend sex by the rhetoric of a grand passion, you may cheapen it as by Fielding's characteristic resort to comic-strip prurience, you may ignore it or jeer at it, you may even in extremity be clinical about it, but you may not regard it as a serious, normal, central preoccupation of mankind, and you may not attempt to understand it.

The first literary effect of such a proscription was to deprive English fiction of normal women. The sphere of decision for women, in Western civilization at least, has always been love and marriage; and if the woman is not permitted to take into account the most serious impulse of her private existence, she may surrender to domesticity or the vapors and become one of Dickens' brave Biddys or dumb Doras, or she may be encouraged to transcend sex before going to the trouble of learning what it is, like George Eliot's Dorothea or Emily Brontë's Cathy or any other Gothic or Romantic heroine. There are even relatively few *interesting* women in English fiction, and most of these are interesting because their authors understand and document the pathology of their reduction: Jane Austen's Emma, Dickens' Estella (his only powerful insight into a woman's sensibility). And there are a very few whose normality has the protective coloration of intelligence and so passes undetected: Jane Austen's Elizabeth Bennet and Anne Elliot, for example. Generally speaking, however, the heroine of English fiction is likely to be a dead loss— think of all the unrememberable Amelias hung like decorative albatrosses round the necks of the heroes of Victorian novels. And then think of Tolstoy's Natasha and Anna, Dostoievsky's women supreme in their passionate abnormality, the whole range of unapologetic women in Stendhal and Balzac and Flaubert, the gallery of unhurried female sensuality in Colette: not only a definable *sex* in contrast to the poor sticks of English heroines, but almost a different species. The English hero, true, has always been allowed some scope of heroic action in adventure (often commercial), in working his way up, in "becoming a success." Still, to eradicate half the human race, and to confine the energies of the other half mainly within the bounds of materialistic aspiration—this is not to survey, through morals and manners, the limits of human possibility. It was this order of things that D. H. Lawrence confronted when he began writing the novel the first part of which eventually became *The Rainbow*.

Literary revolutions are as various and frequent as political elections: some are important, most are not. When what has been called the Flaubertian tradition (a French import which, though it deeply influenced two representatives of his own "native" tradition, Dr. Leavis regards with a somewhat xenophobic distaste) was introduced into English fiction, and such novelists as James, Conrad, Ford, and Joyce adopted and developed the techniques available to a conscious craftsmanship in fiction, one important and irreversible revolution had occurred—the most important, some critics believe, in the history of English fiction. Certainly, it produced important and original work, even though it has inflicted upon us, unavoidably, all the gimmickry of craft-conscious and myth-mongering and symbolifying criticism, as well as some of the doleful justification for such criticism in those pointless manipulations of technique into which the tradition may tempt the novelist: Conrad, for example, somberly picking his way through the underbrush of half a dozen intervening points of view, in that disastrous virtuoso exercise *Chance,* to report on a man's tying a shoelace.

To this tradition, and to the revolution it achieved, Lawrence does not belong. Joyce belonged to them, but he participated in another literary revolution, the revolution against the Anglo-Saxon (and Irish) censor; and here he and Lawrence may be said to have stood in a common cause. Joyce's publishing and distributing difficulties with *Dubliners* and *Ulysses* strikingly resemble Lawrence's with *The Rainbow* and *Lady Chatterley's Lover.* Nevertheless, there is censorship and censorship. When Judge Woolsey issued his celebrated decision admitting *Ulysses* into the United States, he remarked, in denying that it came within the legal definition of obscenity, that its effect on the reader was more likely to be "emetic" than "aphrodisiac." The interesting judicial principle was thus established that, for the Anglo-Saxon commonwealth, to vomit is, if not positively healthier, at least less baneful than to engage in sexual intercourse. The judge rightly inferred that Joyce's sexual imagery and naughty language were no vital threat at all to Anglo-Saxon mores, but only the signs by which a whole culture manifested its nausea and self-disgust. The Joycean Revolution of the Word has brought freedom, it is now obvious, mainly for cynical clinicians and cautious pornographers, the freedom to spit and hiss (and leads directly to such a May-fly oddity of literary entomology as the San Francisco Renaissance). Today, a quarter-century after the canonization of Molly Bloom, the Woolseyan principle continues in force: *Lady Chatterley's Lover,* which audaciously attempted to rehabilitate sexual imagery and the old Anglo-Saxon words as signs of health and tenderness (and which, by the way, succeeded), has not yet been legally published or sold in the United Kingdom, but, as the present volume goes to press, Lawrence's novel is for the first time being publicly distributed in the United States.

Still, *Lady Chatterley's Lover* is, by the pressures of its subject and of the lateness of its hour, as close to being hortatory as a work of art can afford to be; even without its four famous words (all of them used much more frequently, of course, in *Ulysses* and in almost any current popular novel), its radical extra-literary intent is clear. *The Rainbow*—which marked the outbreak of the Lawrencean revolution—is in fact a more dangerous work because it is less open to philistine retaliation, because it bases itself confidently on no exhortation at all, only on the assumption that sex is a serious, normal, central preoccupation of mankind. After its early skirmish with suppression (which showed, not how acutely prescient, but how very silly, English censors could be in 1915), *The Rainbow* has been widely accessible in print, and is even becoming generally accepted—at least the first half of it—as a brilliant record of English manners and morals over three generations, a *really* great English family-chronicle novel, not less respectable and beyond comparison better than anything in this line by Arnold Bennett.

True enough, there is, beside it, no family-chronicle novel in English that deserves mention; and anything that will certify the respectability of *The Rainbow* is to be prized, just as we ought to prize Lawrence's subliterate reputation as a sensational novelist for making more of his fiction accessible in cheap paper-back American reprints than that of any other major English author. *The Rainbow* is not, after all, so respectable as Galsworthy: there are reasons for Lawrence's notoriety, as well as for his boring and disappointing the common reader to whom he is notorious; and the reasons are all in *The Rainbow*. Nothing promises to be more, and proves on inspection to be less, sensational than this family-chronicle novel which assumes not only that generations are generated, but that the relationship between husband and wife is the central fact of human existence, that the living nucleus of this relationship is the act of sexual union, that the act of sexual union is infinitely serious, complex, and difficult, and that an act of such radiant significance must be fairly treated by the honest novelist.

Graham Hough, however, disapproves of Lawrence's candor. In *The Dark Sun* (1956), he says: "As for physical passion . . . no one should try to present it as . . . [Lawrence] does, and traditional literary good sense has always known it." This appeal to timeless good taste would be plausible if it were not for the very special conditions against which Lawrence had to contend. Most authors of the past, and of other cultures, who have dealt with physical passion have not, indeed, presented it directly. Chaucer did not, nor did Colette; but the reason is that neither needs to: for Chaucer, the sacramental nature of passion and, for Colette, the various joys of an indulged sensuality are self-evident and unchallenged; medieval Catholic humanism and modern French hedonism meet in their conviction of the power of sexual gratification, which can bring to peace and stillness men and women alike. Lawrence, very much on the other hand, has a unique problem: he must reassert this life-renewing power against two centuries of a culture and literature that have muffled and denied its very existence, and he can reassert it only by presenting its actuality as a reminder to the deaf and blind. Lawrence's terrible candor is necessary only because there has been so mendacious and destructive a silence; and yet, because it is so peremptorily called for, it not only reclaims old truths but rushes on to make discoveries. The long reign of English philistinism —in both life and letters—is Lawrence's provocation and his unexampled opportunity.

Of course Lawrence has the advantage of springing from the country community of English workingmen-farmers, a community not bound or even much influenced by the shopkeeper code, and he comes to maturity at a time when the whole structure of class and community is about to encounter the disintegrating shock of the World War I. In his historic moment, Lawrence has before him the life of the last English community: not the manners of the province (which are in any case the manners of the provincial petty bourgeoisie and minor gentry), but a life rich in productive labor and in continuity with the passing seasons, rooted in the earthly and physical, inarticulate without grossness or stupidity, a life seemingly permanent yet fated to pass away in the general breakdown of codes and communities and to be replaced or transcended—if by anything—by individual aspiration. It is this process, over three generations, which is the subject and theme of *The Rainbow;* the process is the most momentous human fact of the past century; and it is a process which, in *The Rainbow,* discloses itself poignantly and most crucially in the sexual histories of individuals. The revolutionary nature of *The Rainbow* is, then, twofold: it is the first English novel to record the normality and significance of physical passion; and it is the only English novel to record, with a prophetic awareness of consequences, the social revolution whereby Western man lost his sense of community and whereby men—more especially, women—learned, if they could, that there is no help any longer except in the individual and in his capacity for a passional life.

As soon as the critic of Lawrence begins to favor such terms as "community" and "passion," he risks being suspected of imagining, obsequiously on cue from his author, a unanimity of social feeling that never was and a potency of personal feeling that never could be, under idyllic and perpetually recurring circumstances in the rural districts of the English Midlands up to, say, the turn of our century. But Lawrence presents no idylls. The community in *The Rainbow,* like every other, is an abstraction from its individuals, who are its only embodiment; and it lives as more than a mere term of discourse only so long as it provides forms and sanctions for the abiding impulses of their separate natures. These impulses are, besides, not all of them communal and sympathetic: Lawrence's individuals are just that, different and distinct from one another except when a strength of sympathy draws them together for moments out of the reciprocal alienations of individuality; and every relationship in *The Rainbow* testifies, not how easy and renewable, but how hard to come by, how precarious, and how irrecoverably unique each instance of passion is, even in a nature as faithful to itself and as sensitively patient as Tom Brangwen's:

Then she said:
"You will be good to me, won't you?"
She was small and girlish and terrible, with a queer, wide look in her eyes. His heart leaped in him, in anguish of love and desire, he went blindly to her and took her in his arms.
"I want to," he said as he drew her closer and closer in. She was soothed by the stress of his embrace, and remained

quite still, relaxed against him, mingling in to him. And he let himself go from past and future, was reduced to the moment with her. In which he took her and was with her and there was nothing beyond, they were together in an elemental embrace beyond their superficial foreignness. But in the morning he was uneasy again. She was still foreign and unknown to him. Only, within the fear was pride, belief in himself as mate for her. And she, everything forgotten in her new hour of coming to life, radiated vigour and joy, so that he quivered to touch her.

It made a great difference to him, marriage. Things became remote and of so little significance, as he knew the powerful source of his life, eyes opened on a new universe, and he wondered in thinking of his triviality before. A new, calm relationship showed to him in the things he saw, in the cattle he used, the young wheat as it eddied in a wind.

And each time he returned home, he went steadily, expectantly, like a man who goes to a profound, unknown satisfaction. At dinner-time, he appeared in the doorway, hanging back a moment from entering, to see if she was there. He saw her setting the plates on the white-scrubbed table. Her arms were slim, she had a slim body and full skirts, she had a dark, shapely head with close-banded hair. Somehow it was her head, so shapely and poignant, that revealed her his woman to him. As she moved about clothed closely, full-skirted and wearing her little silk apron, her dark hair smoothly parted, her head revealed itself to him in all its subtle, intrinsic beauty, and he knew she was his woman, he knew her essence, that it was his to possess. And he seemed to live thus in contact with her, in contact with the unknown, the unaccountable and incalculable.

They did not take much notice of each other, consciously.

"I'm betimes," he said.

"Yes," she answered.

He turned to the dogs, or to the child if she were there. The little Anna played about the farm, flitting constantly in to call something to her mother, to fling her arms round her mother's skirts, to be noticed, perhaps caressed, then, forgetting, to slip out again.

Then Brangwen, talking to the child, or to the dog between

his knees, would be aware of his wife, as, in her tight, dark bodice and her lace fichu, she was reaching up to the corner cupboard. He realized that he lived by her. Did he own her? Was she here for ever? Or might she go away? She was not really his, it was not a real marriage, this marriage between them. She might go away. He did not feel like a master, husband, father of her children. She belonged elsewhere. Any moment, she might be gone. And he was ever drawn to her, drawn after her, with ever-raging, ever-unsatisfied desire. He must always turn home, wherever his steps were taking him, always to her, and he could never quite reach her, he could never quite be satisfied, never be at peace, because she might go away.

At evening, he was glad. Then, when he had finished in the yard, and come in and washed himself, when the child was put to bed, he could sit on the other side of the fire with his beer on the hob and his long white pipe in his fingers, conscious of her there opposite him, as she worked at her embroidery, or as she talked to him, and he was safe with her now, till morning. She was curiously self-sufficient and did not say very much. Occasionally she lifted her head, her gray eyes shining with a strange light, that had nothing to do with him or with this place, and would tell him about herself. She seemed to be back again in the past, chiefly in her childhood or her girlhood, with her father. She very rarely talked of her first husband. But sometimes, all shining-eyed, she was back at her own home, telling him about the riotous times, the trip to Paris with her father, tales of the mad acts of the peasants when a burst of religious, self-hurting fervour had passed over the country.

Tom Brangwen's apprehensions are not, after all, merely the customary timeless ones of husbands, but unprecedented seismic shocks: *The Rainbow* is recording a community in its last flare of vitality and gradual dying away, and all relationships and feelings are shaken by the great change. The foreignness of Tom's wife represents, disturbingly enough, the essential distance between all men and especially between the sexes; but it is already a terrifying difference beyond natural difference. Tom is no simple farmer: his aspiration toward the irreducibly alien woman is an inarticulate but not unconscious aspiration toward the experience of a life beyond the receding satisfactions of a community in process of dissolution. Until he meets Lydia he refuses, in drink and solitude, the only life his community offers him. Now, his dissatisfactions are new, and the brave chances he takes are new.

It was the coming of the colliery, years before, bringing canal and railways through the Brangwen land, which cut across the past and offered a promise of the future:

> As they drove home from town, the farmers of the land met the blackened colliers trooping from the pit-mouth. As they gathered the harvest, the west wind brought a faint, sulphurous smell of pit-refuse burning. As they pulled the turnips in November, the sharp clink-clink-clink-clink-clink of empty trucks shunting on the line, vibrated in their hearts with the fact of other activity going on beyond them.

Tom, the young farmer awakened to a troubled sense of the restrictions of the Brangwen life, comes eventually into his own vision of a life beyond, once he has had his encounter with the complaisant pretty girl and his little talk with her Frenchman escort, the "ageless" and "monkey-like," gracious and imperial gentleman from elsewhere. When Tom sees the foreign lady walking toward him on the road, he knows that she is the awful chance he must take, and the best he can do. Yet the impulse outward moves, necessarily, more rapidly than the possibility of comprehending and fulfilling it: the breakup of the community is too sudden and unanticipated as railways and canals cut across the enclosed spaces of the mind, and the individual is freed from traditional unquestioned preoccupations in order to think and do—what? Tom Brangwen seeks out and lives with strangeness; but his satisfaction and his anguish remain equally resistant to statement or analysis, shy of words, still therefore plausibly connected with the old inarticulate traditional world. His steadiness, halfway between two worlds, is constantly in danger from the incompleteness of its commitment to either; it can be shaken, as by his stepdaughter, Anna, whom he desperately loves but who has come too far from the past to rest in mute suspensions of judgment:

She tried to discuss people, she wanted to know what was meant. But her father became uneasy. He did not want to have things dragged into consciousness. Only out of consideration for her he listened. And there was a kind of bristling rousedness in the room. The cat got up and stretching itself, went uneasily to the door. Mrs. Brangwen was silent, she seemed ominous. Anna could not go on with her fault-finding, her criticism, her expression of dissatisfactions. She felt even her father against her.

Individual aspiration, once it is released, has no certain or obvious goal; and how can it be held in check somewhere, how can one keep it from making all action or repose seem premature and insufficient, how can the skeptical analytic mind be quieted? In fact, even for Tom these questions have force, the speechless remoteness of his marriage—for all of its passion—is finally not enough, his pathetic paternal jealousy of his stepdaughter's choice of a husband poisons even as it recalls to him his sense of his own life:

What was missing in his life, that, in his ravening soul, he was not satisfied? He had had that friend at school, his mother, his wife, and Anna? What had he done? He had failed with his friend, he had been a poor son; but he had known satisfaction with his wife, let it be enough; he loathed himself for the state he was in over Anna. Yet he was *not* satisfied. It was agony to know it.

Was his life nothing? Had he nothing to show, no work? He did not count his work, anybody could have done it. What had he known, but the long, marital embrace with his wife! Curious, that this was what his life amounted to! At any rate, it was something, it was eternal. He would say so to anybody, and be proud of it. He lay with his wife in his arms, and she was still his fulfilment, just the same as ever. And that was the be-all and the end-all. Yes, and he was proud of it.

But the bitterness, underneath, that there still remained an unsatisfied Tom Brangwen, who suffered agony because a girl cared nothing for him. He loved his sons—he had them also. But it was the further, the creative life with the girl, he wanted as well. Oh, and he was ashamed. He trampled himself to extingish himself.

So Tom Brangwen dies, drunk as Noah to forget the wearying puzzles of his middle age, drowned in the flood of rain, and his women mourn him:

> They cleaned and washed the body, and laid it on the bed.
>
> There, it looked still and grand. He was perfectly calm in death, and, now he was laid in line, inviolable, unapproachable. To Anna, he was the majesty of the inaccessible male, the majesty of death. It made her still and awe-stricken, almost glad.
>
> Lydia Brangwen, the mother, also came and saw the impressive, inviolable body of the dead man. She went pale, seeing death. He was beyond change or knowledge, absolute, laid in line with the infinite. What had she to do with him? He was a majestic Abstraction, made visible now for a moment, inviolate, absolute. And who could lay claim to him, who could speak of him, of the him who was revealed in the stripped moment of transit from life into death? Neither the living nor the dead could claim him, he was both the one and the other, inviolable, inaccessibly himself.
>
> "I shared life with you, I belong in my own way to eternity," said Lydia Brangwen, her heart cold, knowing her own singleness.
>
> "I did not know you in life. You are beyond me, supreme now in death," said Anna Brangwen, awe-stricken, almost glad.

This is Everyman, not at all the conventional individualist hero of English fiction; and Lawrence, anticipating perplexity, provided his critics with a long peg on which to hang their theories about *The Rainbow* and *Women in Love*. "You mustn't look," he wrote to Edward Garnett, who had been disappointed to find no trace of *Sons and Lovers* in the new work, ". . . for the old stable *ego* of the character. There is another ego, according to whose action the individual is unrecognizable, and passes through, as it were, allotropic states which it needs a deeper sense than any other we've been used to exercise, to discover are states of the same single radically unchanged element." And he goes on to make obligingly explicit the analogy of diamond-carbon to the mode of characterization he has just begun to feel at home in. Now this tip from the essentially kindly Lawrence to his bewildered English friend is a useful one, for the elucidation of *Women in Love* especially, as Mark Schorer has pointed out (in Hoffman and Moore, *Achievement of D. H. Lawrence,* 1953, pp. 163–77). It is nevertheless not so simple, or perhaps even so accurate, as it looks; and it does not indicate anything nearly so unprecedented—if one takes into account Continental fiction—as Lawrence appears to think.

The trouble is that, in this formulation, Lawrence does not yet seem to have made clear to himself why the old mode of characterization is being discarded and how the new mode functions, and what sort of novel employs one or the other. *Sons and Lovers* is—like *A Portrait of the Artist as a Young Man*—a willful and confused post-Victorian novel of youthful longing and self-discovery, written by a young man whose *parti pris* rejects or ignores the values of the community which has helped to make him; *The Rainbow,* on the other hand, is an elegiac novel about the dissolution of a community whose values, even as these pass away, the author neither rejects nor ignores but seeks to understand and somehow, for his characters' sake, to transcend. The characters (Mr. Morel excepted) in *Sons and Lovers* are post-Victorian individualists colliding with an angry young individualist of a hero; the characters in *The Rainbow* breathe and move, as long as they can, in the large atmosphere of a community. Not that Tom Brangwen is less *individual* than, say, Paul Morel; quite the contrary, he is more honestly and totally imagined, and therefore more human and more of a man. If the novelist creates his characters as more or less aggressive bundles of recognizable traits, as egos stabilized by manners and morals, and his novel as a sequence of collisions between such bundles, he will produce the kind of novel that Lawrence is now giving up, the novel preoccupied—whether in affirmation or in protest—with manners and morals, the class novel, the standard English novel. If, however, the novelist creates his characters in a life-size medium, fictional and communal, which nurtures, provokes, and makes room for the strength of impulse, he will produce a novel like *The Rainbow*—or *Anna Karenina,* or *The Idiot,* or *The Red and the Black.* Characters in novels such as these are not caricatures or even conventional heroes, mere victims or arbiters of manners and morals, they are passions and first principles; and they are all the more human and individual for being so. Nor, of course, is Lawrence's new mode of characterization unprecedented or revolutionary, it is only not very English.

What *is* revolutionary in *The Rainbow*—what makes Lawrence, in perhaps the most important sense, the only modern novelist—is not the mode of characterization, but the new awareness which finds this mode necessary: the awareness that with the dying away, in the age of technology, of genuine communal relations between men, with the inevitable thwarting of what Lawrence was later to call "the societal impulse," the only hope for man lies in those remaining potentialities of human relationship which depend for their realization on the fullest (not necessarily the most various or complicated) possible realization of the sexual impulse. Lawrence, being English, had in this respect no choice but to be revolutionary. English novelists, as spokesmen for the most advanced middle class in the world, had since Defoe been advocating the simplest escape from the intolerable human problems posed by industrialism—the escape into materialist success, the pursuit of what Dickens' Wemmick poignantly euphemises under the phrase "portable property"; but with the end of the expansive Romantic phase of English industrialism, no serious English writer could any longer believe in this escape and pursuit, as Dickens and others before and after could believe in it once it had been sweetened by contrition, materialist benevolence, and marital union with another form of portable property. (We cannot imagine a French or an Italian or a Russian Lawrence, just as we cannot imagine an English Dostoievsky, though the awareness of which Lawrence is both creator and instrument has, finally, as much to say to the Continent as Dostoievsky has to say to the English.) For Lawrence, then, the hope, in fact the last resort, of modern man is—the unhappy word stares at us as it did at Lawrence's censors—sex: not as cold appetite, not as self-imposed exile from the teeming world, not as the exploiting of sensation or the temporary allaying of an itch, but as the bond of tranquillity and faith between man and woman, those polar opponents, and the last renewable proof of human community.

The Rainbow is midpassage and arrival. Tom Brangwen still has roots, connections, the virtue of quietness in solitude; of these vestiges of community Anna and Will still keep something by, as it were, barely remembering them, Anna in her slovenly cheerful maternity, Will in his mute satisfaction with manual labor or minor artisanship. Only Ursula—modern woman and therefore, in her unforeseen and disastrously unprepared-for homelessness, true representative of modern mankind—has nothing at all of what, outside themselves, sustained the two generations before her. And for all three generations the unmapped territory to be explored, with increasing desperation and hope, is sex.

Tom Brangwen has a real marriage, notwithstanding its ultimate vulnerability to the stress of uncomprehended change; his apparently unwarrantable youthful waiting for a strangeness beyond his ordinary experience is rewarded and vindicated, and his life is transfigured by the reality of passion. If his marriage fails to give him everything, it nevertheless gives him much, even enough to make him at length unhappily sensitive to the unknown vibrations of what he must do without.

For Anna and Will, on the other hand, marriage seems at first sunnier and more simple. They have moved very far out of the shadow of the old Brangwen world; Anna, at least, is impatient with established sanctities; and both of them rejoice on their prolonged honeymoon in an uninhibited mutual exploration of sexuality, day after day of vital time-dissolving ease:

> As they lay close together, complete and beyond the touch of time or change, it was as if they were at the very centre of all the slow wheeling of space and the rapid agitation of life, deep, deep inside them all, at the centre where there is utter radiance, and eternal being, and the silence absorbed in praise: the steady core of all movements, the unawakened sleep of all wakefulness. They found themselves there, and they lay still, in each other's arms; for their moment they were at the heart of eternity, whilst time roared far off, forever far off, towards the rim.
>
> Then gradually they were passed away from the supreme centre, down the circles of praise and joy and gladness, further and further out, towards the noise and the friction. But their hearts had burned and were tempered by the inner reality, they were unalterably glad.
>
> Gradually they began to wake up, the noises outside became more real. They understood and answered the call outside. They counted the strokes of the bell. And when they

counted midday, they understood that it was midday, in the world, and for themselves also.

It dawned upon her that she was hungry. She had been getting hungrier for a lifetime. But even yet it was not sufficiently real to rouse her. A long way off she could hear the words, "I am dying of hunger." Yet she lay still, separate, at peace, and the words were unuttered. There was still another lapse.

And then, quite calmly, even a little surprised, she was in the present, and was saying:

"I am dying with hunger."

"So am I," he said calmly, as if it were of not the slightest significance. And they relapsed into the warm, golden stillness. And the minutes flowed unheeded past the window outside.

Then suddenly she stirred against him.

"My dear, I am dying of hunger," she said.

It was a slight pain to him to be brought to.

"We'll get up," he said, unmoving.

And she sank her head on to him again, and they lay still, lapsing. Half consciously, he heard the clock chime the hour. She did not hear.

"Do get up," she murmured at length, "and give me something to eat."

"Yes," he said, and he put his arms round her, and she lay with her face on him. They were faintly astonished that they did not move. The minutes rustled louder at the window.

"Let me go then," he said.

She lifted her head from him, relinquishingly. With a little breaking away, he moved out of bed, and was taking his clothes. She stretched out her hand to him.

"You are so nice," she said, and he went back for a moment or two.

Then actually he did slip into some clothes, and, looking round quickly at her, was gone out of the room. She lay translated again into a pale, clearer peace. As if she were a spirit, she listened to the noise of him downstairs, as if she were no longer of the material world.

In such moments as Lawrence here presents, there can be no "characters" in the conventional fictional sense: the mode of characterization is dictated by the focus of attention, which here is on a core of impulse anterior to personality. It is, of course, easy to misunderstand such a passage in the context of English fiction, especially that sort of woman's fiction of which *Jane Eyre* is a quasi-serious instance: the emotion of romantic love reduces heroine (or hero) to a fluttering impotency—especially in anticipation—that may resemble a reduction to impulse. But the conjugal satisfactions of Tom Brangwen, or Anna, or Will, are not reductive at all; they liberate universal human powers; far from making romantic victims they make those relations between people without which there are only egos in collision and no persons. Nobody, it is true, can live indefinitely at such a depth of impulse; and the comic ascension of Anna and Will to the level of a more mundane appetite testifies not only to the existence of a daylight world in which we are all, more or less, scrupulously differentiated fictional characters, but also to that respect for full human truth which disciplines even the most rhapsodic utterances in this novel. The careful reader never forgets that *The Rainbow* is, in one large and traditional aspect, a great realistic novel: Tom Brangwen's life outside marriage, for example, is registered with an immediacy and resonance that would establish him as one of the great figures in English fiction even if he were nothing more; and one thinks of such superb set-pieces as Tom's efforts at comforting the child Anna while Lydia is bearing his first child, Tom's drunkenly inspired eulogy of marriage, his death in the flood—a luminous pertinence of detail, a fidelity to locale, a sternness of pathos not readily matched in any other fiction. Nevertheless, as the rhythm of the style—always near, when not actually, the rhythm of rhapsodic utterance—persists in implying, life is renewable only and perpetually at the springs of impulse, in celebration and praise, where we are less unique than human; and only to the degree to which we have renewed ourselves there, can we breathe and move as individuals in the daylight world.

Renewal, the gift and aim of life, becomes in modern marriage less and less the gift of repose, more and more pressingly the aim of conscious and personal exploration: woman is less passive and man more anxious, approaching an uneasy identity of roles. Lydia is still withdrawn and enigmatic, a woman of the old dispensation, unharried, immured in domesticity and unamenable

to self-questioning; so Tom is the explorer—joyous or baffled
—in this first marriage, moving doubtfully at the rim of awareness. Anna, on the other hand, has come awake, because the invasion of all things by mechanism and the conscious mind has
made Lydia the last possible woman of her kind: having lost
what her mother unquestioningly had, Anna must make up for
it by becoming explorative in her own right, the free companion
of her husband. But, after the shared bliss of the honeymoon,
the difficulties of the new dispensation become gradually manifest. When the communal sanction for marriage is dissipated
and only free and equal individuals remain, the burden on acci-
dents of personality grows suddenly enormous. The tempera-
mental difference between Lydia and Tom were unbridgeable,
and of no significance to Lydia. Yet Will's soft inarticulateness
drives the skeptical articulate Anna wild, and Anna's attacks on
her husband's temperament drive him into retaliatory fury:

> She . . . clung to the worship of human knowledge. Man
> must die in the body but in his knowledge he was immortal.
> Such, somewhere, was her belief, quite obscure and unfor-
> mulated. She believed in the omnipotence of the human mind.
>   He, on the other hand, blind as a subterranean thing, just
> ignored the human mind and ran after his own dark-souled
> desires, following his own tunnelling nose. She felt often she
> must suffocate. And she fought him off.
>   Then he, knowing he was blind, fought madly back again,
> frantic in sensual fear. He did foolish things. He asserted him-
> self on his rights, he arrogated the old position of master of
> the house.
>   "You've a right to do as I want," he cried.
>   "Fool!" she answered. "Fool!"
>   "I'll let you know who's master," he cried.
>   "Fool!" she answered. "Fool! I've known my own father,
> who could put a dozen of you in his pipe and push them down
> with his finger-end. Don't I know what a fool you are!"

In the perilous colloidal tension of modern marriage, too
much depends on merely personal qualities. And—at least for
persons living in the delusive afterglow of the old world, still
unalert to the swarming problems of consciousness—too much

depends on the increasingly elaborate and conscious satisfactions of sexuality: the man, having lost his inherited mastery, comes to depend on these as on a drug, and the woman comes to resent what she will eventually regard as his infantile male weakness. Variety, the avoidance of monotony, becomes more and more a brutal conjugal compulsion. At length, reciprocally excited by Will's brush with infidelity, Anna and Will give themselves to the pleasures of a sort of democratic sexual cannibalism, to the fetishistic daylight fevers of sensuality, the manipulation of bodies as instruments for pleasure; and if Lawrence's imagery in this passage plainly obliges us to find the experience analogous to the Fall, it obliges us also to see the new experiences as a necessary expansion of man's knowledge in the time of another forced departure from the garden. Still, Anna and Will never reclaim their honeymoon fulfillment of passion or seem capable of the reconciliation between passion and sensuality; and their lives dwindle away in subtle disorganization, in the minor consummations and complaints of Anna's role as the fecund housewife and Will's as a woodwork teacher for the town, "very happy and keen in his new public spirit." Since their imperfect truce is the first modern marriage, it is appropriate that they bring into being the first complete modern woman, totally dispossessed and therefore totally explorative.

The child Ursula still has her father's environing and sometimes overpowering love; and she has, also, in conversation with her grandmother, a window on the certainties of the past even as the thought of growing up without such certainties begins to trouble her:

. . . Ursula asked her deepest childish questions of her grandmother.

"Will somebody love me, grandmother?"

"Many people love you, child. We all love you."

"But when I am grown up, will somebody love me?"

"Yes, some man will love you, child, because it's your nature. And I hope it will be somebody who will love you for what you are, and not for what he wants of you. But we have a right to what we want."

Ursula was frightened, hearing these things. Her heart sank, she felt she had no ground under her feet. She clung to her grandmother. Here was peace and security. Here, from her grandmother's peaceful room, the door opened on to the greater space, the past, which was so big, that all it contained seemed tiny; loves and births and deaths, tiny units and features within a vast horizon. That was great relief, to know the tiny importance of the individual, within the great past.

Lydia's wisdom in old age is wasted on her granddaughter, and reverberates outward into the large implications of the novel. One of the dangers of marriage in the time of a breaking of bonds is, as Lydia suggests, that a man may be driven to seek in a mate not a distinct and different person as generous and needy as himself, but only what will compensate him, somehow, for his sense of loss—though, tragically, he must have both in order to have either. The marriage of Anna and Will is, at last, a deadlock because neither wife nor husband has the generosity and wisdom to acknowledge and accept the unbreakable differentness of the other; and Tom's response to Lydia's strangeness—at the beginning so compelling an attraction for him—is, at last, to drift back into confusion and the oblivion of drink. Moreover, the grandmother's words to the child Ursula are a prophecy; for Skrebensky will desperately seek in Ursula (as Will sought in Anna) only what might make up for his unmanning sense of loss, and Ursula herself will not understand, not at least till very late, that her promiscuity with Skrebensky is no generous gift of love but only a confession of mutual weakness, no passionate resolution but an increasingly unsatisfactory escape into sex from the unprecedented problems of the modern consciousness.

In the new world there are no landmarks or guideposts, the great past is no longer even a memory, everyone is free and dispossessed; so Ursula's life becomes, necessarily enough, a kind of adventure in limbo. Yet it is this concluding section—in bulk, more than half—of the novel that has been most vexatious and unrewarding for readers; and any effort to assess *The Rainbow* bumps hard against it. No doubt, the section is less satisfying than most of what has come before: it is unduly repetitive, it is occasionally content to make points by assertion rather than by incident, it sometimes mistakes mere detailed documentation for thematic illustration and development, its tone sometimes verges on stridency. There are, after all, too many and too similar descriptions of Ursula and Skrebensky making hopeless love; the career of Ursula as a teacher, however interesting it may be in its own right, is recorded at too much length and with too little relevance to the theme of the novel; and then Lawrence, in his haste to dismiss dry book-learning, tries to palm off on us so trivially literary a truism about college life as this:

> College was barren, cheap, a temple converted to the most vulgar, petty commerce. Had she not gone to hear the echo of learning pulsing back to the source of the mystery?—The source of mystery! And barrenly, the professors in their gowns offered commercial commodity that could be turned to good account in the examination-room; ready-made stuff too, and not really worth the money it was intended to fetch; which they all knew.

When Lawrence settles for this sort of thing, we are persuaded that he is no longer, for the time being at any rate, attending to the seriousness of his theme. It is perhaps more to the point to agree with Dr. Leavis that Lawrence, his mind already on the very different second novel which had detached itself from his original conception of a single novel on marriage, was trying to finish *The Rainbow* with less sympathy than conscientiousness: in this view, the frustrating account of Ursula's long and strenuous career of frustration may be taken as the result of Lawrence's prudent desire to save her consummation for *Women in Love.*

Still, *The Rainbow* is, finally, not about consummation but about promise. The rainbow that Ursula sees at the very end of the novel need not be dismissed as a despairing symbolic stroke to allow a nominal conclusion and to release Lawrence for *Women in Love;* though the two novels are obviously related in ways more important than the continuance of several characters through the second, it may be that those readers who find the end of *The Rainbow* wanting have turned their minds prematurely to the next book, and are expecting what it is not in the theme of the earlier novel to give. No doubt Lawrence's original intention was to write a single novel which would encompass and illustrate in the lives of a family the great social and psychological change of our century, and which would conclude with a treatment of such individual problems and individual solutions as, indeed, are treated in *Women in Love*. But it must have become eventually clear to him that the breakdown of community was a subject in itself, and that it culminated appropriately in the coming to consciousness of emancipated, modern woman. If Lawrence had ended the novel with modern woman numbed in her grimace of freedom, he would have been merely cynical; if he had ended with Ursula still unsure of her feelings for Skrebensky, the novel would trail off in a puzzle. The novel does, in fact, end as Ursula, having freed herself of her struggle with Skrebensky, is for the first time genuinely free not only of the unrevivable past but of those false ties she has tentatively accepted in place of it. To require any more—at least schematically—is to require an unequivocal happy ending, and even in *Women in Love* or *Lady Chatterley's Lover* Lawrence is not so obliging as that.

The fault is, then, not of scheme but of execution: much of the last half of *The Rainbow* seems to have been written with a slackening of Lawrence's attention to proportion and detail. Yet much is finely done. Something as difficult, for instance, as the relationship between Ursula and Miss Inger comes off without damage to our sympathy for Ursula, and with strong pertinence to the theme. In a time when the injunctions of community and family have been broken, when the individual is responsible only to himself and to his own impulses, why should not Ursula first admire and then fiercely love the handsome, independent woman who so resembles what she herself wishes to be? And why should the warmth and physical responsiveness of her feelings be curbed? No mere prohibition will do, for sanctions and prohibitions alike have gone under. It is only by living through the experience that Ursula can judge its sinister misleadingness for her: to be free like Winifred Inger is to take pleasure only in the thrill of physiological or mechanical process, to handle and reject, to give nothing, to hate one's humanness and to deny the possibility of relationship—as Ursula discovers during the visit to her uncle's colliery:

> His real mistress was the machine, and the real mistress of Winifred was the machine. She too, Winifred, worshipped the impure abstraction, the mechanisms of matter. There, there, in the machine, in service of the machine, was she free from

the clog and degradation of human feeling. There, in the monstrous mechanism that held all matter, living or dead, in its service, did she achieve her consummation and her perfect unison, her immortality.

The narcissistic delights of homosexuality are not enough, even for Winifred Inger; even she must make a commitment to something outside herself, and she finds her consummation and her unison, her immortality, in the machine. But Ursula continues to seek hers in the flesh. Perhaps the repetitive savageries of Ursula's sexual encounters with Skrebensky are partly justifiable on the ground that with Skrebensky Ursula's attempt is so much more plausible and at the same time so much more exacerbating: at least Skrebensky is a man and no narcissistic projection of herself, though she can master and break him; at least Skrebensky is not positively evil, though he is weak and inchoate. If we do not lose sympathy with Ursula for her annihilating cruelty toward Skrebensky, it is because we are convinced that she suffers in the grip of an impulse which is, if it can ever be fulfilled, the sanest and most healing impulse accessible to her; if she appears at moments in the guise of a female spider devouring her sexually spent and useless mate, she is in any case obeying a brute instinct more vital than Skrebensky's attachment to political abstractions or Miss Inger's attachment to mechanism. Ursula's quest is desperate, so therefore are her feelings often; but the discoveries she must make cannot be arrived at by theorem, and she has no immediately recognizable allies. To contain and to be blocked from fulfilling so mastering an impulse is, finally, punishment and promise enough, as Lawrence indicates in the marvelous passage in which Ursula has her heart-stopping encounter with the stampeding horses, hallucination or reality:

She knew they had not gone, she knew they awaited her still. But she went on over the log bridge that their hoofs had churned and drummed, she went on, knowing things about them. She was aware of their breasts gripped, clenched narrow in a hold that never relaxed, she was aware of their red nostrils flaming with long endurance, and of their haunches, so rounded, so massive, pressing, pressing, pressing to burst the grip upon their breasts, pressing forever till they went mad, running against the walls of time, and never bursting free. Their great haunches were smoothed and darkened with rain. But the darkness and wetness of rain could not put out the hard, urgent, massive fire that was locked within these flanks, never, never.

The new woman is too strong, and the new man is too weak, the woman suddenly conscious of long-sleeping powers and the man suddenly confronted with a rival. It is as if, for the new broken reed of a man like Skrebensky, all the long history of patriarchal Western civilization—its dream of wholeness and community, its exaltation of the family and of romantic love— has been man's dogged postponement of woman's inevitable supremacy. It all leads to Skrebensky, totally dependent, beaten child and rejected lover, hearing his doom on the final morning-after:

> He tapped at her bedroom door at the last minute. She stood with her umbrella in her hand. He closed the door. He did not know what to say.
> "Have you done with me?" he asked her at length, lifting his head.
> "It isn't me," she said. "You have done with me—we have done with each other."
> He looked at her, at the closed face, which he thought so cruel. And he knew he could never touch her again. His will was broken, he was seared, but he clung to the life of his body.
> "Well, what have I done?" he asked, in a rather querulous voice.
> "I don't know," she said, in the same dull, feelingless voice. "It is finished. It has been a failure."

In this contest—though Skrebensky thinks otherwise—there is no kindness and cruelty, only life and death, all and nothing; the issue is beyond the condescensions of charity, and the time is very late. There must be, somewhere, men to face up to the new dispensation: men like Tom Brangwen, who did much and might have done more had he known better what had overtaken him. Anna, in paralyzing contempt of Will when he tried to assert an authority he had already yielded by his unmanly surrender to her flesh, cried out that her stepfather "could put a dozen of you in his pipe and push them down with his finger-end." The new woman is strong in her power to wound and even to kill man's spirit if she has no male counterforce to match her. Yet life somehow continuously renews itself: in a time of human degradation, the unique powers of woman have at last asserted themselves; and such powers, coming so unexpectedly out of the very sources of life, cannot be without a commensurate object and response. What remains, in the compulsive ugliness of modern industrialism, as all values except those preservable by the conscious individual are swept away, is promise:

> In everything she saw she grasped and groped to find the creation of the living God, instead of the old, hard barren form of bygone living. Sometimes great terror possessed her. Sometimes she lost touch, she lost her feeling, she could only know the old horror of the husk which bound in her and all mankind. They were all in prison, they were all going mad.
> She saw the stiffened bodies of the colliers, which seemed already enclosed in a coffin, she saw their unchanging eyes, the eyes of those who are buried alive: she saw the hard, cutting edges of the new houses, which seemed to spread over the hillside in their insentient triumph, the triumph of horrible, amorphous angles and straight lines, the expression of corruption triumphant and unopposed, corruption so pure that it is hard and brittle: she saw the dun atmosphere over the blackened hills opposite, the dark blotches of houses, slate roofed and amorphous, the old church-tower standing up in hideous obsoleteness above raw new houses on the crest of the hill, the amorphous, brittle, hard edged new houses advancing from Beldover to meet the corrupt new houses from Lethley, the houses of Lethley advancing to mix with the houses of Hainor, a dry, brittle, terrible corruption spreading over the face of the land, and she was sick with a nausea so deep that she perished as she sat. And then, in the blowing clouds, she saw a band of faint iridescence colouring in faint colours a portion of the hill. And forgetting, startled, she looked for the hovering colour and saw a rainbow forming itself. In one place it gleamed fiercely, and, her heart anguished with hope, she sought the shadow of iris where the bow should be.

Steadily the colour gathered, mysteriously, from nowhere, it took presence upon itself, there was a faint, vast rainbow. The arc bended and strengthened itself till it arched indomitable, making great architecture of light and colour and the space of heaven, its pedestals luminous in the corruption of new houses on the low hill, its arch the top of heaven.

And the rainbow stood on the earth. She knew that the sordid people who crept hard-scaled and separate on the face of the world's corruption were living still, that the rainbow was arched in their blood and would quiver to life in their spirit, that they would cast off their horny covering of disintegration, that new, clean, naked bodies would issue to a new germination, to a new growth, rising to the light and the wind and the clean rain of heaven. She saw in the rainbow the earth's new architecture, the old, brittle corruption of houses and factories swept away, the world built up in a living fabric of Truth, fitting to the over-arching heaven.

The pledge of the future is Ursula's knowledge of what is terrible about the present, and her knowledge derives from a power of passion which must at length be consummated because it would otherwise have had no cause to spring into being. Dostoievsky called the Russians the "god-bearing" people, those who carry the secret of life within them and preserve it for that remote apocalypse when all the world will be fit to receive it. At the conclusion of *The Rainbow*, Ursula is the single god-bearing person left in the world. It is a tribute to the prodigious optimism and persuasiveness of Lawrence's vision that the secret she holds seems worth the keeping till the world is fit to receive it.

Angelo P. Bertocci

SYMBOLISM IN *WOMEN IN LOVE*

It is not until chapter XXVIII, "In the Pompadour," that Birkin abstracts completely into the language of theory the compulsive vision irradiating the whole of *Women in Love*. It is the vision of modern man and modern society with little time left to choose between death-in-life and, indeed, the imminent destruction of civilization, and the radical renewal and reintegration of a whole mode of being that is salvation. The moment is well chosen. The action of the novel has reached a great divide: the two couples, Ursula and Birkin, Gudrun and Gerald, have been united in their contrasting ways and in the final chapters, "Continental" and "Snowed In," will be put to the trial by ice. Birkin's message itself is dramatized; it is in the form of a letter to Halliday and the "Crême de Menthe" crowd. The young man, himself an effeminate figure of decay, declaims Birkin's analysis of the present crisis amid the jeering comments of the coterie. Among them is Pussum, that modern embodiment of the West African wooden figurine which itself had objectified the very state of being denounced in the letter. To add to the tension, the letter is read in the presence of Gerald, Birkin's friend. But it is Gudrun who acts, in a state no doubt partly of jealousy of Pussum, who had for a night been Gerald's mistress and has just flaunted that fact, partly out of loyalty to her sister

Angelo Bertocci, Professor of Comparative Literature at Boston University, was educated at Boston University (B.A.), Harvard (M.A.), and Columbia (Ph.D.), as well as at the Université de Grenoble, and is the author of *Charles De Bos and English Literature* (1949) and of numerous articles and reviews in such journals as *Yale French Studies, Romanic Review,* and *Comparative Literature;* he contributed some of the translations to *From the N. R. F.* (1958) and has translated a third of Gide's *Pretexts* (1959).

Ursula who is now Birkin's wife, but chiefly with that ambivalence of attitude that has characterized her throughout. She hardly knows whether to be angry at what she considers Birkin's promiscuous sermonizing or afraid of the portent for herself in that letter. At any rate, she snatches it away and walks off with it amid the jeers of the crowd and then holds on to it in that *amor fati* that is to grow upon her among the snow-clad mountains.

The message, pronounced against an opposition making for "irony," is briefly that modern society is dominated by the desire for destruction which in the individual is "ultimately a desire for destruction in the self." This means a return to the original rudimentary conditions of being along the Flux of Corruption. It promises, "beyond knowledge, the phosphorescent ecstasy of acute sensation," which is a kind of *fleur du mal,* a "flower of mud," born of sex used as a reductive agent. It invites us "to *lose* ourselves in some ultimate black sensation, mindless and infinite."

The message turns out to be a program for Gerald and Gudrun under the influence of snow and of that artist in corruption, Loerke, the "wizard rat that swims ahead" "in the river of corruption just where it falls over into the bottomless pit." When the trial by ice is over and Birkin looks half in disgust and half in despair upon the frozen stallion that is Gerald, his prophetic words to Gerald come to the reader's mind: "I suppose you want the same . . . only you want to take a quick jump downwards, in a sort of ecstasy—and he [Loerke] ebbs with . . . the sewer stream." Gerald is always the diver and for the last time he has let himself fall into the *cul de sac* of snow where, only a little way farther up, opens the imperial road to Italy. And Birkin takes recourse in the final bitter consolation of the religious when they see man forsaking God. It is the thought that God does not need man and that the "creative mystery" will, as ever, bring to birth "new species . . . more lovely . . . always surpassing wonder." Even in Lawrence the vision of betrayal, for (in spite of the jeers of his enemies and of his own self-criticism) Birkin always remains the *Salvator Mundi,* the vision of death is capped by a Resurrection, or, better, a recurring Re-creation.

To seem to make "the head of the corner" the "stone" that Dr. F. R. Leavis, that master builder in things Lawrencean (and not the least in his study of *Women in Love*) [1] has "rejected" might seem an unnecessary challenge to critical wisdom. Nevertheless, I think it will not do to call Birkin's letter "Lawrencean self-parody." The hoots are those of Birkin's former friends and associates to be sure, but their jeers are to be taken at a discount, for these individuals have already been shown as marked for death. Gudrun's snatching the letter from Halliday's hands has more organic relation to the novel than would the mere survival in Lawrence's memory of the scene when Katherine Mansfield impounded a Lawrence book at the Café Royal.

Dr. Leavis' interpretations at this point suggest too much preoccupation with Middleton Murry's assertion that Lawrence is no artist (even if that constitutes, at the present stage of civilization, his unique greatness) or T. S. Eliot's belief that Lawrence is not sufficiently the artist. Strategy for Lawrenceans no longer requires a defensive-offensive against Murry and Eliot. Birkin's letter and its presentation is quite sufficiently dramatized. But it is no mere parody, or if there is parody, it is parody of tone and not of substance. The proof of this is the way the novel turns out. Further proof is the lifting of the outcome for Gerald, who is Birkin's chief concern as well as the bearer of the social-industrial theme, to the level of religious despair and religious affirmation at the end of the novel. Or is Birkin, at this moment, once more exhibiting his unlovely *Salvator Mundi* propensities? If so, the central situation in the novel would descend, at the very last moment, into bathos.

It is easy to understand how defenders of Lawrence should center their attention on what can be related to the actualities of our personal and social existence, or to what in his vision can be verified in the objectivities of our common life. They want to save him from the connotations, for some people, of the word "prophet." Yet it seems to be a fact that any drastic vision of social death and renewal is a religious vision, as Rousseau's was a religious vision. Nor was Lawrence's desire to save mankind any more intense nor explicit in his conscience as a man than Dante's. One need not feel uneasy, therefore, because the novelist, at the proper moment, makes explicit what had been more largely implicit in the texture and structure of the novel. It is one of the ways of binding an esthetic structure, and Dante uses it. If Birkin occasionally gives the impression that heaven and earth have important stakes in the outcome of the action, Dante goes even further when he declares that heaven, too, has set a hand to his work.

The important question is always, esthetically, whether what seem like propositions can be seen as part of a texture. The answer in *Women in Love* I think is very largely "yes," and the novelistic structure deserves all Dr. Leavis' praise. This is especially true if more attention is paid to Lawrence's symbolism, and from this Dr. Leavis shies away. To define "symbol" as what merely "stands for," and to suggest that in Lawrence we have far more complex significances than symbol can handle, is to ignore a distinction between symbol and allegory made by Goethe and Coleridge. Indeed, what Dr. Leavis uses as an example of symbol—the passage where Gerald, sitting in the canoe with Gudrun, feels his distance from her ("Water-Party")—would, from this point of view, be considered an example of "symbol" which, failing to be realized, falls into mere "allegory."

It is my belief, then, that *Women in Love* is best seen as taking its origin in religious vision, as any drastic proposal for destruction and re-creation, be it Rousseau's or Marx's, is the translation of religious vision into action. I do not speak specifically of the vision of the Hebrew prophets, or the Christian vision, for I am not persuaded by efforts to make of Lawrence almost a Christian. It seems more likely that, as Birkin says of Ursula's relation with her father, that his is a "love of opposition." But like the Hebrew-Christian, Lawrence has the religion of the "one thing needful." Happiness on earth, even existence itself whatever it may be, true productivity and creation, depend upon the faith with which men and women consent to meet in a Third, a principle of being which is neither of the participants. And the way for man is woman, and for woman man.

Thus the religious quality of Lawrence's vision makes for expression, and sometimes a straining toward expression, which carries characters and situations beyond the "universality," let us say, of a Homer at one end or of a good modern realist at the other. To realize this means a clearer understanding of problems of characterization and action in Lawrence's novels. For these problems will go with an art of symbol more radical than Dr. Leavis, or even Graham Hough perhaps, are ready to admit.

What this means is that Lawrence uses not merely the symbols at hand which seem natural to all expression and which have been developed in social experience, but that he strives to create new fusions of meaning and even to *enforce* new meanings based upon created premises. I hope that all this will be clearer after illustration. I will therefore proceed, without seeking otherwise to define symbol, to show how symbol functions in *Women in Love.* Does the novel, or any important portion of it, *behave* like a symbolic work?

Where there is symbol, a kind of magnetic field of incident, image, and rhythm is set up, drawing to itself clusters of interrelated suggestion. Of course the bond of the logical relation of ideas is not completely missing; on the other hand the images and rhythms are not to be thought of as wild vines intertwining about a supporting line of logic, embellishing it with their foliage and giving it the factitious air of a living thing. Rather does image call to image, scene to scene, rhythm to rhythm, as color calls to color, the same or the opposite, in a painting. There is "logic" here, but the logic is not merely discursive. What seem necessities are set up for reasons that are more than the logically necessary reasons. The effect of discursive relations is linear, of symbolic relations the effect is circular. It suggests a to-and-fro in all directions at once. What is "evermore about to be" but is not yet, calls its parts organically into being.

Again, where a structure is truly symbolic, any vigorous cutting should seem to live by the life of the whole because it is constituted by the meeting of the forces of the whole on their way to other and busier intersections. I propose to examine "Water-Party" (Chapter XIV) because of the very challenge of its contrast to the snow and ice images of the final extended carnival at the ski lodge. This chapter is also the culmination of that first rhythm of action bringing commitment of the women, now "in love," to their men. I shall work backward and forward from this center, enough to show that it is indeed a "center." Of course, any intersection in a symbolic structure—and this is a way of defining symbol—seems "the center."

ii

The world of the colliery has been invited to the annual ritual of the "Water-Party" at Shortlands. The affair is an appeasement of conscience for the elder Crich, his way of sharing with his miners the products of what, in spite of himself—for Crich is not the man to look too closely at what his "love" destroys, be it his wife or his colliers—he knows is their enslavement. But the man responsible for the water, and anxious to avoid any accident, is Gerald, he who has carried organization of industry to the point of death for the spirit in exchange for the certainty of *panem et circenses*. And Gerald has already been presented in some sort as a master of the watery element. In "Diver" (IV) though the "morning was full of a new creation," he had been present as a "white" figure, launched in a "white" arc through the air, moving in the "translucency of the grey, uncreated water," that "whole otherworld" which he dominated "just himself of the watery world," "immune and perfect," "like a Nibelung," and loving the "violent impulse of the very cold water against his limbs, buoying him up." This Nibelung, master of water and cold, had exacted a cry of admiration from Gudrun, envying him "this momentary possession of pure isolation and fluidity." He has "go," the sisters agree, though Ursula adds that "it goes in applying the latest appliances." And then, she adds, as though it were relevant, a dark "non sequitur": "You know he shot his brother?"

At the water-party the two girls have succeeded in obtaining a release from this redoubtable master of waters with his right hand bandaged, for it had been "trapped . . . in machinery." They had rowed off in rejection of the collier crowd for a little idyll of happiness around the bend. Ursula had sat "unconsciously crooning her song, strong and unquestioned at the center of her own universe," but Gudrun, as ever suffering from "the sense of her own negation," and demanding "the other to be aware of her," dances as though possessed before Highland cattle which usually frighten her. A little later Gerald's sister Diana, that other "negated" being, as Birkin says, will dance perilously on the top of the boat, tumble into the water, and drown carrying her rescuer down with her.

For Gerald and Gudrun things have not as yet gone so far. There is a quarrel as he takes the part of the cattle being driven "mad." Gudrun strikes him a first blow and prophesies a last. He does not contradict her statement. As he had involved her somehow in the submission to which he had reduced the red

Arab mare (IX), so now her aggression strikes the spark of a declaration of love from him. Gerald, a "terrible swooning burden on his mind," grasps her hand "as if his hand were iron." Thus begins the long imprisonment that Gerald's love will bring Gudrun, in a novel rich with suggestions of imprisonment due to profane love.[2] Gudrun's "blood ran cold," but she acquiesces softly.

Gerald walks on beside her, "a mindless body." Then the author comments: "He suffered badly. He had killed his brother when a boy, and was set apart, like Cain." As often happens when Lawrence is building up his texture of meanings, this second seeming irrelevance, coming after the first, Ursula's reference to that fatal shooting, now drops into its place. He is a threat to Gudrun as well as a man somehow consigned to death. Even though she will indeed strike the last blow later in the snow after he has almost strangled her, yet Gerald will be his own murderer up in that *cul de sac* of snow. For Birkin has already detected the death-wish in Gerald.

As they lower a canoe into the water soon afterward, Gudrun refers again to the wounded hand. She continues to have power over them both. As they paddle, he who "was set apart, like Cain," and who in "Diver" had felt perfect and immune in the water, now feels the distance between himself and Gudrun. She assures him of her nearness, "Yet we cannot very well change, while we are in the water." And now Gerald, "who always kept such a keen attentiveness, concentrating and unyielding in himself," melts "into oneness with the whole" (always in this novel a bad sign) as in "pure, perfect sleep . . . and perfect lapsing out." [3] Gudrun cannot avoid a certain wistfulness even now. Later, on the night that Gerald comes from his father's grave with clay-clogged feet to take her, he certainly does not give sleep to his beloved. He "destroys" her into consciousness. Her awakened consciousness apropos of Gerald will, at the end of the novel, be translated into the awful vision of the clock-face of existence.

But even this relative contentedness now in the canoe is broken by Gudrun's uneasy feeling that someone is in need of Gerald and calling for him. "Then as if the night smashed, suddenly there was a great confusion of shouting, warring on the water." "Wasn't this *bound* to happen?" says Gudrun, her heart grown "cold, because of his sharp, impersonal face. It was as if he belonged naturally to dread and catastrophe, as if he were himself again."

Thus the momentary promise of a true polarity between Gerald and Gudrun in their canoe is dissipated. Just before this, in that magically "illusive" scene with the lanterns, Gerald and Gudrun had stood together "in one luminous union, close together and ringed round with light" in the primrose yellow with butterflies hovering about them. (Generally it is Ursula who is associated with yellow and primrose and gold and who "drifts off like a butterfly.") But a second lantern had shown a cuttlefish with a "face that stared straight from the heart of the light, very fixed and coldly intent." And Gudrun had insisted on exchanging the lantern for one of Ursula's which, Birkin remarked, suggested "the heavens above, and the waters under the earth." It was the cuttlefish that in "Moony" (XIX) Ursula was to see in the bright moon under stoning, "shooting out arms of fire like a cuttle-fish, like a luminous polyp." Tonight, for Gudrun, everything speaks of the death for which she has affinity.

A far different fate, however, awaits Birkin and Ursula. As deep calleth unto deep so one image in the reader's mind, coming later, gives meaning to an earlier image. In "An Island" (XI), Birkin and Ursula had set out on Willey Water, in a leaky punt. "It will float us all right," he had said. He wanted no *Paul et Virginie,* no Watteau picnics. Indeed Ursula had shrunk from the "little jungle of rank plants before her, evil-smelling fig-wort and hemlock." But Birkin, determined as ever to encompass all experience, had "explored" it. They quarreled bitterly about love; never had Ursula found him so insufferable. Yet, at one point, when he is dropping daisies on the pond which float away, face up, like "points of exaltation" here and there, she felt "some sort of control was being put on her." And when they were once more on the "free land" Ursula saw that the boat of purple chocolate paper which she had made and dropped carelessly into the water was escorting the daisies and that they had become a convoy of rafts. Surely these two people seem marked for salvation. We feel the full force of this incident only when the Gudrun-Gerald-in-the-canoe episode provides its pendant and contrast.

To return to the scene of the accident, Gerald and Gudrun

hear the voice of Winnie, imploring help for her drowning sister, "Get her out." It is the same Winnie whom Gudrun is later to tutor to please the dying elder Crich and to yield to her seemingly ineluctable urge to imprisonment. It is that same charming child who makes evilly satirical caricatures of her pets, who mocks as a Gudrun mocks, as a Loerke mocks, and yet who loves her rabbit Bismarck, so "mysterious" and individual and untamed, even though she cannot resist the temptation to "do" him too, as she had "done" her Pekinese Looloo.

But images of prison and oppression, of death and fate, accumulate. The "beauty and subjection of his loins," as Gerald climbs hopelessly with his bandaged hand into the boat from which he has dived, becomes a sign for Gudrun of the "terrible hopelessness of fate," the end of a "great phase of life," indeed the "final approximation" of life for her. And though it is now she who yearns for "connection with him, across the invisible space of water," she feels an unbearable isolation as she hears the "decisive, instrumental voice." Death has made Gerald revert to mechanism and mechanism in that water means isolation and death.

Now when Gerald climbs back to the boat, it is "slowly, heavily, with the blind climbing nature of an amphibious beast, clumsy, his head blunt and blind like a seal's." He has discovered "a whole universe under there; and as cold as hell." Again he insists on the "cold" of the water. "It is so cold, actually, and so endless, so different really from what it is on top, so endless—you wonder how it is so many are alive, why we're up here." "I'm afraid it's my fault. But it can't be helped . . . I could go on diving, of course—not much, though—and not much use—." The situation is the reverse of that in "Diver." The watery realm of immunity and perfection in isolation is the realm of death and cold as hell. But he lingers on, doing what he can. And Birkin must pull him away, this "instrumental" Cain of modern life, who has killed his brother and feels responsible for his sister, scolding him, "You waste yourself . . . to put a mill stone of beastly memories round your neck."

Thus the "water-party" has ended in death by water. There have been some happier results too. Ursula finds herself "deeply and passionately in love" with Birkin. But Gudrun, though shocked and frightened, has been left with a commitment to

Gerald and only one problem: "the real thrill: how she should act her part."

In this same chapter, Gerald and Gudrun had come upon Birkin discoursing to Ursula on Aphrodite born of the "first spasm of universal dissolution"—then the snakes and swans and lotus—marsh flowers—and Gudrun and Gerald, all issuing from "the process of destructive creation," when the "stream of synthetic creation lapses." He had smelled the little marsh, for him a kind of Stygian swamp, where seethed the "river of darkness . . . putting forth lilies and snakes, and the *ignis fatuus*" with the *"fleurs du mal"* that is the best modern civilization can do. Where are the roses "warm and flamy" with which Ursula identifies her happiness? Ursula objects to this obsession with death; Gerald coming up, chimes in his support of Ursula. "I only want to know what we are," Birkin had insisted, the Hamlet of this unreal and death-dealing carnival on the water.

iii

Thus an examination of "Water-Party" has confirmed suspicion. It is a living cross section of an organic unity. All the major motifs of the novel are here, in full sight or by implication. Moreover Birkin's marsh with its "alarming" odor, its unhealthy flowers and reptiles, is watered by the "black river of corruption which has unfathomed depths of death by perfect cold."

But let us try the water again, this time in an earlier chapter, at "Breadalby" (VIII). The pond into which Hermione has marshaled her more docile guests is turned into an alarming aquarium where "great lizards" like Sir Joshua "crawled about," belonging to a primeval world. A Miss Bradley, "plump and big and wet, looked as if she might roll and slither in the water almost like one of the slithering lions in the Zoo." As for the little Contessa, who can compare with her for evocative but unflattering animal names except those other denizens of the underworld, the young man who is being forced to marry in "A Chair" (XXVI), that silky "dark-eyed, silent rat," and, of course, that reptilian nonpareil of a Loerke who bears the full brunt of Lawrencean intemperance in epithet? The Contessa is at her most charming when "small and like a cat, her white legs twinkling as she went, ducking slightly her head," she stands "like a tiny figurine of ivory and bronze, at the water's edge," watching, of course, those lovely shapes of dissolution, "the swans which came up in surprise." [4] In her refusal to give herself though taking amusement from everything, she is, like Loerke, a "weasel," and in the water she "sits like a rat." Lawrence is prone to "see" and "feel" his characters not only in their psychological individuality but also, and sometimes more emphatically, in relation to the central problems of existence. Not that he creates mouthpieces for preconceived ideas, but his vision of character seems to originate in an intense vision of particular qualities of existence, to which the author reacts in attraction and repulsion. Hence a certain patterning of characters and epithets, visible in the instances of the Contessa, the young man of "A Chair," Loerke, and one might add Pussum, to mention only minor figures. Hence, too, a certain narrowing of focus, a loss at times in three-dimensional quality of character in return for a gain in intensity. Lawrence, like Dostoevsky, often "dis-realizes" his characters and for the same reason: their source is not in a "philosophy" but in a religious vision of good and evil. It is not that they "stand" for such and such ideas but they do "stand" in relation to intensely felt reaction to ultimate qualities of existence. To be sure, they are usually endowed with enough psychological characteristics to make them viable in the ordinary sense. But all characters are created characters and Lawrence's quite properly bear the stigmas of his vision. Thus even Lawrence's humor is bound by his fundamental feeling. It is amusing to see Sir Joshua Malleson with his "eighteenth-century appearance," the center of "talk going on, ceaselessly, Joshua's voice dominating," reduced to a great lizard of the primeval world even before he discourses on the *"social* equality of man." These "saurians" in their rites of immersion have something amusing about them, and yet are presented also, in Gudrun's words, as "terrifying." Among them is Gerald who has made a "scarlet silk handkerchief around his loins" do very well for a bathing suit. Looking "white but natural in his nakedness," he flaunts himself in the sun, dives, and dominates the scene from the wall at the end of the pond, as the "shoal of seals" breaks to gather around him. To the silent Ursula with his "really yellow hair, his figure so full and laughing" he seems Dionysius. (It is the Dionysius in Gerald that Birkin cannot save, he who loathes the Dionysian ecstasies and prefers a "dry soul.") Near Gerald-

Dionysius leans Hermione, earlier called "Cassandra," she who with her insane and obscene will has insisted on this water-party over the refusal of Birkin and the Brangwen sisters. In her sinister "grace" she was "frightening, as if she were not responsible for what she might do," but Gerald laughed all the more, in his *amor fati* at her "convulsive madness."

Hermione belongs to death. In her the analytic and discursive reason is keen enough to desire the spontaneity it lacks, but having no true source of life in itself, it tries to create through will power. Hence her awful weariness and fatigue of utterance, and her chanting intonations as though of a priestess more than a little mad. As she sits "erect and silent and somewhat bemused, and yet so potent, so powerful," Birkin sees her and those about her as figures "in the hall of kings in some Egyptian tomb, where the dead all sat immemorial and tremendous." [5]

Through Hermione, too, another land of death comes into view, to be added to West Africa, with the "beetle-like face" of the totem and Egypt, with its "ball-rolling scarab." In an earlier skirmish with her, as Birkin was copying a picture of a goose given to Hermione by the Chinese ambassador, he had filled her with despair as he had described too recognizably the centers the Chinese live from, "the hot, stinging centrality of a goose in the flux of cold water and mud . . . fire of the cold-burning mud —the lotus mystery." So truly does a novel become for Lawrence a scheme of colors and animals, flowers, and sensations transformed, as in the lines just quoted, into a landscape of the soul that it becomes almost inevitable that, if Hermione is to make an attempt on Birkin's life, it will be with a Chinese ball of lapis-lazuli. And if Birkin, refusing to be murdered, is to find healing in nature, it will be on the "wet hillside," where fine soft wet grass will be more delicate than the touch of any woman, but where nevertheless he will seek its opposite, the "sting on the thigh" of the firs and the "light whip of the hazel" on the shoulders.

It was Birkin who had seen the social game as played at Breadalby in all its mechanical perversity: "The game is known, its going on is like a madness, it is so exhausted." Yet the social ritual at Breadalby, too, barely escapes a termination, like "Water-Party," in death.

iv

To continue to follow the traceries of relationships would be tedious. Yet I must at least point to some images found in "Water-Party" and "Breadalby" in order to insist on the richness of symbolic context.

The "whiteness" of Gerald everywhere emphasized (together with his "softness" and the "softness" of Gudrun) might seem a puerile analogy to the snow-death near Innsbruck. But connect it with his Nibelung and Nordic quality, "the strange white wonderful demons from the North," relate it to the "vast abstraction of ice and snow" and the "mystery of ice-destructive knowledge," and a major pattern is seen developing.[6]

Even in other contexts "whiteness" exploits the same suggestion. Thus in "Moony" it is the "white and deathly smile of the moon," the Syria Dea, the "white body of fire" in the water that "leaping up white," in fragments like "white birds," refuses to be violated. When its white petals take the rose shape, then especially must this whiteness be destroyed, for the rose is life-giving and Ursula sees herself as a rose of paradisal bliss. Is it the peace of death that the moon recovers as its rose recomposes itself? At any rate, Birkin has fought well against the "moon-brilliant hardness," mocking the "magic peace" of the woods. The alternative was the "lovely golden light of spring," transfused through Ursula's eyes, "though this was a paradisal bird that could never be netted, it must fly by itself to the heart." [7]

But "whiteness," because it belongs to death, can even be related to the flowers of mud, and—of all seemingly antithetical things—to mechanism. Thus in "Sketch-Book" (X) the image of lotus and other *fleurs du mal* is taken up and woven further into the pattern. This time Gudrun is "seated like a Buddhist" as she stares fixedly at the water-plants that rise from the "festering chill": "She *knew* how they rose out of the mud." Then a "man in white" appears rowing on the water, to her "keen frisson of anticipation." Gerald, she recognized, "was her escape from the heavy *slough* of the pale, underworld, *automatic* colliers" (italics mine). He started out of the mud. He was "master." As he bent forward rowing, there was a "whiteness he seemed to enclose." Yet he "seemed to stoop to something"; and soon he will be made to stoop for Gudrun's "Sketch-Book" in the water, while his "white loins" were "exposed" behind him.

The images in this context reach out toward Birkin's letter calling for "positive creation, relations in ultimate faith, when all this process of active corruption, with all its flowers of mud, is transcended." Again, Pussum is a "flower of mud," also a "red lotus in dreadful flowering nakedness." Another "mud-child" is Loerke, though he will also be, in his way, a master of the snow.

In Gudrun's knowledge of the mud, much as she may seek to escape the vision of the Thames mud in "Water-Party" and the crowd that evokes it, lies her destiny. Hence the strange attraction, after all, to the "automatic colliers," the cinema where with the engineer Palmer she may sit half-fascinated and half-repelled. Gerald's kiss under the bridge will be a collier's kiss; he will take her with the mud from his father's grave on his boots; and in the dawn, as he puts on trousers and braces, what saves him from her ridicule is his resemblance to a collier.

This knowledge, deep in her bones, of how things grow out of mud will attract her to a new master Loerke, the genius of the mud and the sewer. And just as in Gerald she sought to be saved from the mud by the master of mechanisms who started out of the mud, so in Loerke she sought that transcendence of man's abjectness through the art of mockery or the mockery that is art. She will reject marriage with Gerald; she sees the futility of creation in mechanism. "Let them become instruments, pure machines, pure wills that work like clock-work, in perpetual repetition," with a "slumber of constant repetition." Yet her own face is like a "twelve-hour clock-dial," she is "unsheathed in sleep, unrelieved, unsaved." But the "female, subterranean recklessness and mockery" revealed in "Breadalby" by her dance as Ruth in her desperate but subtly malevolent clinging to Ursula as Naomi, finds its affinity in Loerke, "absolute in himself," promising nothing but the wakefulness of exacerbated sensation. And he is even more the slave of mechanism than Gerald; his art is the *fleur du mal* of mechanism in its tendency to exploit and abandon its models in the very flush of youth and in its effort to transmute subjection to mechanism into some kind of a victory by the alchemy of an inhuman art.

For Gudrun this abandonment to Loerke and to the ultimate

"reduction in sensation" is the other side of her transport before the snow peaks and ridges which "glowed with living rose, incandescent like immortal flowers against a brown-purple sky." To Gerald she seems to be seeking to "gratify herself among the rosy snow-tips" leaving him utterly alone and with a mad desire to destroy the scene and Gudrun with her "strange religion." But this is more *amor fati* coupled, with the ambivalence that especially characterizes Gudrun, with the last despairing hope of salvation. Even the "rosy pistils" of the snow peaks will reject her, for she has not learned Ursula's lesson of the "catkins." She is more envious than indignant at Gerald's stallion-like promiscuousness; with her incapacity for marriage, she has chosen the *Glücksritter,* and she will re-enact the ride of the little girlish figure on the huge horse.

Nevertheless, in one of the finer pages of the novel, where Lawrence succeeds completely in becoming a "changer" like Birkin, capable of giving everything its due thanks to the centered strength of vision, a foretaste of Gudrun's union with Loerke at its best is presented in a vividly imagined scene. The section seems to balance both Gudrun and Gerald's moment of unity and Birkin's and Ursula's earlier consummation scene at the end of "Excurse."

In the snow Gerald has been "happy by himself" as he had been in the water in "Diver," "isolated as if there were a vacuum around his heart, or a sheath of pure ice." With Gerald, the instrumentalist, the toboggan had been a means of dangerous exploration of earth and air and sky and "carried the souls of human beings into an inhuman abstraction of velocity and weight and eternal, frozen snow." Gudrun and Gerald had been "brought into perfect static unity" but "unseeing and unwitting." And Gudrun had had the "complete moment" of her life; she had "fused like one molten, dancing globule." The scene had looked "like a garden, with the peaks for pure flowers and her heart gathering them." Yet she had had "no separate consciousness for Gerald," and even her joy had been "like a fine blade in his heart."

Gudrun's toboggan scene with Loerke effects a sharp contrast. For Loerke, "pert as a pixie," the toboggan went "wildly and gaily, like a flying leaf." When they pitched over, he made ironical remarks, the kind he would make "as he wandered in hell."

And this gave them amusement, careless and timeless, and seemed to lift them above the "dreariness of actuality." The *"comble de joie"* was a large thermos flask, a packet of Keks, and a *Schnapps,* heidel-beer, "from the bilberries under the snow." "How *very* perfect it was, this silvery isolation and interplay," Gudrun had thought.

But this momentary release through fancy, using snow and even the products from under the snow, could not in fact deal with the facts of life, "the monotony of contingencies." Gerald appears, Loerke is beaten to the ground, Gudrun strikes her last blow, and is almost strangled to death, and Gerald climbs under the "unremitting" light of a "small bright moon" forbidding sleep until he lets himself fall, within the reach of the road outward, in the final cradle of snow, the *cul de sac,* where "something broke in his soul, and immediately he went to sleep."

v

It is time to pull away from the compulsive magnetism of the field of forces that is *Women in Love* to essay some conclusions valid at least for this novel. The theme of death-in-life with its counter-theme of the life-still-possible for the saving remnant seems to have been, in Lawrence's consciousness, a core of intuitive force, an intensely radiant focus reaching out to assimilate and fuse idea, image, character, episode, and scene. In the number of chapters which we have explored, attracted especially by water-situations, we have seen water, boating, diving woven together with the denizens of river and pond, earth and sky, with the cold fires of the marsh, with the lily and the lotus and other *fleurs du mal,* with whole landscapes of static corruption, West Africa, Egypt, China, and the religions of Buddha, the Magna Mater, and the Mater Dolorosa. We have been taught to see in terms of water and mud and flower and whiteness and soft blondness and snow. As the reader advances he carries with him not merely a line of action or a "tenor" of ideas but also a sensuous vocabulary of images with its own syntax and reaching out toward a perfection of its own "logic." He has the experience of an ever-expanding *globe* of apprehension where the whole that, in one sense, is to be paradoxically integrates into itself the part that is. I submit that this is the experience of the symbol.

But what is the mode of this symbolism? It is less the symbolism of the Metaphysicals, with their "image of thought," than that of the Romantics, of Shelley, Keats, Coleridge, and Wordsworth with their "image of impression." [8] Like Baudelaire in "L'Albatros," Lawrence will work with the illustrative image which presents the sensuous equivalent of an idea easily expressible in itself in order to insure a certain support for it in sensation, emotion, and prestige. In "Mino" (XIII) didactic illustration becomes excessive and perhaps humorless: Birkin is to be to Ursula as Mino to the fluffy female with her incipient promiscuity. On the other hand in "Class-room" the catkins are at once plausible action, illustration, and the base for the meaning of the "pistils" of the mountain peaks late in the novel.

The best Baudelaire is in such a poem as "La Chevelure," where the hair of the beloved becomes the means by which we conceive an exotic seascape and an oasis which is the paradise of memory. It points toward that order "anywhere out of this world," of *"luxe, calme et volupté,"* toward which the poet is ever *en voyage.* Lawrence's symbols, as I have shown, often behave in this way.

For the novelist that is Lawrence the symbols must of course advance the action. Symbolic episodes such as that of the red Arab mare and the rabbit, among other functions, serve to carry forward the reader's perception of Gudrun's most secret processes of development. From a half-frightened and subjected admiration, she evolves to a connivance with Gerald in tyranny over the quick and the individual and to a cynical self-recognition in a universe of cruelty and death. Furthermore, since Lawrence's expression is always straining toward the symbol, it is only in the light of such more fully developed episodes that the reader can find his way into scenes as that of the conflict, immediately after the *Schuhplatteln,* between "Gudrun's ordinary consciousness and his [Gerald's] uncanny, black art consciousness."

To illustrate briefly from a minor instance. Pussum at the Pompadour is described as "leaning forward, her dark, soft hair falling and swinging against her face. There was something curiously indecent, obscene about her small, longish dark skull, particularly when the ears showed." The reader is not made to *see* what makes Pussum look "indecent, obscene," and even less why such a quality is connected with the ears showing. It is thanks to other contexts where the image is more fully fleshed, indeed it is because of the magnetism of the whole system of symbols, that we grant our poetic faith to such moments instead of accusing Lawrence of exploiting illegitimately his vague "somethings." The *created* meanings have provided the faith for the *enforced* meaning.

Our samplings, I submit, like Harry T. Moore's in the study of *The Rainbow,* reveal Lawrence as one of the workers in *symbolisme.*[9] One may argue that Lawrence moves toward even that form of *symbolisme* that seems his antipodes. Mallarmé with his apparently sterile love of a very suggestion of the suggestive, for the rose that is "absent" from all bouquets, relies increasingly on what I should call *enforced* meanings written in some ultimate abstraction of shorthand. He tends to forget that his "enforced" meanings, to be poetic meanings at all, must, though the shadow of a shadow, live by the antecedent fleshed and created meanings. The petal or the fragrance of the rose evokes the rose only for one who has seen the rose. Lawrence, though like any symbolist working toward some more efficient language of poetic abstraction, stops far short of the falling-off place because of his very distrust of abstraction. Even his flame must be a living flame. He will never seek life in that perfect cold whose *"azur"* haunts Mallarmé's imagination. Nevertheless, like any symbolist, he runs Mallarmé's risks. Lawrence fails when he seeks to enforce meanings which he has not created or when he yields to a didactic passion for the explication, forgetting meanings he has already created dramatically.

Fundamentally, Lawrence, like the major writers of his time, belongs to *symbolisme* in that common effort on the part of poetry, as Valéry said, to take back its own from music. Perhaps, in the end, amid the confusions of the *symbolistes* themselves as well as of theorists of the symbol, *"reprendre à la musique leur bien"* is the clue to the true meaning of this way of seeing and working. *Symbolisme* seems to have been a conscious and determined effort, based essentially upon Romantic theory and Romantic experimentation, to elaborate all those possibilities of language, its syntax, and its structures that will distinguish poetry from prose even when it is well written. It has sought to attain in varying degree to the "condition of music," that is, not merely vowel and consonant music, not merely melodic line, but a structure suggestive of fugue and sonata and other musical forms, in the hope that poetry may "mean" and "be" as music means and is. The new ideal spread from poem to novel. *Women in Love,* in Mark Schorer's words, bears "perhaps, a more immediate relationship to the traditional art of dance than to the traditional art of fiction . . . in the shifting allegiances between the members, and the configuration of characters." [10] A full study of *Women in Love* I think would show something of the dance in the shifting allegiances and the configuration of images.

For Lawrence understood the theory of language as paradox and gesture, though also holding to expression as simple, sensuous, and passionate. Birkin, seeking analogies between love, sleep, and death, realizes that "there was always confusion in speech. Yet it must be spoken . . . [though] to give utterance was to break a way through the walls of the prison as the infant in labor strives through the walls of the womb." And Ursula, listening, knows that "words themselves do not convey meaning, that they are but the dumb gesture we make, a dumb show like any other."

The reason for this sense of the inadequacy of vocabulary and syntax, as I have suggested, is that, though Lawrence is ardent in his desire to help shape the affairs of men in this world, his commission, as it were, lies in the religious vision. The search for an appropriate language is a characteristic result of the religious impulse, an attempt to make a gesture toward some newly sensed relation between the seen and the unseen, the social and the overriding reality upon which both a man's integrity and the good society are based. But for Lawrence even the new language is the language of men and not of angels.

NOTES

[1] *D. H. Lawrence: Novelist* (New York: Alfred Knopf, 1956). All references will be to the chapter on *Women in Love* (IV).

[2] One thinks of the elder Crich who had tamed the "hawk" that was his wife. The earliest image of imprisonment is that of Laura Crich.

[3] Sleep is for Birkin, too, related to love and death, little as he may understand the relationship. But for him sleep is more than a "lapsing out" as for Gerald; it is a death into birth and new life, a vulnerability like a babe's to experience and not a drug. Elsewhere, the paradisal state between lovers is described as without thought or desire or will, "to be perfectly still and together, in a peace that was not sleep, but content in bliss . . . this was heaven: to be together in happy stillness." The scene on the water is to be contrasted as an ideal opposite to Birkin's and Ursula's state of love.

[4] Hermione earlier in this chapter, speaking of the swans, had told with

vengeful glee how the "ousted lover had sat with his head buried beneath his wing," after being defeated in combat for the sole female. She herself loves to exert power over the stag; she fondles and dominates her kitten Micio. In this control over the "young, animal-like spontaneity and detachment" which Birkin loves, and which he exhibits at his work, she belongs with the mechanists and the dealers in death. Lawrence uses animals in a dual role: they are valued for their spontaneity and they are used, as in this context, to suggest "reduction in sensation."

[5] In the much discussed passage in "Excurse" (XXIII), the "Egyptian" quality in Birkin is presented in a favorable light. But the Egyptian quality of "pure concentration in darkness" is positive when counterbalanced in Birkin by a "Greek" quality of "lambent intelligence."

[6] Gerald's "whiteness" of body develops into the "magic, hideous white fire," the "white-cruel-recognition" in "Rabbit" and becomes even a "white aura, as if he were a visitor from the unseen" when Gerald first kisses Gudrun.

[7] Lawrence insists in many passages on the "strange golden light" radiating from Ursula. Like Novalis' "beloved object," who also can be reached only through an "accord" (*Stimmung*), she seems to be the "center of a paradise." But at times this same quality of luminousness can ring her round in "supreme repudiation" and "perfect hostility."

[8] There is an excellent discussion of the difference in R. A. Foakes, *The Romantic Assertion* (New Haven: Yale University Press, 1958), pp. 32–34.

[9] Frederick J. Hoffman and Harry T. Moore, *The Achievement of D. H. Lawrence* (Norman: University of Oklahoma Press, 1953).

[10] *Ibid.*, p. 169.

V. de Sola Pinto

LAWRENCE AND THE NONCONFORMIST HYMNS

From July till September, 1928, D. H. Lawrence was staying with his wife at a chalet at Gsteig bei Gstaad in Switzerland. The Lawrences were visited there by their American friends Earl and Achsah Brewster and by Lawrence's sister Emily (Mrs. King), whom he called Pamela, and her daughter Margaret (see Nehls, III, 228–29). In spite of his failing health, Lawrence seems to have been in an exuberant and creative mood at Gsteig. He was working on the novel called *The Flying Fish,* which he had started on his way back from Mexico; he was painting in water colors, and he wrote a number of articles for newspapers which were collected in the volume called *Assorted Articles* published in 1930. Mrs. Brewster tells us that the little party at Gsteig "sang much that summer," and quotes some of the ballads that Lawrence delighted in singing. Possibly the singing brought to his mind the hymns of his childhood, and the presence of his sister also helped to recall the Eastwood days and the Congregational chapel which he attended with his family. One of the best of the essays that Lawrence wrote at Gsteig was the beautiful and revealing "Hymns in a Man's Life" (*A.A.,*

Vivian de Sola Pinto, poet, Restoration scholar, and Fellow of the Royal Society of Literature, who was graduated from Christ Church, Oxford, after war service at Gallipoli and in France, is Professor of English at Nottingham University, where he is arranging the Lawrence commemoration exhibition of 1960; Professor Pinto's book on the Earl of Rochester, first published a quarter of a century ago, has just been reprinted. The Lawrence material in his essay is published with permission of the Lawrence Estate (represented by Laurence Pollinger, Ltd.), Alfred A. Knopf, Inc., and William Heinemann, Ltd.

In the essay, Nehls refers to *D. H. Lawrence: A Composite Biography,* by Edward Nehls, 3 Vols. (Madison: University of Wisconsin Press, 1957–59). *A.A.* is the abbreviation for *Assorted Articles,* by D. H. Lawrence (London: Martin Secker, 1930).

p. 155). This article was first published in the London *Evening News* on October 13, 1928. Lawrence gave the original manuscript draft of the article to Mrs. King, from whom the Library of the University of Nottingham acquired it in 1956. It consists of three leaves torn from a large quarto exercise book (26 x 20 cm), probably the "copy book with green emerald covers" given to him by a child for a Christmas present (see Nehls, III, 228). The manuscript in Lawrence's beautiful clear script covers the whole of both sides of each of the three leaves. A number of passages and single words have been scored through, and usually, though not always, corrections have been written above them. The deleted matter can, for the most part, be read fairly easily through the scoring out. Most of the corrections are obviously improvements. One passage, however, may have been deleted less on artistic grounds than because it might offend the susceptibilities of a newspaper editor. This is the passage illustrating the different meanings of the word "knowing," the omission of which with its typically Lawrencean sexual and Biblical allusions in the printed text is, perhaps, to be deplored:

> We admit there are two ways of knowing a woman. "Oh I know her very well, we've had many a long talk together."— "And as he went, a strange woman sat by the road, And he went in unto her and knew her." *

This is the only passage in the manuscript scored through in pencil. It may be conjectured that its omission was a last-minute alteration due perhaps to the advice of Frieda or Emily or because he realized that the "Biblical" quotation was inaccurate and he had no means of verifying it at Gsteig.

Dr. F. R. Leavis has written that "the Chapel, in the Lawrence circle, was the centre of a strong social life and a still persistent cultural tradition." The importance of "Hymns in a Man's Life" lies in the fact that it is a revelation of Lawrence's aware-

---

* This sounds like a text from the Old Testament but actually there is no text exactly corresponding to it. It is probably based on imperfect memory of Gen. XXXVIII, 16, where the meeting of Judah with Tamar disguised as a harlot is described as follows in the Authorized Version: "When Judah saw her, he thought her to be a harlot: because she had covered her face. And he turned unto her by the way, and said, Go to, I pray thee and let me come in unto thee." It may be noted that in Moffatt's translation, which Lawrence probably knew, Judah is described as stepping aside to Tamar "by the roadside."

ness of his debt to this "persistent cultural tradition," a living tradition of popular poetry, which, in his own phrase, was "woven deep" into his consciousness and gave his art a strength and a vitality unparalleled in the English literature of the twentieth century.

The first thoughts of an artist like Lawrence are always worth preserving, and it has, therefore, been thought worth while to print the complete text of the draft of the essay from the manuscript (Nottingham University Library MS 1480, La, L3). The deleted matter is enclosed in square brackets. Where substituted words or passages are written above the deletions in the manuscript, the deleted matter is printed after the substituted words or passages which are marked with asterisks. Variations in the manuscript from the printed text in *Assorted Articles* are indicated in footnotes. Minor variations in punctuation, which are fairly numerous, are not recorded. Lawrence numbered the pages of his manuscript after the first page. His page numbers are given in round brackets in the following text. An appendix is added on the hymns quoted in the essay. Roman index figures against the hymns quoted or mentioned by Lawrence refer to the notes on the hymns in the appendix. The following text is printed by permission of the University of Nottingham and the Estate of D. H. Lawrence.

HYMNS IN A MAN'S LIFE

D. H. LAWRENCE

Nothing is more difficult than to determine what a child [what a child] takes in and does not take in, of its environment and its teaching. [It is hard for a man who has had what is called a religious upbringing to get the viewpoint of a man who has not been brought up "religiously."] This fact is brought home to me by the hymns which I learned as a child, and never forget.[1] They mean to me almost more than the finest poetry, and they have for me a more permanent value, somehow or other. It is almost shameful to confess that the poems which have meant most to me, like Wordsworth's *Ode to Immortality* and Keats' Odes and pieces of *Macbeth* or *As you Like It* or *Midsummer Night's Dream,* and Goethe's lyrics like "Über allen Gipfeln ist

[1] *A.A.* "forgot."

Ruh," and Verlaine's "Ayant poussée la porte qui chancelle" [2]—
all these lovely poems which after all give the ultimate shape to
one's life; all these lovely poems, woven deep into a man's consciousness, are still not woven so deep in me as the rather banal
nonconformist [3] hymns that penetrated through and through my
childhood.

> Each gentle dove
> And sighing bough
> That makes the eve
> So fair to me.
> Has something far
> Diviner now
> It draws me back [4]
> To Galilee—
> O Galilee, sweet Galilee
> Where Jesus loved so much to be,
> O Galilee, sweet Galilee
> Come sing thy songs again to me! [1]

(2) To me, the word Galilee has a wonderful sound. The Lake
of Galilee! I don't want to know where it is. I never want to go
to Palestine. Galilee is one of those lovely* glamorous* [mys-
terious] worlds, not places, that exist in the golden haze of a
child's half-formed imagination. And in my man's imagination
it is just the same. It has been left untouched. With regard to
the hymns which had such a profound influence on my childish
consciousness, there has been no crystallising out, no dwindling
into actuality, no hardening into the commonplace. They are the
same to my man's experience as they were to me nearly* forty*
[twenty] years ago.

The moon, perhaps, has shrunken a little. One has been forced
to learn about orbits, eclipses, relative distances, dead worlds,
craters of the moon, and so on. The crescent at evening still

[2] *A.A.* prints the titles of the works that Lawrence mentions, "Ode
to Immortality," "Macbeth," etc. in inverted commas as well as the
first lines of the German and French lyrics. Lawrence in his manuscript
makes the scholarly distinction of underlining the titles (italicized here)
and putting the first lines in inverted commas.

[3] *A.A.* "Nonconformist."

[4] *A.A.* "To draw me back."

startles the soul with its delicate flashing. But the mind works automatically, and says: "Ah, she is in her first quarter. She is all there, in spite of the fact that we see only this slim blade. The earth's shadow is over her."—And willy-nilly, the intrusion of the mental processes dims the brilliance, the magic of the first apperception.

It is the same with all things. The sheer delight of a child's apperception is based on *wonder:* and deny it as we may, knowledge and wonder counteract one another, so that as knowledge increases, wonder decreases. We say again: Familiarity breeds contempt. So that as we grow older, and more familiar with phenomena, we become more contemptuous of them.—But that is only partly true. It has taken some races of men thousands of years to become contemptuous of the moon, and to the Hindu the cow is still wondrous. It is not familiarity that breeds contempt, it is the assumption of knowledge. Anybody who looks at the (3) moon and says: "I know all about that *poor* [barren] orb" is, of course, bored by the moon.

Now the great and fatal fruit of our civilization, which is a civilization based on knowledge, and hostile to experience, is boredom. All our wonderful education and learning is producing a great sum-total of boredom. Modern people are inwardly thoroughly bored. Do as they may, they are bored.

They are bored because they experience nothing. And they experience nothing because the wonder has gone out of them. And when the wonder has gone out of a man, he is dead. He is henceforth only an insect.

[Now] When all comes to all, the most precious* element* [thing] in life is wonder. Love is a great emotion, and power is power. But both [true] love and [true] power are based on wonder. Love without wonder is a sensational affair, and power without wonder is mere force and compulsion. The one universal element in consciousness which is fundamental to life, is the element of wonder. You cannot help feeling it in a bean as it starts to grow and pulls itself out of its jacket. You cannot help feeling it in the glisten of the nucleus of the amoeba. You recognise it, willy nilly, in an ant busily tugging at a straw, in a rook, as it walks the frosty grass. They all have their own obstinate will. But also, they all live with a sense of wonder. Plant conscious-

ness, insect consciousness, fish consciousness, animal consciousness, all are related by one permanent element, which love may
call the religious element inherent in all life, even in a flea: the
sense of wonder. That is our sixth sense. And it is the *natural*
religious sense.

Somebody says that mystery is nothing, because mystery is
something you don't know, and what you don't know is nothing
to you. *But there is more than one way* [5] [But there are two
ways] of knowing. [We admit there are two ways of knowing
a woman. "Oh I know her very well, we've had many a long
talk together."—"And as he went, a strange woman sat by the
road, And he went in unto her and knew her"—].

Even the real scientist works in the sense of wonder. The
pity is, when he comes out of his laboratory he puts aside his
wonder (4) along with his apparatus, and tries to make it all
perfectly didactic [wonderless]. Science in its true condition of
wonder is as religious as any religion. But didactic science is as
dead and boring as dogmatic religion. Both are wonderless and
productive of boredom, endless boredom.

Now we come back to the hymns. They live and glisten in the
depths of the man's consciousness in undimmed wonder, because
they have not been subjected to any criticism or analysis. By
the time I was sixteen I had criticised and* got over* [dismissed]
the christian dogma. It was quite easy for me, my immediate
forbears [6] had already done it for me. Salvation, heaven, virgin [7]
birth, miracles, even the christian [8] dogmas of right and wrong
—*one soon got them adjusted* [those were soon dismissed].
I never could really worry about them. Heaven is one of the*
instinctive dreams* [poetic fancies]. Right and wrong is something you can't dogmatise about, it's not so easy. As for my soul,
I simply don't and never did understand how I could "save" it.
One can save one's pennies. But how can one save one's soul?
One can only *live* one's soul.

So that the miracle of the loaves and fishes is just as good
now as when I was a child. I don't care whether it is historically
a fact or not. What does it matter? It is part of the genuine won-

[5] This is the only substituted passage written in pencil and the two
following deleted passages are the only passages scored out in pencil.
[6] *A.A.* "forebears."
[7] *A.A.* "Virgin."
[8] *A.A.* "Christian."

der. The same with all the religious teaching I had as a child, *apart* from the didacticism and sentimentalism. I am eternally grateful for the wonder with which it filled my childhood.

> Sun of my soul, thou Saviour dear
> It is not night if thou [9] be near— [ii]

That was the last hymn at the Board School.[10] It did not mean to me any christian dogma, or any salvation. Just the words "Sun of my soul, thou Saviour dear," penetrated one with wonder, and the mystery of twilight. At another time the last hymn was:

> Fair waved the golden corn
> In Canaan's pleasant land—
> [When full of joy this shining morn
> We viewed the* smiling* pleasant land].[iii]

(5) And again I loved [the] "Canaan's pleasant land." The wonder of "Canaan," which could never be localised.

I* think it was good to be* [I am glad I was] brought up a protestant;* and among protestants*, [And I am glad I was] a nonconformist, and [And] among nonconformists,[11] [I am glad I was] a Congregationalist. Which sounds pharisaic. But [No] I should have missed bitterly a direct knowledge of the Bible, and a direct relation to Galilee and Canaan, Moab and Kedron, those places that never existed on earth. And in the Church of England* one could hardly have escaped those snobbish hierarchies of class, which spoil so much for a child.* [it is hardly possible to escape the sense of class division and snobbism] And the Primitive Methodists, when I was a boy, we were always having "revivals" and being "saved." [12] And I always had a horror of being saved.

So altogether, I am grateful for my "congregational" [13] up-

---

[9] *A.A.* "Thou."

[10] *A.A.* "board school." This is the Beauvale Elementary School, which Lawrence attended.

[11] *A.A.* gives capitals to all the names denoting sects: "Protestants," "Nonconformists."

[12] *A.A.* prints a comma here followed by "and."

[13] *A.A.* prints "Congregational" and "Nonconformist" with capitals throughout.

bringing. The congregationalists are the oldest nonconformists, descendants of the Oliver Cromwell Independents. They still* had* [have] the Puritan tradition of no ritual. But they avoided the personal emotionalism which one found among the Methodists, when I was a boy.

I liked our chapel, which was tall and full of light, and yet still: and colourwashed pale green and blue, with a bit of lotus pattern. And over the organ-loft: "O Worship [14] the Lord in the beauty of Holiness," in big letters.

That was a favourite hymn too.

> O Worship the Lord, in the beauty of holiness,
> Bow down before him,[15] his glory proclaim
> With gold of obedience and incense of lowliness
> Kneel and adore him, the Lord is his name.— [iv]

I don't know what the "beauty of holiness" is, exactly. It easily becomes cant or nonsense. But if you don't think about it—and why should you?—it has a [sensuous] magic. The same with the whole verse. It [easily] is rather bad, really: "gold of obedience" and "incense of lowliness." But in me, to the music, it still produces (6) a sense of splendour.

I am always rather glad we had the Bristol hymn-book,[16] not Moody and Sankey. And I am glad our Scotch minister [17] on the whole avoided sentimental messes such as "Lead Kindly Light," [v] or even "Abide with me." [vi] He had a healthy preference for healthy hymns.

> At even when the sun was set,
> The sick, oh Lord, around thee [18] lay.
> Oh, in what divers pains they met!
> Oh, in what joy they went away.[vii]

And often we had: "Fight the good fight with all they might." [viii]

In Sunday School I am eternally grateful to old Mr. Remington with his round white beard and his ferocity. He made us sing! And he loved the martial hymns:

[14] *A.A.* "worship."
[15] *A.A.* prints "Him" and "His" with capitals throughout the quotation.
[16] See Appendix.
[17] The Rev. Robert Reid, see Nehls, I, 541.
[18] *A.A.* "Thee."

> Sound the battle-cry
> See the foe is nigh
> Raise the standard high
> For the Lord—.[ix]

The ghastly sentimentalism that came like a leprosy over religion
had [y] not yet got hold of our colliery village. I remember when
I was in Class II in the Sunday School, when I was about seven,
a woman teacher trying to harrow us about the Crucifixion. And
she kept saying: "And aren't you sorry for Jesus? Aren't you
sorry?" And most of the children wept. I believe I shed a croco-
dile tear or two, but very vivid is my memory of saying to myself:
"I don't *really* care a bit"— And I could never go back on it. I
never *cared* about the crucifixion,[19] one way or another. Yet the
wonder of it penetrated very deep in me.

Thirty six years ago, men, even Sunday-School teachers, still
believed in the fight for life and the fun of it. "Hold the fort, for
I am coming—." [x] It was far, far from any militarism, or gun-
fighting. But it was the battle-cry of a stout soul, and a fine thing
too.

> Stand up, stand up for Jesus
> Ye soldiers of the Lord— [xi]

Here is the clue to the ordinary Englishman—in the nonconformist hymns.

APPENDIX

"The Bristol hymn-book" to which Lawrence refers at the top
of page 6 of "Hymns in a Man's Life" would appear to be *The
Bristol Tune Book* first published at Bristol in 1863. "Moody
and Sankey" are the well known American evangelists D. W.
Moody and I. D. Sankey, whose *Gospel Hymns* were immensely
popular in the eighteen-eighties and eighteen-nineties on both
sides of the Atlantic.

The Rev. R. R. Turner of Paton Congregational College, Nottingham, and the Department of Theology in the University of
Nottingham has kindly lent me his copy of the third edition of
The Bristol Tune Book published in 1881, which was probably
the edition used at the Congregational chapel at Eastwood when

---

[19] *A.A.* "Crucifixion."

Lawrence was a boy. *The Bristol Tune Book* is not strictly speaking a hymn book but a book of hymn tunes, giving music for 751 hymns used in Congregational churches. The words of the first verses of some of the hymns are printed with the music. For the following notes I have also made use of *The Companion to Congregational Praise* by K. L. Parry, Independent Press, 1953, kindly lent to me by Mr. Turner, and the invaluable *Dictionary of Hymnology* edited by John Julian, revised edition, John Murray, 1908. *The Bristol Tune Book* (1881) is referred to as *B.T.B.*, *The Companion to Congregational Praise* as *C.C.P.* and *The Dictionary of Hymnology* as Julian.

NOTES

[i] "Each gentle dove." This hymn called "Evening" is by Robert Morris, and was published in H. R. Palmer's *Songs of Love for the Bible School*, 1874, and I. D. Sankey's *Sacred Songs and Solos*, 1881. It does not appear in *B.T.B.* and is not listed in *C.C.P.* See Julian, 1581 (i).

[ii] "Sun of my soul, thou saviour dear." This hymn is really a cento of verses from John Keble's "Evening" in *The Christian Year*, beginning "Tis gone, that bright and orbéd blaze." This cento or selection of verses from Keble's famous hymn was, according to Julian, "repeated in numerous hymnals." It seems to have been a favorite in late Victorian Congregational Churches, as it appears with three different tunes in *B.T.B.*: No. 75, "Hursley"; No. 399, "Saxby"; No. 403, "Whitburn." (Julian, 1178 (i).)

[iii] "Fair waved the golden corn." This hymn called "Child's Hymn" by J. H. Gurney first appeared in his *Psalms and Hymns for Public Service*, 1851. It was sung to the Elizabethan tune called St. Thomas by Giles Farnaby, which appears as No. 54 in *B.T.B.* without any words. (*C.C.P.*, 647; Julian, 474 (ii).)

[iv] "O Worship the Lord in the beauty of holiness." This hymn, called "Epiphany; or Divine Worship," by J. S. B. Monsell was first published in his *Hymns of Love and Praise*, 1863. It appears with the tune "Sanctissimus" by W. H. Cooke as No. 638 in *B.T.B.* (*C.C.P.*, 275, Julian, 855 (i).)

[v] "Lead Kindly Light." The famous hymn by Cardinal Newman: it appears as No. 618 in *B.T.B.* with the tune "Sandon." (*C.C.P.*, 622; Julian, 667 (i).)

[vi] "Abide with me." This very popular hymn by H. F. Lyte appears as No. 625 in *B.T.B.* with the tune "Eventide." (*C.C.P.*, 622; Julian, 706 (ii).)

[vii] "At even when the sun was set." This hymn by H. Twells appears with two settings in *B.T.B.*: No. 381; "Angelus," and No. 404 "Zoreth." (*C.C.P.*, 632; Julian, 88 (ii).)

[viii] "Fight the good fight with all thy might." This famous hymn by J. S. B. Monsell first appeared in his *Hymns of Love and Praise*, 1863, and passed into many popular collections. It is not in *B.T.B.* (*C.C.P.*, 512; Julian, 673 (i).)

[ix] "Sound the battle-cry." This hymn called "Christian Courage" by W. F. Sherwin first appeared in his *Bright Jewels,* 1869, and was reprinted in *The Sunday School Hymnary* and other collections. It does not appear in *B.T.B.* or in *C.C.P.* See Julian, 1702 (i).

[x] "Hold the fort for I am coming." Not in *B.T.B.* or *C.C.P.* According to Julian a Moravian Missionary Hymn. See Julian, 739 (i).

[xi] "Stand up, stand up for Jesus." This hymn called "Soldiers of the Cross" by Dr. George Duffield of Philadelphia, seems to have been originally an American antislavery hymn. It first appeared in *Lyra Sacra Americana,* 1868, and, according to Julian, "passed in an abbreviated form into many English collections" (*C.C.P.,* 519; Julian, 315 (ii).)

Diana Trilling

A LETTER OF INTRODUCTION
TO LAWRENCE

Dᴇᴀʀᴇsᴛ ɴᴏʀᴍᴀɴ [Podhoretz]:

When I saw you the other day, you asked me how my Lawrence introduction was going, whether I had finished it yet, and
you forced me to the unhappy admission that it was going not at
all, despite a hundred beginnings and the absolute need to be
done with it this summer. Your response was what I should have
foreseen it would be, one of those generational leers of yours:
you knew all about me and my generation—oh, this statistical
urgency of yours!—what made us comfortable and what strained
us, what constituted a subject-matter and what put a block in
the road. You immediately knew what was standing in my way:
I was afraid to write about Lawrence because he used to be so
important to me, as to most of my friends, and I used to think
his ideas were *true*. Now I didn't think so any more and I was
afraid to confront the reasons.

Well, for the moment I offered no dissent because—it's probably a mistake for me to confess this to you—it had seemed to
me, too, that my inability to get the job done was a "resistance,"
a refusal of self-knowledge, and it would be fairly clear that what
I would be resisting in any essay on Lawrence would be an assess-
ment of my present-day feelings about him and the disclosure of

---

Diana Trilling, formerly fiction critic for the *Nation* and a Guggenheim
Fellow, edited the *Viking Portable D. H. Lawrence* (1947) and is widely
known for her critical articles in *Partisan Review, Commentary,* and
other periodicals. This essay, written in the form of a letter to Norman
Podhoretz, a representative critic of the post-Lawrence generation, is
part of Mrs. Trilling's Introduction to her edition of *The Selected
Letters of D. H. Lawrence,* copyrighted, 1958, by Diana Trilling and
reprinted here by permission of the publishers, Farrar, Straus and
Cudahy.

whatever changes had taken place in me since I first read him with the sense that he was *my* author. He's not at all my author any more, that's sure. It doesn't occur to me to pick him up for pleasure, to learn something that would make my life nicer or bigger, although there never was an author who consciously undertook to make life so large. When I read Lawrence today it is to add to my knowledge of him, not to my imagination of me, and this change might certainly have its disconcerting personal implications.

But then, what do you read Lawrence for, Norman, you who were so barely born the year he died? To learn about you? I doubt it. The situation is as archeological for you as it is for me; there are always these unfathomable reaches of history which you in some subtle fashion put between yourself and anything that happened before this very instant. I'm talking not only of you, of course, or of the things you've written, but of an anxiety about time which seems to me to be common among your literary contemporaries: you all have this sense of time as a kind of cultural bulldozer laying total waste to the land with each flip of the calendar, you're as sensitive to the shifts in decades as we were to the passage of a century. For all of you an examination of yourselves as you were yesterday is like an adventure into a lost civilization. It's what accounts of course for your shared precocity, the speed and thoroughness with which you leave your yesterdays behind you. But it's also what accounts for your *schmerz,* the big hole at the center of your present which you wait for the future to fill. You like to blame this emptiness on your immediate culture rather than on a defect in your historical connection. Your refusal of any but your strictly contemporary experience, a refusal which is implicit in your compulsive historicity—this is the way it was in the '20s, this is the way it was in the '30s—is resistance in its essence, a rejection of the very idea of self-knowledge whose core, after all, is a recognition that the human circumstance is not one's own invention.

But to get back to my difficulties with Lawrence. It was surely quite possible that I was reluctant to retrace my experience of so personally involving an author. It had also occurred to me that perhaps I had talked myself out: it always makes an interesting speculation why an author is suddenly revived; in the last year or two Lawrence has strangely reappeared in our conversational lives, people seem to be clumsily edging up to the notion that perhaps here is a man who still has something to say to us. But now I know this isn't the explanation either, I've discovered what has really been troubling me. It's not that I hesitate to re-examine Lawrence's ideas—and we of course mean his sexual ideas—and I find I have more things I'd like to say than there are people to listen. But they're of a random personal kind that balks at the conventions of a formal literary essay, it's the literariness that stops me, the orderliness of presentation and the pedagogic attitude conventionally required of an introduction. I've actually written of Lawrence only once before but I become claustrophobic at the thought of plowing over the same old ground again, about how Lawrence was born in 1885 and died of tuberculosis in 1930 and how he was the son of a coal-miner father and a schoolteacher mother and how he loved his mother too much and it made him nervous and about how he was a poet and therefore mustn't be read literally, but a poet without an esthetic other than his doctrine, his doctrine *was* his esthetic, and about how his doctrine has been distorted by people who haven't bothered to read him thoroughly and about how his doctrine has been misread even by people who have read him more or less thoroughly because it assaults their most precious assumptions, etc., etc. It isn't that the old ground is no longer fertile; there's not an inch of it but would yield. And I don't ignore the requirements of conscience in writing about Lawrence, the need for a special sanity and balance of the sort we like to think is pedagogic and which does of course finally rest on one's willingness to school oneself in what Lawrence actually wrote and intended: there are so many and such assorted irresponsibilities Lawrence has suffered. But surely one can be as responsible outside as within the established forms, just as one can often best comprehend an object by the full indulgence of one's subjectivity, Lawrence in his travel writing being a classic instance. I'm all at once impatient of an objectivity which adds up to little more than submitting to a convention of literary address and moderating one's voice. I especially want to take Lawrence, who is always written about so grimly, out of the study into the living room where I can be easy and unsolemn, or I want to write a letter, this letter. Lawrence needs to be gossiped about, he was that kind of man and writer; he needs to be come at with as much human immediacy as one can manage.

There's the matter of Frieda Lawrence, for instance. She was a Lawrence *fact,* a human fact of the greatest significance in Lawrence's literary career. How can one write about the author of these letters and ignore the wife who was so consistently at his shoulder when he was writing most of them? It's absurd the way criticism and even biography are willing to explore every influence that touches a writer except the woman he marries. Why are Lawrence's letters so wonderful, the best in modern literature and second only to Keats's in the whole history of English literature, except that they are so absolutely personal, so close to home, so miraculously without an eye to posthumous publication? If we don't hesitate to read a man's mail, if we don't hesitate to read letters even as personal as these of Lawrence, why should we scruple to read such a public statement as his choice of a wife? I want to start with Frieda and throw her out as an institutional piety; instead I'll embrace her for the big, significant, soft, silly reality she actually was. It's no accident that a man marries the woman he marries and if he's a writer, sooner or later he'll somehow explain his choice in his books. But sometimes it's easier, and it should always be thought more respectable, to get at the books through the wife than at the wife through the books.

I'll begin with Frieda, then, and tell you what I think of her but you must keep in mind that I *really* know nothing about her, I've never even known anyone who met her. I think Frieda was a bit of a swamp, and this, dear Norman, is literary criticism, impressionistic to be sure, but literary criticism nonetheless, whatever its high savor of gossip; it has directly to do with the kind of writer Lawrence was. She had a swampy mind and spirit, she had no intellect, no real intelligence, yet she had wits; she was shrewd like so many Continental and so few American women, she had her own kind of innocence but it was not of the sort which is so continuing and inexplicable a fact of our American ineptitude. No American woman, no matter how gifted in masochism—and we make a female specialty of it in this country, it's part of our pioneer heritage—could have been married to Lawrence without going mad; perhaps even a Frenchwoman married to Lawrence would have gone mad. It took a German woman like Frieda to stay entirely sane and make a successful career of the lunacy of her marriage.

Now we must remember that in a way she had been bred for her fate, unlike our Bennington girls, the ones who look to art and lunacy for their personal salvation. For our poor girls, the lunatic life of art has only a negative force, it's the obverse of the mental health culture in which they have been reared. But Frieda, being German, had a large cultural support when she chose Lawrence. Lunacy *was* mental health in postwar Germany and so far as Frieda is concerned it doesn't make the least bit of difference that she was chronologically prewar, almost forty and long removed from Germany by the time the war ended; she seems to me to have been entirely typical of Germany in the years after the first war—being an aristocrat, she was no doubt ahead of herself; the upper classes, especially in Europe, always move in advance of their national culture, they can afford to take more chances. To make a successful life on the slippery edge of madness was the progressive thing for someone of Frieda's background to do, like wandering around with a knapsack or painting wooden bowls. Essentially there was a good deal of the *Wandervogel* in Frieda throughout her life and Lawrence liked it in her although it also made trouble between them as it would no doubt have gone on to make trouble for Lady Chatterley and Mellors if the book hadn't ended when it did: you'll remember Constance Chatterley and her sister had had German, not English, young womanhoods. Was it Frieda or was it Lawrence —I think it was Frieda—who said she had been in a sleep when Lawrence found her, the wife of a Nottingham professor of languages, pouring tea while her three children romped on the lawn? She had whiled away some of the tedium of faculty life with an inconsequential adultery or two, but we can guess that it wasn't sex that had impelled her to her infidelities any more than it was sex speaking when she invited Lawrence to stay the night in the absence of Professor Weekley—not sex, that is, in primary terms. Do I do Frieda an injustice?—I always have this impression that it was art or, rather, creativeness that was the great imperative for her; sex was just a secondary gain in the life of self-expression. Lawrence brought Frieda into the full tumultuous tide of creative living, eventually he made her famous, which was its own immaculate pleasure, but right from the start he gave her the creative status which Weekley couldn't provide, he made her the woman behind his genius which is so much more what women seem to want than being geniuses themselves. We have it in Frieda's own words in her foolish memoir of her husband where she says, with the catastrophic naïveté which is her style, "I had always regarded Lawrence's genius as given to me. I felt deeply responsible for what he wrote." More revealing than the remark itself is its context, an account of Lawrence's relation with Mabel Dodge Luhan; it seems that Mabel and Lawrence wanted to do a book together, it was to be about Mabel, and Frieda explains her position: "I did not want this. I had always regarded Lawrence's genius as given to me." It's from passages like this that I draw my impression that for Frieda art rather outranked sex. But Lawrence could have been a bad artist and it would have been all the same to Frieda so long as he was for self-expression in the largest possible quantity; she had no taste, as we mean the exercise of artistic judgment. But then neither had Lawrence; Lawrence never thought of art in terms of taste any more than he thought of art in terms of permanence. The value for Lawrence of a created work lay not in its lastingness or in its conformity to esthetic standard but in its rightness at the moment and for its creator, in its usefulness as a form of personal communication. He cared just as much about his painting as about his writing and he wasn't a very good painter; and he could devote himself to embroidery and the decoration of little boxes with the same casual gravity he gave to his major literary efforts. Is it funny that I use the word "casual" of Lawrence? It's the accurate word. Certainly there was never a writer who took himself so solemnly as a human being but so unsolemnly as an artist.

I don't for a moment mean that Lawrence was unsolemn about the content of his books or even about their method. He was always the subject of his books and he regarded himself as the most serious subject in the world. And he was a very conscious artist, he was anything but the primitive some of his critics have made him out to be; nothing could have been more intellectualized than his theory of the unconscious source of art. But he never "saw himself" as an artist, only as a person and workman; although his extraordinary gifts were recognized unusually early in his career, it never occurred to him to suppose they earned him any privilege in society. Writing was simply the way he made his living as someone else made his by carpentry or ditch-digging and he did it as competently and quietly as if ours were a world in which as much status accrued to a carpenter as to a literary celebrity. Because he attracted to himself a group of followers for whom he was prophet and savior, and manifestly enjoyed the role, we tend to accuse him of playing artist to the philistines. But this is a mistake, he never bullied people with his artistic superiority, only with his messianism, he never asked or claimed a superior social or personal place on the basis of his talents or their recognition. As an artist he was the most unassuming man who ever lived. It is also a mistake to think of Lawrence, as we are likely to, as one of those instances of unacknowledged or unrewarded genius whose recollection is supposed to fortify the rising artist against a life of failure. Lawrence suffered enormous hardship; he was ill, he was poor, he had great trouble with the press, he was persecuted by the law, he was accused of being a German spy in the war, with alarming regularity his best friends became his public enemies. But there have been few serious let alone revolutionary artists whose right to special critical notice was won so fast and surely. He stopped teaching with the publication of his first novel, *The White Peacock,* which, incidentally, had been taken by the first publisher who saw it, and never again attempted to earn his living except by writing—in any writer's life this implies a large demand on society and a considerable victory if it is managed even meagerly. And despite the hostility which he generated every step of his way, the sheer power of his gift imposed itself unusually early, demanded and received its acknowledgment no matter how grudging or unsympathetic. From the very beginning he was always thought of as a genius and, after all, that isn't the common way we mask our dislikes.

But I have wandered too far from Frieda and her first marriage and Professor Weekley. Poor Professor Weekley: I gather he was something of a scholar, he wrote a whole series of books on etymology, but I'm afraid this doesn't make him the less dim. As he comes through the letters and biographies he seems to have been a person of low emotional intensity and high self-conscious principle who, having once laid successful claim to a woman of spirit, felt he owed it to himself never again to settle for less. I can scarcely suppose he was quite as awful as Lawrence pictures him in the letter to Amy Lowell where he describes Frieda's interview with him when she returned to England in 1914, two years after the elopement. It's a brilliant letter but somehow Lawrence's effort to make Weekley into the very image of castrated middle-class respectability, calling Frieda a prostitute and refusing her all communication with her children, doesn't ring entirely true for me; I have an idea that Lawrence is projecting into Weekley an aspect of his own judgment on Frieda and himself. Lawrence had been miserable about his equivocal situation with Frieda in the two years between the elopement and their marriage; whenever he thought people mistakenly assumed they were married, he hurried to set the record straight. He had wanted this married woman and he had had the courage to take what he wanted, perhaps it was even an important condition of his love for Frieda that she was already another man's wife and a mother; he overrode Frieda's hesitations in fine style and got her to run off with him. But he hated living with her without marriage, it shocked him and he expected others to be shocked. The worst of which I seem to be able to accuse Weekley in the scene Lawrence recreates is a certain hamming and an inadequate imagination in supposing he could outmatch Lawrence by taking a high moral line: this was Lawrence's game and was there anyone to beat him at it? I didn't guess it from Lawrence's reports of Weekley, actually I learned it from Harry Moore's biography, but I suppose I should have been able to figure out that Weekley wanted Frieda the more, not the less, because she had left him for Lawrence: twenty years later, when Lawrence died, Weekley asked her to come back to him and I find this touching, it quite rounds out my image of him, that he had held on to Frieda all these years as the test of his manliness. It's like something in a Lawrence novel, isn't it, but Weekley was precisely like someone in a Lawrence novel, one of those men who need a woman like Frieda to validate their masculinity. Lawrence needed a woman like Frieda himself, to validate his masculinity too, which not only identifies him with Weekley but also with all his other Weekley characters, including Clifford Chatterley, all the frightened insufficient men in his novels who depend on women for their strength. This of course is the confusing thing about Lawrence and his books. Everybody knows Lawrence was representing an image of himself in the game-keeper Mellors in *Lady Chatterley's Lover*. But Lawrence was not only Mellors in that novel, he was Clifford Chatterley as well. Lawrence is not only the heroes in his fiction but the villains too, which is what licenses the cruelty in his books. This is what licenses Lawrence's quite extreme cruelty to Clifford Chatterley: Chatterley is himself.

I'm convinced Frieda was the best possible, indeed the only possible wife for Lawrence. She had a lot of strength, she was *there,* yet she was sufficiently amorphous to mold herself to any notion of femaleness Lawrence needed to impress upon her. She must have been an awful nuisance the way he couldn't even write a letter without her telling him where she agreed and disagreed and adding her own postscripts à la Lawrence, and it's embarrassing how she tried to ape his style. *His* style, of all things for a German lady to ape! But he loved it, of course, when they were newly together—he was twenty-seven when they eloped, she was thirty-three and she must have been still open and sweet-looking then; she aged badly, from the pictures one gathers she became both sharp and overblown, a bit witchlike—and it was very shrewd of him to have chosen her, very therapeutic. Do you remember his remark about how he believed in art, not for art's sake, but for his own sake? "One sheds one's sicknesses in books, repeats and presents again one's emotions in order to master them." His marriage as well as his art was a place where he repeated and presented again his emotions in order to try to master them; it was a proving ground for the material of his books and he was very fortunate to have found a woman who was sufficiently passive and masochistic to accept this therapeutic use of her. Not that Frieda was quiet or withdrawn, she was far from being one of those docile women who confirm their femininity by a refusal of self-assertion; in fact, she seems to have made her presence known a good deal more noisily than many women who have far less instinct for emotional subservience. She could lose her temper at will and act rudely; she seemed to equate smashing dishes and throwing things with both class and femaleness, like those movies of ten or fifteen years ago in which the well-reared heroine finally captivates her lover by breaking a vase over his head. But Lawrence was no mean hand at making scenes himself and if we are even partly to trust the memoirists, he could be savage and ugly whereas Frieda was only elaborate. There's the bad story, for instance, that Witter Bynner tells in *Journey with Genius* of Lawrence having the bootblacks of Chapala arrested and jailed —they hadn't the money to pay their fines—because they had come to solicit business on the terrace of a hotel where the Lawrences were dining and where the youngsters were supposed not to intrude. I can't think Bynner was making up that story any more than I can suppose Mabel Dodge Luhan was wholly fabricating her account, in *Lorenzo in Taos,* of the evening she and Lawrence danced around her living room, bumping into Frieda and her partner as often and hard as they could in a kind of hysteria of jealousy until all four of them were black and blue and breathless. Frieda was too much a born lady to take out her angers on a lot of poor ragamuffins just as she was too much a born fool not simply to sit down instead of letting herself be bumped. I'm afraid Lawrence could be unpleasant like few people one wants to respect; it's hard to put from one's mind the letter he wrote Katherine Mansfield: "I loathe you. You revolt me stewing in your consumption. . . . The Italians were quite right to have nothing to do with you." That was in 1920 when Katherine Mansfield was very ill and Lawrence had not yet learned of his own tuberculosis. But perhaps he already had his premonitions; as I say, one can only be that cruel if it is oneself who is attacked. But surely no one but Frieda could have lived with such a man and it's no use Aldous Huxley telling us how sweet and gentle Lawrence could be, we know from the letters that he was capable of sweetness and gentleness, they're full of the evidence of his endearing human qualities. But he was also half crazy and Frieda knew it and was able to sustain it. If Frieda had had a mind, she would of course have lost it trying to understand Lawrence, and Lawrence would have been ruined both as a person and a writer. Frieda was Lawrence's therapy but fortunately she didn't cure Lawrence, a cured Lawrence would have been no Lawrence at all. In her mindlessness, she held Lawrence together, that was all, and she performed a great service to literature.

But of course I am using the word "mind" here in a way that is almost as confusing as Lawrence's use of it when he took his doctrinal stand against the mental consciousness. To be sure,

Frieda had no intellect in the sense that Lawrence had such a first-rate endowment of mental power: T. S. Eliot to the contrary notwithstanding, Lawrence was a very well-educated man with a quite remarkable capacity for quick learning, especially in his earlier years he read widely and closely. Frieda had a perfectly competent organ of understanding in her head, it was just that it operated behind rather than in advance of her feelings, she felt her way with Lawrence instead of thinking her way. "To know the *mind* of a woman," Lawrence wrote in a letter to Dr. Trigant Burrow, "is to end in hating her. . . . Between man and woman it's a question of understanding *or* love. . . ." It would have been closer to the matter if he had written that to know the mind of a man is to end in hating him since obviously Lawrence was much more concerned to defend men against being understood by women than to defend women against being understood by men; we know that from as far back as *Sons and Lovers*. It wasn't intellect, however, that he wished to preserve from comprehension. In the same letter to Dr. Burrow he goes on to define love as the "pre-cognitive flow" and we are at once aware of what it is he means by mind and what he opposes to understanding. Love is the state of affectional, quite animal connection between two people such as exists between mother and child in the child's infancy; understanding is the operative force which enters into this relationship when the social connection replaces the earlier physical connection. In all his adult life, in all his life with Frieda, Lawrence looked to reproduce the non-cognitive connection of this earliest love experience, his infant experience. It is what he meant by the blood consciousness which he offered as his alternative to mental consciousness, the opposition which plays such a basic part in his attack upon modern civilization. Frieda had enough intelligence of feeling—female intuition, if you will—to recognize Lawrence's need for the kind of love he had once known in the infancy of his life and enough undifferentiated maternal impulse to satisfy this need as far as it can ever be satisfied in a grown man. She couldn't make Lawrence happy, no woman could have, but better than anyone we can imagine she met the first enormous requirement Lawrence imposed on her, it is the same requirement he imposes on us as his readers—that we suspend the usual exercise of reason and the usual impulses of common sense and self-protection in order to receive such beneficence as this man of genius has within his giving. Frieda was knowing, as a mother is, but we can put it that she didn't have to understand what she knew about Lawrence any more than a mother has to understand what she knows about her infant; and that is why she didn't have to end in hating Lawrence and in destroying him and herself.

But she had her bad times nonetheless, of this there can be no question; the two of them had a great talent for making each other miserable. Lawrence might write of himself, "I shall do my work for women, better than the Suffrage," but even Frieda must have had her moments when she would have settled for the vote and a less strenuous husband, especially in the war years. Those war years! It's odd, the way the biographers always take what Lawrence says at its face value when they come to dealing with the depression he ascribes to his hatred of the war, and skip the looming fact that the outbreak of the war and the outbreak of Lawrence's first period of acute emotional disturbance coincide almost exactly with the legitimization of his union with Frieda. The final divorce decree came on May 28, 1914; Frieda and Lawrence were married on July 13, 1914. For two years they had been in exile from England, now they could be legal and they returned to England, to set up life together as a respectable married couple. And war was declared!

For all their self-revelation, there are extraordinary reticences in Lawrence's letters. There is no hint, for instance, in the Huxley volume of what we learn from Moore's biography, that all the time Lawrence was writing *Sons and Lovers* in Italy he was in correspondence with Jessie Chambers, the Miriam of the novel, sending her his manuscript so that she could verify or correct his account of their earlier relationship. It's one of the creepiest episodes in Lawrence's history, the two of them, Lawrence and Frieda, sitting there poring over Jessie's detailed revisions of Lawrence's earlier love affair while back in England, alone, Jessie dug and dug, dredging up every last memory as she cherished it, insisting that Lawrence do her the justice in fiction that she felt he had denied her in real life. What price both art *and* truth! Maybe—we hope—Lawrence was ashamed of himself and that's why he doesn't tell Garnett, say, what he's doing. But this isn't the only place where the letters can be misleading if they are taken as the sole or chief biographical source. If we compare the poems in the *Look! We Have Come Through!* volume with the letters Lawrence wrote in the same period, the correspondence is far from adequate in suggesting the torments Lawrence apparently went through in his life with Frieda after their elopement, Frieda insisting, for one thing, that a mother has a perfect right to miss her children. Instances like these warn us that the books and letters not only must be read together if we are properly to understand either but also that there is still room for conjecture all around the biographical record; they license my suspicion that Lawrence's recorded feelings about the war—the many letters he wrote about his hatred of the war and the famous passages in *Kangaroo*—were very possibly a cover for other emotions he was experiencing at that time of which he was not permitting himself so much awareness.

To feel, as I do, that it was not the war alone but the fortuitous combination of war and his marriage that brought Lawrence so close to the breaking point after he returned to England in 1914 is obviously not to minimize the violence of his response to the war. Anyone who allows himself fully to contemplate the organized butchery in which whole societies can indulge themselves is bound to be pushed toward insanity, and Lawrence was not one to spare himself, or us, any final confrontation. Then too, in his inordinate reaction to the simple routines of physical examination, we necessarily read Lawrence's unconscious fear of the homosexual temptations of army life: surely more than even extraordinary sensitivity is involved in Lawrence's horror because he had to queue up with the other men and submit to medical examination, including an inspection of his genitals. The fact of his marriage to Frieda—I don't mean the mere mention that the marriage has taken place but what it weighed as an emotional event—is conspicuously missing from his correspondence that fall and winter. War, war, war is his obsession, we hear its rumble even through some of the best descriptive writing he ever did and some of his most beautiful passages of nature writing.

In terms of his well-being, I think it was disastrous for Lawrence to have married; it would have been better for him if he had continued to live with Frieda without institutionalizing the relationship. To legalize their union was to bring Lawrence's sexual feeling for Frieda into the atmosphere of social regularity and conventional family emotion; that is, it brought sex into established connection with love—you know, like the song: love and marriage go together like a horse and carriage. Lawrence wanted Frieda to love him like a mother but the moment they were bound together in the institution of marriage, it was as if Frieda was institutionalized in the mother position, it was as if she had become the very mother person from whom she had been supposed to detach him. You remember how, in writing about the Morel boys in *Sons and Lovers,* Lawrence said, "As soon as the young men come into contact with women, there's a split. William gives his sex to a fribble and his mother holds his soul." Well, the split was bad and Lawrence had looked to Frieda to put the pieces together, to unite soul and body as Jessie Chambers had been incapable of doing. But in actuality this was not at all the service Frieda had performed. On the contrary, she had kept soul and sex apart or at least unlegalized in their union, until now the marriage took place and sex and love were presented to Lawrence in the person of a wife. I think it was this institutionalized conjunction of sex and love that threw Lawrence into the despair of the war years. The conflict raging in the world was an externalized expression of the private sexual struggle which was to absorb so large a part of his emotional energies for the rest of his life.

This is no irrelevant private point I'm making, no psychoanalytical advantage I'm trying to take of Lawrence, need I make that clear? The conflict which was crystallized in Lawrence when he and Frieda finally married seems to me to be the essential conflict, and contradiction, that runs through all his work. Lawrence wanted to rid sex of its usual paraphernalia of love emotions, he wanted the sexual relation to be rid of the "mental" trappings which he felt were so destructive of the dark mysterious physical connection. But he also wanted love to be totally assimilated into the sexual experience, he feared to give the sexual emotions any autonomy unless they were sanctified by love. It was a conflict so strong and so deeply rooted in his own personal history that it was impossible of resolution and it accounts, in my opinion, for our inability ever finally to understand what Lawrence is driving toward in his fiction, our inability ever to parse either his plots or his characters and finally say, with any conviction of accuracy, just what it is he *approves* in the relations between his heroes and heroines. We know of what Lawrence disapproves, we know he disapproves of all assertions of will and all sexual behavior which has mere sensation as its goal. But even here he is ambiguous, flagrantly so at times. In the character of Mellors, for example, it's impossible to distinguish what Lawrence would call an assertion of will from what he presents to us as an expression of the gamekeeper's inviolable masculinity and wholly admirable pride. And surely it is difficult to rid Mellors' exercises in sensuality of the charge that they are efforts—and why not, indeed?—to achieve new sensations, new thrills. It's striking that Lawrence never tells us what Mellors and Constance Chatterley actually do on their big sensual excursion; this is the one sexual scene in *Lady Chatterley's Lover* where Lawrence himself did the expurgating. We can conjecture that he drew back at this point as much because he realized he was violating a cardinal tenet of his own faith—his injunction against sensation-seeking—as because of his puritanism.

Whoever has read Lawrence with any thoroughness and tried to grasp his sexual doctrine must at last ask himself, what did Lawrence *really* want of the relationship between a man and a woman, not in metaphoric terms—in the realm of metaphor we accept the fact that we are expected to make our own interpretations and that we may be mistaken—but in didactic terms. (This is another of the contradictions in Lawrence: so much a poet, he yet insists that we read him as a preacher.) Does he want sex without love? Obviously not. Does he want love without sex? Obviously not. Does he want sex and love together? Well, yes and no. Certainly he wants them in conjunction more than he wants them separate, and yet when he puts them in conjunction he is at once and quite automatically driven to attack the quality either of the love or of the sex. The answer is, I'm afraid, that he wants neither sex nor love but some combined transcendence of both, a transcendence that has its source and fulfillment only in phantasy. This transcendence he calls marriage. "Your most vital necessity in this life," he wrote Dunlop, the friendly consul at Spezia, "is that you shall love your wife completely and implicitly and in entire nakedness of body and spirit. . . . You asked me once what my message was . . . This that I tell you is my message as far as I've got any." And you recall that little story he wrote called "Love" in which the girl refuses adoration, appreciation, caressing, anything we commonly think of as love-making. She doesn't want her sweetheart to touch her and yet it's not that she is averse to sexuality, it's just that she wants no demonstrations either of physical or spiritual courtship, all she wants is marriage. Marriage was Lawrence's message. But no marriage on land or sea, Norman; no marriage you or I have ever known, no marriage he had ever known. Lawrence spoke about marriage as he spoke about a return to the dark gods of an earlier civilization than our Hebraic-Christian civilization, as a metaphor against loneliness. His message makes no reasonable sense: when was there ever an entire nakedness of body and spirit between a man and a woman, it's rather dreadful to contemplate. But of course his message makes sense as poetry, as an overleap of the imagination in order to dramatize the insufficiency of our ordinary civilized sexual relationships.

I read Lawrence today and I'm utterly confounded by the effect he had on me and my friends when we first read him: we thought his metaphors were translatable into a program for practical conduct! We knew he addressed himself to us not on behalf of a new way of acting but a new way of being. We understood, of course—after all, we weren't stupid—that his sociology, his politics, his anthropology, his religion were all of them directed only to the quality of being which Lawrence hoped to produce; we never read *The Plumed Serpent* as a defense of Hitler or Mussolini, we knew he didn't mean us to run around like Aztecs or Incas or whatever they were. Yet in the sexual sphere we seemed to find in his books a literal sanction which literally is not there—the sanction for a free, even an experimental sexuality, and we recognized neither the contradictions in his doctrine nor its abstraction from reality. Since Lawrence's morality had to do with the kind of person one is and since all this thinking had as its object the discovery of a better way of being, both of which preoccupations are of course wholly in line with the concerns of the romantic poets, we read Lawrence like the last of the romantics, a bit on the mystical side but still the most intense and personal of the romantic idealists, the one who imposed on us the heaviest burden of self-consciousness and self-realization, as it used to be called. In our effort to meet his high challenge to self-awareness, we failed to perceive that there is no world for Lawrence's people, that they are isolated in their intensity, and that he doesn't permit *us* to live in the actual world—this and his profound sexual puritanism, the fact that he licenses sex only as a sacrament.

You're wiser in your generation, Norman, than we were about Lawrence; no, not wiser, keener. Having been born in the years of the economic depression gives you a keener nose for reality and a quicker instinct to protect practice against theory, which is also why you're less generous than we were. You're more acute in your reading of Lawrence because you're less generous in your imagination of heroism; transcendence worries you, perhaps a little too much. You immediately smell out Lawrence's remoteness from actual life and his restrictiveness, you know that if you take him literally he would pull you after himself into some unwholesome morass and that he doesn't represent the romantic ideal of freedom. Steve Marcus, for instance, says that after a bout of Lawrence he always turns to Colette: we would have scorned such an idea, thought it frivolous, but Steve is right of course and we were wrong: as a sexual writer, Colette is exactly the indicated antidote to Lawrence. And yet I wonder. I wonder if this reality principle of yours doesn't define a weakness as much as a strength. At least we hoped ourselves capable of ultimate emotion, ultimate vision, ultimate experience and, measuring our capacity, we were willing to make mistakes; we didn't enter maturity, like you who, born in the depression, still remain determinists of every kind except economic, all set to accept whatever limitations on our being and call them our fate. We didn't invoke reality only as a negative force, only as a restriction of possibility; there were times when we supposed reality was on our side. Dear Norman, there surely is much to be said for a view of life, like Lawrence's, which not only refuses the simple on the sole ground that it is less than the complex but which also insists that we make our own conditions and that our fate can be grand. . . .

Katherine Mansfield

A LETTER ABOUT THE LAWRENCES

[Zennor, St. Ives, Cornwall]
Thursday [11 May 1916]

I AM quite alone here for all the day so I shall write to you. I have not written before because everything has been so unsettled; now it is much more definite. I wish I could come and see you instead of writing; next month I shall come to London probably for a little time and then we shall be able to meet and talk.

You may laugh as much as you like at this letter, darling, all about the COMMUNITY. It *is* rather funny.

Frieda and I do not even speak to each other at present. Lawrence is about one million miles away, although he lives next door. He and I still speak but his very voice is faint like a voice coming over a telephone wire. It is all because I cannot stand the situation between those two, for one thing. It is degrading— it offends one's soul beyond words. I don't know which disgusts me worse. When they are very loving and playing with each other or when they are roaring at each other and he is pulling out Frieda's hair and saying "I'll cut your bloody throat, you bitch" and Frieda is running up and down the road screaming for 'Jack' to save her!! This is only half of what happened last Friday night. You know, Catalino, Lawrence isn't healthy any more;

Katherine Mansfield (1888–1923), native of New Zealand and one of this century's most famous short-story writers, author of *In a German Pension* (1908), *Prelude* (1911), and other volumes, was the wife of John Middleton Murry and a member of the Lawrence group; the late S. S. Koteliansky, to whom this letter was written, was a Russian exile living in London and a close friend of Lawrence's. Katherine Mansfield's letter is published here by permission of the Estate of John Middleton Murry.

he has gone a little bit out of his mind. If he is contradicted about *anything* he gets into a frenzy, quite beside himself[,] and it goes on until he is so exhausted that he cannot stand and has to go to bed and stay there until he has recovered. And whatever your disagreement is about he says it is because you have gone wrong in your sex and belong to an obscene spirit. These rages occur whenever I see him for more than a casual moment[,] for if ever I say anything that isn't quite 'safe'[,] off he goes! It is like sitting on a railway station with Lawrence's temper like a big black engine puffing and snorting. I can think of nothing, I am blind to everything, waiting for the moment when with a final shriek—off it will go! When he is in a rage with Frieda he says it is she who has done this to him and that she is "a bug who has fed on my life." I think that is true. I think he is suffering from quite genuine monomania at present, through having endured so much from her. Let me tell you what happened on Friday. I went across to them for tea. Frieda said Shelley's Ode to a Skylark was false. Lawrence said, "You are showing off; you don't know anything about it." Then she began. *"Now* I have had enough. Out of my house. You little God Almighty[,] you. I've had enough of you. Are you going to keep your mouth shut or aren't you." Said Lawrence: "I'll give you a dab on the cheek to quiet you, you dirty hussy." Etc. Etc. So I left the house. At dinner-time Frieda appeared. "I have finally done with him. It is all over for ever.["] She then went out of the kitchen and began to walk round and round the house in the dark. Suddenly Lawrence appeared and made a kind of horrible blind rush at her and they began to scream and scuffle. He beat her—he beat her to death—her heart and face and breast[,] and pulled out her hair. All the while she screamed for Murry to help her. Finally they dashed into the kitchen and round and round the table. I shall never forget how L. looked. He was so white—almost green[,] and he just hit, thumped the big soft woman. Then he fell into one chair and she into another. No one said a word. A silence fell except for Frieda's sobs and sniffs. In a way I felt almost glad that the tension between them was over for ever, and that they had made an end of their 'intimacy.' L. sat staring at the floor, biting his nails. Frieda sobbed. . . . Suddenly, after a long time—about a quarter of an hour—L. looked up and asked Murry a question about French literature. Murry replied. Little by little, the three drew up to the table. . . . Then F. poured herself some coffee. Then she and L. glided into talk, began to discuss some "very rich but very good macaroni cheese." And next day, whipped himself, and far more thoroughly than he had ever beaten Frieda, he was running about taking her up her breakfast to her bed and trimming her a hat.

Am I wrong in not being able to accept these people; just as they are—laughing when they laugh and going away from them when they fight? *Tell me.* For I cannot. It seems to me so *degraded*—so horrible to see I can't stand it. And I feel so furiously angry: I *hate* them for it. F. is such a liar, too. To my face she is all sweetness. She used to bring me in flowers, tell me how 'exquisite' I was—how my clothes suited me—that I had never been so 'really beautiful.' Ugh! How humiliating! Thank heaven it is over. I must be the real enemy of such a person. And what is hardest of all to bear is Lawrence's 'hang-dog-gedness.' He is so completely in her power and yet I am sure that in his heart he battles his slavery. She is not even a good natured person really; she is evil hearted and her mind is simply riddled with what she [calls?] "sexual symbols." It's an ugly position for Lawrence but I can't be sorry for him just now. The sight of his humiliating dependence makes me too furious.

Except for these two [. . .], nothing has happened here. A policeman came to arrest Murry the other day, and though I stared him off he will have to go, I think.

I am very much alone here. It is not a really nice place. It is so full of huge stones, but now that I am writing I do not care, for the time. It is so very temporary. It may all be over next month; in fact it will be. I don't belong to anybody here. In fact, I have no being, but I am making preparations for changing everything. Write to me when you can and scold me.

Goodbye for now. Don't forget me.

I am always
[Kissienka?]

Derek Patmore

A CHILD'S MEMORIES OF D. H. LAWRENCE

Even as a child I was surrounded by a literary environment. My mother's friends were usually writers, poets, or painters. The beautiful wife of a rising young business man, who himself cared little for the arts, and known in her own right as Brigit Patmore, she had become the friend and encourager of a group of young authors and poets, many of whom became famous later on. At this period, just before the outbreak of the First World War in 1914, a number of young Americans had started to discover London. Amongst these were men like Ezra Pound, and a shy, good-looking young poet from St. Louis called T. S. Eliot, who was working in a bank and writing poetry in his spare time, and both these poets had become part of my mother's circle. At the same time, she used to talk of another remarkable new friend—D. H. Lawrence, the son of a miner, who had left his native Nottingham and who was already beginning to attract interest as a novelist and poet in literary circles.

These were the days which saw the rise of the Imagist poetry movement and the publication of the *Georgian Poetry* books, under the editorship of Edward Marsh. New ideas and movements were in the air and the literary world had not been disillusioned by war. It was the time when Wyndham Lewis was fighting for new forms in art and launching his Vorticist style with his review *Blast;* and the period when the Russian Ballet had just burst upon an astonished London public and people had become intoxicated with the barbaric colors and designs of the Russian

Derek Patmore, son of Brigit Patmore and great-grandson of Coventry Patmore, of whom he has written a biography, is a writer of travel books, including *Images of Greece* and *Italian Pageant,* and collaborator with Margaret Steen on the play *French For Love.* The present reminiscence of Lawrence is from Mr. Patmore's forthcoming autobiography, *Private History.*

designer Bakst. As a friend of Ezra Pound and of Ford Madox
Hueffer, then wielding great literary influence as the Editor of
the *English Review,* to which D. H. Lawrence also contributed,
my mother was swept into that eager young group of English
and American poets and writers who sought to free poetry from
its traditional bonds and create new verse forms.

Unfortunately, I only have a child's memories of D. H. Lawrence. But I do remember the warm, humane presence of his
wife, Frieda, and I have a distinct recollection of Lawrence himself—a slight man with a personality emanating secret fires. Although my own memories of this great writer are few, I heard
much about him from my mother later on. She met D. H. Lawrence soon after he first came to London from Nottingham. He
was still an unknown and extremely poor young man, but already confident of his own genius. She tells me that in those
days he looked rather ordinary with his reddish hair and clipped
moustache, his really remarkable feature being his eyes which
were a deep blue with curious reflections of light. He rarely
spoke about himself or his work, but he had a subtle way of
drawing out other people's confidences, and he always succeeded
in gaining them because he had a genuine interest in other people's lives.

"Sometimes I used to take Lawrence and Frieda to lunch,"
she tells me, "and I noticed with amusement that even then he
would always take control and order the meals. For example, if
I wanted white wine he'd order red. He had a unique way of
describing everything he saw. His perceptions were extraordinary, and his language was different from other people's. He
even made you see flowers on a table in a new light. Although
he read enormously he never used literary allusions in his conversation. He almost had the direct speech of a peasant. After
his first successes, he began to dress in an unusual manner for
those days. He was fond of wearing bright blue and brown cor-
duroy suits with colored shirts to match, and this made him conspicuous when we went out in public. He himself seemed oblivious
of the stir he created on these occasions. But our lunches used
to be great fun for he was a wonderful mimic and he was fond
of acting. He also had a remarkable ear for music and caught
sounds and tunes immediately."

My mother remained friends with D. H. Lawrence and his

wife until the time of his death. She even nursed him and worked with him during his last days on the island of Port-Cros in the south of France, and although there were long periods when they did not meet they often wrote to each other.

"We lost sight of each other during the First World War," she tells me, "but I saw quite a lot of him afterwards when he was living in London—in Mecklenburg Square. By this time, he looked ill and rather tragic. For he had suffered a certain amount of persecution during the war because of his German wife and because of the controversial quality of his writings. He'd grown very thin, and with his beard he now looked like a tormented prophet. But even then he didn't like flattery, and he was always embarrassed if you praised his books. It was only in his last years that he seemed to crave for public recognition, and he once said to me that he would have liked the critics to have acclaimed *Lady Chatterley's Lover* as the greatest novel of the century. . . .

"Many writers have given the impression that Lawrence was malicious and quarrelsome, but I always found him extremely kind and eager to help. He was obviously devoted to his wife, Frieda, and she formed the mainstay of his whole life. Frieda understood him, and she had an amusing way of talking about his work. I once heard her exclaim: 'Oh, Lorenzo, *how* I suffered when you killed your mother'—obviously meaning *Sons and Lovers*."

Thus D. H. Lawrence and his writings played an important part in my early life. I was proud when he gave a "quick, friendly portrait" of my mother as Clariss Browning in his novel, *Aaron's Rod,* and when *Lady Chatterley's Lover* was first issued in a private edition in Florence by Pino Orioli, I helped to distribute copies in Great Britain. Indeed, after the novel had been banned copies used to be sent to my flat in 4, Millman Street, Bloomsbury, and I used to feel rather like a secret agent handling this so-called "immoral" book. I was also fortunate to receive one of the first copies of the limited edition, signed by Lawrence himself, and when I read it I could not understand what all the fuss was about—but then I had long been an enthusiastic admirer of his writing and felt particularly in sympathy with his views on sex and life. I was not my mother's son for nothing!

Brigit Patmore

A MEMOIR OF FRIEDA LAWRENCE

MY FATHER used to say that I was an *atavismus."*
Frieda said this with a little throat-chuckle. Her chin was
raised, the cigarette between her lips pointed up in the air, and
as she moved her head in time to a tune she heard but we did
not, the straight little cigarette-baton reminded me . . . of
what? yes, it was the long beak of a humming bird on the hibiscus
hedge outside our faraway bungalow on Tobago.

I think I know what her father meant. She was not just a
"throw-back," she was free in time in a wild-happy, loving-wild
way. She knew the conventions but would not mind breaking
them if she thought it necessary. When not bothered by other
people she was enchanted and enthralled by the world. She
should have been allowed to walk through life joyfully, grace-
fully as a deer, with raised head and sensitive nostrils discover-
ing warning scents, passes through a sun-gold wood. Her never-
blunted sense of loveliness made her an exciting companion.
There was passion at times in her green eyes and a generosity one
imagines a lion must have.

Women with such gifts should be praised, but no one speaks,
they are avidly acceptable as the dawn but as quickly forgotten.
Men have a peevish quality that is forever demanding attention
and receiving it and criticizing . . . criticizing.

Brigit Patmore, a native of Ireland, author of a volume of short stories,
Impassioned Onlooker (1926), and of a novel, *No Tomorrow* (1929),
is well known in London literary circles; an Ezra Pound letter mentions
her as one of the charming people on this planet; John Cournos in his
Autobiography spoke of her as "one of the two most beautiful women
I met in London"; and Lawrence presented a friendly vignette of her
as Clariss Browning in his novel *Aaron's Rod*. Her essay is an appendage
to her "Conversations with Lawrence," which appeared in the *London
Magazine,* June, 1957, and was reprinted in Vol. 3 of Edward Nehls's
Composite Biography.

The only time Frieda spoke to me about her father was to remember a tragedy of his young manhood, and she still suffered with him:

"So young. . . . He was sharing quarters in barracks with another officer. They were gay, they enjoyed life, they loved the army. Well, it happened one winter night they brought two girls back to their room. Of course it was forbidden, but how irresistible *that* is! The girls stayed and stayed until it was too late to get them out secretly, so it was decided to keep them there all night. The young officers had to take their men out for a route march at dawn. In the dark, when they left, the girls were sleeping and everything seemed all right, but Brigit, can you imagine their horror—these two young men, when they got back . . . the girls were dead! Suffocated by fumes from the stove! For years my father suffered with remorse. I can't understand why it didn't ruin his career, but it didn't. I suppose they had to go through some stiff punishments. . . . One has to pay always."

Frieda was not a talkative woman, but her silence was never dull and she was too well-bred to show boredom, and if sometimes her thrown-back head looked dreaming, her essence was so alive and conscious that it was stimulating, not depressing. One enjoyed her sudden exclamations, like: "How I suffered, Lorenzo, when you killed your mother." It must have been wonderful to write with someone who lived in one's characters so vividly.

And another time: "That was when Katherine Mansfield sang 'Frankie and Johnny were lovers.' Do you remember her deep voice, Lorenzo?"

She had a way of referring to Lady Ottoline Morrell or the Hon. Dorothy Brett as "the Ott" or "the Brett" in what sounded a slightly contemptuous tone. She was never spiteful about women, although the wife of a famous man has often reason to be. Fame brings to writers in particular a monstrous regiment of women. First, the invasion was by post, letters of admiration, of wonder, or pathetic revelations, or confessions, or requests that the great author should read "something I have written." Women do not ask for anything but to be noticed.

Naturally it is good for an author to receive praise, and Lawrence liked it as much as anyone, but his burning interest in people and a real courtesy made him answer letters. Then came the serious attack—invasion of his home—not difficult in this case because Lawrence had no protection of secretaries or servants, and also really desired to know different examples of human beings.

But for the wife? In Frieda most women saw a stoutish German woman, carefully *not* seeing her beautiful ankles, graceful walk, and charming smile. Indeed, the wife of a great man seems to be regarded—perhaps a hidden jealousy is here—as an over-privileged creature never quite worthy of her position. Take no notice of her is the usual decision.

Frieda's sense of humor, her carelessness of other people's opinions, and her pleasure in Lorenzo's success made her able to ignore what would have enraged some wives. Only when a few tried to get too clinging did she protest. Although the most unobservant person could surely not have helped seeing that for Lawrence Frieda was the only woman.

Pino Orioli told me that once when a clever, attractive woman of notorious sex life was visiting in Florence and wished to meet Lawrence, he said to Pino: "Don't let her touch me! Don't let her touch me!"

Magnanimous was an epithet one could rightly apply to Frieda. In the Retiro Gardens of Madrid there are unimaginable pale roses, pink, primrose yellow and white, open-petaled and immensely large, a few feet from the earth: they filled one with wonder and gratitude: these ungrudging roses are the flowers I would make hers, they are so remindful of her blonde fairness.

Once I was telling her one of the many things that made me love Lawrence. Back in the First World War we were, four of us, having tea in a young Russian's rooms in Bloomsbury. Lorenzo carried the kettle to the gas-ring by the fireplace, I lit the gas and only tiny little flames appeared. Before putting the kettle over them, Lawrence said: "They're like a kitten's upturned paw." It was so exact, the soft blue round things.

"Oh yes, he made everything live so close to one. If you have lived with an artist other men are so *boring!*"

In rare fractious moments he sometimes said: "Don't speak with a cigarette in your mouth, Frieda!" And she would take not the slightest notice and yet once, after a rather gruff criticism of his, to my surprise Frieda rose with great dignity, saying as she walked out of the room: "You are a cad, Lorenzo." He too seemed surprised, as if she had missed her cue. How different was her voice when one heard her going into his room before breakfast: "How is my *pigeon* this morning?"

She sailed over small matters like a ship gliding over weeds. One does not know how she achieved this calm. I never saw her fussing about anything. Once I was trying to help her in the kitchen, and while stirring a sauce, cried out in horror: "God! Frieda, it's going into lumps!" And she answered in her soothing oboe voice, "Never mind. It will come out all right. Just go on stirring."

Notwithstanding her calm, Frieda claimed that when two people loved each other quarreling was natural, and when I said I couldn't bear to quarrel, she said: "Then you don't care for them enough or are frightened of losing them."

There seems to be a secret pleasure in the reporting of the flare-ups between these most suited lovers, perhaps also an unconscious hope that they might be separated, for the world is always jealous of a happy mating. What I saw of them I never thought these quarrels were real, but aggravated by tensions caused by the persons present. Writers are masters of words and use them keenly and with pleasure, mostly not realising how hurtful they sound.

"Do you know, Brigit, people are very cruel. In hotels sometimes when Lorenzo wasn't so well and coughed a lot, there would be complaints and we would be asked to leave." I was so shocked that she added: "Oh, I've learned to meet all sorts of situations." And I know she straightened them out with dignity and tact. How could Lawrence have coped with life without her?

In Frieda's opinion I was too gentle. One of her surprising statements was: "Brigit is our little lamb of God waving her flag." When had she noticed this sign in the Inns of Court?

It is impossible to imagine Lawrence's life without Frieda: he, so sensitive, so disciplined by the harsh demands his genius made on his unbelievable crowd of intuitions and perceptions, needed not only to rest in her love but also on her passionate joy in the quick harvest of her senses. Small wonder that in those evenings of song by the fire "Au près de ma blonde qu'il fait, fait bon" was always sung.

Elizabeth Mayer

AN AFTERNOON WITH D. H. LAWRENCE

I⊤ WAS on a Sunday in September 1927 when, for the first and the last time, I met and talked to D. H. Lawrence. We had been for long years friends of his sister-in-law, Else Jaffe, who had often spoken to us about him and given us his books to read, she being an excellent translator of several of his novels into German. Our meeting took place in her charming little summer house in Irschenhausen, in the Isar Valley, a short train ride from Munich, where we lived. Frequently we had spent some weeks in summer with our children in the bungalow, which Else generously placed at our disposal whenever she traveled somewhere else. I remember that in 1927 we left Irschenhausen a little earlier, because she expected the Lawrences.

When, on that Sunday, we walked slowly up the last hilly ascent from the main road, past the peasant's cottage (who provided the summer guests with milk and butter) and past the familiar pond with the white ducks, we noticed that on either side of the path chicory (its German name so much more poetical: *Wegwarte:* she who waits by the road) already had spread out its light blue flower-stars: a harbinger of fall. Soon we saw the tall pines rising like a dark protective screen behind the bungalow.

On the porch Lawrence was sitting, laying out his favorite patience, called, at least by him, the Demon. He looked frail and not well, a cough frequently interrupting his talk. But his beautiful blue eyes were alive and full of spiritual strength, and

---

Mrs. Elizabeth Mayer, a resident of New York City and a well-known translator from the German, was a friend of Hans Carossa, Rainer Maria Rilke, and other noted German authors.

one detected a twinkle of humor in them. Though probably loathing too many visitors, he welcomed us with gentle warmth, the German he spoke being sometimes quaint but expressive and rather picturesque. The three sisters were round him, Frieda, Else, and Johanna, and one could see how fond he was of them and how well they took care of him. Because of the condition of his lungs he was not supposed to talk much, so we left him for quite some time to finish his patience, and only our ten-year-old son stayed with him on the porch, watching the cards, exchanging now and then an expert's remark with him and, in general, overawed to be in the presence of a real poet.

My husband, who was a psychiatrist, talked with Else and Frieda about Lawrence's health, urgently advising them to consult a good lung specialist in Munich, Dr. Hans Carossa, himself a well-known poet and our friend. Then we joined again the group on the porch. Else encouraged me to tell Lawrence about my translations of contemporary Italian writers into German: Alvaro, Buonaventura, Tecchi, and others, and Lawrence showed great interest. He asked me if I knew the work of Verga, whose *novella, Cavalleria Rusticana,* he was translating. Some years before, in 1921, he had translated Verga's *Little Novels of Sicily,* and in 1922, the year Verga died, the first of the trilogy of great novels: *Mastro Don Gesualdo.* Lawrence advised me to translate Verga, who was then fairly unknown in Germany, and to start with the short stories about the lives of Sicilian men and beasts.

We had a lively conversation on the trials of a translator, particularly on the difficulty of translating dialect. I am sorry that I did not keep a diary at that time and did not make notes immediately after this talk. But everything, especially the essential point Lawrence made, is still clear in my mind. Roughly, Lawrence said that the major problem in handling dialect is how to avoid the two oversimple and absolutely wrong solutions: the first, to translate the dialect of the original into another dialect which is spoken in a geographically existent region (in my case it was Germany) and in a particular locality. For example, one must never have Sicilian fishermen talk like fishermen of the North or the Baltic Sea, or have Sicilian peasants express themselves in the equivalent German or Austrian country idiom. Every dialect has inevitable overtones of the landscape, the character of the people and their native customs, inherent to their special locality and radically different from another and foreign region. Morals and manners, valid in Sicilian terms, would seem absurd when twisted into the sounds of a German way of life. On the other hand, it would be just as wrong to transplant the real Sicilian, together with his native peculiarities, into the German speaking ambience and simply verbally reproduce his dialect: it would not ring true at all. Lawrence's advice therefore, was to avoid both cheap solutions and to try to *invent* a new dialect, coined in German words but free from any reference, from any flavor of a special region, yet preserving the flavor of some sort of relaxed, uncitified, untutored mode of speaking. Of course, he did *not* suggest an artificial or synthetic dialect.

In his *Little Novels of Sicily* he has certainly solved this problem remarkably and, with his imaginative insight, has caught the tone of a dialect and so has preserved the freshness of the original.

Our talk had lasted quite a while, and we then took a short walk in the woods. We were all silent to spare Lawrence from talking, and enjoyed the scent of the pines, the dry resilient soil underfoot, the wild flowers and mushrooms, which Lawrence liked so much, and the occasional glimpse of the shy, graceful deer.

Looking back, I often think with gratitude of this afternoon, of Lawrence's illuminating advice, evoking imagination and therefore relevant not only to the translation of dialect—and of the gentle kindness he showed to a novice in the field of translation. He stimulated and encouraged me, and I like to think of him as a kind of "patron saint" of my work.

Richard Aldington

THE *COMPOSITE BIOGRAPHY*
AS BIOGRAPHY

LODOVICO ARIOSTO opens the last canto of his *Orlando Furioso* with a pleasant fancy. The years of concentrated work needed to bring his poem to completion are likened to a long ocean voyage, and when at last he sees land and his port ahead he gladdens himself by imagining how friends and colleagues will press to greet and to congratulate him when they hear of his successful arrival. It is true that in the contemporary literary dogfight any such generous approval of a living writer seems unlikely, but in studying Mr. Edward Nehls's monumental "composite biography" of D. H. Lawrence, which now fills three large volumes, the parallel often came to my mind. During the years of work on his book Mr. Nehls has made many new friends and acquaintances, who will be happy to welcome him as he brings his literary ship triumphantly into port after the long and arduous voyage.

By skill, enterprise, intelligence, and much hard work, Mr. Nehls has made himself one of the leading American authorities on the life and works of D. H. Lawrence. One might requote the old Oxford joke, and say that what he doesn't know about the subject "isn't knowledge." At a time when literature is being more and more forced relentlessly into journalism, when in so-

---

Richard Aldington, one of the notable authors of the English-speaking world, was a leader of the group of Imagist poets before World War I, author of the internationally best-selling novel, *Death of a Hero* (1929), and of several famous biographies, including one of Lawrence, *Portrait of a Genius, But . . .* (1950). His essay serves as the Introduction of Vol. 3 of Edward Nehls's *D. H. Lawrence: A Composite Biography,* copyright, 1959, by the University of Wisconsin Press, and reprinted here by permission of the copyright owners, the Regents of the University of Wisconsin.

called "creative writing" the applause and the rewards so often go to mere entertainment, which is often unworthy and sometimes downright depraved, it is a pleasure as well as a welcome duty to give all due praise to a work of conscientious and disinterested scholarship such as Mr. Nehls's *Composite Biography of D. H. Lawrence*. It is only fair to include in this praise the University of Wisconsin Press, which has made the achievement possible.

Biography is "the history of the lives of individual men" according to the dictionary—to which I should add the words "and women." Like most definitions this admits, and has admitted, of different interpretations. If in England you raise the subject of biography, almost certainly you will be referred to Boswell's *Johnson*. But in that work the last twenty-one years of Johnson's life receive between four and five times as much space as the fifty-four which passed before Boswell met him. The proportions are all wrong, and Boswell was not so much a biographer as the supreme genius among literary reporters. His book would have been as valuable—perhaps more so—if he had limited it to *Conversations with Johnson*. It is obviously in the same class as Eckermann's *Conversations with Goethe* and Stanhope's *Conversations with Wellington*.

Is biography an art or a science? An excellent topic for a prize essay! Roughly speaking I should say that the French tend to treat it as an art and the Germans as a science, as we might expect. Both conceptions, valid in themselves, tend to fall into excess. In France we have had the deplorable *vies romancées* (recently revived as *vies passionées*), which attempt to turn biographies into novels, and too often only succeed in combining the defects of both forms. In the solemn pursuit of minute and complete *"data"* the Germans fell into such absurdities as the thesis on Dickens (reported and probably invented by Ford Madox Hueffer) amazingly entitled *Die Schwester von Mealy Potatoes*. Mealy Potatoes was one of the boys who worked with David Copperfield at the factory, and since he had already been the victim of a Ph.D. thesis, this one was devoted to his little sister who "did imps in the Pantomime."

We must not forget the nineteenth-century British *Life,* which often burgeoned into a *Life and Times of* . . . , the strange composition too advantageously spoken of as "the standard biography," which Lytton Strachey has mocked so wittily and cogently:

> Those two fat volumes, with which it is our custom to commemorate the dead—who does not know them, with their ill-digested masses of material, their slipshod style, their tone of tedious panegyric, their lamentable lack of selection, of detachment, or design? They are as familiar as the *cortège* of the undertaker, and wear the same air of slow, funeral barbarism.

To crown all, we have among us some who would discourage all biography as "trash," above all in the case of writers. "You can always tell a bad critic," they assert, "because he begins with life." Even more easily can one "tell" a pedant, who begins with words and ends with words and never touches life at all. And yet these would-be disparagers cannot deny that biography has had an immense influence on the Western world for nearly two millennia. I will give you, not one example, but four—Matthew, Mark, Luke, John.

And then came Mr. Nehls with *une idée geniale,* a biographical idea of genius to deal with a genius. Why not? yes, why not re-create the strange, fascinating saga of Lawrence by bringing together in chronological order the relevant available evidence, not only from others but from Lawrence himself, and allowing it to speak for itself, with no narrative and strictly "factual" notes. An excellent idea. The work of "bringing together" the material from which to select what is essential must indeed have been arduous, since it included a search through all Lawrence's voluminous works and the many books and studies and reminiscences about him, with the addition of a further search for new material which involved much correspondence, and a considerable period in England to collect personal testimonies. The achievement is of permanent value, and all thorough students of Lawrence in the future will be indebted to Mr. Nehls.

No doubt this method would not be equally successful for all lives. Applied, let us say, to Jane Austen, a satirical, intelligent maiden lady, whose life, however, was not only blameless but circumscribed, the method would very likely bring only limited results. On the other hand if it had been applied to Queen Vic toria, hundreds of volumes would not contain the results. But in the case of Lawrence this method has proved most successful in bringing out the varying aspects of a tempestuous and adventurous life, of a vehement and contradictory character, as well as the occasions for writings which are among the most remarkable of our century.

True, the available material is so abundant that Mr. Nehls has been compelled to select carefully, in order to keep his book within reasonable limits. Inexorable limits of space have forced him to draw but sparingly on the Lawrence letters and writings generally. I know Mr. Nehls regrets this and share his feelings, for the books and letters bring us most interesting information about the "inner man" when the testimonies of witnesses and similar evidence tend inevitably to tell us most about the "outer man." Moreover in the nature of things such testimonies must be read with critical care, since in some cases they tell us far more about the writer than about Lawrence, and in still others are obviously inaccurate or prejudiced. On the other hand it is illuminating (and sometimes funny) to see the results produced by the impact of Lawrence's personality on other people, even if they go no further than the resentment of wounded vanity, the blunders of misunderstanding, or the fussing of local patriotism. All were worth recording, and all have their value. Not the least valuable is the hagiography of faithful females. If a man finds only one woman to take him seriously until he dies, he is lucky; and Lawrence found more than one.

Socrates in the Platonic dialogue prays that "the inner and the outer man may be at peace." It seems unlikely that Lawrence ever made the same prayer, but he certainly should have done so. Was there ever a man so often at loggerheads with himself, or with the world about him and his few devoted friends in particular? His mother once told him his life was "battle, battle, battle," and years afterward he announced that his future life-program would be "retire to the desert and fight." (Of course, he and she meant Blake's "mental strife," for he was not interested in the strife which results when the guns begin to roll.)

There was a strange perversity in the man, apparently noticeable in his father too, which impelled him to insult and to wound those who could harm him as well as those who tried to help him, and at times a species of megalomania under the influence of which he conceited himself the judge and master, not only of those he knew, but even of the world in general. And yet at those moments when the inner man and the outer man were at peace, he was the most affectionate, charming, amusing, fascinating, and inspired of beings. Katherine Mansfield has fortunately left a record of one such happy moment of time:

> He was just his old, merry, rich self, laughing, describing things, giving you pictures, full of enthusiasm and joy in a future where we become all "vagabonds." . . . Oh, there is something so lovable about him and his eagerness, his passionate eagerness for life—that is what one loves so.

Yet, yet and yet . . . only sixteen months later that same "merry, rich self" could find it in his heart to send her that dreadful unpardonable letter which she mentions:

> Lawrence sent me a letter to-day. He spat in my face and threw filth at me and said: "I loathe you. You revolt me stewing in your consumption. . . . The Italians were quite right to have nothing to do with you," and a great deal more.

Three years later she was dead of consumption, just as he tried to renew a friendship whose loss he must have regretted by—sending her a postcard from her native city of Wellington, New Zealand!

Other ugly incidents, which Mr. Nehls most rightly has not tried to conceal or to gloss over, are recorded of Lawrence, but few quite so gratuitous and "repulsive" as the letter to Katherine Mansfield. After his death, when Frieda published her naïve but honest and very valuable book about Lawrence she related the incident of his throwing a glass of wine in her face because he was jealous—and how absurdly and irrelevantly jealous he could sometimes be!—of her love for her daughter. With that courteous chivalry which marks the modern "press," the London journalists made banner headlines of it, and disregarded all the good she had to tell—so true it is that we get from life and books what we bring to them.

Lawrence appears as a character in several contemporary novels, which is not to be wondered at, seeing how freely he made use of his friends for satirical fiction. To my mind the best of them are Aldous Huxley's, the Rampion of *Point Counter*

Point, and better still the Kingham of *Two or Three Graces.*
This is a vivid but good-natured skit on the irritating side of
Lawrence as it affected those of his men friends who did not lend
themselves to the semi-homosexual relationship he tried unsuccessfully to set up with Murry and others. "I exasperated him,"
says the 'I' of the story, "but he continued to frequent my company—chiefly to abuse me, to tell me passionately how hopeless
I was. . . . I winced, but all the same I delighted in his company. We irritated one another profoundly; but we were friends."

And again later on in the same story: ". . . what in other
men would have been a passing irritation held in check by self-
control, to be modified very likely by subsequent impressions,
was converted by Kingham, almost deliberately, into a wild fury
which no second thoughts were allowed to assuage. . . ."

Traces of this violent habit may be found throughout Lawrence's life story, and Mr. Nehls most rightly has allowed them
to be recorded by the victims, who have not all been "assuaged"
by the passage of thirty or forty years. But this is not all—in
addition, there was Lawrence's extraordinary faith that by writing and publishing his books he would immediately have a decisive influence on human society and the course of history. When
Frieda, in Bavaria in 1912, had a fit of acute "miserables" at the
enforced separation from her young children, he told her vehemently: "Don't be sad. I'll make a new heaven and earth for
them, don't cry, you see if I don't." And two years later his country was at war with hers.

Even after the war he retained this unfounded belief. In that
wonderful Introduction to Maurice Magnus' *Memoirs of the Foreign Legion,* he brings up the topic of war in this outburst:
". . . never again shall you fight with the foul, base, fearful
monstrous machines of war which man invented for the last
war. You shall not. The diabolical mechanisms are man's and
I am a man. Therefore they are mine. And I smash them into
oblivion."

As we all saw in 1939–45. True, he goes on to say that "many,
most" men are with him, but the delusion of immense personal
power is none the less present and deplorable. The war of
1914–18 raised Lawrence's inner conflict to a state of frenzy,
which may be studied in his letters to Bertrand Russell, the publication of which was the most severe blow Lawrence's repu-

tation ever suffered. They are not only absurd, but even ig-
nominious when he drops to the point of asking Lord Russell
to bequeath him money! Frieda's attempted get-out—that Lawrence knew Russell had no money—is very feeble. If he knew
that, why did he ask for it? And, then at another time he wrote
to ask Lady Ottoline Morrell to subsidize his artists' colony of
"Rananim," which is at best a reflection of the "Pantisocracy"
of the youthful Coleridge and Southey.

These are undeniable facts. The mistake (which Mr. Nehls
has entirely avoided) is either to ignore them as some books
on Lawrence have done, or else never to get beyond them, as the
case is with other books or statements about him. Certainly it is
absurd to represent him as a kind of "messiah," blameless and
crucified, but it is equally absurd to see him as a little Satan, "a
force for evil," or a person with a hatred for all mankind, and
still more absurdly, as a Nazi!

That such resentment against Lawrence can still flare nearly
thirty years after his death gives one a most favorable idea of
the force and influence of his character. Lawrence can only be
estimated fairly by those who have rid themselves of uncritical
hero-worship and prejudiced resentment, whether personal or
otherwise. It seems to me that the Danish artist K. Gótzsche expressed a good deal of the truth about Lawrence as a person in
a few colloquial sentences:

> He seems to be absolutely nuts at times, and to have a hard
> time with himself. He over-estimates himself. He thinks he
> can show by his feelings what people think and do. At other
> times he is so reasonable and so overwhelmingly good that
> there is no end to it.

I should say myself that the third sentence is rather off the
mark. I should prefer to say: "He thinks that by writing and
publishing his feelings about what people think and do he can
influence their lives and even change the world."

Unfortunately, the "overwhelmingly good" side of Lawrence
has been far less amply recorded than the disagreeable and hysterical side, perhaps because human vanity is so easily offended
and so implacably resentful. Well, he is not the first of whom
it might be said:

C. N. WRIGHT'S DIRECTORY

OF THE

PARISHES, TOWNSHIPS, AND HAMLETS

'WELVE MILES ROUND NOTTINGHAM

MARKET PLACE.

—◦◦◦◦—

OFORD, LENTON, SNEINTON, HYSON GREEN, BULWELL, CARRINGTON & BASFORD

being in the MUNICIPAL AND PARLIAMENTARY BOROUGH OF NOTTINGHAM, will be found as usual in the THREE CLASSIFICATIONS OF NOTTINGHAM.

he names marked * in the following Lists, unless otherwise specified, have their places of business at Nottingham.

STWOOD is a parish and large and improving age, situated on the top and sides of a considerable eminence on the Alfreton road, Erewash river, tingham and Cromford canals, and borders of byshire. It is a mile from the Langley Mill ion, on the Erewash Valley branch of the Midland way, half-a-mile from the Eastwood station, on Great Northern Co.'s line from Nottingham to xton, 8½ miles N.W. from Nottingham, 10½ from by, and 135 from London, and in its own division the County Council. It is in the Rushcliffe divi-, Broxtowe hundred, Basford union, County Court rict and rural deanery of Mansfield, and diocese Southwell. St. Mary's Church is an imposing, modious, and substantial stone edifice, chiefly of Early Decorated style. It was re-built on the ndations of an old one in 1858, the late J. P. mptre, Esq., and the late rector, being the largest scribers. It comprises chancel, clerestoried nave, es, north and south porches, and massive embat-tower, with pinnacles, clock, chimes and peal of bells. An organ was presented by the late Mr. Bullock in 1873. The Registers date from 1711, se of an earlier date having been destroyed by a which occurred at the rectory house in that year, certified by an entry signed by Henry Peter nel, then rector. Among other mural monu-ts in the south aisle is one to the Rev. Henry stern Plumptre, M.A. (father of the present rector), d son of John P. Plumptre, Esq., of Fredville, ington, Kent, for 36 years rector of this parish, died April 22nd, 1863; also one to George kering, an earnest promoter of the erection of the church, and for many years rector's warden. re are also several good memorial painted win-s. The rectory, valued at £650 a year, with good lence, is in the gift of Charles John Plumptre. A handsome Congregational chapel was erected 868, at a cost of £3,000. It is in the Gothic e, with spire, and built of Bulwell stone. The sleyan chapel, built 1876, will accommodate about persons. There is also a large Baptist chapel, a place of worship for the New Testament Dis-es. There are National, British, and some private ols. Coal mines have long been extensively ked in this and the adjoining hamlets. The etery opened in June, 1889, contains four acres, has a frontage and entrance from Church street. Eastwood and Greasley Mechanics' Hall was ted in 1863, at a cost of £1,000, raised by sub-ption, the library containing nearly 3,000 vols.

It also includes a news room, a hall for meetings and entertainments, science classes, and billiard tables. The Victoria Hall on the Mansfield road will hold 500 persons. It belongs to Mr. Pearson, builder. There is a coffee tavern in the main street. A fair and statutes for hiring servants are held in November, and a market is held every Friday and Saturday evening. Area, 951a. 0r. 35p.; rateable value, £12,500. Present estimated population over 5,000.

New Eastwood lies on the southern part of the parish, and is approached from Church street.

BURIAL BOARD.—Rev. H. W. Plumptre (chairman), Messrs. James Noon, H. Saxton, Alfred W. Brentnall, Fras. Purdy, Henry Hodkin, Thos. Ball, Thomas Fulwood and Edw. Lindley. *Clerk*, John Farnsworth.

ST. MARY'S CHURCH.—Services, Sunday 10-30 and 6-30; Wednesday 7 p.m. Communion first Sunday morning and third Sunday evening in month. Rev. H. W. Plumptre, M.A.; *Curate*, Rev. B. Lumb; *Wardens*, Messrs. J. Haslam and F. Cornell; *Hon. Organist*, Mrs. Plumptre; *Clerk*, John Wheatcroft. Hymnal Companion.

ST. MARY'S MISSION HALL, Church street, New Eastwood. Service, Sunday at 3 p.m., and Thursday at 7 p.m.

CHAPELS—CONGREGATIONAL: Services, Sunday 11 and 6-30; Tuesday, 7-30 p.m. Rev. J. Loosmore. *Organist*, Mr. James Carver; *Keeper*, Thomas Fullwood.—WESLEYAN: Services, Sunday 11 and 6; every alternate Wednesday at 7 p.m.; *Keeper*, Isaac Cliff.—PRIMITIVE METHODIST: Sunday 2-30 and 6; every alternate Monday at 7 p.m.; *Keeper*, Jph. Hewitt.—CHRISTIAN MEETING HOUSE, Victoria Street: Sunday 10-45 and 6; *Elder*, Mr. Daniel Leivers.—THE SALVATION ARMY meet every week evening and on Sunday at the Victoria Hall, Mansfield road.

OUR LADY OF GOOD COUNSEL CHURCH (Roman Catholic), Derby rd.—Rev. Isc. Jas. Hanks (Nottm.) Services, every alternate Sunday at 9 and 11 and every Sunday evening at 7; *Caretaker*, Thomas Hopkin.

POST, MONEY ORDER AND TELEGRAPH OFFICE.—Henry Hopkin, Nottingham road, sub-postmaster. Letters from Nottingham delivered at 7-30 a.m. and 4-45 p.m.; box cleared at 9-45 a.m., 5-45, and 8-30 p.m. on week-days only. Open on Sundays for Telegraph business only, 8 to 10 a.m.

Wall Letter Box at bottom of Church street, New Eastwood, cleared 9-30 and 5 on week-days only.

Eastwood.

Ainger Wm, G. N. R. station master, Langley Mill lane

Allen John, sweet shop, Princess st

Archbold John, engineer *at B. W. & Co.'s*, h *Beauvale*

Argyle Thomas, tinner and general dealer, Nottingham road

Askew Charles, clerk and coal agent, Nottingham road

Ball Thomas, secretary to Phoenix Coffee Tavern, h Queen street

Barber & Bowly, solicitors, Church st (Th. 11-8) & *Fletcher gate, Nottm.*

Barber Mrs. Mrgrt. Annie, Church st

Barber, Walker & Co, colliery proprietors, offices, Mansfield road, Edward Lindley, manager

Barlow George, weighing machine clerk, Langley Mill

Barlow Mrs. Mary Jane, mistress National Infant school

Bentley Mrs. Eliza, miller, New Manley's mill

Boot Charles, chimney sweeper and soot merchant, Nottingham road

Brentnall Alfred Woolston, cashier *at B, W. & Co.'s*, Cocker house

Brookes Wm, caretaker at Cemetery

Buckley Wm, fancy repository and smallware dealer, Nottingham rd

Bullock Mr. Joseph, Nottingham rd

Bullock Joseph, boiler & chain mkr

BUTTERLEY COMPANY, owners of Plumptre, &c., collieries

Carlin Geo picture frmr, Nottm rd

Carlin Robert, bill poster, Nottm rd

Carnill Samuel, watchmaker, Nottingham road

Chambers Alfred, underviewer, Mansfield road

Chambers Enoch, clerk *at B. W. & Co.'s*, Lynn Croft

Chambers Frederick, commercial traveller. Alexandra street

Chambers Geo, gnl dlr, Mansfield rd

Chatterley George, sec to Mechanics' Institute and clk *at B. W. & Co's*, Nottingham road

Cleland Mrs. Priscilla, South terrace, Church street

Cliff Isaac, engine fitter, Victoria st

Cockburn Robert, M.P.C.V.S, veterinary surgeon, Nottingham road

Crockett William Norris, manager *at Bennerley & Erewash furnaces*, h Church street

Cullen George Henry, Robin Hood mantle factory, Nottingham road

Day William, sweet shop, Church st

Dixon Mr. William, Church street

Fletcher John, hairdresser and tobacconist, Nottingham road

Forbes Duncan Macdonald, M.D., surgeon and grazier, Church st

Frear Wm, sergeant, Police station

Frost Wm, spice dlr, 15 Scargill st

Gall James, manager, Nottingham Joint Stock Bank, Church street

Gaunt Mrs. Mary, Nottingham road

G. N. R. STATION, Langley Mill lane, William Ainger, station master

Greatorex Miss Sarah, dressmaker and milliner, Church street

Greenhalgh John, perambucot manufacturer, Nottingham road

Goodburn Samuel, auctioneer, draper, furniture and gnl dlr, Market pl

Hall John & Son, gunpowder manufacturers, McDonald & Skelton, Market place, agents

Hanson John, Manchester warehouseman, Nottingham road

Harris Mrs. Julia, bookseller and printer, Nottingham road

Harrison Alderman Robert, colliery manager, The Grange

Harrison Mr. Thomas, Church st

Haslam George, estate agent

Haslam Jas, canal agt, Langley mill

Haywood Mrs. Ann Elizabeth, wardrobe dealer, Mansfield road

Hill George, clerk *at B. W. & Co.'s*, h Wellington street

Hogg Mr. Robert, Church street

Holderness George, master of British school, h Queen street

Holmes Jph, furntr dlr, Nottm. rd

Hopkins Mrs. Emma, wine and spirit merchant, Church street

Hopkins James, jun, fishmonger and fruiterer, Nottingham road

Hopkin Hy, bootmaker, stationer, and sub-postmaster, Nottm. road

Hopkin Elisha, house agent and rent and debt collector, Nottm. road

Hopkin William Edward, post office assistant, Church street

Johnson Arthur, brass founder, Nottingham road

Leakey Charles J, assistant to Forbes and Dixon's, surgeons, Church st

Leivers George, 'bus proprietor, Victoria street

Leivers Wm, 'bus, &c., proprietor, livery stables, Victoria street

Letts Mr. Joseph, Alexandra street

Lindley Edward, manager, *at Barber, Walker & Co.'s*

Lumb Rev. Barker, curate St. Mary's, h Alexandra street

Meakin Mrs. Elzh, confr, Nottm. rd

Meakin Jph, dyers' agt, Mansfld rd

MECHANICS' HALL AND INSTITUTE, Mansfield rd; Geo. Chatterley, sec.; Charles Askew, librarian; caretaker, Mrs. Elizabeth Varley

Mellors George, beer retailer, china and glass dealer, Nottingham rd

M.R. RECEIVING Office at W. Leivers', Victoria street

Munro-Walker Mr. Edward Lionel, Eastwood hall

Naylor Hy, sweet shop, Albert street

Naylor John, hard confr, Mansfield road

Naylor Mrs. Mary, paper hanging, oil and lamp dlr, Nottingham rd

Newton Mrs. Elzh, hrblst, Church st

Newstead Henry, sweet shop, The Breach

Nix Ths. Morley, tax collector and estate agent and regr of births, &c, Greasley sub-district (8 to 9-30 a. m.) Mansfield road

NOTTINGHAM AND DISTRICT BANK LTD. (Br.), Market place, Saml Attwood, manager

NOTTM. JOINT STOCK BANK (Br.) Church st; James Gall, manager

Phoenix Coffee Tavern, refreshment and boarding house, Nottingham road, Wm. Wright, mgr and sec

Plumptre Rev. Henry Western, M., Rectory, Church street

POLICE STATION, Nottingham road, William Frear, sergeant

Pollard John, news agent, Princess

Purdy Wm, herbalist, Scargill street

Riley Ths, Nottm. Wtrwrks insp

Rollin William, milliner and fancy draper, Nottingham road

Roberts Geo, net maker, Church st

Sheldon John, Master of National school, Church street

Shepherd Miss Ann, South terrace, Church street

Singer Manufacturing Co, Nottm road; William Manning, manager

Slater John, cottager and road maker, Loscoe wharf

Sleath John, herbalist, Mansfield

Sleath Wm, clock and watch maker, Mansfield road

Smedley John, v, *Sun Commercial Hotel*, Market place

Smith David, clothier, Nottm. rd

Soar John, grocer and earthenware dealer, Scargill street

Toplis Misses Elizabeth and Ann, Albert house, Church street

Townsend William, printer, stationer, &c, Nottingham road

Travers William, clerk *at B. W. & Co.'s*, Nottingham road

Turner Tom Newsom, C.E. and M.I.M.E, engineer, Upland house, Nottingham road

VICTORIA HALL, Mansfield road, John Pearson, proprietor

Waldron Henry, Alexandra street

Walker Mrs. Alice, spice and provision dealer, 76 Princess street

Walker James Frederick, colliery agent, Church villa, Nottm road

Walker Wm, collry mgr, The Grange

WATER DEPARTMENT, Nottingham Corpn, Nottm rd; Ths. Riley, insp

Watts Geo. H, clothier, Nottm.

Wheatcroft John, parish clerk, Queen street, Nottingham road

Wheeler Charles Robert, water maker, Nottingham road

Wilbraham Geo, tobcnst and water maker, Nottm. rd, and at *Heanor*

Wilcockson John, clerk and coal agent, Alexandra street

Wilcockson Sml, plmbr, Mansfield

Wild Alfd, clk at *Brbr, Walker & Co*

Williamson John, ironmonger, manager, Nottingham road

Winn Hy, clothier, Nottm. road

Wyld Alfred, clerk *at B. W. & Co.*, Wellington street

Wyld Henry, wine and spirit merchant, Nottingham road

ÆRATED WATER MANUFACTURERS

Skelton John H, Market place

BAKERS.
Bricknell Thos, & grcr, Mansfield rd
Severn Miss Mary Elizabeth, and confectioner, Nottingham road
Sisson Enoch, Princess street

BLACKSMITHS.
Chambers John, Nottingham road
Marriott Levi, Albert street
Swaby Frank, Nottingham road

BOOTMAKERS.
Allcock Wm, & furntr dlr, Nottm rd
Beardsley Richard (dealer), Nottm rd
Copkin Henry, Nottingham road
Leeds & Leicester Boot Co, Church street, Benjamin Geo. Little, mgr
Leivers Charles, Mansfield road
Platts Ths. (dlr) & clothier, Nottm rd
Robinson Mrs. Emma, Nottm rd
Shipstone Edward (rpr), Scargill st
Smith George, 21 Princess street
Smith James, Church street

BUTCHERS.
Barker Chas. Evans (pork), Market pl
Bradbury Evelyn, Nottingham road
Bricknell Thos. (pork), Mansfield rd
Chambers Robert, Nottingham road
Chambers Thomas, Green hills
Chambers Thomas, jun, Church st
Clay David, Nottingham road
Clayton Wm. (pork), Nottingham rd
Hogg Lewis, Nottingham road
Langley Mill and Aldercar Co-operative Society (branch), Nottm rd
Moss John (pork), Victoria street
Noon James, Church street
Roberts Alfd, and grzr, Mansfield rd

CHEMISTS.
Bostock Thos. Henry, Market pl
Chambers James (pharm), Nottm rd
Skelton John Hardy, Market place, with Alexandra street

COTTAGERS.
Bell Geo, & beer retlr, Loscoe wharf
Comb John
Leivers William, Langley Mill lane
Severn William, Old works
Water Wm, & rope mkr, Loscoe walk

DRAPERS.
Carlin George, and habdr, Nottm rd
Chambers George, and general dealer, Mansfield road
Jordan Geo, and outfitter, Market pl
Townsend Benjamin, Nottm rd

DRESSMAKERS.
Bradshaw Mrs. Eliza, 42 Scargill st
Chester Misses Eliza and Mary, 24 Wellington street
Cooper Miss Mary Elizabeth Ann, 26 Princess street
Lindford Mrs. Charlotte, South ter
Naughton Miss Ann Ellen, Church st
Pearson Mrs. Ellen, Princess street
Pilkington Mrs. Eliza, Nottm road
Pilkington Miss Emma, Nottm rd
Purdy Mrs. Frances, Nottingham rd
Sellars Miss Annie, Church street
Walker Miss Kate, Church street
Walsh Mrs. Hannah, The Breach

FARMERS AND GRAZIERS.
Barber, Walker & Co.
Bartley Mrs. Eliza, Newmanley
Chambers Thos. & butcher, Breach
Hogg Robert, Church street

Jacques Thomas, bailiff to Barber, Walker & Co.
Meakin John, and horse dealer, Hill Top house, Nottingham road
Noon James, Church street
Smedley John and v, *Sun Commercial hotel*, Market place

GENERAL AND HARDWARE DEALERS AND IRONMONGERS.
Farnsworth John, and assistant overseer, New Eastwood
Fletcher Barnett, New Eastwood
Greenhalgh John, and furniture dealer, Market place
Hodgkinson Wm. Dennis, Nottm rd
Hogg Robert, Church street
Hudson John, Nottingham road
Pilkington Mrs. Sophia, Nottm rd

GRAZIERS.
Bostock Thomas, Nether green
Chambers Mrs. Elizabeth, Breach
Cook John
Forbes Duncan Macdnld, Church st
Hill George
Hopkin Mrs. Emma, and spirit merchant, Church street
Roberts Alfd, & btchr, Mansfield rd
Rogers William

GREENGROCERS.
Hopkin Jas, & fishmonger, Nottm rd
Leivers Benjamin, Nottingham road
Marriott John, Victoria street
Marriott Levi, and fishmonger, Scargill street
Mellors Thomas, Nottingham road

GROCERS AND SHOPKEEPERS
Marked † are also Beer Retailers.
†Bostock Thomas, and cottager, Nether green
†Bircumshaw Isaac, Bridge terrace
Blount Mrs. Mary, New Eastwood
Bricknell Ths, & baker, Mansfield rd
†Chambers Mrs. Elzh, The Breach
Clifton Mrs. Elzh, Nottingham rd
Cornell Frederick, Nottingham rd
Cullen Bjn. & Thos, Market place
Day William Thomas, Church street
Draper John, Nottingham road
Fulwood Thomas, 44 Scargill street
Griffiths Thomas, Nottingham road
Hudson Jno, & genl. dlr, Nottm rd
Knighton Mrs. Hrt, Nottingham rd
†Lancaster James, Market place
Langley Mill and Aldercar Co-op Society (branch), Nottingham rd, Arthur Linwood, manager
Marriott Levi, Scargill street
Moss John, Victoria street
Noon Jas, and butcher, Church st
Purday George, Nottingham road
†Saxton Hy, Church st & Victoria st
Severn Miss Mary Elizabeth, and baker, Nottingham road
†Sisson Enoch, Princess street
Skelton John Hardy, Market place
†Soar John, and earthenware dealer, Scargill street
†Twigger Frederick, Victoria street
Wagstaff Arthur, Princess street
West James, Nottingham road
†Whittle Mrs. Lydia, and baker, Mansfield road

HABERDASHERS.
Carlin George, and hosier, Nottm rd
Chambers George, Nether green
Pilkington Mrs. Sophia, Nottm road
Townsend Bjn, Nottingham road

HAIRDRESSERS.
Bentley George, Princess street
Fletcher Jno. & news agt, Nottm rd
Wesson Jph, and tobcnst, Nottm rd

INSURANCE AGENTS.
Accidental, F. Cornell, Nottm road
Liverpool, London & Globe (F & L), Joseph Marsh, Nottingham road
Northern (F & L), Jas. Gall, Church st
Prudential, Thos. Nix, Mansfield rd
Queen, William Lambert, Hill top
United Kingdom Temperance and General, H. Hopkin, Nottm road

JOINERS AND BUILDERS.
Durant William, and contractor and undertaker, Albert street
Newton Wm, bricklayer, Nottm rd

PAINTERS AND DECORATORS.
Marsh Jph, and plumber, Nottm rd
Carver James, Nottingham road

PLUMBERS AND GASFITTERS.
Carver James, Nottingham road
Wilcockson Samuel, Mansfield road

PUBLICANS.
Bell George, cottager and beer retailer, Loscoe wharf
Bostock Thomas, bhs, *Thorn Tree*, Nether green
Chambers Thomas, v, *Palmerston Arms*, The Breach
Clayton William, and farmer and v, *New Inn*, Langley Mill lane
Martin Samuel, bhs, *Miners' Arms*, Mansfield road
Rolling George, v, *Lord Nelson*, Nottingham road
Smedley John, v, *Sun Commercial Hotel*, Market place
Smeeton Mrs. Eliza, v, *Wellington*, Nottingham road

SADDLERS.
Hirst John Thomas, Nottingham rd
Pollard John, Mansfield road

SCHOOLS.
British, Geo. Holderness and Miss Margaretta Rees
Cope Miss Mary, Nottingham road
Dowle Chas. Hugh (boys'), Nottm rd
Hamlyn Mrs. Rebecca, Eastwood hse schl, boarding and day, Nottm rd
National, Church street, J. and Mrs. Sheldon; infant school, Mrs. Mary Jane Barlow

SURGEONS.
Barber Robt. David, M.R.C.S., L.S.A, Church street
Forbes (Duncan Macdonald) & Dixon (Francis), surgeons, Church street

TAILORS.
Bothamley James Fdk, Mansfield rd
Clarke Fnk, & woollen drpr, Mrkt pl
Clarke William, and woollen draper, Victoria st and Nottingham road
Knighton John, and woollen draper, Nottingham road
Winn Henry (outfitter), Nottm road

CARRIERS.
Leivers G. ('bus), to Nottm daily

Leivers Wm. ('bus), to Nottm daily and to and from Langley Mill station, and to G.N. railway station, Kimberley, on Sunday evngs

New Eastwood.

Bentley John, farmer

Blount Mrs. Mary, shopkeeper
Clifton Geo, grazier and v, *Moon and Stars*
Cooke George, shopkeeper
Cooke John, farmer
Farnsworth John, assistant overseer
Fletcher Barnett, hrdwr dlr & shopr
Harvey Jno, p.c. | King Jph, cottgr

Oxley John, smallware dealer
Peet John, auctioneer
Rogers William, farmer
Sellars Miss Annie, dressmaker
Sellars George, sharpener at Coll Church street
Steeples Mrs. Patience, sweet sh
White Miss Hannah, dressmaker

THESE PAGES FROM WRIGHT'S *Directory* (*ca.* 1892) give us the Eastwood of Lawrence's childhood, which is the Bestwood of *Sons and Lovers* and the setting for various other of his stories and novels. The names are familiar to readers of Lawrence, who will at once note Chatterley and Mellors (*Lady Chatterley's Lover*), Leivers (*Sons and Lovers*), Sisson and Bricknell (*Aaron's Rod*), and many others. Lawrence's habit was to help himself to the names of his former fellow-townsmen and apply them to fictional characters of a quite different sort. Some of the people listed here are the originals of those characters: George Henry Cullen, for example ("Robin Hood mantle factory, Nottingham road"), became James Houghton (pronounced Huffton), proprietor of the Manchester House shop in *The Lost Girl;* and the Alfred Woolston Brentnall, listed as cashier for Barber, Walker and Company ("colliery proprietors"), became Mr. Braithwaite, who in *Sons and Lovers* tormented Paul Morel when he called for his father's pay on Friday afternoons. Note, too, that Lawrence's long-time friend, William Edward Hopkin, is registered as "post-office assistant"; he also figures in Lawrence's writings, as Willie Houghton in the play *Touch and Go* and as Lewis Goddard in the unfinished novel *Mr. Noon*—and note that the name Noon also appears in this *Directory.* Other pages, not shown here, list the residents of parishes and districts adjoining Eastwood—Greasley, Moor Green, Beau Vale, Hill Top, Brinsley, and Lynn Croft, and here the *Directory* contains other Lawrencean names. In the constablewick of Brinsley, for example, the name John Lawrence appears; this is the author's grandfather. And throughout these towns and villages, names come up out of Lawrence's pages: Birkin and Crich (*Women in Love*), Saxton (*The White Peacock*), and all the others, indicating once again how closely Lawrence was bound to his native region.

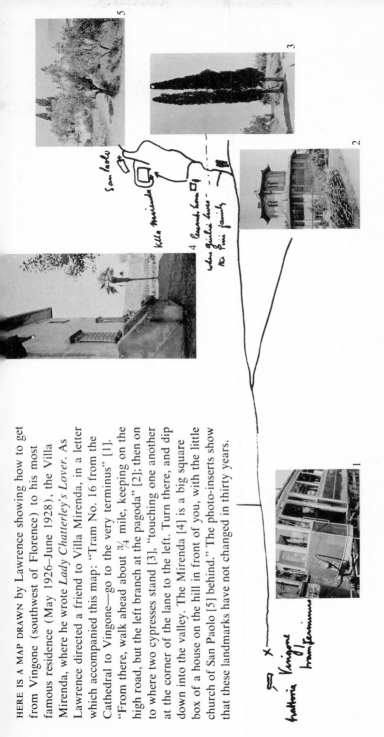

HERE IS A MAP DRAWN by Lawrence showing how to get from Vingone (southwest of Florence) to his most famous residence (May 1926–June 1928), the Villa Mirenda, where he wrote *Lady Chatterley's Lover*. As Lawrence directed a friend to Villa Mirenda, in a letter which accompanied this map: "Tram No. 16 from the Cathedral to Vingone—go to the very terminus" [1]. "From there, walk ahead about ¾ mile, keeping on the high road, but the left branch at the pagoda" [2]; then on to where two cypresses stand [3], "touching one another at the corner of the lane to the left. Turn there, and dip down into the valley. The Mirenda [4] is a big square box of a house on the hill in front of you, with the little church of San Paolo [5] behind." The photo-inserts show that these landmarks have not changed in thirty years.

THE ROAD TO MIRENDA

Music for "David"

D. Lawrence

Villa Mirenda
Scandicci
Florence.

16 Oct 1926

Dear Atkins

I enclose the music I
have written out for *David*. It is very
simple — needs only a pipe, tambourines,
& a tom-tom drum. I hope it will do.

Let me know when you
get the thing going a bit. I hope I can
come to London & help, later, if you think
it really worth while. If only one can
get that feeling of primitive religious

passion across to a London audience.
If not, it's no good.
I'm wondering what sort of cast
you are planning.

Yours Sincerely
D.H. Lawrence

LETTER from Lawrence to Robert Atkins, long associated with the Old Vic
as actor and director, who was staging Lawrence's play *David* in London.

The evil that men do lives after them;
The good is oft interred with their bones.

But in Lawrence's case the best of the "good" has not been lost, and lives on, in writing which taken as a whole forms so original and beautiful a contribution to English literature in this century. How regrettable it is that many of his books are out of print, even in his native country, where some of his finest work must even now be sought for in the second-hand book market. Thus are great writers honored! And let us always keep in mind that if Lawrence had not been a great literary artist we should not still be talking about him.

Lawrence's "proletarian origin" has been held to explain some of the disagreeable traits in his character, such as his ingratitude (as if he gave nothing!), his censorious attitude, his intense class consciousness, his endless abuse and wrangling. But others cannot be so easily brushed off. How, for instance, do we explain the undoubted homosexual streak in him which combines unpleasingly with his vehement and obsolete assertions on the necessity for a woman's "submission"—and that, absurdly enough, in an epoch and country where the "suffragette" movement for the emancipation of women was becoming irresistible? (By the way, he took that particular pig to the wrong market when he married Frieda.) How can we explain his strange power delusions? So far, the professional psychologists do not seem to have found any very valid explanations of these or other traits in him. One doctor is said to have found telltale symbols of Lawrence's horrid impulses in the various dishes forming a meal eaten by Birkin and Ursula in *Women in Love*. I cannot be positive, but my impression is that, as so often in his novels, Lawrence did not invent the meal but simply remembered it— and hence it can have no psychological significance whatsoever.

Even more interesting, and so far as I know almost ignored as well as unexplained, is the remarkable "moon madness" which sometimes possessed Lawrence during a full moon. The synchronization with the full moon may be a coincidence, but the seizures certainly happened. They are reported from his point of view in *The Trespasser* and *Women in Love* (see the very odd chapter called "Moony") and from the point of view of a distressed and unwilling witness by his first sweetheart, Jessie Chambers, who reports two or three such occasions. It is interesting, if only as one more instance of that extreme sensibility which brought Lawrence so much suffering as well as so much joy and beauty.

Among all the writers and painters of his time Lawrence was pre-eminently one "for whom the visible world existed." The tag is musty, but nothing else so well expresses him. Not even Théophile Gautier who invented it, nor Goethe its greatest exponent before it was invented, deserved the phrase more than Lawrence. Oscar Wilde, who was fond of applying it to himself, was a *poseur* compared with Lawrence who was as alert and sensitive to every changing aspect of the living world about him as Walter Pater claimed to be. Norman Douglas—sometimes obtuse about Lawrence, and often hostile—speaks approvingly of "his blithe and childlike curiosity." The phrase is true so far as it goes, but it does not go nearly far enough. It is not enough to explain how it was that for twenty years Lawrence continually renewed himself and poured out so vivid and original a stream of experiences.

It is not a question of "descriptions of scenery," as one writer disparagingly puts the matter, not even of "giving pictures" as Katherine Mansfield wrote—it *is* the living world, that vivid moment of transitory but intense awareness which Goethe thought the real inspiration of poetry. And, apropos that, how strange it is that Lawrence claimed he detested Goethe so much. Perhaps it was because in some of the innumerable striking phrases Goethe hit out we detect something like a prophecy of Lawrence. Deploring the fashionable art of his old age Goethe said it lacked "mind, *naïveté* and sensuousness" and though some might question Lawrence's full right to the first, few will deny the other two qualities. Goethe spoke of the English as "practical and pedantic," and it was against an excess of their practicality and pedantry that Lawrence reacted so strenuously and bitterly. "Freedom," says Goethe, "consists not in refusing to recognize anything which is above us, but in respecting something which is above us; for by respecting it, we raise ourselves to it"—which protests against the ignominy of "democracy" Lawrence sedulously inculcated, though prone perhaps to imply that he was the "something above." Goethe prefigured Lawrence's contempt for petty critics, and his determination to go his own way in spite of them—"we will keep to the right way, and let others go as they choose." Lawrence may not have known of it, but he certainly seemed to believe wholeheartedly Goethe's assertion: "What we agree with leaves us inactive, but contradiction makes us productive." Most striking is Goethe's insistence on the "value of the present moment," that "representative of a whole eternity" and true inspiration of poems. "The world is so great and rich, and life so full of variety, that you can never want themes for poems. But they must be 'occasional' (*Gelegenheitsgedicht*), that is to say, reality must give both impulse and material for their production." There Goethe expresses in aphorism very much what Lawrence said in his preface to the American edition (1920) of *New Poems*.

Pondering over Lawrence's contradictions and perpetual self-contradictions one is inclined to say in despair that it is virtually impossible to generalize about him. Still, one aspect much in his favor seems beyond dispute. He was not mealy-mouthed, he was not a timeserver or a flatterer, and he was not a careerist. He lived and died poor, the more honor to him. If he had cringed and conformed, if he had climbed the social ladder prudently, if he had used others for his advancement and then dropped them when they ceased to be of service, there is no saying how high he might have risen in the magazine and high-royalties world. His awkward efforts "to cultivate the right people" always ended in mutual explosions of bad temper. There was no taming him. The Sun-God, Lord of Song, uses such devices to protect his few favorites from the contaminations of conformity, respectability, and success.

Martin Green

THE *COMPOSITE BIOGRAPHY*
AS COMPOSITION TEXT

I want to claim that Edward Nehls's composite biography of Lawrence, and most especially Volume I, if for practical reasons we must choose one, is an incomparable text for the obligatory course in English composition which begins college education in America.

I shall do no more than mention its potentialities for that first half of the course which is usually devoted to training the students in the recognition of and response to better habits of language—better for the purposes of analysis, discussion, and persuasion. With its extraordinary range of kinds of language, from the tape-recorded interview to the most pretentiously diagnostic biography, with every intellectual and social manner represented, it will be easy to make students see which kinds carry most conviction. And it will be a natural development to discuss, on closer reading, both how kinds of conviction can differ and how many of the verbal guarantees of logic, lucidity, objectivity —the qualities they are concentrating on—are in fact made good by the total performances; how in fact to distinguish those fusions of discipline and liveliness which are the only effective guarantee. The book seems to me to be incomparable for these purposes mostly because it is such a treasure-house of language in operation, in the act of ordering experience; one can find here examples of every way, illegitimate and legitimate, of rendering and rationalizing an impression; because Lawrence incompa-

---

Martin Green is a native of London who, after attending Cambridge and London University, took his Ph.D. at Michigan, where he won three Avery Hopwood Creative Writing awards; he is now teaching at Wellesley College and has written for *Harper's,* the *Chicago Review,* and *Partisan Review.*

rably challenged all these people, and not even the most sophisticated were able to deal with the challenge, at all convincingly, by any of the easy or commonplace modes of discussion.

To be as concrete as possible, as an example of the kind of exercise one could make up from the book I would offer asking one's students to comment on the logic and coherence of this passage, which comes from the piece by Mrs. Minchin I talk about at length later, and which could be paralleled by several passages by Helen Corke, Rachel Annand Taylor, and others:

> It so happened that the Lawrences were spending a great deal of time with us, and my father bitterly resented this intrusion. He told me I was harbouring a man of dubious character who wrote scurrilous books, etc., etc., and it was my duty to send him away at once. I was never quite sure, but I rather think there were some high words between them and my father ordered him out. I remember D. H. was raging and making scathing remarks, but at the time I was unaware of any friction and thought it was a shew of temperament on the part of D. H. I took no notice of my father's agitation and remarks, but just went on as usual, trying to keep things on as even a keel as possible.

This is an elementary exercise, of course, but there is plenty of material in the biography for more difficult ones, and elementariness, of the right kind and in the right complex of other qualities, is perhaps the rarest of all the virtues from this point of view. Most essay anthologies fail, for this purpose, by their impeccability, at least in the face of any critical apparatus the students can successfully manipulate against them; and their own papers are not suitable material for enthusiastic and joyful dissection. The right other qualities add up, perhaps, to "reality," as opposed to the "artificiality," of the handbook exercise; this is real speech, and real confusions, guaranteed as such by our knowledge of its occasion and purposes, and the character of the speaker, and thereby of the kind one is oneself guilty of.

Nor shall I defend in detail the claim that this text leads on easily to all kinds of research work suitable for the source paper. Within the book itself are endless opportunities for comparison and correlation, and admirable examples of scholarship in operation. And from it one can work out into Lawrence's own letters and papers, his novels, the conditions of life in which he grew up, the intellectual climates of his times, the different groups with which he mixed, the countries he visited; or into the books from which the extracts come, the lives of the writers from other points of view, their novels or their philosophies, and so on. The book is a corridor full of doors all of which open on other corridors; Lawrence, like Gudrun, had touched the whole pulse of social England.

Perhaps, though, we should not pass over these matters so quickly that we don't lay some stress on the opportunities you have to refine crude presuppositions about "the people" as congenitally sincere, or "education" as eradicating all intolerance, etc., etc. These opportunities, moreover, are almost uniquely appropriate to the course because of the concretely verbal nature of the evidence. The deepest dilemma of the English composition course, and it takes a practical form in the bewilderment and resentment of the students as well as a theoretical form for the teachers as they plan it, is that it attempts to interfere in the students' thinking and even feeling as well as in their writing; that though it is announced as something as recognizable and harmless as writing papers (getting all your commas in the right place, as Holden Caulfield says), it's taught as if it were a general education course, *the* general education course for the vast majority of students, and consequently for the thinking half of the nation. This extra enormous responsibility constitutes both the glory and the misery of the teaching, and in order to prevent the course from splitting into two parts, one legitimate and one illegitimate, at least in the students' minds, the teacher must deal exclusively, but very inclusively, with language. Language, in this sense, includes much that used to be called style; a person's language is his characteristic choice of words, phrasings, constructions, allusions, images, tones, and arguments, from the point of view of persuasion; all this is examined and estimated as a more or less effective means of persuasion—effective in a fine critical sense, of course. So that though the teacher continues flatly to reject flat statements of opinion and feeling, he does so on the grounds that they are unconvincing, not that they are untrue, or illogical, or illiberal. This still leaves him, of course, with a task greater than all the labors of Hercules—he has to create around him, out of more or less nothing, a climate of opinion in which the fine critical sense can operate as something more than his whim—but it solves the first and greatest dilemma. This being so, Mr. Nehls's volume is better, even in this area of ideas, than those anthologies which feature, for instance, Arnold's debate with Huxley, or Newman's with Kingsley, because the opinions this book expresses and provokes are much more effectively dealt with in terms of language, not of logic. Logic, in the form of such examples of full-dress debate, and in the form of handbooks of pure reason, is the other method the course can use to improve the students' thinking; but the teachers are not trained in logic, the course again breaks in half, and above all the students can't be turned into logicians in a course, and the struggle to do so, the degree of success one *can* achieve, leaves them not really any better able to read or write.

And I think one could claim that this volume will solve the problems of interest and continuity better than any collection of essays, however ingeniously and thematically arranged. The interest eighteen-year-olds take in a person with ideas strikes me as more often intelligent and profitable than that they feel for abstract theory. And Lawrence has something for everyone; so much—biographically, philosophically, esthetically—that one can move around him for a year without getting bored, and at the same time feel oneself to be moving steadily forward, penetrating further into a single, though infinitely complex, phenomenon.

But all these advantages look minor and accidental once one begins to realize how magnificently, in its dramatization of the artist's relation to his material, the book serves the purposes of that second half of the course which introduces the students to more complex uses of language—those of "creative" writing. It is here that this text is incomparable in the way you can move to and fro between it and the stories, essays, poems, plays, novels, in which Lawrence rendered his experience. You move to and fro in twenty different ways, not only because Lawrence treated the same material in different modes and from different points of view from time to time—compare *Women in Love* with the play *Touch and Go,* or the treatment of Jessie Chambers in *The White Peacock* and some of the stories with that in *Sons and Lovers*—but because the writers in the biography wrote their accounts of him before, during, and after their relationship—

before, during, and after their reading *his* account of *them*. The mere juxtaposition itself of such material should raise, and in those happiest forms which bring the answers with them, all the questions one could wish to handle about truth and untruth in literature, imagination and invention, compassion and sentimentality.

Once again the evidence is entirely a matter of language; and the issues are brought to dramatic, combative life, both by Lawrence's sharpness of tone about his characters, the unmodified challenge of his assertions about them, and by their effort of self-defense and counter-accusation in writing about him and his books. For instance, when the students learn that the character Halliday in *Women in Love* in some sense "was" Philip Heseltine (Peter Warlock), a composer and critic, a man of intellect, achievement, importance, and when they read Cecil Gray's indignant account of the relationship between him and Lawrence, their first reaction, I suggest, will be to condemn Lawrence. They will think Lawrence's description of him a caricature: "Gerald looked at Halliday for some moments, watching the soft, rather degenerate face of the young man. Its very softness was an attraction; it was a soft, warm, corrupt nature, into which one might plunge with gratification." This judgment of him will seem too vivid to be either valid or decent. But here the biography supplies us with a passage from a letter of Heseltine's to Delius that shows Lawrence doing no more than taking seriously facts which Gray no more than ignored.

> . . . I feel that I am, and have been for years past, rolling downhill with increasing rapidity into a black, shiny cesspool of stagnation—and with every day the difficulty of pulling up and reversing becomes more apparent. . . . I am in a state of flux—my mind is a whirlpool of alternating excitement and depression.

Evidence of this kind, produced at the right moment in the right way, can undermine a whole area of prejudice, a powerful force of unconscious resistance to literature. And Lawrence's treatment of Bertrand Russell as Sir Joshua Malleson in the same novel will far more certainly seem unfair to them because Russell is far more established and eminent a fact. This will lead the way, of course, to a discussion of what fairnesss, in such a case, means

—what the artist's greatest purposes and responsibilities *are*— but it will be possible to point out that with every advantage of situation in the debate, as the victim, as the philosopher, as writing forty years later, as dealing with facts not fiction, Russell still involuntarily substantiates Lawrence's charges of harshness —"his harsh, yet rather mincing voice, endlessly, endlessly, always with a strong mentality working," and dryness and stiffness —"like compressed tabloids," and destructiveness—"This powerful, consuming, destructive mentality." Knowing himself diagnosed thus, in impugning the diagnosis, he can produce sentences like these, whose texture and movement could not be stiffer, harsher, more destructive:

The world between the wars was attracted to madness. Of this attraction Nazism was the most emphatic expression. Lawrence was a suitable exponent of this cult of insanity. . . . This seemed to me frankly rubbish, and I rejected it vehemently, though I did not then know it led straight to Auschwitz.

Or take the portraits of Witter Bynner and Willard Johnson as Owen Rhys and Bud Villiers in *The Plumed Serpent,* very brief sketches, focused on one quite esoteric feature, their reaction to a bullfight. Lawrence has really only one point to make about them, that they delight in such strong sensations at the expense of a necessary integrity.

She was really very angry, too, with Owen. He was naturally so sensitive, and so kind. But he had the insidious modern disease of tolerance. He must tolerate everything, even a thing that revolted him. He would call it Life! He would feel he had *lived* this afternoon. Greedy even for the most sordid sensations. . . . At about seven o'clock Villiers came tapping. He looked wan, peaked, but like a bird that had successfully pecked a bellyful of garbage.

"Oh it was GREAT!" he said, lounging on one hip. "GREAT! They killed *seven* BULLS."

"No calves, unfortunately," said Kate, suddenly furious again.

He paused to consider the point, then laughed. Her anger was another slight sensational amusement to him. . . .

"Oh but!" he began, making a rather coy face. "Don't you want to hear what I did after! I went to the hotel of the chief toreador, and saw him lying on his bed all dressed up, smoking a fat cigar. Rather like a male Venus who is never undressed. So funny!"

This seems to me a particularly challenging case, because Lawrence's tone is at its most intemperate here at the same time as his interest in the characters is at its most brusque. It is not like the case of Rico Carrington in "St. Mawr," for instance, where Lawrence takes some delight in the character, developing him in several relationships, some of which demonstrate his superiorities. Here, in *The Plumed Serpent,* one very readily suspects mere intolerant offhand categorization; one never hopes, at least, to use these cases to persuade beginning readers that such anger, and such intolerance, may be fully intelligent and judicious. But put beside these passages Willard Johnson's essay in Volume II:

A strange setting for a strange drama. Lawrence and Bynner really liked one another—and yet hated each other, too. . . .

The result, from my point of view, was highly amusing. Here's the way the thing worked out: I became the secretary and confidential companion to both of these writers who were making "copy" as fast as they could out of the situation. All summer long, I was the reservoir for the accumulated wrath of both in saga and song, in invective and confidential confession, in cold-blooded discussion and hot-blooded reaction.

I don't mean to speak unkindly. They were not exploiting their emotions—it was simply their natural safety valve they were using.

There they were: Lawrence sitting under a tree at one end of the village writing a novel in which Bynner is made to appear as one of the characters; Bynner sitting, stripped to the waist, on the Japanese hillside at the other end of town, acquiring his vacation tan, and relieving his mind of all his ideas about Lawrence. And there was I at a typewriter on a balcony of the hotel overlooking the same lake on which both of them rested their eyes between paragraphs, the lake across which oriental sailboats flew. There was I, copying both manuscripts and chuckling quietly to myself—not at all worried over what both Lawrence and Bynner were writing about me or, indeed, saying, as they buried their hatchets, occasionally, and went off on an excursion together.

"Owen had no soul, only a slow, soft caving-in at the centre of him where soul should be," wrote Lawrence—and my fingers flew over the typewriter keys in my bird-like delight over the situation.

This is as lurid a glimpse of sensationalism as the bullfight episode in the book, and sends us back to that, I would suggest, with more interest in both the characters and the writer.

This kind of juxtaposition seems to me not only profitable as sharpening responses to language and deepening responses to literature, but exciting as a debate in which the artist as truth-teller, with a single sentence, discharged forty years ago, slays before our eyes the still-living, infinitely armed and practiced Goliath, who has in fact watched it coming all that time. I mean that I think the students will be engaged by the spectacle, engaged in deciding for themselves the possibilities and responsibilities of these complex uses of language.

These are all, though examples of something very big, in themselves small points, and the biography gives us more than that, gives us opportunities and means for dealing with very major problems in particular novels. For example the passages from *D. H. Lawrence: A Personal Record,* by E. T. (Jessie Chambers), illuminate not only the character of Miriam in *Sons and Lovers,* and Paul Morel's relations with her, but the whole nature of his quest for self-realization throughout the book. One of the commonest misinterpretations which distort and over-simplify the novel for the beginning reader is to take Paul as a Freudian case who would have quite simply loved and married Miriam if he hadn't been sexually involved with his mother. It is difficult, moreover, to dispel this purely from the book itself, because Lawrence himself flirts with the theory. But it becomes very clear from Jessie's anecdotes, and above all from the way she tells them—and this evidence has all the weight of inadvertency, of being, in fact, dead against her interests and purposes—that Mrs. Morel's "jealousy" had ample non-Oedipal justification—that the effect of Jessie's influence over him *was* to alienate him from his family. The anecdote she tells on page 56 of the biography is an example of this. Asked by his married sister, in his mother's presence, when he was coming to visit her, Lawrence replied *"jamais"* with a "swift smile" at Jessie, and translated it as "some time"; and she concludes "We set out together and had our marvellous walk as far as the field path. At the gate Lawrence leaned towards me and said, 'I shall come up tomorrow—early.' " No wonder there was what she calls "an undercurrent of hostility" towards her in the Lawrence family. But even more important is that thinness of tone which over and over obtrudes and makes clear how little such a woman could even at the time have satisfied Lawrence, makes clear in a language we are used to what Lawrence renders in his own far richer and stronger, but at first sight ambiguous, mode. I mean, for instance, her references to money and rank. When Lawrence "with the spectacle of London's opulence before us" exclaimed "I'll make two thousand a year," Jessie said "Will you?" indifferently. "I didn't care whether he made two thousand pounds or two thousand pence. I had never imagined Lawrence making money. I thought he would aim at something finer and more original." And when he said to her that "How that glittering taketh me" was true of him, she says, " 'Does it?' I had replied. 'I'm afraid it doesn't take me.' 'I know,' and he hung his head, 'But . . . it does me . . .' " One recognizes here very clearly the quality of being too "good," too intense, never natural and jolly, that Lawrence complained of in her, and which her own account further shows as horribly impoverishing their major encounters. When he said he didn't love her, and couldn't continue to see her with any implication that he did, and that they must decide what to do, " 'There's nothing to decide,' I said, 'We'll have nothing more to do with one another.' " And when he spoke of seeing her on another footing, "I maintained that there was no footing at all, it would be better to drop everything. But he would not hear of it." And she recounts all this so many years later with no admission that she was throwing all the guilt of their mutual failure—so much of it hers—on to him. Or take the incident—so rich in self-ignorance —of her reaction to his diagnosis:

> "It comes to this, you know," he said. "You have no sexual attraction, at all, none whatever."

I had only the vaguest conception of his meaning, and thought he was telling me that I was unattractive in a general way. I did not feel greatly perturbed, and said,
"Well, how can I help it? Is it my fault?"

Anecdotes of this kind make the book a lot easier to understand and to sympathize with for those who react at first against the endorsed "egotism," "sensuality," and "cruelty" of the hero. And when students come to Jessie's summing up of her relationship with Lawrence and his version of her in *Sons and Lovers,* they are forced to choose between the more and the less valuable and illuminating accounts in a way which clarifies and crystallizes their own total judgments. When she says she "had always believed that there was a bond between us, if it was no more than the bond of a common suffering. But the brutality of his treatment seemed to deny any bond," what could better diagnose the bond or justify the brutality? And when she says he left out "the years of devotion to the development of his genius —devotion that had been pure joy," it is easy to get students to tell you the discomfort and unnaturalness of relation this hints at for them. She dismissed him finally, when the novel came out, as a "philistine of the philistines. . . . His significance withered and his dimensions shrank. He ceased to matter supremely." By the end of the course you should be able to get students to tell you what is the matter with that as language, and thence to return to a clearer understanding of the character and the novel.

Not that Jessie is without her insights, not to mention her information, and what made her important to Lawrence is reflected in her prose equally with what made her impossible.

The invisible barrier that had been raised between us seemed to be freezing the springs of my spontaneity; and the necessity to repress my vital feelings made me cramped and negative. But I could see no way of escape. His attempts to understand me intellectually were paralysing, and the denial of love took all the meaning out of life. I would often wake with a start just before dawn when the air was filled with the unearthly twitterings of the birds, and, realizing instantly the blight that had settled on my life, feel like a castaway on some inhuman shore.

And indeed, though the main value of the book does seem to me its justification of the creative act against all kinds of common complaints and resistances, it is a magnificently varied and living thing, and many of its finest moments belong purely to the writers themselves. There are moments of the purest pathos, some, like the one above, wholly intentional and controlled, others, like the next one, a good deal the result of a failure in control; a contrast the teacher can find very useful. In the memoir by Cecily Lambert Minchin, she begins by being hostile to Lawrence: "Regarding the short story attributed to us: It was sheer fantasy really," and twice ascribes his scraping acquaintance with her and keeping up the friendship to his "looking for copy." But as the memoir continues, relating one incident and another, you come across sentences like "It was fun really," and "One could never be dull in Lawrence's company, or Frieda's, for the matter of that. They were so full of fun and life, and I regret that we were so busy and had so little time to spend with them." And these reflections develop as it were involuntarily out of reliving events the *memory* of which had merely caused resentment. And by the end we get:

> We missed the Lawrences very much. It was a real parting of the ways. D. H. wrote several times and begged us to contemplate going to Mexico with them. It was a pity we did not take him more seriously. At any rate I for one would have gone willingly. But . . . always we had letters saying, "Write, do write," but when they went that life ended for us. How dull it was when he had gone. Always there was some inspiration. We painted tin boxes and bowls at his instigation. To this day I have one bowl on which he painted a grape vine only there was no time to finish the grapes. He signed it on the bottom with his signature in pencil which probably has worn off now. . . . How I would love to have had the chance of their company now. I could appreciate everything and enjoy every minute of it, but I feel now I was probably a bit of a snob and was too timid, thereby giving a false impression. I remember . . . [Here, as all the time, she wanders off into a foolish and irrelevant anecdote, and then, after a few pious remarks about Lawrence's "genius," and how we need more like him, she concludes the memoir with the magnificent final sentence]

> . . . So that was the end for us, and life has knocked many corners off since.

In Volume II you get a comparable ending to May Eva Gawler's account:

> I said good-bye that afternoon, and we hoped to meet again, but we didn't. However, the memory lingers on.
> Yes, I met Lawrence, but it was many years ago.
> And now I am old.

But it is in conjunction with a novel like *Aaron's Rod* that the biography, in this case Volume II, is at its most useful, because of the number and the interest of the portraits from real life, out of which so much of the novel's meaning is constructed. The biography offers thirteen such identifications from "among the possibilities," including Norman Douglas, Augustus John, Richard Aldington, H.D., Cecil Gray, and others, and it is in terms of these people, largely, that the postwar mood in England and Italy is analyzed. They are taken to represent a whole world through which Aaron travels in his search for a mode of being that will satisfy him. But Lawrence's diagnostic, almost case-history treatment of them loses half its force of relevance and insight when read by people who don't know the type of mind analyzed, or its usual panache and acclaim. If you have never read Norman Douglas, that is, and don't know his reputation for lusty paganism, the portrait of James Argyle loses half its point, remains at best a symmetrical diagram; and if you are told he was a novelist and essayist of considerable reputation you can only suppose he may have been right to claim that Lawrence misrepresented everyone, that, in Sir Compton Mackenzie's words, "he had a trick of describing a person's setting or background vividly, and then putting into the setting an ectoplasm entirely of his own creation." But the biography gives us a picture of these people as they appeared to the rest of the world, in fact as they appeared to themselves, and yet manages to corroborate Lawrence's representation of them. Take for instance Norman Douglas, who is introduced like this.

> "He'll never forgive me. Depend on it, he'll never forgive me. Ha-ha! I like to be unforgiven. It adds *zest* to one's intercourse with people, to know that they'll never forgive one.

Ha-ha-ha! Little old maids, who do their knitting with their tongues. Poor old Algy—he drops his stitches now. Ha-ha-ha! —Must be eighty, I should say."

Aaron laughed. He had never met a man like Argyle before —and he could not help being charmed. The other man had a certain wicked whimsicality that was very attractive, when levelled against someone else, and not against oneself. He must have been very handsome in his day, with his natural dignity, and his clean-shaven strong face. But now his face was all red and softened and inflamed, his eyes had gone small and wicked under his bushy grey brows. Still he had a presence. And his grey hair, almost gone white, was still handsome.

Now despite Douglas' assurances that Lawrence misunderstood everything, partly because of his primitive provincial mind, and partly because of his need to caricature all those who had helped him, it seems to me that we hear the same wicked whimsicality here, the same complacent abruptness, the same "civilized" "paganism."

Would Lawrence never learn to be more succinct, and to hold himself in hand a little? No; he never would and he never did; diffuseness is a fault of much of his work. In *Women in Love,* for example, we find pages and pages of drivel. Those endless and pointless conversations! That dreary waste of words! To give your reader a sample of the chatter of third-rate people is justifiable; ten consecutive pages of such stuff is realism gone crazy. . . . An American friend tells me that Lawrence's romances have been of incalculable service to genteel society out there. The same applies to genteel society in England. Scholars and men of the world will not find much inspiration in these novels. Lawrence opened a little window for the bourgeoisie. That is his life-work.

And Douglas himself invites us to compare Lawrence's account of the character called Sir William Franks in the novel with the original's "comments on this proceeding." Sir William Franks is described as very rich, very courteous and hospitable, but old and frail and disturbed at Aaron's indifference to the standards of material and social reward according to which he has lived his life and achieved his success. Though personally generous, his imagination has limited itself to cramped and stuffy patterns in courtesy, honor, duty, humor, and such matters. Douglas invites us to compare this account of him with a letter of "Sir William's," apparently confident we shall realize the injustice, or worse, Lawrence had done him.

> He also described the conversations at the dinner table and afterwards, all of which, according to him, were on a despicably low intellectual level. He also portrays myself and my wife, and I grieve to say that we did not impress him at all favourably, as I appear in his pages as a kind of physically decrepit and vulgarly ostentatious plutocrat. My wife he thought proper to compare to Queen Victoria, which, however gratifying to my loyal British sentiments, was unflattering in the sense that he was evidently not alluding to the admirable qualities which Queen Victoria possessed in such abundant measure, but rather to her physical shortcomings. [This is not true, nor that Lawrence portrayed him as vulgarly ostentatious.] . . . Now, I have no objection to make to his chronicling his impressions with sincerity, but I can never pardon him for the fact that the considerable number of pages which he devoted to us, as well as the whole of the book, were so insufferably dull. If he had at least made me out an amusing jackanapes I would not have minded it, but, that I should have been the source of inspiration of such shockingly wearisome tirades, somewhat humiliates me.

One can sympathize quite fully with Sir William's indignation, but were it not for Lawrence's portrait of him one would set him down, on the evidence of his own letter, as a much more pompous and uninteresting bore than he really was. The ectoplasm of Lawrence's creation seems to me very much at home in its setting, and the chapters of pure reflection and speculation in *Aaron's Rod* can acquire much greater force and richness of meaning from this documentation of the episodes from which they derive.

I offer these as a few tastes of the uses to which the book might be put. And if it isn't the best of all possible texts let us at least grant that it is incomparable with any other such book that *could* be written about any other such writer; because Lawrence so took up the challenge of other people's lives and so forced on them the challenge of his own that he aroused them all to significant language.

James L. Jarrett

D. H. LAWRENCE AND BERTRAND RUSSELL

THE story of the relationship between D. H. Lawrence and Bertrand Russell is the story of a brief friendship and a long quarrel. As a quarrel between rival philosophies of life (to employ a strange but useful locution) it may well be interminable. I will try to show that it is important. But perhaps interesting quarrels can come about only between men who are, potentially, friends—or at least between those who are in significant agreement on certain matters.

The friendship began early in 1915, when Russell and Lawrence met at the home of their mutual friend, Lady Ottoline Morrell. Almost immediately these men, one a mathematician and philosopher in his early forties, the other a writer of fiction and poetry nearly thirty, took to each other. Letters began. They wanted to do something together. Perhaps a lecture series. But Lawrence was awed by the eminent scholar with his learning and wit, social poise and savoir faire. "Your letter," Lawrence wrote early in their relationship, "was very kind to me, and somehow made me feel as if I were impertinent—a bit. You have worked so hard in the abstract beyond me, I feel as if I should never be where you have been for so long, and are now —it is not my destiny." [1] A few weeks later, Russell invited him to Cambridge and, early in March, Lawrence went, though with trepidation. Maynard Keynes records his memory of Lawrence as that of a morose and irritable dissenter. "Most of the talk . . .

James L. Jarrett, formerly a member of the Philosophy departments at Utah, Columbia, and Michigan (where he received his Ph.D.), and formerly President of the Great Books Foundation, is co-editor of *Contemporary Philosophy* (1954), co-author of *Language and Informal Logic* (1956), and author of *The Quest for Beauty* (1957); in 1959 he became President of Western Washington College, Bellingham, Wash.

was *at* Lawrence and with the intention, largely unsuccessful, of getting him to participate. . . . I came away feeling that the party had been a failure and that we had failed to establish contact." He goes on to wonder why Lawrence should have acted as he did, and answers: "It [the whole Cambridge milieu] was obviously a civilization, and not less obviously uncomfortable and unattainable for him—very repulsive and very attractive." [2]

The night before there had been a dinner attended by G. E. Moore and the mathematician Hardy. Apparently it was also unsatisfactory, for Lawrence is reported as having said of the Cambridge-Bloomsbury crowd that they were done for.

Nevertheless Lawrence and Russell continued to exchange letters and occasionally to meet. Lawrence reported on the progress of a long, rather metaphysical essay he was writing and which he calls his "philosophy," though he uses apologetic quotation marks and a parenthetical "forgive the word." But gradually he became less apologetic. He began to tell Russell that he ought to leave Cambridge as there was an increasing chance that Trinity College should insist on his doing. At one point Russell sent him a copy of Burnet's *Early Greek Philosophy* and it had a surprisingly strong effect on Lawrence, who wrote, "I have been wrong, much too Christian, in my philosophy. These early Greeks have clarified my soul. I must drop all about God." [3]

By July, Russell was sending along outlines of his lectures to Lawrence who was, for some reason, shocked to find his collaborator defending democracy and socialism. The outlines were sent back riddled with corrections, objections, and proposals for big changes, but Russell did not sufficiently comply, so by September Lawrence was writing, "You simply don't speak the truth, you simply are not sincere." That letter ends, "Let us become strangers again, I think it better." [4] But it was not yet the end, even though the joint lecture series was abandoned. (Russell's lectures were later printed as *Why Men Fight.*) Lawrence continued to scold, but also to excuse himself and to propose meetings. Finally, Russell did not answer any more and the friendship was over a year after it started. Lawrence had written twenty-three letters in all, Russell perhaps a similar number which have not, unfortunately, survived.

But the two were not to forget each other. Russell appeared a few years later as Sir Joshua in what is perhaps Lawrence's finest novel, *Women in Love*. Sir Joshua is a dry, learned Baronet who is forever making witticisms at which his own hearty, harsh horse-laugh is heard above the crowd. And it is said that his "mental fibre was so tough as to be insentient"; yet he was perfectly happy. There seems to have been comparatively little acerbity in Lawrence's memory and summary of his one-time friend; a year before his death, he wrote, "I was glad to hear of Bertie Russell. Perhaps he and his Dora will do something, after all—better than his donning away in Cambridge." [5] If to us it hardly seems that Russell had been only sleepily donning away all those years during which he published *Justice in War-Time, Political Ideals, Mysticism and Logic, Roads to Freedom, Introduction to Mathematical Philosophy, The Practice and Theory of Bolshevism, The Analysis of Mind, The Problems of China, The Prospects of Industrial Civilization* (with his Dora), *The ABC of Atoms, Icarus, The ABC of Relativity, What I Believe, On Education, Why I am Not a Christian, The Analysis of Matter, An Outline of Philosophy,* and *Sceptical Essays,* to mention only the books—if, I say, we think of Russell as having been well employed in these years, we must realize that, to Lawrence, Russell's was essentially a great wasted talent, wasted because Russell would not dive down deep enough, would not, as Lawrence said to him, stop "being an ego and have the courage to be a creature." [6] For Lawrence's burning zeal, Russell was insufficiently metaphysical, shallow in his criticisms, altogether too easily satisfied with reforms of society that Lawrence could regard as only the most trivial oil-can-and-screw-driver tinkering with a vast machinery that must, the lot of it, be melted down in the deepest and hottest crater of our being. For Lawrence, Russell was, first of all, a great personal disappointment. He thought for a while, as he thought from time to time throughout his life, that he had found someone to join him in the sworn *Blutbrüderschaft* that was one of his obsessive desires. But more important, Russell remained for him an epitome of the abstract intellectual who "stands too much on the shore of this existing world. He must get into a boat and preach from out of the waters of eternity, if he is going to do any good." And then he adds, wistfully, "But I hope he isn't angry with me." [7]

Russell *was* angry, more than angry. For a while Lawrence almost broke through the crackling curtain of wit and democratic noblesse oblige, almost made him mistrust the adequacy of his own program and method. As he wrote in his *Portraits From Memory:*

> I liked Lawrence's fire, I liked the energy and passion of his feelings, I liked his belief that something very fundamental was needed to put the world right. I agreed with him in thinking that politics could not be divorced from individual psychology. I felt him to be a man of a certain imaginative genius and, at first, when I felt inclined to disagree with him, I thought that perhaps his insight into human nature was deeper than mine. It was only gradually that I came to feel him a positive force for evil and that he came to have the same feeling about me.[8]

Russell was annoyed at this young upstart telling him that (and what) he must preach, the "must," Russell says, "having thirteen underlinings."

Russell went on to say that he found it "difficult now to understand the devastating effect" that a certain letter of Lawrence's had upon him. "I was inclined to believe that he had some insight denied to me, and when he said that my pacifism was rooted in blood-lust, I supposed he must be right. For twenty-four hours I thought that I was not fit to live and contemplated committing suicide."[9] The tone is a little jocular after forty years, but it seems likely that Russell *was* at that extremity. Yet his recovery was quick, and he decided to have done, once and forever, with this morbidity. He had been attracted by this passionate poet, but now he saw him, he thought, for what he was, a misanthropist, an irrationalist, an impractical but altogether fanatic proto-Fascist. Dynamic, stimulating, yes, but as Russell wrote:

> This is not to say that there was anything good in his ideas. I do not think in retrospect that they had any merit whatever. They were the ideas of a sensitive would-be despot who got angry with the world because it would not instantly obey. When he realized that other people existed, he hated them. But most of the time he lived in a solitary world of his own imag-

inings, peopled by phantoms as fierce as he wished them to be. His excessive emphasis on sex was due to the fact that in sex alone he was compelled to admit that he was not the only human being in the universe. But it was because this admission was so painful that he conceived of sex relations as a perpetual fight in which each is attempting to destroy the other. . . . The world between the wars was attracted to madness. Of this attraction Nazism was the most emphatic expression. Lawrence was a suitable exponent of this cult of insanity.[10]

I believe these are the harshest words Russell ever hurled at an opponent in a lifetime of polemic.

This then is the brief friendship and the long quarrel. It is an interesting bit of literary gossip. Yet I cannot help seeing more in it. We are, after all, not thinking here of a brush between two nincompoops, nor even of a minor skirmish in the "ancient quarrel between poetry and philosophy." Right now, perhaps, Russell is a bit out of favor, having, as someone said of G. B. Shaw, outlived the age for which he was born too soon. And then there is the fact that professional philosophers have been all too ready to smile off Russell's "popular" writings, an attitude even invited by some of his own disclaimers. Yet surely this is one of the massive intellects of our age, one of those who have made a difference—a free, agile, astonishingly versatile mind that has unself-consciously swung from mathematical logic to science fiction, from university podium to political soapbox, from the imprint of academic presses to that of Haldeman-Julius and the Sunday supplement.

Lawrence too is sometimes shrugged off as one who clutters his pornography with tiresome metaphysics, as an opinionated scribbler and poetaster, as one whose work culminates, in the words of a recent editor of *Punch,* in "the phallic idiocy of *Lady Chatterley.*" And yet his popularity right now among the reading public and his acclaim among responsible critics is at a new high. His name has been made into an adjective, and he has been called the greatest imaginative novelist of our generation.

So let us look closer at these two men, not with a view to

patching up their quarrel, but the better to understand what each stood for, and beckoned toward.

Russell distinguishes two meanings of the word "philosophy." According to the view which has prevailed through the ages, the philosopher's job is "to combine a doctrine as to the nature of the universe and man's place in it with a practical ethic inculcating what was considered the best way of life." [11]

Combine, yes, or yoke together by whatever violence our rhetoric can command, but remembering always that the one unforgivable sin is to pretend to derive one's description of the way things *are* from one's desire as to how they *should* be. About a period of his adolescence Russell says, "For three years I thought about religion, with a determination not to let my thoughts be influenced by my desires." [12] It was a determination he has renewed and reiterated at frequent intervals throughout his philosophic career, and he has always reserved his sharpest stings for those he found projecting their wishes onto an innocent and neutral reality. One of the reasons why the philosophic temperament is rare is that it includes a positive "inability to believe contentedly except on what appear to be intellectual grounds." [13] Yet this much ought properly to be an aim of all schools: the "habit of weighing evidence, and the practice of not giving full assent to propositions which there is no reason to believe true," [14] however much one would *like* them to be true. In promoting such a virtue one is at once scoring against the superstitions and fanaticisms which are at the root of most evil, and promoting positively that spirit of toleration which is a mark of civilization.

Call the roll then of the customary beliefs which are comfortable, heartening, or consoling, and exercise not your will to believe but your will to doubt. If proper care be not taken, these wishful beliefs will be bolstered by an epistemology itself invented especially for the purpose. Thus intuitive knowing, self-evident truths, and supernatural revelation will be invoked to provide a world made over into something close to heart's desire. Against all such, the truth seeker can but turn a stern face. Science has not yet provided and may not for a long time provide answers to certain of our more insistent questions. Many of them are in likelihood unanswerable by the empirical means of observation and verification, but "Whatever knowledge is attainable, must be attained by scientific methods; and what science cannot discover, mankind cannot know." [15]

First to go, in the universal stable cleaning, will be all the beliefs in a supernature. The gods, life before birth and after death, telic qualities in inorganic nature, divine or other cosmic support for the good and condemnation of the bad—all such, though not known to be definitely excluded from the appointments of the universe, are insufficiently supported by admissible evidence to earn the assent of rational man.

Russell is not altogether of a mind as to the extent of this loss for himself. If he sometimes manifests a homesickness for the religious beliefs of childhood, and sometimes presents a grim spectacle of a universe stripped of divinity, he also takes an unmistakable delight in iconoclasm. Indeed, he probably believes that religions are on the whole iniquitous quite apart from their being without cognitive foundation. In one place he says, "I am myself a dissenter from all known religions, and I hope that every kind of religious belief will die out." [16]

If supernatural religious comfort must be eschewed, neither is there any secular universal morality to fall back upon. However desirable a world in which men might live in peace and harmony, such a world cannot be grounded in the superior rationality of such a desire. "There is no such thing as an irrational aim except in the sense of one that is impossible of realization." [17] If someone, a Carlyle, for example, "finds people repulsive, no argument can prove to him that they are not so." [18] In a late work, Russell finds it possible to assign meaning to the expression "objectively right act," namely, as "that which best serves the interest of the group that is regarded as ethically dominant." But the comfort is cold, for "this group will be differently defined by different people in different circumstances. . . . Is there any theoretical ground for preferring one of these groups to another as the basis for the definition of 'objective rightness'?" Russell answers, "I do not see that there is." [19]

He admits that some of his feelings are so strong as to impel him toward an ethical absolutism—surely cruelty is intrinsically evil and not just an object of this or that person's aversion—but once again feelings must not dictate to reason, and reason does not come to the support of ethical intuitionism.

Nevertheless, one need not despair. Even deprived of religious and ethical absolutism, a man of good will and clear head is not helpless. Probably men differ less about ethical ends than is supposed, even though this be a matter of good luck and not of good cosmic management. What one can do is to present ideal conditions in the characters of men and institutions, persuasively hope for concurrence, and then proceed to argue for effective means to their realization. Although there is no reason to hope for support from afar, there is also no reason to dread transcendental malevolence.

A fruitful grouping of ethical philosophers might proceed according to whether their principal concern is with doing good or living well. No one has ever accused Russell of being a do-gooder, even on a theoretical level. As to living well, he has rejected hedonism in words that remind us of his godfather, John Stuart Mill:

> If we were really persuaded that pigs are happier than human beings, we should not on that account welcome the ministrations of Circe. . . . We do not, in fact, value pleasures in proportion to their intensity; some pleasures seem to us inherently preferable to others.[20]

He seems to think that the values of intelligence and esthetic sensibility are hardly reducible to pleasures, yet are important ingredients in the good life. Living well is partly a matter of individual attitude, partly of satisfactory social institutions. What is wanted is a free and just state, a fair and productive economy, and reasonable laws and customs governing such institutions as marriage. In such a social environment a man dedicated to love and reason should, with a little luck, live very well indeed.

There are two cardinal principles to Russell's free democratic society. (1) Authority ought to be kept as closely responsible to the people over whom it is exercised as is consistent with reasonable efficiency. Thus, though world government is indeed necessary for peace, the powers of such government ought to be restricted; so too, the most localized government. (2) The powers invested in leaders should never exceed what is necessary for securing justice, conservation, and the encouragement of creativity.

Few men have more persistently urged vigilance in the restraint of despotic political and economic power. Few have had so sharp an eye for detecting and denouncing dictatorship. But Russell is no anarchist. There are many legitimate governmental functions, but "Political ideals must be based upon ideals for the individual life. The aims of politics should be to make the lives of individuals as good as possible." [21] And Russell never tires of insisting that it is quite within the abilities of social intelligence to effect remarkable results. In a sanguine outburst, he once wrote:

> If a majority in every civilized country so desired, we could, within twenty years, abolish all abject poverty, quite half the illness of the world, the whole economic slavery which binds down nine-tenths of our population; we could fill the world with beauty and joy, and secure the reign of universal peace.[22]

But supposing all this were accomplished, what constitutes and what frustrates living well for the individual? Russell specifies the main causes of unhappiness as being ill health, poverty, and an unsatisfactory sex life.[23] Elsewhere, and much later, Russell has named the chief obstacles to a new era of well-being: "the evil passions in human minds: suspicion, fear, lust for power, hatred, intolerance." [24] Again, he says that good nature is the moral quality the world most needs, "and good nature is the result of ease and security, not of a life of arduous struggle." [25] He has listed the four characteristics "which seem to me jointly to form the basis of an ideal character: vitality, courage, sensitiveness, and intelligence." [26] And he gives as the purpose of education, civilization,

> a term which, as I mean it, has a definition which is partly individual, partly social. It consists, in the individual, of both intellectual and moral qualities: intellectually, a certain minimum of general knowledge, technical skill in one's own profession, and a habit of forming opinions on evidence; morally, of impartiality, kindliness, and a modicum of self control. I should add a quality which is neither moral nor intellectual, but perhaps physiological: zest and joy of life.[27]

Instead of assuming the task of preparing a concordance of these several gospels, let us concentrate on Russell's famous formula: "The good life is one inspired by love and guided by knowledge." [28] Love is always one of the great values to Russell; it is praised in all its meanings. His book *Marriage and Morals* contains some of his violet-ink rhetoric on love between man and woman, which is praised as the source of the most intense delights that life has to offer. "Passionate, mutual love while it lasts puts an end to the lonely longing for affection" that blights so many lives. It is "mental quite as much as physical," and so important, not only in itself, but in its effects, that those who miss it are inclined "toward envy, oppression, and cruelty." "The love of man and woman and the love of parents and children are the two central facts in our emotional life. . . . To fear love is to fear life, and those who fear life are already three parts dead." [29]

A satisfactory marriage is possible if personal attitudes, economic conditions, and civil laws are changed to meet the demands of reason. Divorce should be possible, at least in the case of childless couples, by mere mutual consent; this in turn would facilitate the setting up of households quite openly regarded as probably temporary. Every effort must be exerted to eliminate woman's economic dependence on man, and her slavery to the onerous duties of housekeeping. Marriage, like the state, is properly rooted in liberty, equality, and fraternity. There must be no interference by husband or wife with the essential freedom of the partner. Their relationship should include a similarity in standards of value, and of course be free of the taboos which have so often surrounded sex. Indeed, Russell has said in so many words, their sexual relations will be both *dignified* and *rational*.

It is less commonly recognized that Russell is an advocate of Christian love, love of neighbor:

There are certain things that our age needs, and certain things that it should avoid. It needs compassion and a wish that mankind should be happy; it needs the desire for knowledge and the determination to eschew pleasant myths; it needs, above all, courageous hope and the impulse to creativeness. The things that it must avoid, and that have brought it to the brink of catastrophe, are cruelty, envy, greed, competitiveness, search for irrational certainty, and what Freudians call the death wish. The root of the matter is a very simple and old-fashioned thing, a thing so simple that I am almost ashamed to mention it, for fear of the derisive smile with which wise cynics will greet my words. The thing I mean—please forgive me for mentioning it—is love, Christian love, or compassion. If you feel this, you have a motive for existence, a guide in action, a reason for courage, an imperative necessity for intellectual honesty. If you feel this, you have all that anybody should need in the way of religion. Although you may not find happiness, you will never know the deep despair of those whose life is aimless and void of purpose; for there is always something that you can do to diminish the awful sum of human misery. What I do want to stress is that the kind of lethargic despair which is now not uncommon, is irrational.[30]

We are back to the ideal of guidance by knowledge, or rationality. It is no exaggeration to say that in Russell the sentiment for rationality amounts to a passion, though this is not to say that he is unwaveringly rational or reasonable in practice, for if carelessness about fact, willingness to rely on parody when a close report of an opponent's theory is called for, a propensity upon occasion to summary dogmatism, and a real laziness about scholarship are inimical to reasonableness in practice, then Russell must stand to this extent condemned. Yet rationality remains his ideal. "The power of reason is thought small in these days," he says, "but I remain an unrepentant rationalist." [31]

Now if the ghost of Lawrence may be imagined as having throughout this account kept up a constant obligato of derision and anguish, we will have made a start on our second man. But let us approach him more positively. He once wrote:

It seems to me it was the greatest pity in the world, when philosophy and fiction got split. They used to be one, right from the days of myth. Then they went and parted, like a nagging married couple. . . . So the novel went sloppy and philosophy went abstract-dry. The two should come together again—in the novel.[32]

So far as I know, Lawrence never claimed that he had effected the reunion, or even that he was trying to; yet I believe that such a reunion does represent one of his aims, and one of his achievements. It does not finally matter whether he "has a philosophy"

or not. There is certainly little system in his thought. He was ig-
norant of and contemptuous of most securely professional philosophy. Consistent with his statement that "the business of art
is never to solve, but only to declare," [33] he was much stronger
at declaration, at assertion, than at clinching or arguing conclu-
sively. Rather, he argued not in propositions, but in rainbows,
phoenixes, crowns, and suns. Yet nearly everything he wrote was
a step, tentative or sure, toward a more satisfactory understanding of the universe and of man's place in it.

First to last, Lawrence was a rebel. He had no sympathy for
organized religion, no respect for any government under which
he lived, no confidence in either capitalism or socialism; he had
contempt for class distinctions, hatred for technology, and little
use for most of the customs of civilization. So widespread was
his rebelliousness that he was impatient with all simple proposals
for reform or revolt. Nothing much was to be accomplished by
just changing the form of government, or by even a radical
overhauling of the economic system, by a new religion, a new
set of marriage laws, or by education reform. All of this can
and should be done; but when this is done, there yet remains
the big job to do. Here if ever is God's angry man; and his anger
is with man for worshipping false gods.

Lawrence's protests can be assimilated to the one great protest against partialisms. Like Molière, he found people ready to
acquiesce in a defined role, to settle for being a miser or a doctor, a lover or a misanthrope, a philosopher or a wife. He wrote,
not to give people a surcease from worry, not to give them a
thrill or an hour's entertainment, but to drive them back against
themselves. We are all fixed, stuck, stalled, and therefore bored.
He accuses us of stripping ourselves of "emotional and imaginative reactions, and feeling nothing. The price we pay is boredom
and deadness. . . . For the sphinx-riddle of man is as terrifying to-day as it was before Oedipus, and more so. For now it is
the riddle of the dead-alive man." [34] And: "There is only one
sin in life, and that is the sin against life, the sin of causing
inner emptiness and boredom of the spirit. Whoever and whatever makes us inwardly bored and empty-feeling, is vile, the
anathema." [35]

To partiality, Lawrence opposes wholeness; to the static, flux
and flow; to contentment, fight; to the ashes of death, the flame

of life. A principal enemy is suggested by the words "mind," "intellect," "reason," "abstraction," and "rationality." "The great quality of mind is finality." [36] And finality is death. Again: *"Knowing* and *Being* are opposite, antagonistic states. The more you know, exactly, the less you *are.* The more you *are,* in being, the less you know. This is the great cross of man, his dualism. The blood-self, and the nerve-brain self. Knowing, then, is the slow death of being. Man has his epochs of being, his epochs of knowing. It will always be a great oscillation. The goal is to know how not-to-know." [37]

He speaks of "thinking with the blood":

> This is why one cannot quite believe in Kant, or Spinoza. Kant thought with his head and his spirit, but he never thought with his blood. The blood also thinks, inside a man, darkly and ponderously. It thinks in desires and revulsions, and it makes strange conclusions. The conclusion of my head and my spirit is that it would be perfect, this world of men, if men all loved one another. The conclusion of my blood says nonsense, and finds the stunt a bit disgusting. My blood tells me there is no such thing as perfection. There is the long endless venture into consciousness down an ever-dangerous valley of days.[38]

In passages reminiscent of Bergson, though arrived at quite independently, Lawrence contrasts intuition with conceptual, abstract reason. It is not that the latter is useless; on the contrary its whole value lies in its usefulness, its instrumental function in arranging the external world to creative life. The reason makes closures, establishes fixities, while the intuitive faculties shimmer around the absolute ongoingness of the living process. An abstraction is always more or less a lie; hence the superiority of art to science. Lawrence says in an essay on the novel:

> Now here we see the beauty and the great value of the novel. Philosophy, religion, science, they are all of them busy nailing things down, to get a stable equilibrium. Religion, with its nailed-down One God, who says *Thou shalt, thou shan't,* and hammers home every time; philosophy, with its fixed ideas; science with its 'laws'; they, all of them, all the time, want to nail us on to some tree or other. But the novel, no. The novel

is the highest example of subtle inter-relatedness that man has discovered. Everything is true in its own time, place, circumstance, and untrue outside of its own place, time, circumstance. If you try to nail anything down, in the novel, either it kills the novel, or the novel gets up and walks away with the nail.[39]

Here is an implicit paradox: what of all these generalizations about the inadequacy of generalizations? Is this something like nailing down a nail? Lawrence would probably admit it, saying that these bits of discursive philosophy were only interim obiter dicta, only clumsy and boorish attempts to say what had been better said, obliquely, in the novels, stories, poems; and what he said of poetry he might have said of all art, that "it makes a new effort of attention, and 'discovers' a new world within the known world." [40]

Similar to the reason-intuition and science-art polarities is the distinction between the conscious and the unconscious. There is the self that we know, the mental, deliberative self with certain public interests and aversions, habits, dispositions, and mannerisms. About this self one knows a great deal, assigns reasons for the way it behaves, and makes predictions about how it is going to behave. But there is another self that Lawrence calls the dark, passional, or bodily self. It is largely unknown, even finally unknowable. As he puts it, *"Know thyself* means knowing at last that you *can't* know yourself." [41] He struggles to say this, to bring the intuition here adumbrated to fruition. Like all artists, he searches for metaphors to present that which is apparently recalcitrant to conceptualization. One he employs is the cross. It is the body, the dark self, and on this cross is crucified the known and daylight self. Yet we will pretend there are no nails, that there is no pain.

One indication of the existence of this unconscious being is the dim awareness that we have a kind of duty to "become oneself," but the expression is misleading if it suggests an already formed inner man, ready to be stripped of his masking shell. What it is, rather, is life, undefined, unfixed, unconceptualized, mysterious.

Lawrence's never-ending struggle down to the dark and blooded being is not altogether solitary. Somehow it is in the deepest intimacy of human relationship that one touches the dark quick of the body. Sex? Love? To these questions, one can only answer "yes"—in a dubious tone. Not *sex* if one is thinking of a Kinsey tabulation. Not titillation of the nerves. And not *love* insofar as that means possessiveness, an impulsion to swallow or be swallowed. Perhaps no writer has been more scornful of love in its usual significations. The men in Lawrence's novels spurn the woman who cries out, "Love me! Say you love me!" And perhaps no writer has made a nicer distinction between kinds of sexual intercourse, ranging from what was to him an abomination, to the rarer kind that is a mystical communion. I do not mean that he finally comes to etherealized love, the step beyond the highest rung of Plato's ladder. It is physical, certainly, sensual, but dark, the touching of the most deeply buried plasms (as he liked to say) of the two selves. And in this touch there is the greatest of all paradoxes: a meeting which establishes separateness. Here is one of his attempts to express the ideal relationship:

> But the love between a man and a woman, when it is whole, is dual. It is the melting into pure communion, and it is the friction of sheer sensuality, both. In pure communion I become whole in love. And in pure, fierce passion of sensuality I am burned into essentiality. I am driven from the matrix into sheer separate distinction. I am become my single self, inviolable and unique. . . . I am destroyed and reduced to her essential otherness. It is a destructive fire, the profane love. But it is the only fire that will purify us into singleness, fuse us from the chaos into our own unique gem-like separateness of being.[42]

This relationship when it is love properly so called, is a rhythm of comings and goings, of meetings and partings. Nothing annoyed Lawrence more than talk of the equality of man and woman. One might as well speak of equality of a pine tree and a lake.

But just as we draw back from acknowledging our unconscious selves, so we substitute comfortable love for the real, searing thing. We take refuge in sentimentalism, which Lawrence defines as "the working off on yourself of feelings you haven't really got." [43] In that same essay he goes on to say:

We all *want* to have certain feelings: feelings of love, of passionate sex, of kindliness, and so forth. Very few people really feel love, or sex passion, or kindliness, or anything else that goes at all deep. So the mass just fake these feelings inside themselves. Faked feelings! The world is all gummy with them. They are better than real feelings, because you can spit them out when you brush your teeth; and then tomorrow you can fake them afresh.[44]

As Lawrence tries to show in *The Rainbow*, our civilization has disintegrated until we are out of touch: out of touch with the natural world, with each other, with our own deeper selves. Love is become rare; deep friendship between man and man, perhaps still more rare; we are become strangers to the physical world, and to ourselves. The cure does not lie in morality, which as it has been usually conceived is mainly irrelevant. No so-called practical proposals will do. Lawrence believed *the* job, his job, was to make us aware of what we are missing and thus to drive us to deeper involvement in life, to completer human relationships, to an immediate sense of belonging to the world of flowers, snakes, turtles, and seas. But morality:

> It is only immoral
> to be dead-alive
> sun-extinct
> and busy putting out the sun
> in other people.[45]

He was impatient with the inevitably slow, compromising processes of politics, and beyond his own immediate affairs, economics remained an uninteresting mystery. He could not abide talk of equality, which for him always meant leveling or even the establishing of equivalences. The word "democracy" seemed to bring to mind mass production, uniformity, dullness. He was willing to agree with socialists who demanded for everyone a fair share of the world's goods, but he could never agree that this was really very important. In politics he was an aristocrat. He did believe in leaders who were more than mere presidents and ministers, but he seemed to value them for the inspiration of their glory rather than for their actual power. There was indeed a time when he essayed a society dominated by strong, dashing, silent supermen who combined in themselves the offices of dictator and high priest, as for example in *The Plumed Serpent*. But it was not long after this was published that he wrote a friend who complained of these notions: "The hero is obsolete and the leader of men is a back number. . . . On the whole I agree with you, the leader-cum-follower relationship is a bore." [46] Even more significant is the fact that Lawrence entirely abandoned that quasi-political tack in his fiction. His last three principal works return the emphasis to personal and religious problems.

I have saved to last what I believe to be Lawrence's most important symbol—most important to him and to an understanding of what he meant. The phoenix, his life-long symbol of resurrection, the bird who dies in flame and whose ashes arise into new life, was Lawrence's call to all who content themselves with mediocrity. "Die, die down to the essential coals of your being and be born again."

Lawrence and Russell. The twice-born man and the once-born man. The apostle of dark and the apostle of light. The aristocratic collier's boy and the democratic Earl. The intuitionist and the rationalist.

Two men with different styles, grievances, remedies, hopes. To Russell, Lawrence was a bigoted, neurotic, sex-obsessed, Fascistic irrationalist. To Lawrence, Russell was a bloodless, self-deceived sophomore playing tiddlywinks with dead ideas. Surely both were wrong, and not *quite* wrong about each other.

Lawrence was politically naïve—and consequently at times insufficiently cautious of the man on horseback. He was unable to foresee that "thinking with the blood," some men's thinking and blood being what it is, could, a few years after his death, inflame the satanic horrors of Nazi Germany. It must be said, however, that Lawrence hated brutality and truly prized freedom; he wanted to be let alone, above all else. His spokesman in *Aaron's Rod* says, "I think every man is a sacred and holy individual, *never* to be violated. I think there is only one thing I hate to the verge of madness, and that is *bullying*. To see any living creature *bullied,* in *any* way, almost makes a murderer of me."

Lawrence was utopian, at times preachy, without concrete suggestions for the parliaments and leagues that so largely matter in the fabric of our social life. And he was cranky, lacking due respect for the great, exaggerating his own powers and the value of his evaluations. He could never believe that women really cared about voting or anything else that excited the feminists. He was, according to Russell's standards of rationality, largely irrational. Worst of all, you might say, he demanded more of life and living than can ever be had.

Then there is Russell, who can be so infuriating in his patness. Does the world have some little problem of peace or injustice? He leaves both fools and angels dawdling at the post to provide us with a four-point program which can be enacted next Tuesday, and that will be that. He is sanguine in his notions of what a little more logic, or intelligence, a little less muddle would do. An analysis of his rhetoric might provide a key to both his strength and weakness: that elegant, clipped, balanced, aphoristic, brittle style occasionally giving way to lush peroration.

But both had extraordinary imaginative daring and creativity. At their best, both made some of the finest English prose of our time. And both were so nearly fearless and so vehement in their attacks on ruling powers and customs that one was jailed and twice deprived of academic positions, and the other reduced to poverty and to virtual exile.

Were they wrong about each other? If so, are they then so different from the profound thinkers of any age? Which great philosopher, for instance, do we trust to give us an adequate account of the theories of his enemies? Lawrence and Russell were far more concerned to advance new ideas than to give scrupulously fair attention to the ideas of the other. And even if they had been right in determining what the other said, no doubt they would still have violently disagreed, these contradictory characters. As Freud superbly said, "Only in logic are contradictions unable to coexist."

NOTES

[1] Harry T. Moore, ed., *D. H. Lawrence's Letters to Bertrand Russell* (New York: Gotham Book Mart, 1948), Letter 2, p. 36.

[2] J. M. Keynes, *Two Memoirs*, "My Early Beliefs" (New York: Augustus M. Kelley, 1949), pp. 78–80.

[3] Moore, *op. cit.*, Letter 10, p. 50.

[4] *Ibid.*, Letter 15, pp. 59–60.

[5] Aldous Huxley, ed., *The Letters of D. H. Lawrence* (New York: Viking, 1932), p. 792.

[6] Moore, *op. cit.*, Letter 22, p. 71.

[7] Huxley, *op. cit.*, p. 240.

[8] Bertrand Russell, *Portraits from Memory* (London: George Allen & Unwin, 1956), "D. H. Lawrence," pp. 104–5.

[9] *Ibid.*, p. 107.

[10] *Ibid.*, p. 108.

[11] Bertrand Russell, *Unpopular Essays* (London: George Allen & Unwin, 1950), "Philosophy and Politics," p. 11.

[12] Bertrand Russell, "My Mental Development," in *The Philosophy of Bertrand Russell*, Paul Arthur Schilpp, ed. (Evanston: Library of Living Philosophy, 1946), Vol. V, p. 8.

[13] Russell, *Unpopular Essays*, "Philosophy's Ulterior Motives," p. 65.

[14] Bertrand Russell, *Free Thought and Official Propaganda* (New York: B. W. Huebsch, 1922), p. 49.

[15] Bertrand Russell, *Religion and Science* (London: Oxford University Press, 1935), p. 243.

[16] Russell, *Free Thought and Official Propaganda*, p. 3.

[17] Bertrand Russell, *Human Society in Ethics and Politics* (London: George Allen & Unwin, 1954), p. 11.

[18] Bertrand Russell, *Why Men Fight* (New York: The Century Co., 1916), p. 33.

[19] Russell, *Human Society in Ethics and Politics*, p. 80.

[20] *Ibid.*, p. 117.

[21] Bertrand Russell, *Political Ideals* (New York: The Century Co., 1917), p. 4.

[22] *Ibid.*, p. 35.

[23] Bertrand Russell, *Education and the Good Life* (n.p.: Boni and Liveright, 1926), p. 62.

[24] Bertrand Russell, *The Impact of Science on Society* (New York: Simon and Schuster, 1951), p. 95.

[25] Bertrand Russell, *In Praise of Idleness and Other Essays* (London: George Allen & Unwin 1935), p. 29.

[26] Russell, *Education and the Good Life*, p. 60.

[27] Russell, *In Praise of Idleness and Other Essays*, pp. 202–3.

[28] Bertrand Russell, *What I Believe* (London: Kegan Paul, Trench, Trubner, 1925), p. 28.

[29] Bertrand Russell, *Marriage and Morals* (London: George Allen & Unwin, 1929), p. 224.

[30] Russell, *The Impact of Science on Society*, pp. 91–92.

[31] Bertrand Russell, *Sceptical Essays* (New York: W. W. Norton, 1928), p. 123.

[32] Edward D. McDonald, ed., *Phoenix: The Posthumous Papers of D. H. Lawrence* (New York: Viking, 1936), "Surgery for the Novel— Or a Bomb," p. 520.

[33] *Ibid.*, "Thomas Hardy," p. 461.

[34] D. H. Lawrence, *Apocalypse* (London: Martin Secker, 1932), pp. 88–89.

[35] *Phoenix*, "The Duc De Lauzun," p. 745.

[36] Lawrence, *Apocalypse*, p. 205.

[37] D. H. Lawrence, *Studies in Classic American Literature* (New York: Doubleday, 1923), p. 124.

[38] D. H. Lawrence, *Selected Essays,* "Books" (n.p.: Penguin Books, 1950), p. 45.

[39] *Phoenix,* "Morality and the Novel," p. 528.

[40] *Phoenix,* Introduction to "Chariot of the Sun," p. 255.

[41] D. H. Lawrence, *Assorted Articles* (New York: Alfred A. Knopf, 1930), p. 235.

[42] Lawrence, *Selected Essays,* "Love," p. 27.

[43] *Ibid.,* "John Galsworthy," p. 224.

[44] *Ibid.*

[45] D. H. Lawrence, *Pansies,* "Immortality" (New York: Alfred A. Knopf, 1929), p. 154.

[46] Huxley, *op. cit.,* p. 711.

Robert E. Gajdusek

A READING OF *THE WHITE PEACOCK*

LAWRENCE once said of *The White Peacock,* "It is a first novel . . . publishers take no notice of a first novel." [1] His observation might well be extended to include critics and scholars who have generally ignored his first book. His later works have been discussed at length, but a lack of comment and study has kept *The White Peacock* from the status it richly deserves.

This remarkable critical omission has been the result of a failure on the part of critics to evaluate the texture and structure of this first novel. An experiment in form, *The White Peacock* is tightly organized, overlaid with an intricate multi-leveled symbolism, and co-ordinated by a complex stream of allusions. In this book Lawrence has also played with forms, introducing an "elegy," a "poem," and a "symphony" into his prose. He delights in musical effects, and to achieve his ends uses rhythms, internal rhymes, repetition of significant elements, alliteration, and assonance. The structure is complex: he underlines his meanings with parallelism and contrast, with an incremental repetition of elements, and with adjective clusters. Using an involved network of allusions drawn from Christian tradition, the Graeco-Roman world, and European culture, Lawrence skillfully expands the dimensions of his plot.

Many of the symbols and most of the themes and preoccupations of the later Lawrence are established in this first novel: his mysticism; his sense of the conflict between mind and in-

Robert E. Gajdusek, who studied with R. P. Blackmur at Princeton, Mark Schorer at California, and William York Tindall at Columbia, is teaching at George Washington University. He has contributed to the *American Scholar* and other American and British journals.

stinct, or knowledge and intuition; his annunciation of paganism and the return-to-earth motif; his preoccupation with white and dark gods; his outrage at the humiliation man suffers before a woman-administered idealism; his movement towards myth— all these are important parts of his early work.

The White Peacock acknowledges and attempts to reconcile the fundamental dualism of his mind. The dark-light, above-below, air-earth, spirit-flesh, God-devil, bird-serpent, fire-ash oppositions are firmly established in the book which is, in many respects, closer than *Sons and Lovers* to *The Plumed Serpent*.

The book also is a biographically revealing study and, for a first novel, remarkable in its emotional maturity. *The White Peacock* shows Lawrence's sympathy for the father-figure and hostility towards the mother-figure. His understanding of the marital conflict is compassionate and he does not conceal from himself that, despite his deep sympathy for the father, he is the accomplice in his destruction. Following his mother's death, which coincided with the publication of *The White Peacock,* Lawrence repudiated the years of labor and the sense of achievement he had discovered in the novel. *Sons and Lovers* is an attempt to shed guilt by revising or rephrasing the image of the mother that *The White Peacock* projected. It is an apology and an expiation, and it seems to me to be farther from the truth of Lawrence's early emotional life than *The White Peacock*.

The story of *The White Peacock,* the tale that hides the moral, tells of the love between George Saxton, a dark, heavy, herdsman figure, and Lettie Beardsall, a charming, cultivated, witty young woman. George, his sister Emily, and his parents live at Strelley Mill; the Beardsalls live near by. The narrator, Cyril Beardsall (obviously Lawrence), is sensitive, interested in literature and painting, and responsive to the world of nature that so fully surrounds life in the English Midlands. His mother, Mrs. Beardsall, is the much-doted-upon mother-figure abandoned by her husband. The father enters the novel only briefly, to see his children, die, and be buried.

As the focus shifts to Lettie, who takes over the mother's role and qualities, Mrs. Beardsall vanishes from the novel as a significant character. Lettie is a capricious, high-spirited, intelligent girl, naturally attracted to the animal vigor and virility of George but also repelled by him as a result of her animosity toward her own father. She is afraid of the man of brute power who is able to dominate and control.

Lettie yearns for a simple, natural response to life, but she fears raw life and moves her experience toward abstraction, to cultural references and heightened idealisms, to a concern with religion and an interest in the arts. The principle of slumbering animal passivity in George—of what becomes a kind of mindless being in Lawrence's later work—frightens Lettie. She begins a campaign to awaken her slumbering savage or barbarian, as he is soon called, by vending him visions—visions of the world of ideas, religion, culture, and sophistication. In the early chapters "Dangling the Apple" and "A Vendor of Visions," she succeeds in casting a spell that awakens George to a new consciousness. After his first taste of Lettie's diet of pictures and songs, the most George can do is awkwardly but prophetically attempt a quotation, "I have supped full . . ." (30).[2] It is Lettie who finishes the quotation, ". . . of horrors," pointing up the *Macbeth* parallel, a forewarning of what is to come.

George, teased into a realization of Lettie's world of abstractions, is moved throughout the novel almost as a passive principal, victimized in a world he cannot comprehend. Lettie, allied with the world of Christian-Platonic idealism and at war with the barbarian in man, attempts to replace vitality in him with idealism, the life of the senses with the life of the mind. Her attempt to supplant his barbarism with her idealism merely creates a dichotomy of the spirit in George. Lawrence leaves no doubt that it is woman who is the agent in effecting this fatal schism in the sensibility of man. In the final chapter Lawrence graphically symbolizes this: George, hovering on the brink between two worlds, is released to his death by Lettie, who makes a broad significant parting in his hair. The attempt to reconcile the aggressive masculine world of active paganism and the feminine world of passive idealism is the attempt to bring man and woman into harmony. George as a character suggests Lawrence's inability to solve the conflict of his own parents.

The struggle for wholeness in George dramatizes the dualism of the world to which Cyril has adjusted. Cyril, in sympathy with the father and allied with the mother, is the adaptable Pandarus go-between of ambivalent sympathies and tastes. Among the women of the novel, he is affectionately known as

"Sybil," the prophetic figure who augments, implements, and oversees the tragedy. He is the supreme type of the artist whose detachment and esthetic distance enable him to be the objective reporter. The ambivalence of his position, however, is best seen in "The Poem of Friendship" chapter, with its suggestions of Greek classical ideals, where he expresses his classical-pagan devotion to George in a passage that usually has been read as a homosexual episode. Despite his sympathy with George's predicament, he is the one to sharpen the knife with which George's symbolic suicide is accomplished.

Leslie Tempest and Annable are the other central figures in the novel. Leslie lives in the faintly aristocratic, mine-owning world of Highclose, a world of church patronage and sophistication. In contrast to George, he is the somewhat effeminate mother-seeking child who, after a brief struggle, accepts tyranny and domination in the husband-wife relationship. It is to Leslie that the frightened Lettie turns when George establishes his manly independence and control in a chapter filled with blood imagery and rough, sanguine virility. Symbolically, she first goes into the dark bottom garden and from there brings Leslie two swollen ripe plums in a leaf. She asks him to eat of a fruit she knows he has not yet eaten: "You have not tasted yet," she laughs (*53*). Leslie assumes the lover role and courts, wins, and eventually marries Lettie.

Annable, the gamekeeper, Cambridge-educated and once a curate, had been married to the Lady Crystabel, who violated his essential nature as she molded him into an art object, a creation of her various idealisms. "She'd got the idea from a sloppy French novel—*The Romance of a Poor Young Man*. I was the Poor Young Man . . . I was Greek statues for her, bless you: Croton, Hercules, I don't know what!" (*149*). Annable—variously called Pan, Pluto, and the Devil—later marries Proserpine, the enslaved-woman figure in the novel, but queen of the infernal regions and wife of Pluto in Greek mythology. Shackled to drudgery and their many children, she laments her fate but believes in it. Her attachment to Annable, despite her complaint, is profound, and his uncivilized children, whose wildness he celebrates, are sympathetically presented. In spite of his understanding of the social world, Annable rejects it and turns to a deep sympathy and fusion with nature. He becomes a human controlling principle in a nature that otherwise runs wild, perverting human passion and endeavor. The rabbits that ruin the crops embody the principle of uncontained prolificity and destructive profusion in nature. Annable is a mythic figure, standing for the bond between humanity and nature that every civilization must establish if it is not to be overrun. The description of Annable's funeral belongs among the great pastoral elegies in English.

Annable and Cyril together establish the white peacock as the basic symbol of the novel. Annable sees a peacock perched on the bowed head of a stone angel in the wild thicket and tangle of the churchyard behind the mouldering Hall church. The bird seems a symbol of the Lady Crystabel, of the pride and vanity proceeding from resplendent and showy idealisms that victimize man. When the bird defecates upon the bowed head, Annable is certain: "Look at it! That's the soul of a woman—or it's the devil!" he cries (147). As Annable tempers the rage inspired by the recollection of his own violation, Cyril suggests that they concede the whiteness of the peacock.

The Lady Crystabel as the white peacock, through the allusion to Coleridge's lamia theme, becomes the plumed-serpent symbol of a bird who has taken a snake under her wings. The bird-serpent combination explicitly appears in the novel two more times. At the beginning of the second chapter, "Dangling the Apple"—the chapter in which Lettie decides to regenerate George and begins to "vend" him her fatal visions—Cyril and Lettie, heedlessly crushing plants as they probe and examine nests, startle young lapwings by their approach. The frightened, bewildered birds "go whining, skelping off from a fancy as if they had a snake under their wings" (11). The heavily scored dangling-apple motif suggests the temptations of the serpent who offers a new knowledge, but Lawrence inverts the Biblical account of the Temptation and the Fall to his own ends, making Lettie, the Christian idealist, the tempter. Frequently in this first novel he achieves his irony through such inversion of myths and allusions. The flight of the lapwings is a warning and contrasts with George's passive acquiescence before Lettie's probing. The serpent-bird is the symbol of the two worlds of earth and air, or flesh and spirit, fatally linked, and it suggests the predominant dualism of Lawrence's later work, culminating in *The Plumed Serpent*. In the first paragraph of the chapter in which the son-figure, Cyril, and the father-figure, George, come into a full undertaking of one another, "A Poem of Friendship," nature as a chorus to the action mourns the impending death that is about to be symbolically accomplished, and a snipe flies round overhead "in great circles, seeming to carry a serpent from its throat, and crying a tragedy" (*217*).

Among the women of the novel, the representatives of the white-peacock symbol are the Lady Crystabel, Mrs. Beardsall, Lettie, Mrs. Wagstaffe, Meg (the woman George marries), Gertie (George's vicious daughter), and most of the girls who attend the parties, the church services, and the giddy pastoral in the meadow. They illustrate the violation of natural man by idealism, and Lawrence shows them oppressing and dominating the truth of nature that man's instinctive being affirms. The father, Cyril, George, Annable, and at times even Leslie are men identified with the earth and sympathy with nature who resist the violation offered them in spurious or deadening idealisms.

The intellectual framework that Lawrence erected for this novel is very impressive. The elaborate structure is reflected on one level in a complex but well-defined symbolism. Actions and qualities, as well as objects, serve as symbols. Stooping or bending toward the earth is connected with a movement back to nature or earth relationship, as it is in Lawrence's later novels. Even the white peacock leans over her victimized male. Lawrence plays with this image of the peacock leaning over and defecating upon an apprehensive bowed angel; he introduces the symbol thirteen times. Annable calls the bird "devil! God!" (*148*). Cyril immediately associates the peacock with the church: "The church is rotten. I suppose they'll stand all over the country like this soon" (*148*). A few paragraphs earlier, he had seen the Hall church standing "above the shrinking head of the traveler" (*146*). When Lettie is bending Leslie to her will, she is described as a big bird perched on the top of a stile, balancing with her hand on Leslie's head. Leslie "was looking up at her anxiously" (*127*). In the "Pastorals and Peonies" chapter, a Miss Denys in heliotrope leans over the recumbent Freddy Cresswell, who has jokingly damned women, and, tapping his head with her silk glove, says, "Consider whom you're damning" (*226*). On the morning of George's ill-fated marriage to Meg, he shows Cyril a white smear on his shoulder; "Look here, a bird has given me luck," he cries (*236*). This playfully ironic extension of an image is not rare in Lawrence's first novel.[3] Heaviness is used to represent man moving toward earth values and resisting or ridding himself of idealisms. Radiance, light, whiteness, ascendancy, and woman, all fused in the peacock symbol of a transcendent, controlling divinity, comprise a complex symbol nexus. As in Lawrence's other symbol conglomerates, any element of the nexus can function individually by virtue of its established reference. The Death-by-Water or Ship-of-Death theme, the wind, the ash tree, the elm tree, the plum, the white peacock, the peewits, the crow, water, wetness or moisture, and mud, as well as nests, eggs, and birds are all skillfully and meticulously developed symbols. Some 145 different trees, shrubs, and plants are introduced; 51 animals are brought in; 40 different birds skim, hover, flit, fly, and wheel through this novel; and many of these function as symbols. There are really few moments in the novel when words are not being used symbolically or with contrived ambiguity.

Most of the action of the novel centers in the woods and fields surrounding Nethermere, the lake toward which the focus of the novel leads. Even the name, Nethermere, Lawrence's original choice for the title of the novel, symbolizes the fatal split, the Anglo-Saxon-French dualism, the dissociation of sensibility, the mother ascendancy over the man, and the oppression man suffers. *Nethermere* is a compound name that breaks readily into *nether,* meaning below or under, and *mère,* the word for mother in French—a language identified in this novel with a type of mother-idealism. *Mere*—Old English for a small lake, pond, or pool—can suggest George's symbolic death under water at the end of the novel as he renounces the Platonic-Christian world for mindless unconsciousness in the waters of Lethe. "A Prospect Among the Marshes of Lethe" is the last chapter. At the end of the novel, George is symbolically both at the bottom of the lake where he has fled from the mother-figure become pirate (he sings the folksong about the pirate Henry Martin) and below the ascendant peacock-mother. The title Lawrence originally had for the novel, probably the title of the version he gave his mother to read, may be translated as "Under the Mother."

Puns, anagrams, and word play are frequent: George Saxton —Saxon; Golaud—GO LauD, laud God; Lettie becomes Lettice

(Lawrence's sister's name), and then lettuce; French Carlin—French and carl or karl; pyeenocks—peacocks; Hilda Seconde—an Anglo-Saxon given name and a French surname, introduced into the novel to suggest the fatal split in sensibility. French Carlin is the name Cyril's father adopts after leaving Cyril's mother, that is, after she has broken his wholeness as a man. The Anglo-Saxon-French dichotomy is only one expression of the bright God-dark God division, most explicitly presented as a Christian-pagan conflict. George, as an unrepentant sensualist, goes to the devil, but as the Bacchus or Pan figure, he goes to Pluto.

Traditional symbolism is distorted by Lawrence's use of church ritual and Christianity itself as personal symbols. He attacks Christian religion fiercely and even with anger throughout this novel. The frightened, mouse-voiced man, who moves into Annable's kennels after the gamekeeper's death, hides behind the *Christian Herald* while pretending to read and substitutes his paper flowers and antimacassars for the other's riotous spawn of children. At the end of the novel, the inheritors of Strelley Mill, disconsolately clutching their prayer books, prepare to go to church while the chorus of nature sobs behind the newly erected barbed wire separating man from earth and inflexibly asserting the broken bond and the established schism. To Lawrence of *The White Peacock,* Christianity was an unnecessary and contaminating idealism, set in opposition to nature and the natural, and allied with high society, patronage, and oppression. The dissemination of Christianity is associated with the vision-vending woman who often uses the piano as the instrument of her evangelism. The piano, used eleven times in the novel, is in every instance associated with woman—or the womanish man—in the evangelical role spinning illusions and creating sentimentality, unreality, or pretense.[4] In the novel, whenever a song is sung by a woman, or a picture is used as an interpretation of life, whenever French is spoken or referred to by any of the characters, and whenever Christianity is embraced, vicarious life comes momentarily between natural man and his true-blooded avowals and earth-contact. The very resplendent spread of the peacock fills the mind of the beholder with visions.

The White Peacock presupposes a familiarity with music—folk songs and ballads as well as opera. The seventeen songs used in the book are usually referred to by title or first line, but the allusions, however slight, involve the total complex situation of the complete songs. The full text of the songs "Should He Upbraid?" and "Gaily the Troubadour" create much of the humor and irony of the novel. The context of Margaret's "Spinning Song" in *Faust* and Wolfram von Eschenbach's *Tannhäuser* aria "O Star of Eve" are integral parts of Lawrence's book. When Lettie sings "Drink to Me Only with Thine Eyes" in the second chapter, she is proposing the total philosophy of the song, not merely the action of the line. Again, when George sings "I Sowed the Seeds of Love," he not only recapitulates his past relationship with Lettie, but warns her of the dangers inherent in the immediate situation prevailing as he sings. Although nothing but the title of the song is given in the text of the novel, Lettie's actions in this chapter can only be understood in terms of her response to the complete message of the song.

The twenty-three references to specific artists and paintings also function allusively. Some knowledge of Beardsley's illustrations for *Salomé* and *Atalanta,* and a recollection of Watt's painting "Hope" and Greiffenhagen's painting "The Idyll" expand the meaning of the book.

Graeco-Roman mythology introduces some forty specific gods, goddesses, and myth figures in contrast to the multiple Biblical references. Each of these references seems carefully and intentionally to introduce its own canon of association and story. The *Odes* of Horace and the Theocritan *Idylls* underlie several sections of the book.[5] Numerous untranslated fragments of Latin poetry intrude into the novel; each is a key to a significant attitude that cannot be understood by simple translation of the fragment. The original context of a passage is of considerable importance. In the chapter "The Fascination of the Forbidden Apple" Lawrence writes, "She answered him in Latin, with two lines from Virgil" (*213*). This is a crucial point in the novel and a crucial answer, yet nothing more of Lettie's answer is given. The key to her answer is found several lines earlier where Lettie remarks, "Let me say farewell—'jamque Vale! Do you remember how Eurydice sank back into Hell?" (*213*). In Virgil's *Georgics* the lines appear:

> Iamque Vale! feror ingenti circundata nocte,
> Invalidasque tibi tendans, heu non tua, palmas! [6]

Her answer then is this statement of Eurydice's helplessness and of her own final withdrawal from George. The novel is filled with similarly demanding allusions.

Literary allusions are plentiful. Milton's "Lycidas," "L'Allegro," and "Ode on the Morning of Christ's Nativity" are extensively involved. In addition to the possible contribution of Schopenhauer's philosophy, there are details which suggest Spinoza's *Ethics.* Cyril is asked if he believes love is a tickling, "Amor est titillatio" (*177*), a phrase from "The Strength of Emotions" which suggests the entire discussion of this chapter in Spinoza. This sort of allusion, where a phrase or a fragment is used as a means of access to a philosophy or a complex dramatic situation, is frequent in *The White Peacock.* Also, remarkably, a good knowledge of Longfellow's *Hiawatha* is helpful. There are scattered allusions to the work, one of the most significant being at Lettie's coming-of-age party where her engagement to Leslie is announced. Will, a close friend, lightheartedly jests, "I skimmed here like Brra-ave on my snowshoes, like Hiawatha coming to Minnehaha" (*110*). Lettie has turned away from George and the natural world, and this glib reference, which ignores the fact that Minnehaha is dead before Hiawatha reaches her, relates to the many death and nonmortal symbols in the chapter: Eurydice, Persephone, Houri, angels, Eskimo's heaven, sainted virgin, etc. Lawrence makes somewhat the same demand in this novel that Joyce and Eliot were later to make in *Ulysses* and *The Waste Land,* and that Joyce had earlier made in *Chamber Music.*

Other works which figure in this first novel are Shakespeare's *A Midsummer Night's Dream, Macbeth, The Taming of the Shrew,* and *The Life and Death of King John;* Spenser's *Faerie Queen;* Tennyson's "The Lady of Shallott"; Wordsworth's Lucy poems and "An Ode on Intimations of Immortality"; Coleridge's *Christabel;* Maeterlinck's *The Bluebird;* Rossetti's "The Blessed Damozel"; Poe's "The Raven"; Dumas' *La Dame Aux Camélias;* Keats's "La Belle Dame Sans Merci"; and Ibsen's *Hedda Gabler.* Maupassant, Machiavelli, Christina Rossetti, Gorky, Hardy, Merimée, Chekhov, Chaucer, Wells, Edward Fitzgerald, Blackmore, Wilde, William James, D'Annunzio, Burns, Shaw, and Dickens are among others whom Lawrence introduces, suggesting through allusion what he does not explicitly state. The ultimate catastrophe of the story is apparent in the first book where, already, allusions establish historical and fictional parallels which spell out the fate of the principals in the novel.

William York Tindall and Mark Schorer have pointed out that there is a strong Greek sense in Lawrence. The inseparability of character and fate is integral to the novel and the character of George is essentially Greek. Nature, in the role of Greek chorus, anticipates the fate of the protagonists: it grieves at every fatal error in judgment and rejoices when human choice reinforces natural and instinctive truth. As George moves away from Lettie and towards Lethe, pagan Fate becomes the controlling God and Christian reference diminishes. Such minor points as the exclamations "By Heaven!" and "By Jove!" underscore the conflict of powers. Lawrence contrasts the Christian God, who now and then ravishes spiritually with the singing of choirs of angels, with the pagan god who ravishes with rape—the white bull of Europa and the white swan of Leda. When, at Lettie's coming-of-age party, Will sings "Don Juan's Serenade" by Tchaikowsky, the women variously exclaim "Choirs of angels!" and "Europa!"—suggesting the two poles of Will's appeal. Will is the effeminate male, split between masculinity and femininity as he is between Christianity and paganism, who compensates for his lack of wholeness by assuming the Casanova-Don Juan role, one Lawrence always detested.

The White Peacock is primarily concerned with the conflict between culture and primitivism, between vicarious life and direct experience, between tradition and man's unimpeded expression—the man-and-woman drama being basically that between ideality and reality, between air and earth, between life as transcendence, escaping into the skies, and life as immanence, rooted in the world. The novel is a philosophical examination of an age. The characters are so consistently symbolic that the tale itself is almost a theologically speculative allegory. Woman's defilement and violation of man mirrors the oppression of humanity by superannuated Christian idealisms in a world where a return to blood-knowledge and an earth-related religion has become imperative. Woman and transcendent Christian principle, equated with culture, sophistication, and the white peacock, victimize man and the principle of immanence respected by the Graeco-Roman religions. Lawrence values the ancient Greeks who brought their gods down to earth where they associated with men and peopled the natural world as dryads, naiads, nymphs and fauns, and sensuous wandering Joves. Lawrence, however, ends *The White Peacock* with George in the realm of the god of death—perhaps a significant exclusion of the rest of the pantheon.

George achieves a sort of Pyrrhic victory at the end of the novel. He has died symbolically by his own hand in the middle of the novel; he awaits an imminent death in the marshes of Lethe, but he has refused the alternative of the white peacock. It is not into Lettie's arms that he flees when she offers them as the alternative for the lean arms of death; he flees from her to a pagan forgetfulness of the world, achieved in the waters of Lethe in the underground kingdom of Hades. In the chapter "Pisgah," George has a vision of the future he would share were he to accept a world determined by Lettie's terms, the white peacock's terms, or Christianity's terms; but he profoundly knows that this is not for him. In the last chapter, "A Prospect Among the Marshes of Lethe," George moves irrevocably beyond the reach of Christian society. He renounces the Biblical vision and accepts the pagan realm of death. There is a certain heroism in George's renunciation of the ascendant peacock figure with its suggestion of the Christian God in Heaven; his plunge into primitive, dark abandonment of consciousness in the pagan waters of Lethe is a judgment of the modern Western world.

The end of Lawrence's novel is the celebration of a choice between two possible solutions. The choice that George accepts does not belong to the novel alone, as Lawrence's career makes evident; it is Lawrence's own choice, deliberately made in his young manhood, and it determines the Lawrence we know. In later years Lawrence tried to effect the synthesis or relationship of two worlds which would be necessary to the creation of a functional myth. He was trying to revitalize Christian idealism by mating it with pagan earth gods. This is explicit in *The Escaped Cock,* where he resurrects Christ to mate him with a priestess of Isis. He was constantly trying to effect his plumed-serpent synthesis and to perfect the imperfect marriage of his parents. Most obviously in *The Woman Who Rode Away* and *The Plumed Serpent,* but implicitly in many other works, Lawrence attempted to fuse transcendent religious principle, symbolized by white woman, with the dark gods of an immanent nature. Even as he refused to let his Christ escape into the skies through crucifixion and resurrection, so he ties the phoenix to its ashes and the bird to the earth creature, the snake. This is perhaps the process of mysticism rather than the vision itself, and it may explain the prophetic role Lawrence assumes.

The flight from Lettie to Lethe is one distinctive feature setting this book off from *Sons and Lovers,* at the end of which Paul turns again "towards the faintly humming, glowing town." [7] Professor Tindall, well understanding the importance of Lawrence's movement from "the plains of heaven" (*24*) to the waters of Lethe, has written: "Lawrence for a time tried to substitute Greek pantheism for the religion in which he could no longer believe." [8] In this first novel Lawrence has renounced the ethos of the Christian tradition and speaks out with great religious force for the resurrection of an older and altered myth.

The careful structure and the meticulous development of symbolism in *The White Peacock* give it an air of tightness or artificiality, the same tightness found in any great work of the intellect (*e.g., The Scarlet Letter*) so organized that no element falls unanalyzed into its place. This novel should lead us to an estimation of Lawrence that revises the myth of the man; too frequently it has been read in terms of the established myth and, naturally, judged by the values of the later Lawrence, it has seemed awkward and jejune. A key to a truer estimate of Lawrence's later technique may lie in a correct estimate of the reasons behind Lawrence's revulsion towards *The White Peacock.*

Lawrence writes in his *Studies in Classic American Literature:*

> The artist usually sets out—or used to—to point a moral and adorn a tale. The tale, however, points the other way, as a rule. Two blankly opposing morals, the artist's and the tale's. Never trust the artist. Trust the tale. The proper function of a critic is to save the tale from the artist who created it.[9]

For none of Lawrence's works should the critic heed this advice more literally than for *The White Peacock.* By Lawrence's expressed attitudes towards *The White Peacock,* the work is an immature and pretentious first novel for which the author felt a chastening shame. Lawrence writes, "I began it at 20—let that be my apology!" [10] He writes his sister Ada, "I don't care much about the peacock, really I don't." [11] He told an admirer that the book "had brought him very little but bitterness." [12]

In spite of the sporadic method of composition which, Lawrence maintained, brought the book to completion, the novel *had* been a major endeavor. He writes, "I had been tussling away . . . getting out *The White Peacock* in inchoate bits, from the underground of my consciousness. I must have written most of it five or six times." He admits that it was the result of "four or five years' spasmodic effort." [13] He told Jessie Chambers that he was putting everything in the book that was part of him.

The acceptance and publication of his novel and his mother's fatal illness coincided. Bitterness and guilt seem to have been the result of this coincidence. Lawrence as Cyril is guiltily allied with the mother-figure, yet Lawrence as author attacks and renounces her through his observation and presentation. Mrs. Lawrence was on her deathbed as the book went to press, and the special copy Lawrence rushed into her hands lay in her lap unread. Lawrence's hostility toward his first novel begins with his mother's death: "She was beyond reading my first immortal work. It was put aside and I never wanted to see it again." [14] Lawrence writes later in an "Autobiographical Sketch": "When I was 25 my mother died, and two months later *The White Peacock* was published, but it meant nothing to me." [15] The psychological situation that may be deduced is painful. The novel places the son-figure, Cyril, in sympathy with the father who flees from woman's domination to his escape in death. The irony of Lawrence's own mother's death after this statement in *The White Peacock* moved him to the recantation and expiation that makes *Sons and Lovers* a profound apology.

Cyril in the first novel is unlike Paul Morel in *Sons and Lovers*. The Paul who hates the father hates the ash tree, the symbol of masculine control, of the husband's retaliation against his wife, and the "harp" for the father's music; the Cyril who loves and sympathizes with the father-figure sees the ash tree as an "emblem" of a necessary "discipline of life" (*151*). Lawrence's anger against the father, notably in *Sons and Lovers,* reverses the attitude of *The White Peacock*. The guilt he had felt for being allied with the mother in the oppression of the father is absolved in part by the writing of *The White Peacock*. This earlier guilt seems to be replaced by a sense of guilt for allowing his mother on her deathbed to become aware of his sympathies with the father.

It is known that Mrs. Lawrence read a first version of this first novel. Jessie Chambers writes: "I asked her what she thought of it, and she replied in a pained voice: 'To think that *my* son should have written such a story,' referring presumably to Lettie's situation." [16] Jessie Chambers' presumption may well miss the point.

There is a mother-son, sister-brother collaboration in the death of the father-figure in *The White Peacock*. Lawrence sees the child in a family situation being used as a weapon against the man. At the end of the novel, Lettie and Meg both stand with their children snuggled against them, "dealing death" to their men. Cyril's position is essentially Lawrence's own position between his parents. He demonstrates his love and sympathy for George, giving him advice and assistance, but he secretly knows he is also a weapon for the mother-figure, in this novel his sister. Cyril's esthetic and spiritual response to life, his culture-oriented personality choices, and his retreat to France, as well as his gradual alienation from nature, announce an active allegiance that is denied, however, by his instinctive sympathy.

Lawrence's search for a synthesis of the ideal world and the real, or for an adjustment between the nether world of the father and the transcendent world of the mother, shows him to be both the troubled youth and the myth-maker. The white peacock, looking forward to the phoenix and the plumed serpent, is the initial symbol of Lawrence's unremitting struggle.

NOTES

[1] E. T. (Jessie Chambers), *D. H. Lawrence: A Personal Record* (London, 1935), p. 189.

[2] References are to page numbers in D. H. Lawrence, *The White Peacock* (London, 1955).

[3] In the rarefied atmosphere of Leslie's home, Highclose, among talk of painting, new music, culture, and Paris, Leslie and Lettie, as they drink to the new year and to "the *Vita Nuova*," are answered by a faint booing noise from the "hooters at the pits"—the voice of Lawrence's father in a well-timed raspberry.

[4] Lawrence's poem "Piano" which "betrays" him back to childhood shows a similar association of the mother with religion, and places the man-child beneath the mother.

[5] The action of the "Pastorals and Peonies" chapter is determined in large part by several of the Theocritan *Idylls*.

[6] Virgil's *Georgics,* IV, 1. 497.

[7] D. H. Lawrence, *Sons and Lovers* (New York, 1951), p. 491.

[8] William York Tindall, "D. H. Lawrence and the Primitive," *Sewanee Review* (April–June 1937), p. 205.

[9] D. H. Lawrence, *Studies in Classic American Literature* (New York, 1951), p. 13.

[10] Aldous Huxley, ed., *The Letters of D. H. Lawrence* (New York, 1932), p. 8.

[11] Ada Lawrence and G. Stuart Gelder, *Early Life of D. H. Lawrence* (London, 1932), p. 76.

[12] Harry T. Moore, *The Life and Works of D. H. Lawrence* (New York, 1951), p. 39.

[13] D. H. Lawrence, *Assorted Articles* (New York, 1930), p. 175.

[14] Moore, *op. cit.,* p. 69.

[15] Lawrence, *op. cit.,* p. 177.

[16] E. T. (Jessie Chambers), *op. cit.,* pp. 116–17.

Patricia Abel and Robert Hogan

D. H. LAWRENCE'S SINGING BIRDS

In E. L. Nicholes' article, "The Simile of the Sparrow in *The Rainbow*," published in *Modern Language Notes* for March, 1949, was expressed what seemed to us then a farfetched connection between the sparrow simile from Bede's account of "The Conversion of Edwin" and a seven-line paragraph from the last chapter of D. H. Lawrence's novel. Miss Nicholes wrote, "An important aspect of the prose style of D. H. Lawrence is his use of animal imagery and symbol, in brief metaphors or in the more extensive and complex images which characterize whole episodes and conflicts."

Since 1949 scholarly investigation has done much to substantiate Miss Nicholes' comment and to refute the charge that Lawrence was a hardy primitive scarcely understanding and little affected by the intellectual milieu of his time. Indeed, increasing familiarity with Lawrence's work tends to persuade the critical reader that Lawrence's creative powers, though not emulative, were to a surprising extent assimilative. Rather than being coincidental, it now seems that the sparrow simile was consciously used by Lawrence. But, and more important, it also seems that the simile was partially misunderstood by Miss Nicholes because it is connected to a complex of imagery in Lawrence's work and thought much more extensive than the one cited instance in *The*

Patricia Abel, who teaches at the University of Nebraska, where her husband is a mathematics professor, has contributed to *Modern Language Notes* and other professional journals. Her collaborator on this article, *Robert Hogan*, is a graduate of the University of Missouri, now teaching at Purdue, who has published in the *Dublin Magazine, Modern Fiction Studies*, the *New Republic*, and in other magazines. The article he wrote with Mrs. Abel was published in *Heft 2, Jahrgang 1958, Neue Folge*, of *Die Neueren Sprachen* (Frankfurt am Main und Bonn), and is here reproduced by consent of the editors of that journal.

Rainbow, a complex of imagery rooted in archetype and myth.

William York Tindall wrote as early as 1939 in *D. H. Lawrence and Susan His Cow* that

> . . . Lawrence thought order to be so alien to life that he could conceive of it as something imposed from without to his soul's impediment. Despite this conviction, however, he appears to have made some attempt to give order to his books by following the pattern of familiar myths as Joyce did in *Ulysses* and Eliot in *The Waste Land.* But his contempt of form and his conviction that truth is enough for beauty prevented Lawrence from making the most of such mythical scaffolds. His use of myth was too desultory to repel confusion.

Yet Maud Bodkin in her *Archetypal Patterns in Poetry* offers several general yet convincing examples of Lawrence's use of the rebirth archetype and comments that "the ancient identifications are alive for Lawrence, felt with an intensity that can secure response from the reader." To investigate further Lawrence's conception of myth, one might compare Miss Bodkin's definition of Jung's "primordial images" or archetypes with Lawrence's statements on the function of myth. Miss Bodkin writes:

> These archetypes Jung describes as "psychic residua of numberless experiences of the same type," experiences which have happened not to the individual but to his ancestors, and of which the results are inherited in the structure of the brain, *a priori* determinants of individual experience.

Lawrence writes:

> Then came the melting of the glaciers, and the world flood. The refugees from the drowned continents fled to the high places of America, Europe, Asia, and the Pacific Isles. And some degenerated naturally into cave men, neolithic and palaeolithic creatures, and some retained their marvellous innate beauty and life-perfection, as the South Sea Islanders, and some wandered savage in Africa, and some, like the Druids or Etruscans or Chaldeans or Amerindians or Chinese, refused to forget, but taught the old wisdom, only in its half-forgotten, symbolic forms. More or less forgotten, as knowledge: remembered as ritual, gesture, and myth-story.

And so, in the intense potency of symbols is part at least memory. And so it is that all the great symbols and myths which dominate the world when our history first begins, are very much the same in every country and every people, the great myths all relate to one another. And so it is that these myths now begin to hypnotize us again, our own impulse towards our own scientific way of understanding being almost spent. And so, besides myths, we find the same mathematic figures, cosmic graphs which remain among the aboriginal peoples in all continents, mystic figures and signs whose true cosmic or scientific significance is lost, yet which continue in use for purposes of conjuring or divining.

Lawrence's definition of myth stands almost immediately parallel to the definition of archetype, and when we note some of his reading in Frazer, Frobenius, Jane Harrison, and Jung himself, the evidence that Lawrence understood the nature of myth and archetype and of their value for literature is quite convincing. Further, when we examine the extensive use and the similar function of the complex of imagery surrounding the singing birds in Lawrence's work, the evidence for Lawrence's assimilation of the use of myth and archetype becomes almost overwhelming.

The peculiar conformation of imagery, centering around "the cock and the singing birds," recurs in the works of several other modern writers. This series of images is apparently felt as a unit and given a surprisingly similar connotation and emotional weight by writers as disparate as W. B. Yeats, T. S. Eliot, Wallace Stevens, and Sean O'Casey. The resemblance is obviously not due to any universal unconscious, but to the interest felt by many contemporary poets, novelists, and dramatists, in the mythological studies of such scholars as Frazer, Weston, and Harrison, an interest felt in the studies in archetype made by Jung, Miss Bodkin, and Northrop Frye. However, to uncover Lawrence's use of this complex of imagery centering around the rebirth archetype, some background is first necessary.

i

The basic conception in the complex of ideas surrounding Lawrence's use of the cock and the singing birds seems to be drawn from the ritual of the worship of Zeus at Dodona, a ritual which served as the germinative impulse for Frazer's *Golden Bough*. This is a rain-making ceremony utilizing the symbol of the death and rebirth of the god, with a final assurance of life and fertility, provocatively explored in C. B. Lewis' *Classical Mythology and Arthurian Romance*.[1]

For the purposes of this comparison, the essential symbols involved are: a chapel or church or grove, which was originally the temple of the god; a gong or bell or cock-crow, which is an apparatus imitative or evocative of thunder; a storm, which is usually a thunderstorm accompanied by wind and lightning, but which is frequently simply rain or running water; a tree full of singing birds, which are probably oracles of the god; and finally the rejuvenation or rebirth.

This combination of ideas is, according to Lewis, a familiar association in early metrical romances, existing as a distorted memory of the then obliterated pagan cults. For instance, in the English romance *Ywain and Gawain*, there is the gong, the storm, and the tree of birds:

> Þat weder made so will of rede
> I hopid sone to haue my dede;
> And sertes, if it lang had last,
> I hope i had neuer þeþ in past.
> Bot thorgh His might þat tholed wownd,
> Þe storme sesed within a stownde;
> Þan wex þe weder fayre ogayne,
> And þareof was i wonder fayne,
> For best comforth of al thing
> Es solace efter myslikeing.
> Þan saw i sene a mery syght:
> Of al þe fowles þat er in flyght
> Lighted so thik opon þat tre
> Þat bogh ne lefe none might i se;
> So merily þan gon þai sing
> Þat al þe wode bigan to ring; [2]

Also, in the *Yvain* of Chrétien de Troyes, there are the storm, the gong, and the chapel. In both cases these figures are associated with the entrance into a new, strange land.

Several distortions varied the myth in these reworkings. The chapel, a relic of the past, became a ruined chapel. As a remnant of a discredited religion, it acquires a sinister and supernatural tone. Also, because of its assimilation in the Arthurian cycle, it became almost automatically equated with the Chapel Perilous of the Grail legend and connected with the Wasteland-Fisher King equation, which was so painstakingly traced to its ritual origins by Jessie L. Weston.[3]

Of special concern for a consideration of Lawrence and other later writers is one version of this formation, the *Wolfdietrich,* in which the singing birds suffer an intriguing alteration:

> Wol zwene und sibenzie este nam er (Wolfdietrich)
> an der linden war,
> Die vogel, die dar uf stuanden, die waren gulden
> gar.
> Sie warn gemacht mit listen und waren innen hol:
> Als si der wint durchwate, ir stimme diu sane wel.[4]

Lewis traces this change in the nature of the singing birds to a well-known tale of a bronze tree overlaid with gold and inhabited by gilded bronze birds in the imperial palace at Constantinople. Perhaps the most familiar use of this facet of the legend is in Yeats' "Byzantium" poems where the cock of Hades is equated with the singing bird. This cock is a natural one and associated with the "mire and blood" of natural fertility. The question of how it originally came to be so associated is seemingly answered by a quotation from Prudentius in Helen Waddell's *The Wandering Scholars:*

> Inde est, quod omnes credimus
> ille quietis tempore
> quo gallus exsultans canit,
> Christum redisse ex inferis.[5]

And here is the cock of Hades. The cock as the announcer of the renewal of the day is an obvious and frequently used symbol of rejuvenation, of course, and, in the Christian context, of resurrection. In "Byzantium" by congruence with the singing birds, the cock finds its way into the central pattern of symbols. Further, this equation of the cock with the fertility myth finds frequent substantiation in Frazer. One example, for instance, is noted near Udvarkely in Transylvanis, when the cock is identified with the corn spirit:

> By being tied up in the last sheaf and killed, the cock is identified with the corn, and its death with the cutting of the corn. By keeping its feathers till Spring, then mixing them with the seed-corn taken from the very sheaf in which the bird has been bound, and scattering the feathers together with the seed over the field, the identity of the bird with the corn is again emphasized, and its quickening and fertilizing power as an embodiment of the corn-spirit, is intimated in the plainest manner. Thus the corn spirit, in the form of a cock, is killed at harvest, but rises to fresh life and activity in the spring.[6]

In the Christianization of the fertility symbol of the cock, an early connection is made with the resurrection. A ballad on St. Stephen the Protomartyr casts an illuminating sidelight on this aspect of the cock. In this ballad a roast capon crows, "Christus natus est" to justify the faith of St. Stephen. In a sense, the bird is here himself resurrected, and we are led directly to D. H. Lawrence's most famous use of this cluster of symbols.

ii

Lawrence has combined these two aspects of the cock, the pagan symbol of fertility and the Christian symbol of resurrection, in the novelette *The Man Who Died,* the first edition of which appeared under the title *The Escaped Cock.* In this story the deserted church and the rejuvenated person, now combined with a rejuvenating, not simply oracular, bird, appear. A thematic connection between the pagan sexuality of the Priestess of Isis and the cock is made, a connection between the woman and the bird that appears also in *The White Peacock* and in Sean O'Casey's *Cock-A-Doodle Dandy.* In *The Escaped Cock,* Lawrence utilizes the cock, which Christ carries under his arm, as a symbol of fertility—

> . . . a young gamecock which looked a shabby little thing, but which put on brave feathers as Spring advanced, and was resplendent with arched and orange neck by the time the fig trees were letting out leaves from their end-tips.[7]

—and of the rebirth of the dead, ecclesiastical Christ into sensuality. In the denouement, Christ passes over the water into a new life.

A curious connection between the singing bird, the cock, and the tree is exemplified by another Lawrence novel, *Aaron's Rod,* in which the flute of the protagonist, Aaron Sisson, appears as a phallic symbol. Both Aaron and the Marchesa del Torre have lost their life-direction and are consumed by a sterile debility. When the Marchesa married, she lost her beautiful singing voice. Aaron on the symbolic level plays his flute, which is spoken of as flowering, and restores her desire and ability to sing. On a literal level they engage in a brief love affair. The connection of the woman with the singing birds and of Aaron's rod with the flowering tree and with the vulgate appellation of the phallus is unavoidable.

This connection of a woman with the bird occurs frequently. Although probably deriving from different sources, the ability of the Fay of Avalon and the Irish Morrigen to change themselves into birds undoubtedly reinforces a very natural extension of the mystery of the birds.[8]

Another provocative connection of the woman with the bird occurs in Lawrence's first novel, *The White Peacock.* Here, Lawrence effectively unites the vital cock, the gong, the storm, the singing birds, and the rebirth with the closely allied "Wasteland" element. The peacock is used in a spatial relationship similar to the cock in Yeats' poem, but with an opposite valence. Cyril, the story's narrator, in a chapter "A Shadow in Spring," finds his way through a gloomy and rotted landscape to a deserted church, where he meets the first of Lawrence's virile gamekeepers, Annable:

> So I left the wildlands, and went along the old red wall of the kitchen garden, along the main road as far as the mouldering church which stands high on a bank by the roadside, just where the trees tunnel the darkness, and the gloom of the highway startles the travellers at noon. Great obscurity rots the Hall church, black and melancholy above the shrinking head of the traveller.
>
> The grassy path to the churchyard was still clogged with decayed leaves. The church is abandoned. As I draw near, an

owl floated softly out of the black tower. Grass overgrew the threshold. I pushed open the door, grinding back a heap of fallen plaster and rubbish, and entered the place. In the twilight the pews were leaning in ghostly disorder, the prayer-books dragged from their ledges, scattered on the floor in the dust and rubble, torn by mice and birds. Birds scuffled in the darkness of the roof. I looked up. In the upward well of the tower I could see a bell hanging. I stooped and picked up a piece of plaster from the ragged confusion of feathers and broken nests, and remnants of dead birds. Up into the vault overhead I tossed pieces of plaster until one hit the bell, and it "tonged" out its faint remonstrance. There was a rustle of many birds like spirits. I sounded the bell again, and dark forms moved with cries of alarm overhead and something fell heavily. I shivered in the dark, evil-smelling place, and hurried to get out of doors. I clutched my hands with relief and pleasure when I saw the sky above me quivering with the last crystal lights, and the lowest red of sunset behind the yewboles. I drank the fresh air that sparkled with the sound of blackbirds and thrushes whistling their strong bright notes.[9]

After Annable has exorcised the peacock by driving it away, Cyril is sensually rejuvenated by the gamekeeper's story of his struggle with intellectuality, with the predatory woman, his wife, symbolized by the peacock, who "defiles" the churchyard, and of his breaking through to sensuality. Cyril returns through a wood reborn from its earlier rot and decay:

The wood breathed fragrantly, with a subtle sympathy. The firs softened their touch to me, and the larches awoke from the barren winter-sleep, and put out velvet fingers to caress me as I passed. Only the clean, bare branches of the ash stood emblem of the discipline of life. I looked down on the blackness where trees filled the quarry and the valley bottoms, and it seemed that the world, my own home-world, was strange again.[10]

Here is the ruined chapel, the gong or bell, the singing birds, the wasteland, and the rejuvenation. The peacock seems to take the same central weight as the cock, but Lawrence reverses the movement to make the renewal dependent upon the removal of the bird, rather than upon its character as a fertility symbol, as in the Yeatsian "life-in-death and death-in-life" dichotomy. In spite of this change, the cock or peacock is yet the daemon through whose influence the rebirth occurs.

This situation lacks the emphasis on water found in the other passages, but includes the "Wasteland" and the figure with whose welfare the health of the land is bound up—Annable, the gamekeeper. Annable, like the Fisher-King, has a wound. Cyril, like Gawain and Perceval, sounds the gong at the entrance of the Chapel Perilous. Although the episode in the Lawrence novel has no storm, there is a wind as there is also in *Cock-a-Doodle Dandy*—a great wind that hurtles the sterile male characters about on the stage—in Wallace Stevens' poem, "Ploughing on Sunday" and, of course, in the "What the Thunder Said" section of *The Waste Land*.

The passage from *The Rainbow* containing the sparrow simile was interpreted by Miss Nicholes as follows:

> Lawrence uses only that part of the passage which presents the visual image—the lighted room with its rows of warriors, the bird finding temporary refuge from the storm. In the original passage (and in Wordsworth's sonnet)[11] the simile is developed and its meaning made general: Man's life on earth is like the flight of the sparrow; man's concern is with the fate of his soul in the time unknown to him. A clear parallel is drawn between Ursula's flight from insecurity back to insecurity and the sparrow's flight through the lighted room. But Lawrence never gets away, in his explicit statement, from the specific situation centering around Ursula. Once he has made use of the concrete symbol he drops the figure. Yet, for the literate reader, the generalization which is so much a part of the original passage has been implied.[12]

Miss Nicholes' conclusion, however, should be weighed against another section of the book in which birds are significantly utilized, the very important chapter called "The Cathedral." In this chapter Lawrence portrays the clashing reactions of Will and Anna Brangwen to Lincoln Cathedral, and Lawrence seems to condemn Will's emotion as too sterile and bloodless. Anna's feelings are compared in a longish paragraph to a bird striving to escape from constriction.[13] Subsequently Will is converted to Anna's point of view:

> Outside the cathedral were many flying spirits that could never be sifted through the jewelled gloom . . . He listened to the thrushes in the gardens and heard a note which the cathedrals did not include: something free and careless and joyous . . . he was glad he was away from his shadowy cathedral.
>
> . . . He thought of the ruins of the Grecian worship, and it seemed, a temple was never perfectly a temple, till it was ruined and mixed up with the winds and the sky and the herbs.[14]

Lawrence's use of the sparrow simile then would seem to indicate not a moment of repose and safety amid insecurities, but an intrusion into a building in which a civilized ritual is in progress and from which an escape must be made. The escape is, of course, back to nature and the natural ritual which takes place in a religious ruin and which may some day rejuvenate that ruin.

The original pattern of the particular symbol cluster of the cock and the singing birds is, thanks to recent scholarship, fortunately clear and, therefore, discernible in much of Lawrence's work. The manner in which the remnants of primitive ritual have been molded into a contemporary revitalization and combined with congruent material and Lawrence's inimitable personality may perhaps suggest that much of Lawrence does not result from "the hot blood's blindfold art" but from a highly intellectual assimilation of myth.

NOTES

[1] C. B. Lewis, *Classical Mythology and Arthurian Romance* (Edinburgh: Humphrey Milford, 1932).

[2] Walter H. French and Charles B. Hale, *Middle English Metrical Romances* (New York: Prentice-Hall, 1930), pp. 496–97.

[3] Jessie L. Weston, *From Ritual to Romance* (Cambridge: Cambridge University Press, 1920).

[4] Lewis, *op. cit.,* p. 80.

[5] Helen Waddell, *The Wandering Scholars* (New York: Doubleday Anchor Books, 1955), p. 19.

[6] Sir James G. Frazer, *The Golden Bough,* abridged ed. (New York: The Macmillan Co., 1951), p. 524.

[7] D. H. Lawrence, *The Man Who Died* (New York: Alfred A. Knopf, 1931), p. 3.

[8] In Sean O'Casey's play *Cock-a-Doodle Dandy*, the cock appears as the alter ego of the girl, Loraleen, who is several times transformed into the bird. Loraleen-the Cock stands for a robust vitality which is opposed to the mental and physical sterility of the male characters.

[9] D. H. Lawrence, *The White Peacock* (Rome: The Albatross, 1949), pp. 167–68.

[10] *Ibid.*, p. 173.

[11] XVI of the Ecclesiastical Sonnets.

[12] E. L. Nicholes, "The 'Simile of the Sparrow' in *The Rainbow* by D. H. Lawrence," *Modern Language Notes*, Vol. LXIV, No. 3 (March, 1949), pp. 173–74.

[13] D. H. Lawrence, *The Rainbow* (Modern Library Edition), p. 191.

[14] *Ibid.*, p. 193.

Nancy Abolin

LAWRENCE'S *THE BLIND MAN:*
THE REALITY OF TOUCH

It is surprising that more has not been written on D. H. Lawrence's short story "The Blind Man." Not only is it a fine piece of writing in its own right, but it also provides commentary on several of Lawrence's most frequently recurring themes, and it is further valuable as an index to some of his most characteristic writing techniques. In this story Lawrence once again examines the problem which most deeply concerned him throughout his life, his conception of the complexity of the relations between men and women. He demonstrates the fact that the devouring intimacy of an all-absorbing "blood" marriage is an unsatisfactory situation; and that the potentially healing power of touch is foredoomed by the unworthy nature of its recipient, as Lawrence shows it operating ambivalently in the dramatic scene between the blind man, Maurice Pervin, and the man who is his opposite in every respect, Bertie Reid.

Bertie, the epitome of Lawrence's cerebral man, is devoid of any connection with a physical contact with life. Held in contempt by even his closest friend, Isabel Pervin, he is a neuter being, unable to approach women physically and at the same time almost annihilated by Maurice's fervent offer of friendship. In contradistinction, Maurice, the emotional and sensual male, who has much in common with the Brangwen men of *The Rainbow,* and who is governed by the strong, hot, provincial blood that

Nancy Abolin, a 1959 graduate of Wellesley College, where she has been doing independent research on Lawrence under the direction of Sylvia Berkman, has attended summer sessions at Harvard, California, and the University of London, and is now a graduate student at Columbia. This essay is her first published writing.

beats in his veins, is nonetheless incapable of reconciling himself
to an existence which permits no extension of the self beyond
that which constitutes the male counterpart to the female half
of the marriage bond. The flow of his blood prescience with the
substantial world is thus at times checked and thrown back
chaotically inside him, making painfully apparent to him his
fatal flaw of dependence upon another person, his wife Isabel.

Isabel is Lawrence's possessive woman with one great article of faith, that husband and wife should be so important to
one another that the rest of the world does not count. Although
she has come closer than ever before to realizing this desire in the
year of her husband's blindness and subsequent retreat into a
world of sensual blood contacts, this very fact now prevents her
from withdrawing into herself, away from her husband, to lux-
uriate privately in the lethargy of her coming maternity. The
strain of her husband's recurrent fits of depression, of forcing
the old spontaneous cheerfulness and joy to continue, sends
dread to the roots of her soul and keeps her from enjoying the
fruit of their newly achieved intimacy in the way that Anna
Brangwen, for example, rejoiced over such experiences in *The
Rainbow*.

Each of the three characters in "The Blind Man" thus represents an incomplete aspect of life, the incompleteness of which
Lawrence condemns. The attempt of the blind man to transcend the limitations of his married life in order to become a
whole human being is doomed to fail, and we are left with this
knowledge at the end of the story.

Almost none of this thematic matter is shown in the action
of the story, which consists of two trips from the house to the
barn and back; nor is it more than suggested in the dialogue. And
the only scene which could be called dramatic, the vivid scene
in the barn where Maurice presses Bertie's hands into his scarred,
blinded eye sockets, is dramatic only because Lawrence has
gradually built up such a clear picture of each of his characters
that we are able to know exactly what this climactic scene means
to each man and how it affects him. Lawrence employs several
devices throughout the story in order to convey this strong sense
of his characters to his reader. One of the most effective, and
perhaps the most typically Lawrencean, is his apprehension of
place and its effect on the characters. He also enriches the texture

of his story and further reveals his characters by making a ritualistically progressive pattern of the simplest, most ordinary series of actions, and by imbuing a number of elements in the story with almost symbolic meanings.

Here, too, each character is portrayed less as an individual creation existing in a single story than as an instrument to express certain views of life and society that Lawrence wished to show in effective juxtaposition with one another, a quality which becomes increasingly apparent in his later work as his novels and tales evolve into the parable form.

It is also characteristic of Lawrence that some degree of familiarity with his other works increases the reader's understanding of the story and intensifies his response to it. How much more significant, and how emotionally charged, becomes the scene between Maurice and Bertie if one is able to recall similar Lawrencean scenes in which dissatisfied men have tried to reach beyond their limitations toward wholeness by means of a *Blutbrüderschaft* through physical contact with another man. As early as *Sons and Lovers* the rivals Paul Morel and Baxter Dawes come to a mutual understanding through their physical struggle; in *Women in Love,* Rupert Birkin tries unsuccessfully to transcend the bonds of his marriage to Ursula and thereby achieve wholeness of self through a *Blutbrüderschaft* with Gerald Crich, a man who is (as Bertie is to Maurice) his anti-self in an almost Yeatsian sense; and in *Aaron's Rod,* Aaron during an illness is rubbed out of physical and spiritual sickness and back into contact with life, into a connection with a man intrinsically different from himself, the writer Lilly.

None of these attempts approaches the ideal relationship that Lawrence describes in *Women in Love* through Birkin, but none of them fails so utterly as the abortive attempt shown in "The Blind Man." In this story there is a sense of desperation. The couple is in the throes of the recoil from a too-intense love intimacy which Lawrence finds inevitable and which here must be resolved quickly, before the baby is born. Maurice needs to provide an outlet for himself which is comparable to the outlet the coming baby has already begun to supply for Isabel and, in perfect accordance with Lawrence's constant demands for wholeness of character, Maurice chooses as a friend a man who is the epitome of everything that he himself is not. It is part of the irony of Lawrence's vision that the very same nature which would make Bertie a complementary fulfillment for Maurice's character also makes him totally incapable of accepting Maurice's urgent and poignant offer of friendship.

The effect of the sparse dialogue on the development of the story is negligible; there is also very little dramatic action in the story. What action there is, however, assumes additional importance because of its ritual implications. The characters move about and meet in their various worlds in a rigid pattern of action which the author has reduced to its barest minimum. The action begins and ends in the severely elegant and highly civilized home that Isabel has cultivated to house the animalistic sensuality of her marriage. The purpose of both of the trips made in the course of the story is to fetch Maurice, whose instinctive tendencies, brought to the fore in him by the advent of his blindness, are in harmony with the life of the stable. Isabel makes the first trip, and Lawrence uses this trip as a means of revealing the basic conflicts between husband and wife. Isabel grows desperate when confronted by the unclothed sensuality of the animal world of which Maurice is an integral part; she must restrain and refine the unseeing passion and dark intimacies she shares with her husband; she does not wish to talk to him or touch him until she can see him, until the slight suggestion of the stable in his voice is dispelled by the atmosphere of the house and the euphemizing spiciness of her pot-pourri bowls.

A subdued interval follows the first trip, in which all three characters subtly reveal themselves and each other within the decorously intimate confines of the house. But harmony is lacking even in this interlude; Isabel is preoccupied with her coming maternity, Maurice longs to escape the intellectual intimacy existing between the two old friends which excludes him and finally drives him out to the stable once more, and Bertie is uncomfortable before the physical fact of Isabel's pregnancy and in the presence of the rich sensual life which the couple shares. The growing tension can be brought to a full dramatic climax only in the realm of the stable, a realm uncamouflaged by the restraints and refinements of civilization. Lawrence has already revealed Isabel to us by exposing her to this world; now the point in the story has been reached where it is necessary to show Bertie and Maurice in conjunction with this world. And, in order to bring about the climax of Maurice's one-sided fulfillment and Bertie's annihilation, Lawrence repeats with increased intensity the pattern which has been established in the preceding action of the story.

Throughout "The Blind Man" Lawrence reinforces what is being said within the structured pattern of the action by occasionally endowing certain "props" with almost symbolic qualities, and by his use of the natural elements to further reveal his characters. The sharply contrasted descriptions of the two dining rooms—the image of the softly glowing round table and old handsome china belonging to the Pervins juxtaposed against that of the long narrow table, white lamp, and large black teapot which serve the ruddy Werthams at "feeding-time"—the atmosphere evoked by these two settings functions importantly as Isabel makes her progression from the Pervin dining room to the first yard of the farm premises, stopping in the Wertham kitchen to talk to the half-animal people there before going on to the second yard which encloses the wholly animal life of the stable. Similarly, Lawrence has Maurice handle two tellingly different representatives of organic life, one in the house and one in the stable. Sitting at the table in the dining room he is handed a little crystal bowl of sweet-scented violets from Isabel's garden under the windows of the house; later, in the stable, his connection with organic life is allowed much fuller statement in the large, half-wild cat which comes to him naturally and claws his flesh affectionately. And, too, Lawrence makes use of the horses, which are just as symbolically suggestive to him here as they are in *The Rainbow* and in "St. Mawr."

Even the weather intrudes upon the characters in such a way that it becomes an integral part of the explication of the story. Throughout, Lawrence describes the outside world of natural elements as dark and violent, for it is a windy, rainy night in November. Once again we are shown, one by one, the response of each of the three characters to this additionally revelatory device. First Isabel goes out into the night and, as we might expect, her reaction to the weather is similar to her reaction to her husband: half she likes it, half she feels unwilling to battle. Maurice of course is unperturbed by the storming elements; his feet have a strong contact with the earth and massively he rises out of it to become a tower of darkness to Isabel. And Bertie too is predictably affected by the wet roaring night: too much moisture everywhere makes him feel almost imbecile, Lawrence tells us, thus clarifying our perception of each character by the use of still another literary technique.

The characteristic techniques which Lawrence uses in "The Blind Man" function primarily to illustrate the different responses of his three characters to various aspects of touch. The physical reality of touch itself becomes a central factor in the story, and we are shown in a number of ways precisely how each character operates in relation to this sensory experience. Maurice is forced by his blindness to live almost entirely by touch; Isabel, although shrinking from physical contact in the barn where it is too nakedly exposed for her delicate sensibilities, is hypnotized by it when its power is somewhat mitigated by the "repose and beauty" of her civilized world; last, and least in Lawrence's estimation, there is Bertie, who has spent his life avoiding any intimate contact and who is destroyed by touch when it is finally forced upon him by Maurice. At the end of the story Maurice returns to the house temporarily fulfilled, standing "with his feet apart, like a strange colossus"; but this transcendence is doomed to be short-lived, for Bertie is at this point "like a mollusc whose shell is broken."

Typically, Lawrence does not attempt to present any resolution at the end of his story; his primary purpose has been to convey a sense of the subtly complex conflicts which, for him, always exist in a blindly intimate marriage relationship and between three such widely divergent attitudes as those which he embodies in the three main characters in "The Blind Man." This purpose is admirably achieved in the story by means of Lawrence's unique literary gifts.

S. Ronald Weiner

IRONY AND SYMBOLISM IN *THE PRINCESS*

THE short story "The Princess" illustrates a character-istic Lawrencean "shift." The movement compares to the Italian relocation in *The Lost Girl,* the Alpine journey of *Women in Love,* the excursion of "The Captain's Doll," and the return to America of "St. Mawr." The shift is not only in scene, but in the way the protagonists and the reader relate the scene, and in the way Lawrence's tone enforces that relation. It is the shift illustrated in a comparison of the following two passages from "The Princess":

> There began a new phase, when the father and daughter spent their summers on the Great Lakes or in California, or in the South-West. The father was something of a poet, the daugh-ter something of a painter. He wrote poems about the lakes or the redwood trees, and she made dainty drawings. He was physically a strong man, and he loved the out-of-doors. He would go off with her for days, paddling in a canoe and sleep-ing by a camp-fire. Frail little Princess, she was always un-daunted, always undaunted. She would ride with him on horse-back over the mountain trails till she was so tired she was nothing but a bodiless consciousness sitting astride her pony. But she never gave in. And at night he folded her in her blanket on a bed of balsam pine twigs, and she lay and looked at the stars unmurmuring. She was fulfilling her role (478).[1]

. . .

S. Ronald Weiner, who teaches at the University of Chicago, has been a Teaching Fellow at Harvard, where he was graduated and where he completed his doctoral dissertation on narrative tone in Lawrence; the present essay is his first publication.

She sat immobile, her cheeks hot, full of conflicting thoughts. And she watched him while he folded the blankets on the floor, a sheepskin underneath. Then she went out into night.

The stars were big. Mars sat on the edge of a mountain, for all the world like the blazing eye of a crouching mountain lion. But she herself was deep, deep below in a pit of shadow. In the intense silence she seemed to hear the spruce forest crackling with electricity and cold. Strange, foreign stars floated on that unmoving water. The night was going to freeze. Over the hills came the far sobbing-singing howling of the coyotes. She wondered how the horses would be.

Shuddering a little, she turned to the cabin. Warm light showed through its chinks. She pushed at the rickety, half-opened door.

"What about the horses?" she said.

"My black, he won't go away. And your mare will stay with him. You want to go to bed now?"

"I think I do."

"All right. I feed the horses some oats."

And he went out into the night.

He did not come back for some time. She was lying wrapped up tight in the bunk (*502–3*).

The clear distinction in tone and relative objectivity of the two passages relates to the sense of "nature" each conveys. In the first passage nature seems to exist only as it has interest for Dollie and her father: it offers a subject for poetry—note the casualness of "lakes or redwood trees"—and "dainty drawings," and it affords recreation. In the second passage nature seethes with intense life; no longer does Dollie merely look at the stars; they seem to look at her. Mars, uniting the themes of passion and destruction, aptly stands out among the vital night-presences. Passion is also suggested by Tansy's loyalty to the stallion—to their suggested "attraction" which contrasts ironically both with her earlier attempt to escape from the Princess, and with Dollie's relationship to Romero. That relationship is also suggested by Dollie's turning to the fire for warmth; indeed, the sentence "Warm light showed through its chinks" points toward the later, "Only through a chink she could see a star" (*503*).

The end of the second passage also emphasizes her separateness and solitariness. The first passage, however, puts emphasis on her essential connection with her father: "He folded her in her blanket." The sentence rhythm of the passage as well as the paragraph structure, moreover, tends to enforce this sense of duality, in the way "something of a poet" balances "something of a painter": his poems, her pictures. The paragraph then splits into separate symmetric comments on Colin and the Princess. Lawrence re-establishes the sense of relation in the last two sentences, especially in the devastating irony of "She was fulfilling her role." "Which role," we wonder, "that of daughter or perhaps of wife?" The irony is disturbing, as was Dollie's refusal to live with her grandparents: "But Papa and I are such an old couple, you see, such a crochety old couple, living in a world of our own" (*477*). Genuine "fulfillment" is, of course, quite impossible in such a "world." The ironic juxtaposition of "fulfillment" and "role" demonstrates perfectly the subtle delicacy of Lawrence's touch in the first part of "The Princess" and clarifies the central opposition in terms of which we must comprehend the tale: the conflict of the Urquharts' illusory self-awareness with the demands of a fuller, less conscious, human existence.

This conflict is suggested in the very first sentence of "The Princess":

> To her father, she was The Princess. To her Boston aunts and uncles she was just *Dollie Urquhart, poor little thing* (*473*).

The poise here of fantasy and vulnerability is characteristic, and we hear it later: "Dear child!" her hostess said of her. "She is so quaint and old-fashioned; such a lady, poor little mite!" (*476*). Lawrence further emphasizes her vulnerability by describing the antipathies she aroused in her travels:

> Encounters like these made her tremble, and made her know she must have support from the outside. The power of her spirit did not extend to these low people, and they had all the physical power (*477*).

The notion of "spirit" and the "lowness" of the physical are, of course, legacies from her father. Colin's disquisition on the self and the demon is the locus of the themes of illusion, vulnerability, and the danger of the "inferior":

> "My little Princess must never take too much notice of people and the things they say and do," he repeated to her. "People don't know what they are doing and saying. They chatter-chatter, and they hurt one another, and they hurt themselves very often, till they cry. But don't take any notice, my little Princess. Because it is all nothing. Inside everybody there is another creature, a demon which doesn't care at all. You peel away all the things they say and do and feel, as cook peels away the outside of onions. And in the middle of everybody there is a green demon which you can't peel away. And this green demon never changes, and it doesn't care at all about all the things that happen to the outside leaves of the person, all the chatter-chatter, and all the husbands and wives and children, and troubles and fusses. You peel everything away from people, and there is a green, upright demon in every man and woman; and this demon is a man's real self, and a woman's real self. It doesn't really care about anybody, it belongs to the demons and the primitive fairies, who never care. But, even so, there are big demons and mean demons, and splendid demonish fairies, and vulgar ones. But there are no royal fairy women left. Only you my little Princess. You are the last of the royal race of the old people; the last, my Princess. There are no others. You and I are the last. When I am dead there will be only you. And that is why, darling, you will never care for any of the people in the world very much. Because their demons are all dwindled and vulgar. They are not royal. Only you are royal, after me. Always remember that. And always remember, it is a *great secret*. If you tell people, they will try to kill you, because they will envy you for being a Princess. It is our great secret, darling. I am a prince, and you a princess, of the old, old blood. And we keep our secret between us, all alone. And so, darling, you must treat all people very politely, because *noblesse oblige*. But you must never forget that you alone are the last of Princesses, and that all other are less than you are, less noble, more vulgar. Treat them politely and gently and kindly, darling. But you are the Princess, and they are commoners. Never

try to think of them as if they were like you. They are not. You will find always that they are lacking, lacking in the royal touch, which only you have . . ." *(475–76)*.

Lawrence's negative attitude toward Colin's philosophy [2] is implicit in the tale itself, in the special force of the passage— achieved through an almost hypnotic series of repetitions of words and phrase structure, and by the felt contrast of "childish" rhetoric and decadent sentiment—and in the gentle irony which informs it: in the suggestion of death joined with egoism and mystery in such phrases as "the last of the royal race of the old people," "only you are royal, after me," "I am a prince, and you a princess, of the old, old blood"; and in the delicate suggestion of disease in reference to an English king's supposed ability to cure scrofula by his "royal touch." Such suggestions seem relevant because the tale as a whole powerfully demonstrates that the maintenance of an illusory self destroys one's real self and the self-respect of others, that in attempting to be an isolated "something," one becomes nothing.

Lawrence renders Colin Urquhart's essential nothingness through the special quality of his characterization: he is a thing of "mist and glamour," a "fascinating spectre," and "a living echo! His very flesh, when you touched it, did not seem quite the flesh of a real man" *(473–74)*. His physical distance and his psychic peculiarities merge in the ironic ambiguity of: "But absent. When all came to all, he just wasn't there. 'Not all there,' as the vulgar say" *(474)*. Lawrence's judgment of that "distance" is decisively established in the opening sketch of the tale, in which the ironic poise of tone is masterly in its constant opposition of the real and the illusory; in the contrast, for example, of "looking at nothing" and "a very attractive body" *(473)*, or, more comically, in the contrast of "shown his knees" and "hushed Ossianic past."

The tone begins to recall Jane Austen and James in:

For the rest, he was one of those gentlemen of sufficient but not excessive means who fifty years ago wandered vaguely about, never arriving anywhere, never doing anything, and never definitely being anything, yet well received in the good society of more than one country *(473)*.

This tone merges wonderfully with the "politeness," "courte-ousness," and "musicality" of this first page, but the hush and the delicacy are exposed as they are rendered, for the initial "bit mad" and "bit off" control our responses. In the second para-graph, moreover, the simple declarative sentences and heavily monosyllabic diction tend to puncture the idea of "royalty." The more complex sentences which begin the third paragraph seem similarly "denigrating" in the way qualifying details blunt initial impressions: Colin is handsome, but with nice *wide* blue eyes that "look at nothing"; "soft hair" tops a "low, broad, brow"; "sum of his charms" seems to call his charms into question and "resonant and powerful like bronze" fuses a sense of distance and immateriality with a feeling of destructive, egoistic insensitivity.

That Dollie is herself one of the destroyed as well as a de-stroyer complicates our response to her. Her presentation is not the same as Colin's; the strokes are subtler, there is less sug-gestion of incongruity. She is not quite real—a fairy, a change-ling—and can be exasperating in her "cold, elfin detachment," but in her exaggerated delicacy she also seems pathetic:

> She was erect and very dainty. Always small, nearly tiny in physique, she seemed like a changeling beside her big, hand-some, slightly mad father. She dressed very simply, usually in blue or delicate greys, with little collars of old Milan point, or very finely-worked linen. She had exquisite little hands, that made the piano sound like a spinet when she played. She was rather given to wearing cloaks and capes, instead of coats, out of doors, and little eighteenth-century sort of hats. Her complexion was pure apple-blossom (*476*).

We know her costumes and manner are based on illusion (*476*), but the Lawrencean control of tone does not permit us to feel it the same way that we feel Colin's fantasies. Many of the details seem double-edged. Her "little collar" both represents her pure delicacy and her imprisonment to illusion. Her play-ing both graces the piano and seems to rob it of potential. Her "apple-blossom" complexion suggests the organic fullness she lacks, and her ultimate destruction emphasizes her sterile per-fection. This is a perfection that enrages "Calibans" (*477*), while she seems bound by a false Prospero who will not say farewell to his art.

Her confusion after her father's death, her ambivalence over the necessity of *doing* something is both comic and pathetic:

> Now her father was dead, she found herself on the *fringe* of the vulgar crowd, sharing their necessity to *do* something. It was a little humiliating. She felt herself becoming vulgarised. At the same time she found herself looking at men with a shrewder eye: an eye to marriage. Not that she felt any sudden interest in men, or attraction towards them. No. She was still neither interested nor attracted towards men vitally. But *marriage* that peculiar abstraction, had imposed a sort of spell on her. She thought that marriage, in the blank abstract, was the thing she ought to *do*. That *marriage* implied a man she also knew. She knew all the facts. But the man seemed a property of her own mind rather than a thing in himself, another thing (*480*).

How ironically right it is, in the light of her father's mystic vagueness, that marriage should impose a sort of "spell." The fusion of comedy and pathos is seen when the Princess is forced to write her age:

> The Princess looked just twenty-five. The freshness of her mouth, the hushed, delicate-complexioned virginity of her face gave her not a day more. Only a certain laconic look in her eyes was disconcerting. When she was *forced* to write her age, she put twenty-eight, making the figure *two* rather badly, so that it just avoided being a three (*482*).

By the peculiar quality of his irony—illustrated in this passage by the way the first two sentences play off against the last two—Lawrence manages to create a character who engages our sympathy and affection, paradoxically, even as she seems somewhat less than human.[3]

Our sense of her core of inhumanity becomes even more marked when the tale shifts to the Southwest and we watch the Princess' complex reaction to Romero. She is attracted by the spark of gentlemanly pride she sees in his eyes—a trait even Colin might have approved—and responds to his "subtle, insidious male kindliness" (*484*), but the oddness of her feeling—as Dr. Leavis tells us, "inevitably odd"[4]—is delicately *there:*

And at the same time, curiously, he gave her the feeling that death was not far from him. Perhaps he too was half in love with death. However that may be, the sense she had that death was not far from him made him "possible" to her (485).

It is only too true that in his rising interest in Dollie, Romero is half in love with the death [5] which is her incapacity for a whole, living relationship. It is precisely that incapacity, moreover, which gives power to the ambiguity of "possible," for the Princess' realization of what may be possible for her, is less than ours:

And yet his presence only put to flight in her the *idée fixe* of "marriage." For some reason, in her strange little brain, the idea of *marrying* him could not enter. Not for any definite reason. He was in himself a gentleman, and she had plenty of money for two. There was no actual obstacle. Nor was she conventional (485).

No, certainly not conventional, we know, but surely there is an obstacle, all the more potent because it is not actual, because it is based on pernicious, egoistic illusion: her inability to relate to another individual, as well as her father's notions of vulgarity.

Despite her reservations, the Princess obstinately presses for an expedition to see wild animals. Dr. Leavis is largely correct in saying that henceforth Lawrence drops the ironic tone which characterizes the first part of the tale.[6] While the tone shifts markedly, however, irony remains in a series of "dramatic connections" between the first and second sections. One such connection is illustrated in the phrases "fairy-like gentleness" and "she felt quite in the picture" in the following passage:

It was a little valley or shell from which the stream was gently poured into the lower rocks and trees of the canyon. Around her was a fairy-like gentleness, the delicate sere grass, the groves of delicate-stemmed aspens dropping their flakes of bright yellow. And the delicate, quick little stream threading through the wild, sere grass.

Here one might expect deer and fawns and wild things, as in a little paradise. Here she was to wait for Romero, and they were to have lunch.

She unfastened her saddle and pulled it to the ground with a crash, letting her horse wander with a long rope. How beautiful Tansy looked, sorrel, among the yellow leaves that lay like a patina on the sere ground. The Princess herself wore a fleecy sweater of a pale, sere buff, like the grass, and riding-breeches of a pure orange-tawny colour. She felt quite in the picture (*494*).

The last phrase of the passage ironically recalls:

> She looked as if she had stepped out of a picture. But no one, to her dying day, ever knew exactly the strange picture her father had framed her in and from which she never stepped (*476*).

Dollie is still very much "framed" in her father's "pictures"; her paradisal imaginings seem over-idyllic and illusory—note how the careful repetition of sentence structure in the second paragraph of the passage tends to enforce this feeling. Nature is neither "little" nor paradisal, and the only "wild things"—we feel the suggestion of almost patronizing neutrality—that appear are two tired-looking Indians attempting to hide the carcass of a dead deer. The Princess' sense of belonging to the scene, moreover, as well as her appreciation of Tansy, is entirely dependent on surface harmony; we are reminded of Rico's initial response to St. Mawr: "He'd be marvelous in a composition. That colour!" [7]

Still another such ironic connection occurs when Romero throws the Princess' pretty clothes into the pond, an action which recalls Colin Urquhart's words: "Let us take it [the legacy of Dollie's Boston grandfather], as we put on clothes, to cover ourselves from their aggressions" (*478*).

An even more basic irony is suggested by:

> He could not conquer her, however much he violated her. Because her spirit was hard and flawless as a diamond. But he could shatter her. This she knew. Much more, and she would be shattered (*508–9*).

The passage recalls: "As a small child, something crystallized in her character, making her clear and finished, and as impervious as crystal" (*476*).[8]

The suggestion of her inner hardness and clarity merges with the major lines of imagery that characterize the Princess: clear, cold, "un-animal" light, and solidity. We are told how her "inward coldness" irritates her American relations (476), and how "strange and *uncanny,* she seemed to understand things in a cold light perfectly, with all the flush of fire absent" (477). She is the "fairy from the North" (478).[9]

The opposed continuities of cold and heat refer ultimately back to:

> She was relieved when her father died, and at the same time it was as if everything had evaporated around her. She had lived in a sort of hot-house, in the aura of her father's madness. Suddenly the hot-house had been removed from around her, and she was in the raw, vast, vulgar, open air (480).[10]

The canyon to which she and Romero journey is decidedly "raw, vast," and being "animal" must in Colin's terms be "vulgar." It is characterized by dark freezing cold in conjunction with animal energy, characteristics which seem to fuse in the vivid description of the bob-cat (501) with its clear revelation of "the dread and repulsiveness of the wild." Paradisal imaginings vanish.

The increasing cold imposes both a physical and a psychic discomfort; a physical numbing, and a sense of loss of consciousness and self:

> She crouched in her dark cloak by the water, rinsing the saucepan, feeling the cold heavy above her, the shadow like a vast weight upon her, bowing her down. The sun was leaving the mountain-tops, departing, leaving her under profound shadow. Soon it would crush her down completely (501).

The Princess' dream recapitulates this fear. The cold destroys her illusions as it numbs her body, and she is left to choose between the icy centrality of her being, and salvation through another's warmth:

> She dreamed it was snowing, and the snow was falling on her through the roof, softly, softly, helplessly, and she was going to be buried alive. She was growing colder and colder, the snow was weighing down on her. The snow was going to absorb her. . . .
>
> What did she want? Oh, what did she want? She sat in bed and rocked herself woefully. She could hear the steady

breathing of the sleeping man. She was shivering with cold; her heart seemed as if it could not beat. She wanted warmth, protection, she wanted to be taken away from herself. And at the same time, perhaps more deeply than anything, she wanted to keep herself intact, intact, untouched, that no one should have any power over her, or rights to her. It was a wild necessity in her that no one, particularly no man, should have any rights or power over her, that no one and nothing should possess her (*503*).

The sentence, "What did she want?" is central to the tale. As Lawrence makes it clear, Dollie does not know what she wants, and Romero's passion hardly clarifies her thoughts:

She had never, never wanted to be given over to this. But she had *willed* that it should happen to her. And according to her will, she lay and let it happen. But she never wanted it. She never wanted to be thus assailed and handled, and mauled. She wanted to keep herself to herself (*504*).

Her confusion is the result of the conflict between the obstinate will of a life based on illusory consciousness—we are reminded of Hermione Roddice—and the promptings of a realer and deeper self, of a layer beneath her father's "demon": "in some peculiar way, he had got hold of her, some unrealised part of her which she never wished to realise" (*509*).

With the dawn, consciousness returns:

She sat up suddenly.
"I want a fire," she said.
He glanced at the chinks of light. His brown face hardened to the day.
"All right," he said. "I'll make it" (*504*).

The irony of her request is emphasized by the way Romero responds to the daylight; sunlight makes his animal warmth less necessary to her, and the Princess turns on him.

The fusion of irony and symbolism the passage presents is characteristic of Lawrence's technique in the tale. Symbol and irony function so well together in "The Princess" because Lawrence has made every section of the tale reflect its basic issues. The great Rockies are not Colin Urquhart's world, but Lawrence

has made the striking natural descriptions express the irresolu-
tion and nervousness that are Dollie's legacy and has, in effect,
translated the ironic opposition of the earlier pages into a symbolic statement of the tense contradictions Colin represents.

The following passage illustrates the way in which the tone
and imagery convey this tension:

> The sun was already on the desert as they set off towards the
> mountains, making the greasewood and the sage pale as pale-
> grey sands, luminous the great level around them. To the right
> glinted the shadows of the adobe pueblo, flat and almost in-
> visible on the plain, earth of its earth. Behind lay the ranch and
> the tufts of tall, plumy cottonwoods, whose summits were
> yellowing under the perfect blue sky.
>
> Autumn breaking into colour in the great spaces of the
> South-West.
>
> But the three trotted gently along the trail, towards the sun
> that sparkled yellow just above the dark bulk of the ponderous
> mountains. Side-slopes were already gleaming yellow, flam-
> ing with a second light, under coldish blue of the pale sky. The
> front slopes were in shadow, with submerged lustre of red
> oak scrub and dull-gold aspens, blue-black pines and grey-
> blue rock. While the canyon was full of a deep blueness.
>
> They rode single file, Romero first, on a black horse. Him-
> self in black, made a flickering black spot in the delicate pallor
> of the great landscape, where even pine trees at a distance take
> a film of blue paler than their green. . . .
>
> They neared the pale, round foot-hills, dotted with the round
> dark pinnon and cedar shrubs. The horses clinked and trotted
> among the stones. Occasionally a big round greasewood held
> out fleecy tufts of flowers, pure gold. They wound into blue
> shadow, then up a steep stony slope, with the world lying
> pallid away behind and below. . . .
>
> . . . high up, away in heaven, the mountain heights shone
> yellow, dappled with dark spruce firs, clear almost as speckled
> daffodils against the pale turquoise blue lying high and serene
> above the dark-blue shadow where the Princess was. And she
> would snatch at the blood-red leaves of the oak as her horse
> crossed a more open slope, not knowing what she felt
> (489–90).

What is characteristic about the passage is conveyed by the words "flickering," "dappled," "speckled"; the sense of "darkness visible" we have throughout the journey through the constant mingling or opposition of light and dark, with an attendant sense of breakdown or vagueness of form, the calling into question of solidity. It is the mood inspired by "pale," "submerged lustre," and "dull gold," or in "The near great slopes were mottled with the gold and dark hue of spruce, like some unsinged eagle . . ." (*493*); or in a phrase like "half-burnished immensity" (*497*); or in a passage like:

> They rode down a bank and into a valley grove dense with aspens. Winding through the thin, crowding, pale-smooth stems, the sun shone flickering beyond them, and the disc-like aspen leaves, waving queer mechanical signals, seemed to be splashing the gold light before her eyes. She rode on in a splashing dazzle of gold.
> Then they entered shadows and the dark resinous spruce trees. The fierce boughs always wanted to sweep her off her horse. She had to twist and squirm past (*499*).

Brief quotation cannot do justice to the subtlety and range of Lawrence's devices in achieving this mood. We may point to the frequency of present participles, the vital activity of the words associated with the things of nature, the pattern of ascent and descent in the journey, all enforcing a sense of jitteriness and nervousness in the landscape itself.

The peculiar quality of "The Princess" passages will emerge more clearly if we compare them with some passages from the superb Southwest descriptions in "St. Mawr":

> It was Autumn, and the loveliest time in the south-west, where there is no spring, snow blowing into the hot lap of summer; and no real summer, hail falling in thick ice from the thunderstorms: and even no very definite winter, hot sun melting the snow and giving an impression of spring at any time. But autumn there is, when the winds of the desert are almost still, and the mountains fume no clouds. But morning comes cold and delicate, upon the wild sun-flowers and the puffing, yellow-flowered greasewood. For the desert blooms in autumn. In spring it is grey ash all the time, and only the strong breath of

the summer sun, and the heavy splashing of thunder rain succeeds at last, by September, in blowing it into soft puffy yellow fire.

It was such a delicate morning when Lou drove out with Phoenix towards the mountains to look at this ranch that a Mexican wanted to sell. For the brief moment the high mountains had lost their snow: it would be back again in a fortnight: and stood dim and delicate with autumn haze. The desert stretched away pale, as pale as the sky, but silvery and sere, with hummock-mounds of shadow, and long wings of shadow, like the reflection of some great bird. The same eagle shadows came like rude paintings of the outstretched bird, upon the mountains, where the aspens were turning yellow. For the moment, the brief moment, the great desert-and-mountain landscape had lost its certain cruelty, and looked tender, dreamy. And many, many birds were flickering around (*The Short Novels,* pp. *123–24*).

She watched the desert with its tufts of yellow greasewood go lurching past: she saw the fallen apples on the ground in the orchards near the adobe cottages: she looked down into the deep arroyo, and at the stream they forded in the car, and at the mountains blocking up the sky ahead, all with indifference. High on the mountains was snow: lower, blue-grey livid rock: and below the livid rock the aspens were expiring their daffodil yellow this year, and the oak-scrub was dark and reddish, like gore. She saw it all with a sort of stony indifference (*The Short Novels,* pp. *142–43*).

In the passages from "St. Mawr," we were impressed by the steadiness of form and light the description imposes; the tone somehow seems firmer, objects harder and more tactile; the participles in the first "St. Mawr" passage do not have the same kind of energy, for they are "placed" in a tight rhetorical pattern imposing a sense of predictable cycle rather than surprise. Shadowiness and dimness are not the delicate things they tend to be in "The Princess," but are like "hummock-mounds," "and rude paintings," very definite and sharp. We lack the nervous tension which the opposition of light and dark imposes in the tale, a tension which is artistically "right," for it reflects the opposition in the Princess herself between her realized and un-realized being, which in turn relates to the opposition on which the astringent irony of the first section is based: the conflict of illusory self-hood (with its relation to "consciousness") and the demands of organic wholeness (with its relation to the uncon-scious).

In speaking of the irony of "The Princess," then, we must realize that it functions not only in terms of the tone with which the tale begins, but also in the symbolic translation of the opposi-tion underlying that tone, the use of ironic links between the two sections, and, finally, in the very contrast of scene and tone between the two sections, a contrast related to the basic opposi-tion of the "hot-house aura" of Colin Urquhart and the "raw, vast, vulgar open air."

The two worlds fuse with powerful irony in the final scene of the tale. After shooting Romero, the Ranger approaches Dollie (we recall the policeman in "The Virgin and the Gypsy"):

> "Hello!" he said, coming towards the hut. And he took his hat off. Oh, the sense of ridicule she felt! Though he did not mean any.
>
> But she could not speak, no matter what she felt.
>
> "What'd this man start firing for?" he asked.
>
> She fumbled for words with numb lips.
>
> "He had gone out of his mind!" she said, with solemn stam-mering conviction.
>
> "Good Lord! You mean to say he'd gone out of his mind? Whew! That's pretty awful. That explains it then. H'm."
>
> He accepted the explanation without more ado.
>
> With some difficulty they succeeded in getting the Princess down to the ranch. But she, too, was not a little mad.
>
> "I'm not quite sure where I am," she said to Mrs. Wilkieson, as she lay in bed. "Do you mind explaining?"
>
> Mrs. Wilkieson explained tactfully.
>
> "Oh yes!" said the Princess. "I remember. And I had an accident in the mountains, didn't I? Didn't we meet a man who'd gone mad, and who shot my horse from under me?"
>
> "Yes, you met a man who had gone out of his mind."
>
> The real affair was hushed up. The Princess departed east

in a fortnight's time, in Miss Cummins's care. Apparently she recovered herself entirely. She was the Princess, and a virgin intact.

But her bobbed hair was grey at the temples, and her eyes were a little mad. She was slightly crazy.

"Since my accident in the mountains, when a man went mad and shot my horse from under me, and my guide had to shoot him dead, I have never felt quite myself."

So she put it.

Later she married an elderly man, and seemed pleased (*Complete Short Stories,* pp. *511–12*).

The rightness and subtlety of detail in this final scene is most impressive: one need only point to the ironic sting of Dollie's sense of ridicule at the Ranger's politeness—her sense of "elevation," we note, has suffered; or to those familiar words "a little mad," or "a virgin intact," or to the apt ambiguity of a word like "affair." [11]

It is also apt that her lips are "numb," for Lawrence has used the word several times previously: there is the incident of the near-frozen chipmunks:

The night had been cold. There was ice at the edges of the irrigation ditch, and the chipmunks crawled into the sun and lay with wide, dumb, anxious eyes, almost too numb to run (*488*).

The Princess' own condition on the journey is not very different: "But with the height, the cold, the wind, her brain was numb" (*498*). We know the icy "cold" and illusion have triumphed, and madness, the destruction of the essential self, seems almost inevitable. We can now feel the irony of the earlier remark: "She realised an implacability of hatred in their turning on her. But she did not lose her head. She quietly paid out money and turned away" (*477*).

Her "turning away" at the conclusion—to the kind of man with whom her desired "abstract" marriage would be possible—is more decisive, and how appropriate it is that she *"seemed* pleased." In these last lines, we have something of a return to the initial tone—reminiscent of Colin—which, combined with the fragmentary, sharply monosyllabic quality of the sentence structure, makes the final scene a superb evocation of the madness it describes. The passage also has the effect of framing the journey and disengaging us from the central violence, even as it emphasizes the meaning of that violence. It also demonstrates the superb use of irony we find throughout the tale, an irony so fluid that it allows "The Princess" both great subtlety and remarkable clarity of contour and structure, a tonality so artfully poised that our emotional response to the characters and the plot is always what Lawrence wishes it to be. It is precisely the "telling," the mastery and subtlety of nuance that makes the tale such a unique experience, and so thoroughly Lawrence's.

NOTES

[1] References to "The Princess" are to page numbers in D. H. Lawrence, *The Complete Short Stories,* Vol. 2, in The Phoenix Edition (London, 1955).

[2] It would be incorrect to argue that Lawrence's objections to Colin are based on a rejection of the notion of individual "specialness"; his work repeatedly proclaims the uniqueness of the individual and each person's obligation to discover and be himself. Colin's discovery of self is a false one, however, based upon an evasion rather than a meeting of reality. His attempt, moreover, to mold Dollie's character in terms of his own illusions rather than let her discover her own true selfhood— her own special demon—represents the type of challenge to individualism by "preconception" and "conscious mentality" that Lawrence despised and attacked in most of his work; *e.g.,* Lady Beveridge's prepossessing ideals in "The Ladybird."

[3] Cf. F. R. Leavis, *D. H. Lawrence, Novelist* (London, 1955), p. 271, where, I am pleased to say, a similar point is suggested: "But, though she may not be fully human, we are made to realize fully that she is a human case."

[4] *Ibid.*

[5] The Keatsian echo imposes a complexity of response based on the thematic similarity of the "Code" and "The Princess": the incompleteness and "peril" contingent upon a commitment to illusion; although the quiet expiration that the poet longs for is scarcely the violent end which is Romero's fate.

[6] Leavis, *op. cit.,* p. 272.

[7] D. H. Lawrence, *The Short Novels,* Vol. 2, p. 16, in The Phoenix Edition.

[8] One could cite many more examples of such "connections": the irony of the phrase *"noblesse oblige"* (in Colin's demon speech) in light of Dollie's fatal rudeness to Romero; and there is Colin's remark: "I could kill any man or woman who is rude to me" *(478)*; and there is "she was . . . like a flower that has blossomed in a shadowy place" *(479)* which, in the light of the "apple-blossom" complexion, and the shadowiness of the canyon, has its impact; *etc.* Consider also Dollie's preference for cloaks over more conventional attire (see passage quoted above, p. 476). We later find that she takes a cloak along with her on

the excursion, wraps herself in it in the cabin, and that it is the only article of her clothing which Romero does not throw into the pond, and in its way seems to suggest the layer of illusion which surrounds her essential being.

[9] Dollie seems to be a distant counterpart of the "arctic" Gerald Crich with whom we associate cold, clear light in contrast to the warm, dark lambency of Birkin.

[10] Note the unquestionable rightness of the word "aura" in the passage.

[11] One hesitates to make trusty old Tansy into a symbol but the ironic charge of the Princess's hallucination would seem to indicate some sort of symbolic reading. The incidents of the tale suggest—and our recollection of "St. Mawr" supports the suggestion—that the horse represents Dollie's own unrealized animal "wildness" and femininity. This interpretation seems to work for the closing scene and to give significance to Romero's throwing her saddle into the pond, to the passage about the "fierce boughs" trying to unseat her and to the remark that Tansy had "the usual mare's failing. She was inclined to be hysterical" (*485*).

Jascha Kessler

DESCENT IN DARKNESS:
THE MYTH OF *THE PLUMED SERPENT*

IN HIS later years, D. H. Lawrence explicitly devoted most of his work to what has been perhaps the most popular of the literary cults of our century, mythology. He was in a sense naturally a writer of myths, as is indicated, for example, by his methodical depersonalization of "character," from *The Rainbow* onward.

Though the myths we have received from various primitive or ancient cultures and the myths contrived by contemporary artists are often quite incongruous in weight and significance, *The Plumed Serpent* is a most curious case; for Lawrence, who believed he had contrived for the modern man a myth of politics and revolution and religious revelation, actually wrote what may be regarded as a cultural myth because of its typically ancient form and symbolism. Quite consciously, Lawrence's chief character, Don Ramón Carrasco, plots, leads, and brings to fruition a revolt in Mexico that is based on a religious myth and acted out as a political myth; this is not only what the book seems to be mostly about, but Lawrence himself, at least for a short while after the novel was published, seems to have believed that its myth could be as real as life itself and not just a symbolic story. (And how prophetic he was!) Yet there is another myth in *The Plumed Serpent* of which Lawrence seems not to have been conscious, so absorbed was his attention by the manifest political-

Jascha Kessler, who teaches at Hamilton College, is the author of essays on Meredith and other writers in various literary journals and of fifty poems published in American, English, and Canadian magazines; his poetry won a Hopwood Award at Michigan in 1952, and he was a Fellow in Writing at Yaddo (1958), where he wrote a novella, a play, and a libretto for an opera.

religious myth he was composing. My purpose here is to explicate
what is truly mythical in *The Plumed Serpent*.

> Kate woke up one morning, aged forty. . . . To be forty!
> One had to cross a dividing line. On this side there was youth
> and spontaneity and "happiness" (*44*).[1]

Also:

> No, she no longer wanted love, excitement, and something to
> fill her life. She was forty, and in the rare, lingering dawn of
> maturity, the flower of her soul was opening. Above all things,
> she must preserve herself from worldly contact. Only she
> wanted the silence of other unfolded souls around her, like a
> perfume (*55*).

Here, in "Fortieth Birthday," the third chapter of *The Plumed
Serpent,* the tale of Kate Leslie's descent into the heart of herself begins. Her *waking up* at forty marks her venture into the
darkness where all our aspirations wait, ready to burst forth
from their inchoate origin and source. She is strongly impelled:
having known all that her society offers womanhood, she has lost
interest in the dull round of daily repetitions. In this chapter
we are informed that she has been married twice and has seen
her two children, a boy and a girl, grow up; that she divorced
her first husband (the father of these children) to marry James
Joachim Leslie, an idealist, a social philosopher, an agitator
in the cause of the new mass democracy; and that Leslie has
recently died—consumed, so Lawrence hints, by his fervid idealism for the welfare of the modern masses. Although Kate passionately desired children from him, Leslie was infertile. Now,
because she has already completed her life, she is prepared for
any challenge, and free to start anew. And so, she suddenly finds
herself in Mexico, her feelings oppressed by its "spirit of place":

> Superficially, Mexico might be all right: with its suburbs of
> villas, its central fine streets, its thousands of motor-cars, its
> tennis and its bridge parties. The sun shone brilliantly every
> day, and big bright flowers stood out from the trees. It was a
> holiday.
>   Until you were alone with it. And then the undertone was
> like the low, angry, snarling purring of some jaguar spotted

with night. There was a ponderous, down-pressing weight upon the spirit: the great folds of the dragon of the Aztecs, the dragon of the Toltecs winding around one and weighing down the soul. And on the bright sunshine was a dark stream of an angry, impotent blood, and the flowers seemed to have their roots in spilt blood. The spirit of place was cruel, down dragging, destructive *(44–45)*.

Why was she there? She had come to the land which, as Lawrence conceives it in this novel, had once worshipped death and sustained life by constant and incomprehensibly wanton and murderous human sacrifice. She herself had come to retire and die; in a sense she was already dead, because what her society called life had lost any meaning for her. But now, on the morning of her fortieth birthday, she realizes, *consciously,* that "she was no longer in love with life" *(54)*, and that to escape her barren ennui she must die to the old self which cannot hold her anymore. "The thing called 'Life' is just a mistake we have made in our minds. Why persist in the mistake any further?" *(55)*. That Kate has reached such a depth of despair is the sign that the stage has been set for her removal from the modern capital of Mexico City which teems with our degenerate life.

In the first chapter, Kate has gone to a bullfight with two American friends who, though they are against this murderous sport "on principle," must have all the "thrills" life offers; they are, in Lawrence's language, two American carrion birds.[2] She leaves, nauseated, after witnessing the disembowelment of two hacks ridden by the picadors. It starts to rain; and she finds herself assisted to a car by one General Don Cipriano Viedma, her future god-man-mate, who appears out of the crowd at the gates.[3] Even though we recognize from the tone of the writing in this chapter that Lawrence is expressing his (editorialized) disgust with bullfighting, the chapter also stands as an efficient symbol of the wanton brutality and of the kind of publicly ritualistic death suitable to a debased Mexico. Kate's immediate loathing for what she considers murderous bestiality presages similar spontaneous reactions against what she is fated to suffer throughout the novel as the otherness of Mexico is gradually pressed upon her with ever-increasing force, and despite her flight from the carnage of the bullring, she will find herself, as she remains in the country, yielding and assenting, unaccountably, to much worse.

The second chapter, "Tea-Party in Tlacolula," presents the hebetude of her alternatives, the death within her and the death without. At the home of a lady archaeologist,[4] she meets with the idle chatter of the European and American time-killers for whom, at forty, she has no more time. She finds herself terribly bored by the rude, arrogant Midwestern *gringos,* Judge Burlap and his prying wife with her "silly social baby-face" *(41)*. But there she also meets, to her surprise, Cipriano, who has brought along his mentor, Don Ramón Carrasco. In Kate's revulsion from her own kind, she is rescued by these two. Indeed, Lawrence loses no time in setting up the final outcome of her incipient relationship with Cipriano:

> She could feel feel in him a sort of yearning towards her. As if a sort of appeal came to her from him, from his physical heart in his breast. As if the very heart gave out dark rays of seeking and yearning. She glimpsed this now for the first time, quite apart from the talking, and it made her shy *(35)*.

The two peculiar men talk of the questions facing revolutionary Mexico, and through their conversation we learn what the political-cum-religious (or vice versa) theme of the book is to be: they believe that Mexico can meet the future only by means of some kind of projection of its psyche.[5] Kate learns more of their scheme as (in Chapter III) she ponders her plight, marooned and inert, in this land of death. She comes across an article in the newspaper, oddly entitled "The Gods of Antiquity Return to Mexico." It relates how, at the little village of Sayula, a golden-bodied, dark-bearded figure stalked from the lake and took some clothing from peasant women washing on the shore. He called himself a messenger of the newly reborn god, Quetzalcoatl. It turns out, furthermore, that Don Ramón's hacienda is nearby. So, Kate simply decides to go there. Her desire is irresistible because she feels "that Don Ramón and Don Cipriano both had heard the soundless call, across all the hideous choking" *(55)* of the death rattle in contemporary Mexico.

At this point, it would be well to pause in order to see the direction in which the opening events of the novel are so surely moving. These trivial incidents can be observed to conform to the pattern of the great myths of mankind.[6] Most primitive and ancient societies devised certain ceremonies for the natural (i.e., biological-psychological) crises in the life of the individual, and these "rites of passage" have certain ritual myths attached to them. The myths are based on a simple formula: *separation— initiation—return,* as Joseph Campbell outlines it.

> A hero ventures forth from the world of common day into a region of supernatural wonder: fabulous forces are there encountered and a decisive victory is won: the hero comes back from this mysterious adventure with the power to bestow boons on his fellow man.[7]

Kate's story in *The Plumed Serpent* comprises only the first two parts of this formula: *separation* and *initiation*. It is not within the scope of my discussion to explain why this is so, but it may be suggested that the third part, the symbolic *return* of the hero, is to be found in a later book of Lawrence's, *The Escaped Cock,* where the awakened Jesus, called "the man," evades his disciples, only to be captured by a virginal priestess of Isis. This girl sees the dismembered Osiris in him, and she gives herself to him in a sacred union so that through him she may receive the power to renew the dying pagan civilization (represented by her mother, a woman interested only in managing vast slave-worked estates). In this fable, the "boon" that "the man" is enabled to give the world by virtue of his return from death is his recognition of the meaning of life, symbolized by Lawrence as a sacred orgasm. For Kate Leslie, however, there is only the going down to the depths, where she comes to rest, finally *and forever,* at the source of all power. I shall trace the events of *The Plumed Serpent,* in what follows, by subsuming them under the various stations of the mythic hero's journey.

The first stage is the *call to adventure,* already summarized as it occurred in the first three chapters. The call "signifies that destiny has summoned the hero and transferred his spiritual center of gravity from within the pale of his society to a zone unknown." This zone is a "fateful region . . . always a place of strangely fluid and polymorphous beings, unimaginable torments, superhuman deeds, and impossible delight." [8] Mexico is so alien to whatever Kate has previously known that she feels anything can happen there. The inhabitants she discovers on her journey are uncreated beings, uncreated (in Lawrence's terms) in the sense of what the industrialized West imagines to be humanity. Therefore, at forty years of age, she hears the call and goes to rent a little house at Sayula.

After the call to adventure, the hero crosses *the first threshold,* where he finds himself in a peculiar region. The crossing of the threshold is usually denoted by a trip across water, Styx perhaps, or the waters of death which Gilgamesh, King of Erech, was ferried over in the Babylonian epic; [9] sometimes the threshold is depicted by womb or rebirth imagery, as in the Biblical tale of Jonah's stay in the whale's belly; but no matter what the special imagery may be, this crossing marks a dying to the old self and figures the promise of rebirth. Lawrence, in one subtly evocative scene, combines the ferrying which separates the old ego from its familiar environs with symbols of rebirth. Kate arrives at Ixtla-huacan, from whence she is to embark upon the Lake of Sayula, at the other end of which lies Sayula village. Significantly, from among the clamoring Indians she chooses a boatman who is crip-pled. His infirmity reveals him (to us, not to Kate) as her Charon. The landscape is strange and uncanny.

> Earth, air, water were all silent with new light, the last blue of night dissolving like a breath. No sound, even no life. The great light was stronger than life itself (*86*).

No sooner have they set their little craft sailing off upon the waters than they are stopped by a swimming Indian who demands a gift from them, some money perhaps, declaring that the lake belongs to "the old gods of Mexico," and that he is "Quetzal-coatl's man" (*87*). This challenge by the messenger of the god confirms our guess that she is now in the special region of her mythic mission (though, again, it does not cross Kate's mind so clearly). Kate says to her boatman, " 'And you? are you one too?' 'Who knows!' said the man, putting his head on one side. Then he added: 'I think so, We are many!' " (*88*).

Throughout this chapter the waters of the lake are curiously described; it is, for instance, "frail-rippling, sperm-like" (*89*); furthermore, the natives who live by it seem unearthly: they reveal

> a strange and mysterious gentleness between a Scylla and Charybdis of violence; the small, poised, perfect body of the

bird that waves wings of thunder and wings of fire and night, in its flight. . . . The mystery of the evening-star brilliant in silence and distance between the downward surging plunge of the sun and the vast, hollow seething of inpouring night. The magnificence of the watchful morning-star, that watches between the night and the day, the gleaming clue to two opposites (*90*).

All this Kate senses in one swift, deep intuition of the Indians and of the landscape "flashing its quiet between the energies of the cosmos" (*92*). When she disembarks, the boatman reaches casually into the shallow water and brings up a little earthenware pot, "ollita," which was originally an Aztec offering to their gods, and gives it to her as the sign of an unspoken understanding.

Once arrived at midpoint, she is disturbed to feel herself on such forbidding ground. She looks from her hotel window out at "the eternal tremble of pale-earth, unreal waters," "filmy water that was hardly like water at all," "the great lymphatic expanse of water, like a sea, trembling, trembling, trembling to a far distance, to the mountains of substantial nothingness" (*93*). She hears frightening stories of lawless massacre and robbery in the vicinity. About to give up the trip and return, perhaps all the way to Europe, she determines—on an impulse—to go all the way down the lake to Sayula and rent her house. On this next leg of her little trip, she suddenly realizes that all the human beings she has ever known, including the pair of Mexicans who are her companions in the hotel's motorboat, were never truly alive.

She . . . realized, for the first time, with finality and fatality, what was the illusion she laboured under. She had thought that each individual has a complete self, a complete soul, an accomplished I. And now, she realized as plainly as if she had turned into a new being, that this was not so. Men and women had incomplete selves, made up of bits assembled together loosely and somewhat haphazard. Man was not created ready-made. Men, today, were half-made, women were half-made. Creatures that existed and functioned with certain regularity, but which ran off into a hopeless jumble of inconsequence (*103*).

Now the object of her quest becomes clear to her: she is seeking *wholeness of being*.[10] Kate's first self-conscious commitment to the search for wholeness takes place upon this spectral Mexican lake which is also, as events are to show, the center from which Mexico's spiritual regeneration is beginning to emanate.

> So in her soul she cried aloud to the greater mystery, the higher power that hovered in the interstices of the hot air, rich and potent. It was as if she could lift her hands and clutch the silent stormless potency that roved everywhere, waiting. "Come then!" she said, drawing a long slow breath, and addressing the silent life-breath which hung unrevealed in the atmosphere, waiting.
>
> And as the boat ran on, and her fingers rustled in the warm water of the lake, she felt the fulness of the ripe grapes. And she thought to herself: "Ah, how wrong I have been, not to turn sooner to the other presence, not to take the life-breath sooner . . ." (*104*).

She shares her lunch with the two "semi-barbarous" boatmen, thinking, "They can receive the gift of grace, and we can share it like a communion, they and I. I am very glad to be here. It is so much better than love: the love I knew with Joachim" (*104–5*). That she should make such a comment on her dead husband, and so casually as it were, by comparing him with the two unfamiliar peons eating her oranges and sandwiches, exposes the mythical character of her action; this notion of hers is especially strange when the reader recalls that Lawrence had remarked previously about Joachim Leslie that "she had loved [him] as much as woman can love a man; that is, to the bounds of human love" (*54*). The explanation is that she is now far outside the bounds of humanity.

Once settled in her house at Sayula with an Indian woman named Juana as her cook, maid, and the scourge of her patience, the second great phase of Kate's descent opens: *initiation*. This is her *road of trials,* "a favorite phase of the myth-adventure" which "has produced a world literature of miraculous tests and ordeals." [11] On this road, Kate will suffer constant annoyance from her servant, a malicious, tricksy witch, who is moreover obviously her *double!*

Juana was a woman of about forty, rather short, with a full dark face, centreless dark eyes, untidy hair, and a limping way of walking.

Juana was going to be a bit of a trial. She was a widow of doubtful antecedents, a creature with passion, but not much control, strong with a certain indifference and looseness.

There was a bit of a battle to be fought between the two women (*107*).[12]

Myths usually provide a ubiquitous helper for the hero on his quest, and when he is en route he is "covertly aided" by this person with "advice, amulets and secret agents." [13] And, in fact, Juana, as Kate's intimate, becomes her source of news and gossip in this alien country; and, Juana, who is also a prototype of the region's inhabitants, acts as her guide through their midst while at the same time shielding her from them. By her reluctance to talk of the doings of the Quetzalcoatl men in Sayula, Juana also arouses Kate's curiosity.

One Saturday Kate goes shopping with her. In the plaza she hears a rather longish sermon which is accompanied by the music of flute and drum. It turns out to be both an exequy on the death of Jesus and of his retinue of godling saints, and an annunciation of the rebirth of the Aztec gods. Then a dance begins: the Indian women take their partners from the silent crowd of stolid men, and before long Juana draws Kate herself into the circle.

"Come, Niña, come!" said Juana, looking up at Kate with black, gleaming eyes.

"I am afraid!" said Kate, and she spoke the truth.

The voice of the criada [Juana] had sunk to the low crooning, almost magic appeal of the women of the people, and her black eyes glistened strangely, watching Kate's face. Kate, almost mesmerized, took slow, reluctant steps forward, towards the man who was standing with averted face.

His hand, warm and dark and savagely suave, loosely, almost with indifference, and yet with the soft barbaric nearness, held her fingers, and he led her to the circle. She dropped her head, and longed to be able to veil her face. In her white dress and green straw hat, she felt a virgin again, a young virgin. This was the quality these men had been able to give back to her (*127*).

These men renew Kate's virginity, literally, because she is in a mythic realm: they are the shades of the mysteriously potent underworld of the unconscious; they are the insubstantial figures forever gliding out of the timelessly primitive heart, abstract in their instinctual quality. Had she been an old-time Puritan instead of the "Celtic Catholic Irishwoman" she was, she might well have seen it, as she joined the circling dancers, as young Goodman Brown in Hawthorne's tale saw it, not as a dancing of the dance of life-renewal in the Bacchic chorus, but as an act of the witch among heathen witches.[14] It depends, of course, on one's perspective. Lawrence's description of her first meeting with these demons of the soul's underworld is quite powerful.

> The outer wheel was all men. She seemed to feel the strange dark glow of them upon her back. Men, dark, collective men, non-individual. And herself, woman, wheeling upon the great wheel of womanhood.
>
> Men and women alike danced with faces lowered and expressionless, abstract, gone in the deep absorption of men into the greater manhood, women into the greater womanhood. It was sex, but the greater, not the lesser sex. The waters over the earth wheeling upon the waters under the earth, like an eagle silently wheeling above its own shadow.
>
> She felt her sex and her womanhood caught up and identified in the slowly revolving ocean of nascent life, the dark sky of the men lowering and wheeling above. She was not herself, she was gone, and her own desires were gone in the ocean of the great desire. As the man whose finger touched her hers was gone in the ocean that is male, stooping over the face of the waters (*128*).
>
> And as she sank into sleep, she could hear the drum again, like a pulse inside a stone beating (*129*).

Kate, in entering the dance, has suddenly come into communion with cosmic forces beating even in stones. In this line of what can only be called poetry, Lawrence has captured a religious idea of great significance; for, taking a Buddhist view of the immanence of soul in all things, he has united it with the Western idea which strives to realize itself in our transcience, while at the same time he has sought to negate the Eastern conclusion that peace comes only with escape into the eternal unity of *Atman* from the fractured multiplicity of material phenomena which spells death.[15]

Now that she is well on her way toward eventual initiation, Kate meets Don Ramón's wife, Carlota. Highly bred, cultured in the European way of life, Carlota is an excellent foil for Kate. Furthermore, whereas Kate has answered *the call,* Carlota refuses it.[16] The irony of her portraiture as Kate's foil comes from the fact that Carlota is a fanatically devout Roman Catholic. Instead of entering into some sort of harmony with her husband's mystical goals, she strives bitterly against him and turns his sons against him too; and, by opposing his vision that man and woman form a *Tao* by uniting in their sexes' rapport (in the greater sense) the masculine and feminine principles of the universe, she destroys the only basis for her being. Consequently, she soon dies, after same galling scenes of connubial struggle for mastery. Though she tries to have her way, Don Ramón, who has attained "detachment," is able to elude her Torquemada-like severity and go forward to his own apotheosis.

Lawrence leaves no possible doubt as to the reason why Carlota *must* die. On a Sunday morning, during the ceremony of the reconsecration of the church at Sayula to Quetzalcoatl, she rises from the crown of kneeling women to scream in protest:

> "No! No! It is not permitted!" shrieked the voice. "Lord! Lord! Lord Jesus! Holy Virgin! Prevent him! Prevent him!" (*341*).

Moaning prayers and imprecations, Carlota crawls toward the altar, where Ramón stands anointed, crowned and gowned in godhood's full panoply.

> Carlota crouched black at the altar steps and flung up the white hands and her white face in the frenzy of the old way.
> "Lord! Lord!" she cried, in a strange ecstatic voice that froze Kate's bowels with horror: "Jesus! Jesus! Jesus! Jesus! Jesus! Jesus!"
> Carlota strangled in her ecstasy. And all the while Ramón,

the living Quetzalcoatl, stood before the flickering altar with naked arm upraised, looking with dark, inalterable eyes down upon the woman.

Throes and convulsions tortured the body of Carlota. She gazed sightless upwards. Then came her voice, in the mysterious rhapsody of prayer:

"Lord! Lord! Forgive!

"God of love, forgive! He knows not what he does. Lord of the world, Christ of the cross, make an end. Have mercy on him, Father. Have pity on him!

"Oh, take his life from him now, now, that his soul may not die."

Her voice had gathered strength till it rang out metallic and terrible.

"Almighty God, take his life from him, and save his soul."

And in the silence after that cry her hands seemed to flicker in the air like flames of death.

"The Omnipotent," came the voice of Ramón, speaking quietly, as if to her, "is with me, and I serve Omnipotence!" (*341–42*).

And when Carlota is carried out of the temple, unconscious after her third convulsion on the altar steps, Kate does not follow, but lingers on the porch to hear the hymn of the "Living Quetzalcoatl." Later, she sits equably by in the death-room as her husband-to-be, Cipriano, curses the comatose (yet still raving) Carlota, who dies

at dawn, before her boys could arrive from Mexico; as a *canoa* was putting off from the shore with a little breeze, and the passengers were singing the Song of Welcome to Quetzalcoatl, unexpectedly, upon the pale water (*351*).

Ramón is quite unmoved by her death: " 'It is life,' he said, 'which is the mystery. Death is hardly mysterious in comparison' " (*350*).

Some hours before Carlota died, Kate had felt love's presence in the dark candle-lit room where Carlota's stertorous breath sounded and her "ghost's" voice mumbled. Kate sat on there after Cipriano's fury had spent itself upon the dying woman and, while they waited for her to pass away, "she felt for his hand."

> All was so dark. But oh, so deep, so deep and beyond her, the vast, soft, living heat! So beyond her!
>
> *Put sleep so black as beauty in the secret*
> *of my belly. Put star-oil over me.*
>
> She could almost feel her soul appealing to Cipriano for this sacrament (*349–50*).

Thus, in witnessing Carlota's haunted death, Kate has entered the last threshold, beyond which the secret mystery will be disclosed to her. She has seen and assented to the perishing of the last version of the former life of the European woman; she has assisted at its extinction, without sympathy, and has found herself desiring a new sacrament. She has passed her tests.

Previously, her greatest trial in this journey of initiation into the Plutonic realm had come when bandits (demons, one might as well say) attacked Jamiltepec, Don Ramón's hacienda. Father Tiverton, who calls *The Plumed Serpent* Lawrence's *"greatest* failure," [17] thinks of Chapter XIX, "The Attack on Jamiltepec," as a sensational, Western-type piece of action-writing, as something to make Zane Grey blush with envy. As a matter of fact, it is written out in sensationally savage detail, and every thrust of knives into throats, every writhing body and drop of streaming blood in the hand-to-hand combat is shocking (*294*). Since Father Tiverton is concerned in his study to interpret Lawrence as a kind of Existential Christian, he does not dwell upon the importance of this episode at the Citadel of Quetzalcoatl. In this mythic interpretation, however, its significance derives from the fact that Kate, who ran away from the bullfight, nauseated, has by this time been drawn to stand and fight (she shoots an Indian at point-blank range) with her new mentors against the savage demons of this land. All through *The Plumed Serpent* conflict is maintained in her mind because of her reluctance to surrender herself utterly to the primordial powers she has nevertheless elected to meet. In Lawrence's terms, the Western, nay Christian, effeteness which warped her away from the duality of life and death is slowly being dissolved. She is growing acclimated, so to speak. But it is not an easy thing for her to do; the habits and social beliefs of a lifetime, indeed the culture of Europe itself personified in her characterization, cannot be discarded in a moment merely by wishing or willing, for it is one thing to apprehend the worthlessness of one's way of life, quite another to relinquish it. The mythological voyage represents the hardships encountered once this effort to change has begun, and it gains its drama by presenting episodes which emphasize the hazards of losing the path through the maze. These episodes are the ordeals.[18]

Yet not all of Kate's ordeals originate from her journey into a land utterly foreign in its ways. She is pursued also by Cipriano, a demon lover who has leaped at her through some fatality of sexual magnetism. It is through him that she will find her ecstasies and momentary glimpses of the wonderful region, "the Pan-world," to use Lawrence's own phrase.[19] Perhaps the strongest substantiation of the mythical quality of Kate's acclimatization to the Mexican hell is the nature of her thought when she begins to know that she can see it through the eyes of its people. Though one may be rather sceptical of Lawrence's supposition that they themselves look at their world in the manner described below, one does recognize that at least Kate has grasped this vision for herself. One day, she is watching a lad pelt a bird tied by a string near the shore of the lake.

And sitting rocking . . . on her verandah, hearing the clap-clap of tortillas from the far end of the patio, the odd, metallic noises of birds, and feeling the clouds already assembling in the west, with a weight of unborn thunder upon them, she felt she could bear it no more: the vacuity, and the pressure: the horrible uncreate elementality, so uncouth, even sun and rain uncouth, uncouth.

And she wondered over the black vision in the eyes of that urchin. The curious void.

He could not see that the bird was a real living creature with a life of its own. This, his race had never seen. With black eyes they stared out on an elemental world, where the elements were monstrous and cruel, as the sun was monstrous, and the cold, crushing black water of the rain was monstrous, and the dry, dry, cruel earth.

And among the monstrosity of the elements flickered and towered other presences: terrible uncouth monsters of rich people, with powers like gods, but uncouth demonish gods. And uncouth things like birds that could fly and snakes that could crawl and fish that could swim and bite. An uncouth, monstrous universe of monsters big and little, in which man held his own by sheer resistance and guardedness, never, never going forth from his own darkness.

Walking forever through a menace of monsters, blind to the sympathy in things, holding one's own, and not giving in, nor going forth. Hence the lifted chests and the prancing walk. Hence the stiff insentient spines, the rich physique, and the heavy, dreary natures, heavy like the dark-grey mud-bricks, with a terrible, obstinate ponderosity and a dry sort of gloom (*218*).

Having been vouchsafed such a vision of the world she is really seeking (rather, the world she has found), it comes about quite naturally that she stay on to have Cipriano, the Indian general, woo her, to witness Carlota strangled by the proliferation of Ramón's hymns [20] and given her deathblow by the founding of the "Church of Quetzalcoatl"; Kate stays on through the assassins' ambush of the villa, through Ramón's assumption of incarnate godhood and Cipriano's investiture as the "Living Huitzilopochtli." She permits herself to be plighted in marriage with him by Ramón in an informal "religious ceremony" in the name of Quetzalcoatl (Chapter XX, "Marriage by Quetzalcoatl"), and finally crosses the last threshold of her quest. Though uneasy with Cipriano, she is quelled by "the black fume of power which he emitted, the dark, heavy vibration of his blood" (*308*). In the realm of reality, Lawrence's narrative would seem sheer, rank, foolish melodrama; but in this Mexican world, Kate is responding, really, not to persons but to *powers*.[21]

Just before the initiatory ceremony of her ritual troth, signalizing her induction into the final mystery, there is an astounding description of the physical and spiritual region she has reached at last. This is well worth reproducing at some length, because it is one of the key passages in the story of the novel as it is being traced here.

As they sat side by side in the motor-car, silent, swaying to the broken road, she could feel the curious tingling heat of his blood, and heavy power of the *will* that lay unemerged in his blood. She could see again the skies go dark, and the phallic mystery rearing itself like a whirling dark cloud, to the zenith, till it pierced the sombre, twilit zenith; the old, supreme phallic mystery. And herself in the everlasting twilight, a sky above where the sun ran smokily, an earth below where the trees and creatures rose up in blackness, and man strode alone naked, dark, half-visible, and suddenly whirled in supreme power, towering like a dark whirlwind column, whirling to pierce the very zenith.

The mystery of the primeval world! She could feel it now in all its shadowy, furious magnificence. She knew now what was the black, glinting look in Cipriano's eyes. She could understand marrying him, now. . . . Once you entered his mystery the scale of all things changed, and he became a living male power, undefined, and unconfined (*308*).

As he sat in silence, casting the old, twilit Pan-power over her, she felt herself submitting, succumbing. He was once more the old dominant male, shadowy, intangible, looming suddenly tall, and covering the sky, making a darkness that was himself and nothing but himself, the Pan male. And she was swooned prone beneath, perfect in her proneness.

He would never woo; she saw this. When the power of his blood rose in him, the dark aura streamed from him like a cloud pregnant with power, like thunder, and rose like a whirlwind that rises suddenly in the twilight and raises a great pliant column, swaying and leaning with power, clear between heaven and earth.

Ah! and what a mystery of prone submission, on her part this huge erection would imply! Submission absolute, like the earth under the sky. Beneath an over-arching absolute.

Ah! what a marriage! How terrible and how complete! With the finality of death, and yet more than death. The arms of the twilit Pan. And the awful, half-intelligible voice from the cloud.

She could conceive now her marriage with Cipriano; the supreme passivity, like the earth below the twilight, consummate in living lifelessness, the sheer solid mystery of passivity.

> Ah, what an abandon, what an abandon, what an abandon!
> —of so many things she wanted to abandon (*309*).[22]

Knowing where she is now, Kate does not revel when Cipriano, "the living Huitzilopochtli," takes it upon himself, after preliminary dressing-up and chanting of hymns, to pass judgment in front of the temple upon the peons who were part of the plot to assassinate Don Ramón. Drums throb in the little square thronged by peasants, and torches give the darkness a macabre illumination:

> The eyes of the three men were blindfolded with black cloths, their blouses and pantaloons were taken away. Cipriano took a bright, thin dagger.
> "The Lords of Life are Masters of Death," he said in a loud clear voice.
> And swift as lightning he stabbed the blindfolded men to the heart, with three swift, heavy stabs. Then he lifted the red dagger and threw it down.
> "The Lords of Life are Masters of Death," he repeated (*379*).[23]

Though Kate tries continually to resist the deathly ways of this Mexican Sheol, we remember the profound quiet that succeeded the carnage of the battle at Jamiltepec, when Don Ramón, lying wounded, asserted that she was indubitably one of them:

> "Good that he is dead. Good that he is dead. Good that we killed them both."
> He looked at her with that glint of savage recognition from afar.
> "Ugh! No! It's terrible!" she said shuddering.
> "Good for me that you were there! Good that we killed them both between us! Good they are dead!" (*295*).

After the executions in the public square, Kate reacts with her flurry of revulsion for the last time; she is "shocked and depressed" (*385*), yet she gives herself nevertheless to Cipriano, body and soul. And even during the last struggle with herself, "She knew that Ramón and Cipriano did deliberately what they did: they believed in their deeds, they acted with all their conscience. And as men, probably they were right" (*385*). Though she continues to argue with herself, questioning their "wills," she finally comes to the conclusion that men and women do not exist in their own right as individuals with selves, but that each lives only in the duality of male-female, life and death, "the morning-star," and that the idolatrized self, "even in the relation to the utmost God," is "still fragmentary and unblest" (*388*).[24]

With this realization, Kate has reached the final adventure preceding the mythic hero's return. In Chapter XXIV, "Malintzi," she is interrupted in her theological musing by Cipriano, who takes her off to the temple, there to become his goddess-mate. She gives her life simply into his pleading hands.

> "Malintzi," he said to her in Spanish, "Oh, come! Come and put on the green dress. I cannot be the living Huitzilopochtli, without a bride. I cannot be it, Malintzi!" (*389*).

In the temple Kate changes her dress.

> When she stepped out she found Cipriano naked and in his paint, before the statue of Huitzilopochtli, on a rug of jaguar skins (*390*).

Together they light the oil lamps and seat themselves, holding hands, side by side on their respective thrones. She has reached the climax of her adventure, "when all the barriers and ogres have been overcome." [25] As Campbell discusses it, this sort of achievement is usually

> represented as a mystical marriage . . . of the triumphant hero-soul with the Queen Goddess of the World. This is the crisis at the nadir, the zenith, or at the uttermost edge of the earth, at the central point of the cosmos, in the tabernacle of the temple, or within the darkness of the deepest chamber of the heart.[26]

Malintzi-Kate is at the center which is all, or almost all, of these places at once. And, at the center of her cosmos, Kate finds the fountain of youth, the secret of renewed life which is the boon the hero must bring back to the world.

After this, Lawrence winds up his novel rather hastily. "A kind of war" breaks out (*420*), but the combination of Ramón's religious inspiration with Cipriano's intensively trained and mobile shock troops sweeps away the feeble resistance of the government:

> The Archbishop was deported, no more priests were seen in the streets. Only the white and blue and earth-coloured serapes of Quetzalcoatl, and the scarlet and black of Huitzilopochtli, were seen among the crowds. There was a great sense of release, almost exuberance (*421*).

The life-giving waters of the World Navel have been released because the heroine has found her way to the beating core of existence where age and death are conquered in herself: she has been taken up to the abode of the gods, as Psyche was taken to Olympus to be united with Cupid forever. In short, Kate marries Cipriano "legally" (*421*).

> The mystical marriage with the queen goddess of the world represents the hero's total mastery of life; for the woman is life, the hero its knower and master. And the testings of the hero, which were preliminary to his ultimate experience and deed, were symbolical of those crises of realization by means of which his consciousness came to be amplified and made capable of enduring the full possession of the mother-destroyer, his inevitable bride.[27]

After her marriage, Kate decides to go back to Europe for a short while because her transformation is making her sick:

> For it was not her spirit alone which was changing, it was her body, and the constitution of her very blood. She could feel it, the terrible katabolism and metabolism in her blood, changing her even as a creature, changing her to another creature.
> And if it went too fast, she would die (*421*).

But at last, in her debate with the man-gods, not god-men now —for they are tired and unsure as they ride the crest of the new Mexican revolutionary wave—she wavers and renounces the last touch of proud, independent European womanhood's self-assertiveness.[28]

> "You don't want me to go, do you?" she pleaded.
> "*Yo! Yo!*"—his eyebrows lifted with queer mock surprise, and a little convulsion went through his body again. "*Te

quiero mucho! Mucho te quiero! Mucho! Mucho! I like you
very much! Very much!"

It sounded so soft, so soft-tongued, of the soft, wet, hot
blood, that she shivered a little.

"You won't let me go!" she said to him (*444*).

And the novel ends with these words. But it is the triumphant
outcome of Kate's quest for life, that is, her quest of perpetual
virginity (it comes to quite the same thing), which explains the
inconclusive nature of the novel on its realistic plane. According to the analysis that has been given here, everything in *The
Plumed Serpent,* all the politics and religious demagoguery, seems
irrelevant when we compare it with the drama of the hidden
primal mythic adventure it subserves.[29] I believe it is for this
reason, too, that criticism has been generally unfair to this book
for so many years. Critics have seized upon the superficial content of the novel and confused it with the story it is really
telling. On the other hand, they have not misled themselves
completely; they have, after all, followed Lawrence's own in-
dications. He himself more than half-believed that the stories
he was telling in his later works were mere scaffoldings for the
great social and religious truths he had to teach.

I hope this attempt to salvage his profoundly moving and
beautiful tale from the clumsy superstructure of the novel's manifest content is of some help in unraveling the dominant tone of
his later works. Kate's quest, reviewed as an adventure which
follows in minute detail the classic pattern of the world's great
myths, is fairly self-explanatory. And there is, in a deep sense,
nothing more in the novel than this story. It might just be noted
once more, however, that although Kate does not return from
the cosmic heart, Lawrence did write out the last part of this
mythic cycle, not as a pseudo-allegorical, or pseudo-realistic,
novel but as a simple tale. In *The Escaped Cock* the hero wakes
from "death" in a cave, and walks abroad, Lawrence-Jesus
full of the secret of life.

NOTES

[1] References are to page numbers in D. H. Lawrence, *The Plumed
Serpent* (New York: Alfred A. Knopf, 1951).

[2] The chapter is called "Beginnings of a Bullfight." The identity of
these two men in real life has been given as Witter Bynner and Willard

Johnson. Cf. Harry T. Moore, *The Intelligent Heart: The Story of D. H. Lawrence* (New York: Farrar, Straus, and Young, 1955), pp. 312ff.

[3] Though Don Cipriano is an Indian, Lawrence here recognizably describes himself; thus, when Cipriano says that he had known Kate's dead husband's brother at Oxford, we may be allowed to suspect that this brother (non-existent in the novel) is a shadowy alias for the sick and dying Richard Lovat Somers of Lawrence's previous novel, *Kangaroo.* This curious matter of 'symbolic hagiography' in Lawrence's later novels is discussed at some length elsewhere. Cf. Jascha F. Kessler, "Ashes of the Phoenix: A Study of Primitivism and Myth-Making in D. H. Lawrence's *The Plumed Serpent*" (Ann Arbor: University of Michigan, 1955), pp. 200–210 [dissertation on microfilm].

[4] William York Tindall makes much of this character, whom he identifies as Mrs. Zelia Nuttal, who was supposed to have supplied Lawrence with the names of the gods in *The Plumed Serpent.* Cf. William Y. Tindall, *D. H. Lawrence and Susan His Cow* (New York: Columbia University Press, 1939). But Moore states that Frieda Lawrence told him they had been to Mrs. Nuttal's for luncheon only three times at most (*The Intelligent Heart,* p. 312).

[5] They are driving at Lawrence's great program for universal spiritual rebirth (cf. Ch. III, *Ashes of the Phoenix*). In *Kangaroo,* the political problems of Western mass democracy were weighed more seriously, that is, in comprehensible terms, because Australia is settled by Europeans; but in Mexico, where there is an indigenous "primitive" population, Lawrence makes his issues somewhat ridiculous by much the same sort of joking as there was in the twenties about the Russian peasant's blunders with machinery of industrial technology. It is simply asserted in the conversation of Ramón that Red Indians and automobiles are forever immiscible, that technology will be forever alien to Mexican souls.

[6] Joseph Campbell, *The Hero with the Thousand Faces* (New York: Pantheon Books, 1949), pp. 3–96. Campbell uses a term he borrowed from James Joyce, and calls this universal pattern of the myth the "monomyth."

[7] *Ibid.,* p. 30. The first part of Campbell's book illustrates this formula with a collection from world-wide sources on the various levels of dream, fairy tale, and epic myth.

[8] *Ibid.,* p. 58.

[9] Cf. F. L. Lucas' translation: *Gilgamesh, King of Erech* (London: The Golden Cockerel Press, 1948).

[10] Campbell summarizes this goal of the mythic hero: "The effect of the successful adventure of the hero is the unlocking and release again of the flow of life into the body of the world. . . . The torrent pours from an invisible source, the point of entry being the center of the symbolic circle of the universe. . . . Beneath this spot is the earth-supporting head of the cosmic serpent, the dragon, symbolical of the waters of the abyss, which are the divine life-creative energy and substance of the demi-urge, the world generative aspect of immortal being. . . . The hero as the incarnation of God is himself the navel of the world, the umbilical point through which the energies of eternity break into time." *The Hero with the Thousand Faces,* pp. 40–41.

[11] Campbell, *op. cit.,* p. 97.

[12] Indeed, the reader may well suspect that Juana, except for racial coloring, is Kate herself.

[13] Campbell, *op. cit.,* p. 97.

[14] This matter of ritual choric dancing, of pagan cult and its transformation in Western Christianity (and Lawrence's translation of it back into paganism is relevant), is dealt with at great length by Jules Michelet, *Satanism and Witchcraft: A Study in Medieval Superstition* (New York: The Citadel Press, 1939). It still has survival in European custom; e.g., in Brittany, where it is called "The Jabadou," and danced at the nuptials of virgins. Cf. Anne de Tourville, *Wedding Dance* (New York: Farrar, Straus and Young, 1953).

[15] This interpretation gives Lawrence full benefit of the doubt. In my study, "Ashes of the Phoenix," I presented quite another case, one more in line with Lawrence's full statements of his own philosophy; cf. Ch. III, Pt. 2, pp. 71–110.

[16] Campbell, *op. cit.,* pp. 59–60: "The myths and folk tales of the whole world make clear that the refusal is essentially a refusal to give up what one takes to be one's own interest. The future is regarded not in terms of an unremitting series of deaths and births, but as though one's present system of ideals, virtues, goals, and advantages were to be fixed and made secure."

[17] Father William Tiverton, *D. H. Lawrence and Human Existence* (London: Rockliff, 1951), p. 71.

[18] "The ordeal is a deepening of the problem of the first threshold and the question is still in balance: Can the ego put itself to death? For manyheaded is this surrounding Hydra; one head cut off, two more appear—unless the right caustic is applied to the mutilated stump. The original departure into the land of trials represented only the beginning of the long and really perilous path of initiatory conquests and moments of illumination. Dragons have now to be slain and surprising barriers passed—again, again, and again. Meanwhile there will be a multitude of preliminary victories, unretainable ecstasies, and momentary glimpses of the wonderful land." Campbell, *op. cit.,* p. 109.

[19] Lawrence's treatment of the lovers, their passion at first sight, may seem worse than melodramatic, bathetic in the extreme, were it not saved, for him at least, by his belief in immortal, vital electric currents, dormant but never dead. If one thinks, in this regard, about the psychoanalytic theory of libidinal cathexes, his description can be given enough credence to sustain one's suspension of disbelief in his unusual statement of the undying powers of Eros and Ananke.

[20] Moore's discussion of the poems, or "hymns," which compares them to Nonconformist hymns, is of value; cf. *The Intelligent Heart,* pp. 315–16.

[21] Lawrence's hint is clear, for he says that Kate is disgusted by people to the limits of her being: "Till she flung herself down the last dark oubliette of death, she would never escape from her deep, her bottomless disgust with human beings. Brief contacts were all right, thrilling even. But close contacts, were short and long revulsions of violent disgust" (*250*).

[22] Also, on the same page, "It was the ancient phallic mystery, the ancient god-devil of the male Pan. Cipriano unyielding forever, in the ancient twilight, keeping the ancient twilight about him. . . . He had the old gift of demon-power."

[28] Quoted from Chapter XXIII, "Huitzilopochtli's Night."

[24] "Now, must she admit that the individual was an illusion and a falsification? There was no such animal." "The individual, like the perfect being, does not and cannot exist, in the vivid world. We are all fragments. And at the best, halves. The only thing is the Morning Star."

[25] Campbell, *op. cit.,* p. 109.

[26] For instance, Cipriano says to Kate: " 'Ramón says he will make the lake the centre of a new world. . . . We will be the gods of the lake.' " (*324*). One might add, to clarify any confusion of sexes in comparing Kate to the heroic soul of the questing male, that there is no need to say, explicitly, "heroine-soul"; for, after all, Lawrence is projecting his myth from his own life: he is at same time both Cipriano and Kate, and Kate, the Goddess of the World, is his creation whom he is marrying as Cipriano. Tindall remarks that in Lawrence's later work all the heroines, the "questing girls," become "the artist's deepest self in search of a subject and a place." Cf. Tindall's Introduction, *The Plumed Serpent,* p. vii.

[27] Campbell, *op. cit.,* pp. 120–21.

[28] *Ibid.,* pp. 193–96, a discussion of the mythic instances of the "Refusal of the Return," which is what has happened at the end of *The Plumed Serpent.* "Numerous indeed are the heroes fabled to have taken up residence forever in the blessed isle of the unchanging Goddess of Immortal Being" (p. 193).

[29] Although, as I have shown in "Ashes of the Phoenix," Lawrence's "religion" and politics, etc., are very significant stuff indeed: a study of it is essential for understanding the later Lawrence and modern intellectual history.

Harry T. Moore

LADY CHATTERLEY'S LOVER AS ROMANCE

At last a publisher in one of the English-speaking countries has dared to bring out the full text of our century's great romance, which has for too long been a smuggler's trophy.

In the novels of contemporary writers of a stature comparable to Lawrence's, love is usually treated shabbily, as something perverse, ironic, or merely annoying. But his *Lady Chatterley's Lover,* a book dealing with love as a serious, major, and sacred theme, was taboo over here and in his native England for the thirty-one years of its existence. Meanwhile, a mutilated edition that sold chiefly as a drugstore paperback had parodied what he really wrote; this emasculated version omits Lawrence's faithful descriptions of the love experience and his use of the four-letter words in a way which he believed was therapeutic. His own attempt to neutralize *Lady Chatterley's Lover,* at the suggestion of his publishers, had ended in a cry of "Impossible! I might as well try to clip my own nose into shape with scissors. The book bleeds."

After he began selling it by subscription, from Italy in 1928, the novel was pirated in America. Since then, the authorized editions printed in English on the Continent have supplied American tourists with a spicy bit of contraband to sneak past the customs. The underground reputation of this book, whose essential innocence should long ago have been quietly accepted, has given it an unfortunate emphasis—unfortunate because, unlike Joyce's *Ulysses,* whose own forbidden-fruit days gave it a lurid excitement for a time, *Lady Chatterley's Lover* is not

Harry T. Moore is a Professor of English at Southern Illinois University. Among other books, he has written two critical biographies of Lawrence and is now editing his collected letters. This essay on *Lady Chatterley's Lover* is reprinted by courtesy of the *New York Times Book Review.*

its author's masterpiece. Earlier Lawrence novels such as *The Rainbow* and *Women in Love,* produced at the summit of his writing power, stand out as far better books. Yet, though these novels have romantic ingredients, *Lady Chatterley's Lover* occupies a special place in the Lawrence canon because it is exclusively a romance.

We may now see clearly that it is the authentic descendant of *Madame Bovary* and *Anna Karenina.* But instead of leading his heroine to her doom, Lawrence shows her the way toward renewed and enriched life. Here, as in so much of his other work, he creates his own variant of the Sleeping Beauty myth, in which a woman in a trance-like state of unfulfillment is awakened by what might be called the Erotic Invader. In story after story ("The Fox," "The Ladybird" and "The Virgin and the Gipsy" are typical), the Erotic Invader breaks through the thorny hedge of an imprisoning relationship to release the dreaming woman or "lost girl."

Lady Chatterley, like so many of Lawrence's stories, is set mostly in the English Midlands. Once again, as the symbol of his antagonism to industrial civilization, he used the mines which blight the earth there and, in Lawrence's view, blighted human beings also. But in attacking industrial civilization and its mechanization of the living, which often took the form of the intellectualizing of natural impulses, Lawrence was not trying to destroy what he called "mind knowledge" but to bring it into balance with "blood knowledge" of the kind celebrated in *Lady Chatterley's Lover.* He made his position clear in his notable essays, "À Propos of *Lady Chatterley's Lover*" and "Pornography and Obscenity," as well as in letters such as the one quoted in Mark Schorer's illuminating introduction to the new American edition: "You mustn't think I advocate perpetual sex. Far from it. . . . But I want, with 'Lady C.,' to make an *adjustment in consciousness* to the basic physical realities."

In a different letter, Lawrence explained that as a young writer he had heard an older author say he would "welcome a description of the whole act," and that this had stayed in his mind until he wrote *Lady Chatterley.* Some critics have attacked this naturalistic impulse in the book because it tries to express what they think is the inexpressible. But after numerous readings others find (as I do) that Lawrence's endowments as an artist—his incandescent gifts as a prose writer, his command of cadences and verbal impressionism—did him more than yeoman service in expressing the very difficult.

He didn't limit himself to naturalism in *Lady Chatterley,* which has the therapeutic overtones mentioned earlier. At times, too, the writing has the quality of sacrament, though that is less apparent here than in many of Lawrence's other works. He once thought of calling this book "Tenderness"—and tenderness is the key to the story.

Only a reading of the book can reveal its power, its depth of complication, its psychological and social intricacy, all of which contribute to the effectiveness of the long, slow process which the gamekeeper and the lady of the manor go through in order to find enrichment in love. Without so full a development of the people and the situation, the love descriptions would be meaningless. So would the unleashing of the four-letter words by Mellors, the gamekeeper, in the presence of Constance Chatterley—words intended to root out and purify feelings long hidden by shame.

The flaw of the novel doesn't lie in this direction but rather in the physical crippling of Sir Clifford Chatterley, who comes home from World War I smashed and impotent. This is a weakness in the story not because it sets up an apparatus for sentimentalism over the betrayal and desertion of Clifford, but rather because it has the effect of removing the target which Lawrence was most of all aiming at. This was the over-intellectualization of such people as Clifford, a colliery owner who becomes a clever writer of the "mind-knowledge" type. Lawrence would have strengthened his story if he had shown that it was such elements, which can exist in men not physically crippled, that drove Connie into the arms of his gamekeeper, the preserver of natural life.

Even if this is not Lawrence's finest book, the text of the full story may have the virtue of encouraging more people to read his other novels, his essays and his poems. *Lady Chatterley's Lover* justifies itself, if not necessarily as a healing book for all readers, at least as our time's most significant romance.

Frederick R. Karl

LAWRENCE'S *THE MAN WHO LOVED ISLANDS:* THE CRUSOE WHO FAILED

D. H. LAWRENCE'S short story "The Man Who Loved Islands" deserves more serious notice than it has received, chiefly for two reasons. First, it affords insight into several of the author's major themes and characters, while lacking the rambling nature of much of his longer fiction; second, it shows Lawrence at his best as a craftsman, at the same time making transparent his inadequacies. "The Man Who Loved Islands" first appeared in the *London Mercury* (August 1927), but has, since then, attracted little attention. Although both F. R. Leavis and Anthony West have kind words to say about the story, neither remarks how carefully this parable of modern man defines Lawrence's artistic achievements and shortcomings, nor how sparely and directly it delineates his central thesis about the fate of a "bloodless" man. For Cathcart, Lawrence's dubious hero, is a composite of everything Lawrence hated: a twentieth-century Robinson Crusoe who is now, ironically, an Englishman without mettle or resolution, one who, possessing only money, tries to regain a personal paradise that constantly eludes him. The story, befitting its opening—"There was a man who loved islands"—is a fable for our time, a loose allegory of wasted Edens and of a sterile world full of personal inadequacies.

Cathcart, the islander who wanted an island "all of his own . . . to make it a world of his own," has everything in his favor except sufficient will and ability. Recognizably lacking these

Frederick R. Karl, who teaches at City College of New York, has published fiction and nonfiction in various literary quarterlies and is author of *A Reader's Guide to the Major Twentieth-Century English Novels* (1959); he is now working on a book on the Victorian novel, some short stories, and a novella whose setting is Italy.

qualities, as well as any live feeling, he tries to command contentment with money. In his dissatisfaction with the world and with himself, he buys three islands, of which the first proves to be his shaky domain, the second his place of refuge, and the third his burial ground. In his compulsive passage from one island to the next, a journey of steady "decline," he is a being torn by a basic contradiction: for Cathcart, constitutionally unable to be self-sufficient, yet desires independence. But in seeking his own soul, Cathcart demonstrates his lack of real blood-feeling; unable to "touch" anyone, Cathcart never comes into a live relationship with either man or the world. By trying to conquer by money what he should touch only through love, Cathcart reveals himself as a "false aristocrat," the man, as Lawrence defines him, who has position because of birth or accident. Furthermore, Cathcart, incapable of fulfilling himself, lacks the ability to fathom his personal resources. This fault in itself isolates him, drives him from the world, as much as the snow that brings him to a white death on the third and final island. For, as Lawrence writes in the story, the islander must realize that his ". . . little earthy island has dwindled, like a jumping-off place, into nothingness, for you have jumped off, you know not how, into the dark wide mystery of time, where the past is vastly alive, and the future not separated off." [1] In brief, man possesses a divine spark which can save him when he honors it, and which, conversely, can destroy him if he dishonors it.

Cathcart's first island was the least remote of the three. A sort of communal venture, with its owner as benevolent commissar, this island—unfortunately for Cathcart—contained mysteries of past blood rituals which seemed to permeate the atmosphere at night. What seemed merely a ruin under the hornbeam tree by day "was a moaning of blood-stained priests with crucifixes in the ineffable night. . . . To escape any more of this sort of awareness, our islander daily concentrated upon his material island. . . . A minute world of pure perfection, made by man himself" (724–25). Dressed in creamy white, the Master oversees his projects and workers, all the while his illusion of perfectibility blinding him to the world in which real

---

[1] *The Complete Short Stories of D. H. Lawrence,* Vol. 3 (London: Heinemann, 1955), p. 724. All references are to this edition.

likes and dislikes exist. He exchanges good will for emotional interchange, and artificial relationships for human touch. When not concerned with his investments, he leisurely labors to classify all the flowers mentioned in the Greek and Latin authors, an activity that seems to satisfy his pseudo-artistic energies. Meanwhile, his fortune is slowly being dissipated by the luxurious island; for in attempting to create a kind of personal paradise, Cathcart has imported a butler, a cook, a skipper for his yacht, a mason, et al. As expenses increase and income diminishes, his delight vanishes; he becomes afraid of his island and unsure of the future. In his now dwindling enchantment, he sees, as symbolic of his own failing situation, a cow that had fallen over a cliff and now lay dead "on a green ledge under a bit of late-flowering broom. A beautiful, expensive creature, already looking swollen. But what a fool, to fall so unnecessarily!" (*730*).

To this angel unexpectedly fallen from grace, the island becomes malevolent. Cathcart cuts back his costs, but the accounts show only deficits. He feels swindled by the help, but as that idea jars his perfect world, he dismisses it. After five years, the island has become such a burden that he transfers it to a company planning to turn it into a handy honeymoon-and-golf resort.

With this unhappy experience behind him, the islander moves —this time to a much smaller outpost, taking with him only five people, including a widow and her daughter. This island, happily, is too small to contain any mysteries, for the sea has washed away all human ghosts and bloody traces of past sacrifices. The Master is here undistracted; in his study he works on his book, giving the manuscript to the widow's daughter to type. Isolated from life and feeling nothing, he seems personally satisfied. But his soul is slowly rotting, as he spins out the "soft evanescence of gossamy" flower lore. He lives insulated, full of illusions, full of what Ibsen had called "Life-lies." Meanwhile, the widow's daughter, named Flora, cherishes him, sucks at his calm by servilely following him. She demands attachment, sex, desire, even love—just when he thought "he had come through, to a new stillness of desirelessness." Eventually, she seduces him, and, ironically, this Flora is to produce a child, the only productive flower for Cathcart. But loving flowers, Cathcart is incapable of loving Flora. He marries with just as little will as he impregnated her, all the time studying maps of other islands, smaller ones, where he can retreat without the nausea of human contact. Shortly, he says farewell to his baby daughter and the ever adoring Flora, whose passion humiliates his sensibilities, and moves to his third island, a rocky crag in the ocean.

Like a celibate saint in the wilderness, Cathcart lives on his third island, inviolate even from the growth of trees or heather. With the loss of Nature follows a complete loss of will—even his book on ancient flowers no longer interests him. He sits facing the sea, "while his mind turn[s] soft and hazy, like the hazy ocean." The sight of a steamer or mailboat outrages him, upsets his calm. Only the great silence of the whispering sea satisfies him. Moreover, the few animals on the island must go, for they intrude on his illusion of nothingness and distract him from his contemplation of self. Although he has a sudden burst of interest to know the names of the birds he sees, this desire to codify Nature, as he had once catalogued flowers, wanes and leaves him. Gradually, all life, including the sea-birds themselves, begins to desert the island. When the mailboat arrives, Cathcart finds it personally revolting to talk to the crew, and the letters they bring are left unopened. His disgust with the world is complete. With Swiftian disdain, he asks: "What repulsive god invented animals and evil-smelling men? To his nostrils, the fishermen and sheep alike smelled foul; an uncleanness on the fresh earth" (742). The mere sight of black heads bobbing in the bay is sufficient to make him swoon, and the shock only leaves him when he realizes the heads are seals, not men.

As winter nears, Cathcart's only satisfaction derives from being absolutely alone—"Only space, damp, twilit, sea-washed space! This was the bread of his soul" (743). Just as he avoids all human contact, so he also disdains the written word in books and letters. Speech itself is depraved. Time stands still; even his periodic illnesses fail to register on his feelings. Then the cold moves in—Cathcart's frozen soul now finds rapport with the frozen waste around him. The whiteness of his own sterility is reflected in Nature's snow, which falls relentlessly on the island. Its whiteness permeates his every activity—Cathcart even drinks hot milk in his cell-like, snow-covered house illuminated with white light.

As the islander is entombed in the heart of this frozen waste, his will suddenly surges up; he realizes that if he is to be buried, "it must be by his own choice, not by the mechanical power of the elements" (*745*). His drive against Nature's forces takes on the cast of a frenzied struggle against implacable and immovable forces, but his lifeless surroundings prevail. Even the still black rocks are "brutally black." Another great storm traps him inside his hut, as the island itself begins to disappear beneath the white hills which rise and fuse with powdered snow. Only then he realizes the hopelessness of fighting against nature—"You can't win against the elements" (*746*). The sea, the whiteness, the cold vastness—all the elements of Cathcart's own soulless existence—close in over him; and the story ends:

> As he looked, the sky mysteriously darkened and chilled. From far off came the mutter of the unsatisfied thunder, and he knew it was the signal of the snow rolling over the sea. He turned and felt its breath on him (*746*).

ii

Lawrence obviously wrote this story as a parable for the twentieth century—Cathcart has much in common with those other Lawrence villains who lack heart or soul, particularly with Gerald Crich of *Women in Love* (1920). In fact, a passage from that novel describing how Gerald too is swept under by snow suggests that in this image Lawrence found a useful equivalent for his own feelings:

> Gerald stumbled on up the slope of snow, in the bluish darkness, always climbing, always unconsciously climbing, weary though he was. On his left was a steep slope with black rocks and fallen masses of rock and veins of snow slashing in and about the blackness of rock, veins of snow slashing vaguely in and about the blackness of rock. Yet there was no sound, all this made no noise.

In desperation and frustration, Gerald had renounced the sheer joy of being alive, and Cathcart has lost touch with his sense of duality—he wants to complete only himself, to be a single egg in his own nest; and this desire for insulation reduces him, first, to the status of an infant in the womb of perfect loneliness, and then leads to a stifling death.

Lawrence believed that even the conquest of the air made the "world smaller, tighter, and more airless"; conquest meant denial of life, for life is relatedness, the giving up of sufficient ego so that man, the sun, moon, flowers, birds, and animals interconnect, as Lawrence said, in fierce living. But Cathcart, like Gerald Crich, Clifford Chatterley, and Skrebensky (*The Rainbow*), among others, tries to be a conqueror of life, and thus becomes a destroyer of self. Accordingly, most of Lawrence's villains have at least this single quality in common: lacking personal resources, they must, to maintain their equilibrium, become materialistic. Perhaps the very role that materialism plays in their consideration is a measure of their inner failing. Cathcart wants both to rough it as an islander and yet to have the comforts and luxuries of an island estate—thus his cook, butler, expensive foods, etc.! Placing much emphasis on physical comfort and deficient in what Lawrence elsewhere has called a spontaneous will, he must, perforce, fear the presence of dark spirits and mysterious past rites on his first island. For the one who isolates himself, Lawrence suggests, if his strength does not come from within, then his soul is out in the dark, "out in the timeless world." It is this "dark" that Cathcart tries to escape, and in so doing he corrupts his ambition to be a real islander, a real Crusoe—one who can sustain existence in the dark. Cathcart, therefore, never faces what Lawrence claims is his real problem: that the desire for personal conveniences and material possessions often debases the individual and makes impossible the realization of self.

Cathcart dissembles his own want of soul by living amidst the illusions of a Paradise of his own making, where he is God, not Adam. This earthly Paradise—recalling the pastoral golden age—contains the seeds of perfectibility, but based as it is on isolation from the traffic of a possibly sordid existence, its terms are necessarily artificial. Thus, Cathcart's relationships are forced and strained, centered as they are on an impossible ideal. By trying to realize an idealized situation—perfect friendship, perfect comfort, etc.—in which reality is ignored, Cathcart must come to grief. Even his knowledge of the soil and of farming methods comes from books, not from life, and the flowers on the island are "used" only for purposes of cataloguing. Accordingly, on the second island, Cathcart loves flowers, but not Flora; he wants servants, but not their physical contact; when sex itself revolts him, his will withdraws completely from any contaminating relationship.

Yet, the Cathcart of the third island is by no means a saint —only externally, in his desire for meditation and isolation, does he resemble one. Had he been truly saintly, Lawrence would have presented him with sympathy, not sarcasm. The saint has will and direction, both of which Cathcart lacks. His relationship with Flora is crucial in this respect. We first meet her as both bend over the golden saxifrage, which Cathcart has found growing on the island. The saxifrage, a flower of no particular beauty, literally means "rock-breaking" (*saxum,* rock; *frangere,* to break); the parallel with Cathcart and Flora is ironical, for the next moment Lawrence presents Cathcart as only the fragment of a rock, broken into pieces, so to speak, by Flora's insistent will which frustrates him. Subsequently, he turns to her because she is there; he has no power of resistance, no rock-like character of his own. Lawrence persists in varying the use of the word *rock* so that its antithesis to Cathcart's own character is apparent. Cathcart is soft, flabby, flexible; yet he seeks existence on three successive rocks. Lawrence can only sneer at this would-be saint who, wanting "the crocus-flame of desire," destroys within himself all semblance of a loving response. Therefore, when Cathcart retires to his third island to meditate, he is the antithesis of the saint, who always has something to give of himself. Cathcart can only receive impressions, which he then translates into his own desire for nothingness, a void in which he cannot be reached or violated.

In his making equivalent purity of self with destruction of self, Lawrence was not, of course, attacking that type of purity which he associated with Birkin (*Women in Love*) or Mellors (*Lady Chatterley's Lover*)—*that* type is religious, unaffected, necessary for an honest and feeling life. But Cathcart's purity is too tarnished by civilization to have value. Purity, in Lawrence's terms, was warmth, not cold. Not without meaning does Cathcart await death in a cold frozen waste. He had, literally, rejected the sun, which means connection, involvement of personality, while ice means entombment, and escape from

reality and sex. A northern type, Cathcart must, like Gerald
Crich, perish through the iciness of his own heart. Just as in
Conrad's "Heart of Darkness" Kurtz's bald head takes on the
hue of ivory, so Cathcart's heart becomes a frozen white.

Lawrence had spoken repeatedly in his letters of the quality
of love which "universalizes the individual," which is "an extending in concentric waves over all people," what he in another
context calls the joining of the "free self with other free selves in
blood consciousness." But Cathcart can love only flowers, and
that love is possessive, womanish, Lawrence says, in the desire
to pluck and trim them. "Most of the so-called love of flowers
today," he adds, "is merely this reaching out of possession and
egoism: something I've got; something that embellishes *me.*"
Afraid to plunge into life ("He who would save his life must
lose it"), Cathcart deludes himself by cultivating flowers which
protect him from the flood of life and allow him to "prowl in
rotten safety."

Published five years after Eliot's *The Waste Land* and thirteen
years after *Prufrock,* Lawrence's story is also concerned with
sterility, futility, cultural despair—but Lawrence finds no way
to fertilize or regenerate Cathcart, and so, unlike the Eliot of
the later poem, his conclusions here are quite negative. Both
writers, however, strike to the heart of the twentieth-century
malaise, with Cathcart a kind of Prufrock with money and position, but perhaps even less resolution. Like Prufrock, who
wishes himself a crab so he can scuttle in isolation, Cathcart
temporarily fights to save himself—so he can catalogue more
flowers and stare once more into the whispering sea. His function in life does not differ from that in death. Surely Eliot's
world, although partaking of the same sterility, is not so bleak.
For Eliot, even at this time, was already a religious writer
concerned with salvation and regeneration, while Lawrence, by
1928, had passed from religion into a type of personal philosophy wherein he was concerned not with redeeming man, but
with examining aspects of modern nullity. The white world of
nothingness—with all its affinities to Melville's *Moby Dick* and
Coleridge's *The Rime of the Ancient Mariner*—can contain
no seeds of salvation so long as it is peopled by Cathcarts, and
here Lawrence gives no alternative to him; his world is, as it
were, our fate. Conversely, Eliot suggests that in death there

is rebirth ("In the end is my beginning"), but Lawrence assumes that only life devoid of meaning is death. In matters of sex, however, both are in agreement. For example, in Part III of *The Waste Land,* "The Fire Sermon," Eliot catalogues a modern love affair—"His vanity requires no response,/And makes a welcome of indifference" and the typist answers, "Well now that's done: and I'm glad it's over." Thus Cathcart conceives his child with Flora: he plants his seed in her with no more enthusiasm than he would plant seeds for his flowers. Incapable of a positive sexual adjustment, Cathcart loses his soul, for as Lawrence wrote in *Phoenix,* "The final aim of every living thing, creature, or being is the full achievement of itself."

iii

"The Man Who Loved Islands," while succinctly presenting important aspects of Lawrence's doctrines, also suggests criteria by which to judge his craftsmanship. It is apparent that Lawrence's most notable artistic successes often occurred in the short story or novella, and that his long novels, although significant and genuine, frequently overstate, repeat, or stress the obvious, excesses not nearly so prevalent in his work in shorter form. "The Prussian Officer," for example, with its control and pungency, is perhaps Lawrence's supreme artistic achievement. Though without making equal claim for "The Man Who Loved Islands," one can rank it artistically with "The Rocking-Horse Winner," "Daughters of the Vicar," "The Fox," and "England, My England," many of whose virtues and vices it also shares.

The most evident, and surely the most destructive, weakness in the story is caused by Cathcart himself. Too much a symbol and too little a person, Cathcart, like many of Lawrence's other villains the author evidently detests, lacks substance and dimension. Lawrence could not overcome the personal problem of the author who must make an essentially negative character come to life despite his obvious soullessness. Cathcart illustrates Lawrence's point too explicitly, and he only exists or stands for something in the author's mind. Lawrence, who could frequently bring objects and people brilliantly to life, cannot make Cathcart flesh and blood. In this connection, one should, to evaluate Lawrence's shortcomings, compare the islander with Conrad's Heyst (in *Victory*), another "islander" who also lacks will and the desire to "relate" himself in human contact, and yet a character fully human. If we carry the comparison one step further and measure Flora against Lena, we can see that Lawrence as well abstracted a woman, while Conrad, although not entirely successful, was able to create the semblance of a woman trapped by circumstances. In Lawrence, the small personal touches which occasionally bring Clifford Chatterley to life while also chastising him are here missing, and with them all possibility of artistic objectivity.

The prose itself, in places evocative and inevitable in its aptness, whips and lashes sarcastically about Cathcart; so even the style further diminishes the islander's stature and makes him like a captive rat running a maze devised by the author. This "trapped" quality is found in several passages:

> The Master pursed his own flexible mouth in a boyish versatility, as he cleverly sketched in his ideas to the other man, and the bailiff made eyes of admiration, but in his heart he was not attending, he was only watching the Master as he would have watched a queer, caged animal, quite without sympathy, not implicated (*729*).

Cathcart has no "extension" values; Lawrence is always catching and ridiculing him, playing with him, as if disallowing all foibles, all vanity: "The Master went for a short cruise in his yacht. It was not really a yacht, just a little bit of a thing" (*729*). Moreover, not satisfied with destroying Cathcart's world, Lawrence toys repeatedly, puppet-master-like, with Cathcart's feelings:

> It is doubtful whether any of them really liked him, man to man, or even woman to man. But then it is doubtful if he really liked any of them, as man to man, or man to woman. He wanted them to be happy, and the little world to be perfect. But anyone who wants the world to be perfect must be careful not to have real likes or dislikes. A general goodwill is all you can afford (*727*).

Attacked and hedged in by Lawrence's sarcasm and invective, Cathcart cannot achieve normal stature, nor less tragic dimension. His flaws are too obvious, his decline too rapid, and his absurdity continually underscored by the author's relentless attack. These faults in Cathcart's presentation are character-istic of Lawrence's work in general—rarely indeed do his "tragic" stories contain tragic characters. The tragedy, rather, is in the conflict implicit in Lawrence's view of the world, *not* in his characters as they relate to the world. Lawrence, as sug-gested, lacked the objectivity that would provide freedom for his characters and without freedom, their problems often be-come more frustrating than tragic, and his fiction in this respect comes closer to doctrine than to art. When, for example, Law-rence has sketched in the *mystique* of the island's past as a place of "priests, with golden knives and mistletoe; then other priests with a crucifix; then pirates with murder on the sea," he turns to Cathcart: "Our islander was uneasy. He didn't believe, in the daytime, in any of this nonsense" (724). Cathcart's prosaic nature must, under Lawrence's assault, reveal its antipathy for poetry, for anything, in fact, that extends beyond immediate self-gratification. All nature and all Lawrence are bracketed against Cathcart; it is no wonder that like Gerald Crich, Clifford Chat-terley, and other similar emotional cripples, he cannot survive.

That "The Man Who Loved Islands" does succeed despite Cathcart's ineffectiveness and thinness is a tribute to Lawrence's powers of description in evoking a world of waste and decline. This story conveys a "logical" situation that remains under firm control from the opening evocation of the island as a place where in early spring "the little ways and glades were a snow of black-thorn, a vivid white among the Celtic stillness of close green and grey rock, blackbirds calling out in the whiteness their first long triumphant calls" (723). Whenever pastoral elements are summoned, Lawrence asserts his genius for bringing even rock to life; conversely, whenever Cathcart appears, the style loses its grace and becomes sarcastic and charged with hatred.

Although in handling Cathcart Lawrence is the grim avenger of his character's ideas, in other areas he respects life and the variety of experience. The minor characters—except for Flora, whose very impassiveness is her only way of seducing Cathcart —retain their dignity as people. Cathcart's various island serv-ants are Lawrence's typical lower-class creations, perceptive and mocking, full of juice and awareness of their own rights:

They handled him [Cathcart] almost tenderly, and almost with adulation. But when he left, or when they spoke of him, they had often a subtle, mocking smile on their faces. There was no need to be afraid of "the Master." Just let him have his own way. Only the old carpenter was sometimes sincerely rude to him; so he didn't care for the old man (727).

As soon, however, as Lawrence temporarily forgets Cathcart, he brightens perceptively, and, so too, the prose suggests the silence and majestic isolation of the island.

Followed summer, and the cowslips gone, the wild roses faintly fragrant through the haze. There was a field of hay, the foxgloves stood looking down. In a little cove, the sun was on the pale granite where you bathed, and the shadow was in the rocks. Before the mist came stealing, you went home through the ripening oats, the glare of the sea fading from the high air as the fog-horn started to moo on the other island. And then the sea-fog went, it was autumn, the oatsheaves lying prone, the great moon, another island, rose golden out of the sea, and rising higher, the world of the sea was white (723).

As an artistic device, the white sea of course foreshadows the vast whiteness which sweeps in upon Cathcart on his third island. Whiteness, as Lawrence uses it, is both reality and illusion: real when it becomes Cathcart's destroyer, illusory when it is the pure whiteness of his "creamy-white serge" that physically distinguishes his figure from the workers. Whiteness enters again when Cathcart dreams of perfectibility—he has white hopes, which can never be realized by an imperfect person. Whiteness, finally, is the color of Cathcart's pure soul, which makes everything he does "automatic, an act of will, not of true desire." Therefore, that whiteness should destroy Cathcart is the paradox of the innocent being slaughtered as the result of their own purity, not despite it. For purity, to Lawrence, is self-denying, life-negating, unless it is purity tempered by the fires of living human contact. The snow, then, like the white sea and moon, is symbolic of Cathcart's own lifelessness; it nullifies his existence and buries him in a tomb of endless desirelessness.

In creating workable situations for his novels and stories,

Lawrence, like Conrad and Hardy, was concerned with what happens when an individual isolates himself from the human community; and on this ground he is less categorical than his two contemporaries. Conrad, with Jim, Heyst, Decoud, Razumov, and others, suggested that self-isolation assumes self-superiority, and in an imperfect world to forsake society's conventions is tantamount to self-destruction. Conrad claimed that all men are united, that one cannot be a Cain wandering the earth; for, eventually, the outcast, after he has been broken or defeated, must return to society. Jim, Heyst, and Decoud die because they run away and realize too late their intransigence. Razumov, in turn, becomes a hopeless cripple before he is reaccepted into the community. The heroes of Thomas Hardy likewise are crushed by a world that seemingly permits little individuality and makes a mockery of man's desires to fulfill his own calling—so Jude, Clem Yeobright, Tess, Michael Henchard, and others!

Lawrence, on the other hand, argues both for isolation and for dependence, both for individual fulfillment and for a strong relationship to society. In discussing Whitman's sense of identifying with the Mass ("Democracy," in *Phoenix*), Lawrence says that Whitman really asks for the nullification of the individual soul. Lawrence insists, rather, that democracy be in "the singleness of the clear, clean self." To look after our neighbors, he suggests, is to deprive them of their freedom, as much as it robs us of ours. Nevertheless, Lawrence is evidently not advocating Cathcart's type of withdrawal. He is implying, however, that the divine spark of life must come from within, and any attempt to stifle that spark is a kind of death, both physical and spiritual. Unlike Conrad and Hardy, he does not feel that the spark of brotherhood is generated by society, and that the individual must at least be aware of society's demands in order to survive. Lawrence realized that even if we grant that Hardy's position is ironical—that his heroes are right in revolting and society wrong in crushing them—still, Clem miscalculates in trying to become a schoolteacher, and Jude is foolhardy in trying to break down institutions that should not concern him. Lawrence would have crushed them also, just as he crushes Cathcart, because they lack the will which would have kept them supreme in themselves, without the necessity of trying to storm society. Lawrence certainly granted the need for man to relate himself to other things—life itself, he said, is a continuum between its various creations. But Lawrence would deny that convention gives one his liberty, and that outside convention is destructive isolation. Jude and Clem, among others, fail, Lawrence suggests in his long essay on Hardy, because they fail in themselves. Both have denied man's other half, the female half —what Lawrence calls the Soul; thus their incompleteness, for they lack the combination of Male and Female, of Spirit and Soul, that gives fullness. Thus, the conventions of society can destroy them. And here, Lawrence can castigate Hardy for permitting his characters to be crushed in a manner so as to make following convention seem a necessary function of life. For the problem is otherwise—the convention is irrelevant when we talk of freedom. *That* quality begins in the individual.

All this has, of course, great importance in "The Man Who Loved Islands." Cathcart becomes Lawrence's classic statement of what has gone wrong with civilized man in the twentieth century. Cathcart, Lawrence claims, is really the *best* the century has to offer, like Egbert of "England, My England"; yet how incomplete and frail he is! Withal his intelligence, fairness, notions of democracy, even resiliency—the true Englishman in his virtues—he lacks Soul, the Female part that would complete him. It is not enough for Lawrence that Cathcart does not hurt anyone else; his type of passivity destroys the individual himself. Rather, Lawrence implies, that Cathcart were less fair and less "English" if he were able to realize himself by being a living person.

This side of Lawrence has been noted by several critics who have interpreted his ideas on individuality and found them nondemocratic, dangerously aristocratic, socially unacceptable. But Lawrence was neither sociologist nor politician and certainly not a significant philosopher; fervent, sensitive, perhaps a little mad when he saw his ideas frustrated or circumvented, he tilted at windmills in his futile idealism. Therefore, Cathcart and his kind must be exposed, for they are the so-called "good" people of this world who are destroying it. Not fortuitously, Lawrence's villains are rarely bad people; their villainy destroys only themselves, rarely others. The "others," like Flora, escape because they are sufficient. Moreover, Lawrence's heroes are frequently unappetizing, for they are too busy saving themselves to be agreeable. Consequently, Lawrence does not seem pleasant or sympathetic even to the serious reader; his earnestness led to dissatisfaction, not to propitiousness. In these terms, the irony of Cathcart's demise is doubled, for he *is* pleasant, *is* amiable, *is* just. Yet because his money has given him a kind of power which he misuses, Lawrence must destroy him before his type becomes powerful.

In this story, all of Lawrence's fears and hopes come together; it is a true microcosm of his work, an epitaph on *The Rainbow, Women in Love, The Plumed Serpent,* and a forerunner of *Lady Chatterley's Lover,* whose ideas it almost entirely encompasses. Still, its artistic virtues are greater than these novels, although it retains in small the defects common to all of Lawrence's work. For this man who preached individuality and self-fulfillment could not, ironically, stop imposing his will on his own characters even if it meant crushing them and destroying their dramatic effectiveness in the process.

Mark Schorer

LAWRENCE AND THE SPIRIT OF PLACE

Poste Restante!

So any knowing correspondent would have labeled the en-
velope of almost any letter he was addressing to D. H. Lawrence.
Poste restante, or *Post-lagernd,* or *Hold until called for*—a half
dozen languages, a dozen countries, but always the same admonition. How many postal clerks the world over must have observed
it, wondered briefly or not wondered about the identity of the
English mister, at last looked him in the face as they handed him
his packet of accumulated mail, and then, once having seen this
improbable addressee, thin and red and dusty and vivid, wondered about him indeed! Certainly the admonition on his letters
was indispensable if the mail was by any chance to reach him.
A paraphrased refrain of Lawrence's correspondence runs like
this: We are here. . . . We leave tomorrow, write me at. . . .
Everything changed, we are still here. . . . Tomorrow we may
be off after all. . . . We are still here. . . . We are off at last,
and in two days will be at. . . . We have come here instead.
. . . We are leaving, I will send address.

The most casual leafing through of Lawrence's letters, the
unpublished together with the published, invokes at once a sense
of the relentlessness of his itinerant life, and ten different leaf-

---

Mark Schorer, Professor of English at the University of California at
Berkeley, now writing a book on Sinclair Lewis, is widely known for
his criticism in scholarly journals and in magazines. He is the author
of *The Wars of Love* (1953) and other novels, as well as of *William
Blake: The Politics of Vision* (1946), and is additionally well known
for his editorial collaboration on *Criticism: The Foundations of Literary
Judgment* (1948). The present essay is his Introduction to *Poste Restante: A Lawrence Travel Calendar,* by Harry T. Moore, published by
the University of California Press and copyrighted, 1956, by the Regents
of the University of California, by whose permission it is reprinted here.

ings through would produce ten catalogues of travel in general like the following, each different from the others only as to details of place. In 1918 Lawrence wrote from England, "Frieda is pretty well—wondering what is to become of us. There are primroses in the wood and avenues of yellow hazel catkins, hanging like curtains." In 1920, from Taormina: "At the moment I feel I never want to see England again—if I move, then further off, further off"; a few months later, from the Abruzzi: "I feel all unstuck, as if I might drift anywhere"; and eighteen months after that, from Taormina again, "Our great news is that we are going to Ceylon." Ceylon promptly proved unsatisfactory: "Here we are on a ship again—somewhere in a very big blue choppy sea with flying fishes sprinting out of the waves like winged drops, and a Catholic Spanish priest playing Chopin at the piano—very well—and the boat gently rolling. . . . We are going to Australia—Heaven knows why." Less than six months later, from Taos, New Mexico: "We got here last week and since then I have been away motoring for five days into the Apache country to see an Apache dance. It is a weird country, and I feel a great stranger still." The stay in New Mexico and Mexico was to be long enough to make of these places as much a home for Lawrence as any he was to know after his native Nottinghamshire, and yet, in 1924, inevitably, he writes: "We are packing up to leave here on Saturday. . . . It is time to go." England again, and then, in late 1925, from Spotorno, south of Genoa, "We got here yesterday—it's lovely and sunny, with a blue sea, and I'm sitting out on the balcony just above the sands, to write. Switzerland was horrid—I don't like Switzerland anyhow—in slow rain and snow. We shall find ourselves a villa here, I think, for the time." The time was short, as usual, and presently they were living outside Florence, and from there in 1927 he wrote: "I have put off coming to England. I just feel I don't want to come north—feel a sort of migration instinct pushing me south rather than north." But in the next year he wrote to Harry Crosby from Switzerland, "I suppose we shall stay a week or two, then perhaps move up the mountain a little higher—my woful [*sic*] bronchials! How are you and where are you and where are you going?" From the south of France less than a year before his death, Lawrence could still write, "I wonder where we shall ultimately settle! At the moment I feel very undecided about everything. I shall send an address as soon as I have one." And then in 1929 he had one, the last: "We have got this little house on the sea for six months, so the address is good. It is a rocky sea, very blue, with little islands way out, and mountains behind Toulon—still a touch of Homer, in the dawn—we like it —& it is good for my health. . . ." But in less than six months the long, circling journey was over.

This odyssey that only death could end, as uneasy as it was adventurous, of the most restless spirit in a world that seems more stable than it is because his restlessness strides and flashes and flies across it—this odyssey, if we are to see it in its multiple and shifting details, demands an itinerary that is fixed at last in print; Lawrence's, more than any other modern literary life, should have a calendar.

The chief reason for this necessity is that all the time that Lawrence was moving, he was also writing, and the settings of his works follow upon the march of his feet. It is in no way surprising, of course, that a writer, and especially a novelist, should assimilate his travels in his works; but there is probably no other writer in literary history whose works responded so immediately to his geographical environment as Lawrence, and certainly there is no other modern writer to whose imagination "place" made such a direct and intense appeal, and in whose works, as a consequence, place usurps such a central role. Often it becomes the major character, as it were, Lawrence's arbiter, disposing of human destinies in accordance with the response that the human characters have made to itself, the nonhuman place. Or one may say that Lawrence's people discover their identities through their response to place, and that, having thus come upon their true selves, they mark out their fate and are able to pursue it to another place—factory or farm, city or country, north or south, England or Italy, Europe or America, death or life.

This catalogue of polarities should suggest what is in fact the one basic polarity that motivated Lawrence's attitude toward place and his use of it in his fiction. It was a polarity in which, as a child and a boy and a young man, his vision was daily

PICNIC, ABOUT 1918, at Mountain Cottage, Middleton-by-Wirkswirth, Derbyshire; Lawrence and Frieda are at the left; Lawrence's old friend, William E. Hopkin, is in the center of the picture.

Hymns in a Man's Life

D H Lawrence

Nothing is more difficult than to determine what a child takes in and does not take in, of its environment and its teaching. This fact is brought home to me by the hymns which I learned as a child, and never forget. They mean to me almost more than the finest poetry, and they have for me a more permanent value, somehow or other. It is almost shameful to confess that the poems which have meant most to me, like Wordsworth's Ode to Immortality and Keats' Odes and pieces of Macbeth or As You Like It or Midsummer Night's Dream, and Goethe's lyrics such as "Über allen Gipfeln ist Ruh," and Verlaine's "Ayant poussé la porte qui chancelle" — all these lovely poems which after all give the ultimate shape to one's life; all these lovely poems, woven deep into a man's consciousness, are not woven so deep in me as the rather banal nonconformist hymns that penetrated through and through my childhood.

> Each gentle dove
> And sighing bough
> That makes the eve
> So fair to me
> Has something far
> Diviner now
> It draws me back
> To Galilee. —
> O Galilee, sweet Galilee
> Where Jesus loved so much to be,
> O Galilee, sweet Galilee
> Come sing thy songs again to me!

A MANUSCRIPT PAGE of Lawrence's "Hymns in a Man's Life," which is the subject of an article by V. de Sola Pinto in this volume.

The Fox.

by D. H. Lawrence.

The two girls were usually known by their surnames, Banford and March. They had taken the farm together, intending to work it all by themselves: that is, they were going to rear chickens, and make a living by poultry, and also by keeping a cow, and raising one or two young beast. Unfortunately things did not turn out well.

Banford was a small, thin, delicate thing with spectacles. She, however, was the principal investor, for March had little or no money. Banford's father, who was a tradesman in Islington, gave his daughter the start, for her health's sake, and because he loved her, and because it did not look as if she would marry. March was more robust. She had learned carpentry and joinering at the evening classes in Islington. She would be the man about the place. They had, moreover, Banford's old grandfather living with them at the start. He had been a farmer. But unfortunately the old man died after he had been at Bailey Farm for a year. Then the two girls were left alone.

They were neither of them young: that is, they were over thirty. But they certainly were not old. They set out quite gallantly with their enterprising programme. They had numbers of chickens, black leghorns and white leghorns, Plymouths and Wyandots: also some ducks: also two heifers in the fields. One heifer, however, refused absolutely to stay in the Bailey Farm fields closes. No matter how March made up the fences, the heifer was out, wild in the woods, or trespassing on the neighbouring pasture, and March and Bancroft were away, flying after her, with more haste than success. So this heifer they sold in despair. Then, just before the other young beast was expecting her first calf, the old man died, and the girls, afraid of the coming event, sold the remaining heifer in a panic: and limited their attentions to fowls and ducks.

In spite of a little chagrin, it was a relief to have no more cattle on hand life was not made merely to be slaved away. Both girls agreed in this. The fowls were quite enough trouble. March had set up her carpenter's bench at the end of the open shed. Here she worked, making coops and doors and other appurtenances. The fowls were housed in the bigger building which had served as barn and cowshed in old days. They had a beautiful home, and should have been perfectly content. Indeed, they looked well enough. But the girls were disgusted at their tendency to strange illness, at their exacting way of life, and at their refusal, obstinate refusal

THE FOLLOWING PAGES are a facsimile reproduction of the manuscript of Lawrence's story, "The Fox," in its first version, apparently written late in 1919 at Middleton-by-Wirkswirth. The original manuscript is the property of the English collector, George L. Lazarus, who now has the finest set of Lawrence materials in the hands of any private collector.

to lay eggs.

March did the outdoor work. When she was out and about, in her puttees and breeches, her belted coat and her loose cap, she looked almost like some graceful, loose-balanced young man, for her shoulders were straight, and her movements easy and confident, even tinged with a little indifference, or irony. But her face was not a man's face, ever. The wisps of her crisp dark hair blew about her as she stooped, her eyes were big and wide and dark, when she looked up again, strange, startled, shy and sardonic at once. Her mouth, too, was almost pinched as if in pain and irony. There was something odd and unexplaining about her. She would stand balanced on one hip, looking at the fowls pattering about in the obnoxious fine sand of the sloping yard, and calling to her favourite white hen, which came in answer to her name. But there was an almost satirical flicker in March's big, dark eyes as she looked at her three-toed flock, pottering about under her gaze, and the same slight dangerous satire in her voice as she spoke to the favoured Patty, who pecked at March's boot by way of friendly demonstration.

Fowls did not flourish at Bailey Farm, in spite of all that March did for them. When she provided hot food for them, in the morning, according to rule, she noticed that it made them heavy and dopey for hours in the morning. She expected to see them lean against the pillars of the shed, in their languid processes of digestion. And she knew quite well that they ought to be busily scratching and foraging about, if they were to come to any good. So she decided to give them their hot food at night, and let them sleep on it. Which she did. But it made no difference.

War conditions, again, were very unfavourable to poultry keeping. Food was scarce and bad. And when the Daylight Saving Bill was passed, the fowls obstinately refused to go to bed as usual, about nine o'clock in the summer time. That was late enough, indeed, for there was no peace till they were shut up and asleep. Now they cheerfully walked around, without so much as glancing at the barn, until ten o'clock or later. Both Banford and March disbelieved in living for work alone. They wanted to read or take a cycle-ride in the evening: or perhaps Banford wished to paint curvilinear swans on porcelain, with green background, or else make a marvellous

2.

fire-screen by processes of elaborate cabinet-working. For she was a creature of odd whims and unsatisfied tendencies. But from all these things she was prevented by the stupid fowls.

One evil there was greater than any other. Bailey Farm was a little homestead, about a hundred and fifty years old, lying just one field removed from the edge of the wood. Since the war the fox was a demon. He carried off the hens under the very noses of March and Banford. Banford would start and stare through her big spectacles with all her eyes, as another squawk and flutter took place at her heels. Too late! Another white leghorn gone. It was disheartening.

They did what they could to remedy it. When it became permitted to shoot foxes, they stood sentinel with their guns, the two of them, at the favoured hours. But it was no good. The fox was too quick for them. So another year passed, and another, and they were living on their losses, as Banford said. They let their farm-house one summer, and retired to live in a railway-carriage that was deposited as a sort of out-house in a corner of the field. This amused them, and helped their finances. None the less, things looked dark.

Although they were usually the best of friends, because Banford, though nervous and delicate, was a warm, generous soul, and March, though so odd and absent in herself, had a strange magnanimity, yet, in the long solitude, they were apt to become a little irritable with one another, tired of one another. March had four-fifths of the work to do, and though she did not mind, there seemed no relief, and it made her eyes flash curiously sometimes. Then Banford, feeling more nerve-worn than ever, would become despondent, and March would speak sharply to her. They seemed to be losing ground, somehow, losing hope as the months went by. There alone in the fields by the wood, with the wide country stretching hollow and dim to the round hills of the White Horse, in the far distance, they seemed to have to live too much off themselves. There was nothing to keep them up - and no hope.

The fox really exasperated them both. As soon as they had let the fowls out, in the early summer mornings, they had to take their guns and keep guard: and then again, as soon as evening began to mellow, they must go once more again. And he was so sly. He slid along in the deep grass, he was difficult as a serpent to see. And he seemed to circumvent the girls deliberately. Once or twice

March had caught sight of the white tip of his brush, or the ruddy shadow of him in the deep grass, and she had let fire at him. But he made no account of this.

One evening March was standing with her back to the sunset, her gun under her arm, her hair pushed under her cap. She was half watching, half musing. It was her constant state. Her eyes were keen and observant, but her inner mind took no notice of what she saw. She was always lapsing into this odd, rapt state, her mouth rather screwed up. It was a question, whether she was there, actually consciously present, or not.

The trees on the wood-edge were a darkish, brownish green in the full light – for it was the end of August. Beyond, the naked, copper-like shafts and limbs of the pine-trees shone in the air. Nearer the rough grass, with its long brownish stalks all agleam, was full of light. The fowls were round about – the ducks were still swimming on the pond under the pine trees. March looked at it all, saw it all, and did not see it. She heard Banford speaking to the fowls, in the distance – and she did not hear. What was she thinking about? Heaven knows. Her consciousness was, as it were, held back.

She lowered her eyes and, suddenly, saw the fox. He was looking up at her. His chin was pressed down, and his eyes were looking up. They met her eyes. And he knew her. She was spell-bound. She knew he knew her. So he looked into her eyes, and her soul ~~pointed~~ failed her. He knew her, he was not daunted.

She struggled, confusedly she ~~came~~ to herself, and saw him ~~making off~~, with slow leaps leaping over some fallen boughs ~~soft, undulating jumps~~. Then he glanced over his shoulder, and ~~ran~~ smoothly away. She saw his brush held smooth like a feather, she saw his white buttocks twinkle. And he was gone, softly, soft as the wind.

She put her gun to her shoulder, but even then pursed her mouth, knowing it was nonsense to pretend to fire. So she began to walk slowly after him, in the ~~this~~ direction he had gone, slowly, pertinaciously. She expected to find ~~him~~. In her heart she was determined to find him. What she would do when she saw him again she did not consider. But she was determined to find him. So she walked about on the edge of the wood, with wide, vivid dark eyes, and a faint flush in her cheeks. She did not think. In strange mindlessness she walked hither and thither.

At last she became aware that Banford was calling her. She made an effort of attention, turned, and gave some sort of a screaming call in answer. Then again she was striding off towards the homestead. The red sun was setting, the fowls were retiring towards their roost. She watched them, white creatures, dark creatures, gathering to the barn. She watched them spell-bound, without seeing them. But her automatic intelligence told her when it was time to shut the door.

She went indoors to supper, which Banford had set on the table. Banford chatted easily. March seemed to listen, in her distant, manly way. She answered a brief word now and then. But all the time she was as if spell-bound. And as soon as supper was over, she rose again to go out, without saying why.

She took her gun again and went to look for the fox. For he had lifted his eyes upon her, and his look seemed to have entered her brain. She did not so much think of him: she was possessed by him. She saw his dark, shrewd, unabashed eye looking into her, knowing her. She felt him invisibly master her spirit. She knew the way he lowered his chin as he looked up, she knew his muzzle, the golden brown, and the greyish white. And again, she saw him glance over his shoulder at her, half inviting, half contemptuous and cunning. So she went, with her great startled eyes glowing, her gun under her arm, along the wood edge. Meanwhile the night fell, and a great moon rose above the pine trees. And again Banford was calling.

So she went indoors. She was silent and busy. She examined her gun, and cleaned it, musing abstractedly by the lamp-light. Then she went out again, under the great moon, to see if everything was right. When she saw the dark crests of the pine-trees against the blond sky, again her heart beat to the fox, the fox. She wanted to follow him, with her gun.

It was some days before she mentioned the affair to Banford.

6.

Then suddenly, one evening, she said:

"The fox was right at my feet on Saturday night."

"Where?" said Banford, her eyes opening behind her spectacles.

"When I stood just above the pond."

"Did you fire?" cried Banford.

"No, I did it."

"Why not?"

"Why, I was too much surprised, I suppose."

It was the same old, slow, laconic way of speech March always had. Banford stared at her friend for a few moments.

"You saw him?" she cried.

"Oh yes! He was looking up at me, cool as anything."

"I tell you," cried Banford — "the cheek! — They're not afraid of us, March."

"Oh no," said March.

"Pity you did it get a shot at him," said Banford.

"Is it it a pity! I've been looking for him ever since. But I don't suppose he'll come so near again."

"I don't suppose he will," said Banford.

And she proceeded to forget about it: except that she was more indignant than ever at the impudence of the beggars. March also was not conscious that she thought of the fox: But whenever she fell into her odd half-musics, when she was half rapt, and half intelligently aware of what passed under her vision, then it was the fox which somehow dominated her unconsciousness possessed the blank half of her musing. And so it was for weeks, and months. No matter whether she had been climbing the trees for the apples, or beating down the last of the damsons or whether she had been digging out the ditch from the duck pond, or clearing out the barn, when she had finished, or when she straightened herself, and pushed the wisps of hair away again from her forehead, and pursed up her

months again in an odd, screwed fashion, much too old for her
ears, there was sure to come over her mind the old spell of the
as it came when he was looking at her. It was as if she could smell him
at these times. And it always recurred, at unexpected moments,
just as she was going to sleep at night, or just as she was pouring
the water into the teapot, to make tea – there it was, the fox, the it
came over her like a spell.

So the months passed. She still looked for him *unconsciously*,
whenever she went towards the wood. He had become a settled
fact in her psyche, a state permanently established, not
continuous, but always recurring. She did not know what
he felt or thought: only the state came over her, as when he
cried at her.

The months passed, the dark evenings came, heavy, dark
November, when March went about in high boots, ankle deep
in mud, when the night began to fall at four o'clock, and the
day never properly dawned. Both girls dreaded these times.
They dreaded the almost continuous darkness that enveloped
them on their desolate little farm near the wood. Banford was
physically afraid. She was afraid of tramps, afraid lest someone
should come prowling round. March was not so much afraid, as
uncomfortable and disturbed. She felt discomfort and gloom in
all her physique.

Usually, the two girls had tea in the sitting room. March
lighted a fire at dusk, and put on the wood she had chopped
and sawed during the day. Then the long evening was in front,
dark, sodden, black outside, lonely and rather *oppressive* inside, a
little dismal. March was content not to talk, but Banford
could not keep still. Merely listening to the wind in the pines
outside, or the drip of water, was too much for her.
One evening the girls had washed up the tea-things in the
kitchen, and March had put on her house-shoes, and taken
out a roll of crochet-work, which she worked at slowly from
time to time. So she lapsed into silence. Banford stared at the
red fire, which, being of wood, needed constant attention. She
was afraid to begin to read too early, because her eyes would
not bear any strain. So she sat staring at the fire, listening

to the distant sounds, sound of cattle lowing, of a dull, heavy moist wind, of the rattle of the evening train on the little railway not far off. She was almost fascinated by the red glow of the fire.

Suddenly both girls started, and lifted their heads. They heard a footstep – distinctly a footstep. Banford recoiled in fear. March stood listening. Then rapidly she approached the door that led into the kitchen. At the same time they heard the footsteps approach the ~~outer~~ back door. ~~of the kitchen~~ They waited a second. The door opened softly. Banford gave a loud cry. A man's voice said softly:

"Hello!"

March recoiled, and took a gun from a corner.

"What do you want?" she cried, in a sharp voice.

Again the soft, softly-vibrating man's voice said:

"Hello! What's wrong?"

"I shall shoot!" cried March. "What do you want?"

"Why, what's wrong? What's wrong?" came the soft, wondering, rather scared voice: and a young soldier, with his heavy kit on his back, advanced into the dim light. "Why," he said, "who lives here then?"

"We live here," said March. "What do you want?"

"Oh!" came the long, melodious wonder-note from the young soldier. "Does not William Grenfel live here then?"

"No – you know he doesn't."

"Do I? – Do I? – I don't, you see. – He _did_ live here, because he was my father, and I lived here myself five years ago. – What's become of him then?"

The young man – or youth, for he would not be more than twenty, now advanced and stood in the inner doorway. March, already under the influence of his strange soft, modulated voice, stared at him spell-bound. He had a ruddy, roundish face, with fairish hair, rather

g, flattened to his forehead with sweat. His eyes were
ue, and very bright and sharp. On his cheeks, on the
sh ruddy skin were fine, fair hairs, like a down, but
arper. It gave him a slightly glistening look. Having
 heavy sacks on his shoulders, he stooped, thrusting
 head rather forward. His hat was loose in one hand.
 stared brightly, very keenly from girl to girl, particularly
 March, who stood pale, with great dilated eyes, in her
tied coat and puttees, her hair knotted in a big crisp
ot behind. She still had the gun in her hand. Behind
r, Banford, clinging to the sofa-arm, was shrinking
ay, with half-averted head.

"I thought my father still lived here? - I wonder if he's
ad."

"We've been here for three years," said Banford, who
as beginning to recover her wits, seeing something
yish in the round head with its rather long, *sweaty smooth!* hairs
stuck with sweat.

"Three years! You don't say so! - And you don't know
o was here before you?"

"I know it was an old man, who lived by himself."

"Ay! - Yes, that's him! - And what became of him then?"

"He died. - I know he died - "

"Ay! He's dead then!"

The youth stared at them without changing colour
 expression. If he had any expression, besides a slight
ffled look of wonder, it was one of sharp curiosity
ncerning the two girls, sharp, impersonal curiosity,
. curiosity of that round young head.

But to March he was the fox. Whether it was the
rusting forward of the head, or the glisten of fine
ritish hairs on the ruddy cheek-bones, or the bright,

keen eyes, that can never be said : but the boy was t[o]
her the fox, and she could not see him otherwise.

"How is it you did n't know if your father was alive
or dead?" asked Banford, recovering her natural sharpn[ess]

"Ay, that's it," replied the softly-breathing youth. "You
see I joined up in Canada, and I had n't heard for th[ree]
or four years. — I ran away and went to Canada."

"And now have you just come from France?"

"Well — from Salonika really."

"So you've nowhere to go now."

"Oh, I know some people in the village. Anyhow, I
can go to the Swan."

"You came on the train, I suppose. — Would you lik[e]
to sit down a bit?"

"Well — I don't mind."

He gave an odd little groan as he swung off his kit. Ban[ford]
looked at March.

"Put the gun down," she said. "We'll make a cup of tea[.]"

"Ay," said the youth. "We've seen enough of rifles."
He sat down rather tired, on the sofa, leaning forward.

March recovered her presence of mind, and went into the
kitchen. There she heard the soft young voice musing.

"Well, to think I should come back and find it like this!"
He did not seem sad, not at all — only rather interestedly surpris[ed]

"And what a difference in the place, eh?" he continued,
looking round the room.

"You see a difference, do you?" said Banford.

"Yes — don't I?"

His eyes were almost unnaturally clear and bright, though it
perfectly, unusually healthy was the brightness of abundant heal[th]

March was busy in the kitchen preparing another meal. It was about seven o'clock. All the time, while she was active, she was attending to the youth in the sitting-room, not so much listening to what he said, as feeling the soft run of his voice. ~~moving upon her.~~ She primmed up her mouth tighter and tighter, puckering it as if it was sewed, in her effort to keep her will uppermost. Yet her large eyes dilated and glowed in spite of her, she lost herself. Rapidly and carelessly she prepared the meal, cutting large chunks of bread and margarine - for there was no butter. She racked her brain to think of something else to put on the tray - ~~f~~ She had only bread, margarine, and jam, and the larder was bare. Unable to conjure anything up, she went into the sitting room with her tray.

She did not want to be noticed. Above all, she did not want him to look at her. But when she came in, and was busy setting the table just behind him, he pulled himself up from his sprawling, and turned to look over his shoulder. She became pale and ~~stupid~~ wan.

The youth watched her as she bent over the table, looked at her slim, well shapen legs, at the belted coat dropping around her thighs, at the knot of dark hair, and his curiosity, vivid and widely alert, was again arrested by her.

She turned round, but kept her eyes sideways, dropping and lifting her dark lashes. Her mouth unpuckered, as she said to Banford:

"Will you pour out?"

Then she went into the kitchen again.

"Have your tea where you are, will you?" said Banford to the youth - "unless you'd rather come to the table."

"Well," said he, " I'm nice and comfortable here, aren't I? I will have it here, if you don't mind."

"There's nothing but bread and jam," she said. And she put his plate on a stool by him. She was very happy now, waiting on him. For she loved company. And

12.

now she was no more afraid of him than if he were her own younger brother. He was such a boy.

"Nellie", she called. "I've poured you a cup out."

March appeared in the doorway, took her cup, and sat down in a corner, as far from the light as possible. She was very sensitive in her knees. Having no skirts to cover them, and being forced to sit with them boldly exposed, she suffered. She shrank and shrank, trying not to be seen. And the youth, sprawling low on the couch, glanced up at her, with long, steady, penetrating looks, till she was almost ready to disappear. Yet she held her cup balanced, she drank her tea, screwed up her mouth and held her head averted. Her desire to be invisible was so strong that it quite baffled the youth. He felt he could not see her distinctly. And ever his eyes came back to her, searching, unremitting, with unconscious fixed attention.

Meanwhile he was talking softly and smoothly to Banford, who loved nothing so much as gossip, and who was full of perky interest, like a bird. Also he ate largely and quickly and voraciously, so that March had to cut more hunks of bread and margarine, for the roughness of which Banford apologised.

"Oh well", said March, suddenly speaking, "if there's no butter to put on it, it's no good trying to make dainty pieces."

Again the youth watched her, and he laughed, with a sudden, quick laugh, showing his teeth and wrinkling his nose.

"It is it, is it", he answered, in his soft, near voice.

It appeared he was Cornish by birth and upbringing. When he was twelve years old he had come to Bailey Farm with his father, with whom he had never agreed very well. So he had run away to Canada, and worked far away in the West. Now he was here — and that was the end of it.

He was very curious about the girls, to find out exactly what they were doing. His questions were those of a peasant: acute, practical, a little mocking. He was very much amused by their attitude to their losses: for they were amusing on the score of ~~this~~ heifers and ~~this~~ fowls.

"Oh well", broke in March, "we don't believe in living for nothing but work."

"Don't you?" he answered. And again the quick young laugh came over his face. He kept his eyes steadily on the obscure woman in the corner.

"But what will you do when you've used up all your capital?" he said.

"Oh, I don't know", answered March laconically. "Hire ourselves out for landworkers, I suppose."

"Yes, but there won't be any demand for women land-workers, now the war's over", said the youth.

"Oh, we'll see. We shall hold on a bit longer yet", said March, with a plangent, half sad, half ironical indifference.

"There wants a man about the place", said the youth softly. Banford burst out laughing.

"Take care what you say", she interrupted. "We consider ourselves quite efficient."

"Oh", came March's slow, plangent voice, "it is not a case of efficiency, I'm afraid. If you're going to do farming you must be ~~all~~ at it from morning till night, and you might as well be a beast yourself."

"Yes, that's it", said the youth. "You are not willing to put yourselves into ~~all~~ it."

"We are not", said March, "and we know it."

"We want some of our time for ourselves", said Banford. The youth threw himself back on the sofa, his face tight with laughter, and laughed silently but thoroughly. The calm ~~amusing~~ scorn of the girls tickled him tremendously.

"Yes", he said, "but why did you begin then?"

"Oh", said March, "we had a better opinion of the nature of fowls then, than we have now."

Again the face of the youth tightened with delighted laughter.

"You have not a very high opinion of fowls now, then", he said.

"Oh no - quite a low one", said March.

He began ~~laughed again~~ ~~silently~~.

"Neither fowls nor heifers," said Banford.

The youth broke into a sharp clap of laughter, delighted. The girls began to laugh too, March turning aside her face and wrinkling her mouth in amusement.

"Oh well," said Banford, "we don't mind, do we Nellie?"

"No," said March, "we don't mind."

The youth was very pleased. He had eaten and drunk his fill. Banford began to question him. His name was Henry Grenfel - no, he was not called Harry, always Henry. He continued to answer with courteous simplicity, grave and charming. March, who was now not included, cast long, slow glances at him from her recess, as he sat there on the sofa, his hands clasping his knees, his face, bright and alert, turned to Banford. She became almost peaceful, at last. He was identified with the fox - and he was here in full presence. She need not go after him any more. There in the shadow of her corner she gave herself up to a warm, relaxed peace, almost like sleep, accepting the spell that was on her. But she wished to remain hidden. She was only fully at peace whilst he forgot her, talking with Banford. Hidden in the shadow of her corner, she need not any more be divided in herself, trying to keep up two planes of consciousness. She could at last lapse into the odour of the fox.

For the youth, sitting before the fire in his uniform, sent a faint but distinct odour into the room, indefinable, but something like a wild creature. March no longer tried to reserve herself from it. She was still and soft in her corner like a wild creature in its cave.

At last the talk dwindled. The youth relaxed his clasp of his knees, pulled himself together a little, and looked round. Again he became aware of the silent, half-invisible woman in the corner.

"Well," he said, unwillingly, "I suppose I'd better be going, or they'll be in bed at the Swan."

"I'm afraid they're in bed anyhow," said Banford. "They've all got this influenza."

"Have they!" he exclaimed. And he pondered. "Well," he continued, "I shall find a place somewhere."

"I'd say you could stay here, only —" Banford began. He turned and watched her, holding his head forward.

"What —?" he asked.

"Oh well," she said, "propriety, I suppose —". She was

rather confused.

"It wouldn't be improper, would it?" he said, gently, surprised.

"Not as far as we're concerned," said Banford.

"And not as far as I'm concerned," he said, with grave naïveté. "After all, it's my own home, in a way."

Banford smiled at this.

"It's what the village will have to say," she said.

"I see," he answered. And he looked from one to another.

"What do you say, Nellie?" asked Banford.

"I don't mind," said March, in her distinct tone. "The village doesn't matter to me, anyhow."

"No," said the youth, quick and soft. "Why should it? — I mean, what should they say?"

"Oh, well," came March's plangent, laconic voice, "they'll easily find something to say. But it makes no difference, what they say. We can look after ourselves."

"Of course we can," said the youth.

"Well then, stop if you like," said Banford. "The spare room is quite ready."

His face shone with pleasure.

"If you're quite sure it isn't troubling you too much," he said, with that soft courtesy which distinguished him.

"Oh, it's no trouble," they both said.

He looked, smiling with delight, from one to another.

"It's awfully nice not to have to turn out again, is it?" he said gratefully.

"I suppose it is," said Banford.

March disappeared to attend to the room. Banford was as pleased and thoughtful as if she had her own young brother home from France. It gave her just the same kind of gratification to attend on him, to get out the bath for him, and everything. Her natural warmth and kindliness had now an outlet. And the youth luxuriated in her sisterly attention. But it puzzled him slightly to know that March was silently working for him too. Still, it seemed, he had not really seen her. He felt he should not know her if he met her in the road.

That night March dreamed vividly. She dreamed she heard a singing outside, which she could not understand, a singing that roamed round the house, in the fields and in the darkness. It moved her so, that she felt she must weep, ~~just it sounded like some angel roaming~~. She went out, and suddenly she knew it was the ~~fox~~ singing. He was very yellow and bright, like corn. She went nearer to him, but he ran away and ceased singing. He seemed ~~sad~~; and she wanted to touch him. She stretched out her hand, but suddenly he ~~hit her wrist~~, and at ~~the~~ same instant, as she drew ~~back~~ stinging ~~round~~, ~~he whistled~~ his brush across her face, and it seemed his brush was on fire, for it slared and burned her mouth with a great pain. She awoke with the ~~tremendous~~ pain of it, and lay trembling as if she were really scared.

In the morning, however, she only remembered it as a distant memory. She arose and was ~~very~~ busy preparing the house and attending to the fowls. Their guest came downstairs in his shirt-sleeves. He was young and fresh, but he walked with his head thrust forward, so that his shoulders seemed raised and rounded, as if he had a slight curvature of the spine. It must have been only a manner of bearing himself, for he was young and vigorous. He washed himself and went outside, whilst the women were preparing breakfast.

He saw everything, and examined everything. His curiosity was quick and insatiable. He compared the state of things with that which he remembered before, and cast over in his mind the effect of the changes. He watched the fowls and the ducks, to see their condition, he noticed the flight of wood-pigeons overhead: they were very numerous; he saw the few apples high up, which March had not been able to reach; he remarked that they had borrowed a draw-pump, presumably to empty the big soft-water cistern which was on the north side of the house.

"It's a funny, delapidated little place," he said to the girls, as he sat at breakfast.

His eyes were wide and childish, with thinking about things. He did not say much, but ate largely: March kept her face averted. She, too, in the early morning, could not

be aware of him, though something about the glint of his
khaki reminded her of the brilliance of her dream-fox.

During the day the girls went about their business. In
the morning, he attended to the guns, shot a rabbit and
a wild duck that was flying high, towards the woods. In
the afternoon, he went to the village. He came back at
tea-time. He had the same alert, forward-reaching look
on his ~~fresh~~ roundish face. He hung his hat on a peg with a
little swinging gesture, ~~almost like playing quoits~~. He
was thinking about something.

"Well," he said to the girls, as he sat at table. "What
am I going to do?"

"What do you mean, what are you going to do?" said Banford.

"Where am I going to stay?" he said.

"I don't know," said Banford. "Where do you think of staying?"

"Well – " he hesitated – "I should like to stay here, if you
could do with me, and if you'd charge me the same as they
would at the Swan. – That's what I should ~~like~~ – "

He put the matter to them. He was rather confused.
March sat, with her elbows on the table, her two hands supporting
her chin, looking at him unconsciously. Suddenly he lifted
his clouded blue eyes, and instantaneously looked straight
into March's eyes. He was ~~startled~~ as well as she. He too
recoiled a little. March felt ~~the same knowing, domineering spark~~
~~leap out of his eyes and the possession of her psyche. She shut her eyes.~~
~~to her. Her consciousness became dim.~~

"Well, I don't know – " Banford was saying. She seemed
reluctant, as if she were afraid of being imposed upon. She
looked at March. But, with her weak, troubled ~~sight~~ eyes, she only
saw the usual semi-abstraction on her friend's face. "Why
don't you speak, Nellie?" she said.
But March ~~remained~~ was wide-eyed and silent, and the
intruder, as if fascinated, was watching her without moving
his eyes.

"Go on – answer something," said Banford. And
March turned her head slightly aside, as if coming to
consciousness, or trying to come to consciousness.

18.

" What do you expect me to say ? " she asked automati

" Say what you think ," said Banford.

" It's all the same to me," said March.

And again there was silence. A pointed light seemed to ~~tou~~ be or ~~into~~ the boy's eyes, penetrating like a needle.

" So it is to me," said Banford.

But he had dropped his head, and was oblivious of what she was saying.

" ~~Banford~~ well I suppose you can please yourself, Henry ," Banford concluded.

Still he did not reply, but lifting his head, with a strange, ~~intent~~ cunning look, watched March, only watched her. S yet with face slightly averted, and mouth suffering, qui aim in her consciousness. Banford became a little puzzled Even she perceived the ~~steady~~ concentration of the youth's eyes, their fixed, ~~impersonal, absorbed~~ knowing, unabashed, unwavering attention, as he looked at March, whose mouth quivered a little, not with tears — indescribably.

" Cut a bit more bread, Nellie ," said Banford uneasi And March automatically reached for the knife. The boy dropped his head again, so that they only saw its ~~shapely~~ round dome.

~~After tea March went out to the out-buildings, bu without a lantern. It was dark and misty. The boy rose and followed her. He came near to her as she was stooping in the wood-shed.~~

~~" Are, say there, Nellie ?" said his soft voice behind he she sank on to the heap of small logs, unable to answer At that moment she wished she felt she could die.~~

~~" Listen to me a minute ," he said. " Just half a minute His voice had become incredibly soft, so that it seemed to be like the softest touch of a cat's paw. " Why won't you marry me ?" he said. " Why won't you marry me ? There's nothing against it." His voice seemed like the drawing of the~~

9.

One or two days went by, and the boy stayed on. Banford was quite charmed by him. He was so soft and courteous in speech, not wanting to say much himself, preferring to hear what she had to say, and to laugh in his quick, half mocking way. He helped a little with the work - but not too much. He loved to be out alone with the gun in his hands, to watch, to see. For his sharp-eyed, impersonal curiosity was insatiable, and he was most free when he was quite alone, half-hidden, watching.

Particularly he watched March. She was a strange character to him. Her figure, like a graceful young man's, piqued him. Her dark eyes made something rise in his soul, with a curious elate triumph, when he looked into them, a triumph he was afraid to let be seen, it was so keen and secret. And then her odd, shrewd speech made him laugh outright. He felt he must go further, he was inevitably impelled. But he put away the thought of her, and went off towards the wood's edge with the gun.

The dusk was falling as he came home, and with the dusk, a fine, cold November rain. He saw the fire-light leaping in the window of the living-room, a leaping light in the little cluster of dark buildings. And suddenly, he wanted to stay here permanently, to have this place for his own. And then the thought entered him like a bullet: why not marry March? He stood still in the middle of the field for some moments, holding the dead rabbit hanging still in his hand, arrested by this thought. His mind opened in amazement - then his soul gave an odd little laugh. And something in him began to burn. He wanted to marry her. Even a sense of ridicule hardly affected him. Secretly, he was keen, subtly and secretly keen, to have her.

He scarcely thought of his intention openly to himself. Yet in his mind he began to scheme, to scheme endlessly: what it would be like; what she would probably say to him; whether he could stay on the farm when he had got his ticket. She would like to be on a little place of his own, to do as he liked - for of all things, he hated most a master. The quick scheming of his mind quickly resolved itself. The sense of ridicule was strongest, there was something ridiculous in the idea, to him. And he was very much afraid that she might reject him. But when he thought of the actual proposal something beat up like a keen and secret desire in him. He knew he could make her obey his will. And again, he burned.

He went about just the same for two more days. Only it was evident he had something on his mind. But his nature was secretive, it would be impossible to speak to him, or even to surmise about him. He seemed to draw a cloak of invisibleness about him. At the end of the second day however he determined to speak. The great nerves in his thighs and at the base of his spine seemed to burn like live wire.

He had been sawing logs for the fire, in the afternoon. Darkness came very early: it was still a cold, raw mist. It was getting almost too dark to see. A pile of short sawed logs lay beside the trestle. March came to carry them indoors, or into the shed, as he was busy sawing the last log. He was working in his shirt sleeves, and did not notice her approa. She came unwilling, as if shy. He saw her stooping to the bright-ended logs and he stopped sawing. A fire like lightning flew down his legs, in the nerves.

"March?" he said, in his quiet young voice.

She looked up from the logs she was piling.

"Yes!" she said.

He looked down on her in the dusk. He could see her not too distinctly.

"I wanted to ask you something," he said.

"Did you? What was it?" she said.

"Why -" his voice seemed to draw out soft and subtle, it penetrated her nerves - "why, what do you think it is?"

She stood up, placed her hands on her hips, and stood looking at him transfixed, without answering. Again he burned with a sudden po

"Well," he said, and his voice was so soft it seemed rather like a subtle touch, like the mental touch of a cat's paw, a feeling rather than sound. "Well - I wanted to ask you to marry me."

March felt him rather than heard him. She was trying in vain to turn aside her face. A great relaxation seemed to have come over her. She stood silent, her head slightly on one side. He seemed to be bending towards her, invisibly smiling. It seemed to her fine sparks came out of him.

Then very suddenly, she said:

"What do you mean? I'm old enough to be your mother."

"I know how old you are", came his soft voice, as it were imperceptibly stroking her. "You're thirty-three - and I'm nearly twenty-one. That's not old enough to be my mother. I knew you'd say that. What difference does it make?"

She could hardly attend to the words, the sound of his voice had such power over her, taking away all her power, loosing her into a strange relaxation. She struggled somewhere for her own power. But she knew she was lost - lost - lost. The wood seemed to rock in her as if in a narcotic dream. Suddenly, again she spoke.

"You don't know what you're talking about," she said, in a brief and transient stroke of scorn.

"Ha! - don't I! Don't I though! Yes I do. Yes I do," he said softly, as if he produced his voice in her blood. "Yes I do know what I'm talking about. I ask you to marry me, because - I want you - you see -"

The swoon passed over her as he slowly concluded. She felt she had been too late, and must give up. She could not help herself - she gave up in a darkness, through which his voice came, resonant in her as if she were its medium:

"I want you - you see - that's why -" he proceeded, soft and he had achieved his work. Her eyelids were dropped, her face half-ave

and unconscious. She was in his power. He stepped forward and put
his arm round her.

"Say then," he said. "Say then you'll marry me. Say - say?"
He was softly insistent.

"What?" she asked, faint, from a distance, like one in pain.
His voice was now unthinkably near and soft.

"Say yes."

"Yes - yes," she murmured slowly, half articulate, as if semi-conscious
and as if in pain, like one who dies.

He held her, and he seemed to glisten above her. He was so young - and
so old. This also seemed to occupy her consciousness: he was so young -
and so old. She was in his power.

He did not kiss her or caress her. Suddenly he pressed her hand,
and brought her to herself.

"We'll carry in these logs," he said. "We'd better tell Banford."
Without knowing, she obeyed him.

It was he who told Banford.

"Well," he said. "What do you think?" And his face glistened
like a were-wolf at poor Banford. He had that power for strangely
smiling without altering a muscle of his face, exultantly, domineeringly
smiling.

"What?" said Banford.

"March and I are going to get married."

"Don't be silly," said Banford.

"No silliness. It's quite right - is n't it March?"
And March, with her wide, dark, lost eyes, and her inscrutable
pale face, glanced at him and answered "Yes."

Banford was utterly overcome. Her eyes nearly fell out of her head.
She laughed, and she was angry. But the boy sat there in his
shirt-sleeves, like a man, and both women were at his mercy. All
the time there was this indescribable shining on his face, a sort of
brutish gleam, which Banford could have vouched for, and which
galled her. But he made her discuss all arrangements with him.
They decided the marriage should take place by special licence, in
a few days time.

Somewhere, Banford now disliked him intensely, almost mystically,
but she did what he wanted. She was quite helpless. And the sight
of the wide-eyed, lost March angered her and almost broke her heart.
But she was powerless as if enmeshed in fine electric cobwebs.

He was very jaunty in his silence as he took all the necessary
measures, very jaunty and self-satisfied, very cocky in his

quiet way. The women were at his mercy. He did not make love to them, he did not even want to be with her very much. He almost kept her at a distance. But he held her completely, none the less.

One day she said to him, as they happened to be busy together.

"You remind me so much of the fox." She put aside her strand of hair wistily. His face turned suddenly on her, with its gleam.

"Which fox?" he said, laughing.

"The one that fetched the fowls."

"Do I remind you of _that_?" he said, laughing strangely, and putting his hand on her arm. She almost winced. But she watched him fixedly. "Do you think I've come for your fowls?" he continued, still laughing invisibly. He put his hand behind her neck and drew her head towards him. He kissed her for the first time, on the mouth. Then he laughed aloud. "Well," he said, "tomorrow we shall be married."

And on the morrow they were married, although to Banford it seemed utterly impossible. Yet it was so. And he seemed so cocky, in a quiet, secret way. And Banford was so curiously powerless against him, and March was so curiously happy. This also angered Banford. She could not bear to see the secret, half-dreamy, half-knowing look of happiness on March's face. It seemed wicked. March seemed to her to have a secret ~~looking~~ wickedness, gentle, receptive ~~glad~~ wickedness, like a dream.

In March, the dream-consciousness now predominated. She lived in another world, the world of the fox. When she dreamed, the fox and the boy were somehow indistinguishable. And all through the day, she lived in this world, the world of the fox and the boy, or the fox and the old man, she never knew which. Her ready superficial consciousness carried her through the world's business all right. But people said she was odd. And she talked so little to her husband. He had to go away ~~and ten days~~ in ten days time after the marriage. She suffered when he was gone, and he suffered in going. But he went in the inevitable ~~determination~~ decision to come back, and his ~~determinations~~ decisions fulfilled themselves almost like fate, unnoticeably, would come home by instinct.

educated, on which his imagination was forced to feed, and which finally formed the core of his intellectual view. It is a polarity that founds itself on the distinction between natural place and natural place corrupted by unnatural circumstance. The early forms of the distinction are literal and simple: from his childhood on, landscape and the country were freedom, the industrial town and the city were mechanical slavery. An early novel like *Sons and Lovers* may be said to base its drama on values symbolized by the contradiction between flowers growing in the sunny fields and woods, and men working in the black depths of coal mines. In *The Intelligent Heart,* Mr. Moore tells us that as a young school teacher Lawrence found only drawing and "nature study" congenial to him. The botanizing impulse throughout his poetry is evident from the start, and his novels from the beginning tended to organize themselves around the poles of place—civilized and wild, city and farm, mine and field. Industrialism, "the base forcing of human energy," almost inevitably made geography the first symbolic statement in anything he wrote, as, likewise, it was to drive him to the remote places of the world. War, the dehumanizing process of society in the destructive mass, always seemed to him a portion of the industrial process, and it is not accidental that Lawrence's hatred of industrial England seems to have reached its height during the war years when, in a letter to Catherine Carswell, he wrote, "I can't live in England. I can't stop any more. I shall die of foul inward poison. The vital atmosphere of the country is poisonous to an incredible degree: to me at least. I shall die in the fumes of their stench. But I *must* get out."

Thus, a polarity that began at the level of visual observation of place grows in the imagination into the difference between entities no smaller than war and peace themselves, and thus "place" can become a major symbol of distinction and judgment in Lawrence's great and sustained concern with "that sacrifice of life to circumstance which I most strongly disbelieve in." It was this sacrifice that made Lawrence sometimes rage in his work as it made him wander in his life, and there is merit in Mr. Moore's argument that there was an impersonality in this rage, that he was "a channel of rage . . . on behalf of life and growth." Lawrence himself said, "I won't have another war. . . . I am not one man, I am many, I am most." Alas!

At the outset, then, England provided the still coupled poles of place, and the earliest work invokes a kind of dream of an older England that is dying as it paints a dark picture of the new England that is death itself. The opening paragraph of Lawrence's first, and very young novel, *The White Peacock,* strikes the note:

> I stood watching the shadowy fish slide through the gloom of the mill-pond. They were grey, descendants of the silvery things that had darted away from the monks, in the young days when the valley was lusty. The whole place was gathered in the musing of old age. The thick-piled trees on the far shore were too dark and sober to dally with the sun; the weeds stood crowded and motionless. Not even a little wind flickered the willows of the islets. The water lay softly, intensely still. Only the thin stream falling through the mill-race murmured to itself of the tumult of life which had once quickened the valley.

Lawrence's insights are still unanalyzed in this novel that is without any formal focus, and yet the suggestion seems clearly there in the picture of the ruined feudal farm, Strelley Mill overrun by rabbits, and in the picture of Annable, who has turned his back on society and lives by choice in primitive squalor, that the fault lies in civilization, that with the invasions of an industrial way of life and the end of that great, slow cultural convulsion which was the Industrial Revolution, human responses have split into warring dualities and have thinned out, sound human passions have been ennervated as natural place has been devastated and corrupted. In his next novel, *The Trespasser,* Lawrence presents two victims of these warring and debilitated responses and shows them fleeing from the dark city to the Isle of Wight, where, wrapped in the hot mists of the island, they make the belated attempt to heal themselves in a feverish, Wagnerian debauch that can only drive the war deeper and that kills one of them. This is a poor novel, but the major importance of the island to its structure as to its meaning foreshadows a major characteristic of the novels that are

to come. It is in the next, *Sons and Lovers,* that Lawrence seems
to push his initial intuition about place and the opposition of
kinds of place into their full cultural and psychological implications. His profound response to the natural world and his
deep loathing for the unnatural things that are done to it now
become articulate in this novel that opposes flower and farm and
field to mine and machine and factory, creativeness and growth
to mechanization and death, men and women struggling to live
in wholeness to men and women determined to die in division.

It is in *Sons and Lovers,* appropriately, that we become aware
of that element at the very heart of Lawrence's genius, the
ability to convey the unique quality of physical experience that
is so central to his power of communicating the spirit of places.
This ability shows best in Lawrence's descriptions of nonhuman
things, in his writings of animals, flowers and grass, fish, birds,
snakes—a genius for identifying and defining the individuated
quality of life, the physical essences of things outside the personality, the not-me, the very *ding an sich.* Some of Lawrence's
poems, notably those in the volume called *Birds, Beasts and
Flowers,* reveal this ability in its most intense purity, but we
see it flashing all through *Sons and Lovers,* in every natural description, and we begin to see how it will come to form the
basis of Lawrence's sense of individual integrity and human
relationships. At one point in the novel, when Paul Morel is
sketching, Miriam asks,

> "Why do I like this so?"
> "Why do you?" he asked.
> "I don't know. It seems so true."
> "It's because—it's because there is scarcely any shadow in
> it; it's more shimmery, as if I'd painted the shimmering proto-
> plasm in the leaves and everywhere, and not the stiffness of
> the shape. That seems dead to me. Only this shimmeriness is
> the real living. The shape is a dead crust. The shimmer is
> inside reality."

The "shimmer," the "inside reality" in human individuals and
relationships, in love no less than in place and natural forms,
Lawrence pursued above all else, and he was implying now and
would soon enough demonstrate explicitly that the several varie-
ties of reality are deeply interdependent. The corruptions of

place and the corruptions of men are a single process, and with these corruptions, the "inside reality" is itself destroyed as place and men yield to the mechanical form, the "husk." Husks, chiefly, Lawrence believed, were modern men, deprived of vital connections with life outside themselves, ensnared in their partial and divisive and mechanized "personalities." To discover a place where the vital connections could be maintained intact was the motive of Lawrence's life as it increasingly becomes the motive of his heroes and heroines.

Before he had finished the final version of *Sons and Lovers,* Lawrence was already traveling and living outside England: the icy blue mountains and the black firs of Germany, the north, help to create the extraordinary, destructive atmosphere of an early story like "The Prussian Officer," and the lemon yellow air of the south, the sharp and yet somehow dreaming pathos of the first travel sketches in *Twilight in Italy.* In short, Lawrence had already started what was to grow into his vast and vastly various compendium of impressions, whether in essay, poem, story, or novel, of places all over the world, continuously supplemented until the every end of his life, and always written with his unique freshness and dash. But he was not yet, nor would he ever quite be finished with England and the primary poles of place, together with their poles of value, that England meant to him.

The next novel, *The Rainbow,* is a slow and careful writing out of the whole long process of the transformation of the old England into the new, and a dramatization of the concomitant alteration in human functions. Perhaps no single passage in Lawrence communicates more fully his sense of the relation of place and character than that idyllic opening description of the old yeoman way of life in Britain:

> The Brangwens had lived for generations on the Marsh Farm, in the meadows where the Erewash twisted sluggishly through alder trees, separating Derbyshire from Nottinghamshire. Two miles away, a church-tower stood on a hill, the houses of the little country town climbing assiduously up to it. Whenever one of the Brangwens in the fields lifted his head from his work, he saw the church-tower at Ilkeston in the empty sky. So that as he turned again to the horizontal

land, he was aware of something standing above him and beyond him in the distance. . . . They felt the rush of the sap in spring, they knew the wave which cannot halt, but every year throws forward the seed to begetting, and, falling back, leaves the young-born on the earth. They knew the intercourse between heaven and earth, sunshine drawn into the breast and bowels, the rain sucked up in the daytime, nakedness that comes under the wind in autumn, showing the birds' nests no longer worth hiding. Their life and inter-relations were such; feeling the pulse and body of the soil, that opened to their furrow for the grain, and became smooth and supple after their ploughing, and clung to their feet with a weight that pulled like desire, lying hard and unresponsive when the crops were to be shorn away. The young corn waved and was silken, and the lustre slid along the limbs of the men who saw it. They took the udder of the cows, the cows yielded milk and pulse against the hands of the men, the pulse of the blood of the teats of the cows beat into the pulse of the men. They mounted their horses, and held life between the grip of their knees, they harnessed their horses at the wagon, and, with hand on the bridle-rings, drew the heaving of the horses after their will.

From this initial condition of natural harmony between man and his environment, the novel traces the disintegration of both men and the environment, the dissolution of harmony, the fre-netic disintegration of life, and concludes with a visionary chal-lenge to new integration under still other circumstances of place, yet to come. In *Women in Love,* a kind of sequel, we observe two couples who are concerned to achieve the new integration: one couple achieves it, the other does not, but the solution no longer lies within England itself. In this novel, England has become the full symbol of mechanization, and it is the Continent that is opposed to it. On the Continent, the poles of place once more became the north and the south, the icy Alps and the golden Italian reaches of hill and flowering plain and Renais-sance city below.

. . . as by a miracle she remembered that away beyond, below her, lay the dark fruitful earth, that towards the south there were stretches of land dark with orange trees and cypress, grey with olives, that ilex trees lifted wonderful plumy tufts in shadow against a blue sky. Miracle of miracles!—this utterly silent, frozen world of the mountain-tops was not universal! One might leave it and have done with it. One might go away.

One might go away! The theme of the life as of the works. For two years now, while the Lawrences roamed the Italian cities with their *pied à terre* a farm house clinging to the hills over the sea at the edge of Taormina, Lawrence wrote two more novels that played their variations on the theme. In *The Lost Girl* the heroine escapes the respectable stultifications of commercialized Nottinghamshire by following an Italian peasant into the hard life of the Abruzzi. The hero of *Aaron's Rod* leaves England for wanderings in Italy that are based on Lawrence's own, seeking his fulfillment in place, and the work is nearly as much travel book as it is novel. In the same period, Lawrence produced his second genuine travel book, *Sea and Sardinia.* As in *Twilight in Italy* he had seen industrial mechanization overcoming feudal Italy, so in his study of the vividly dark island, so long isolated from the culture of continental Europe, he sees Sardinia after it has been drawn into the despoiling tensions of continental war. Place, in Lawrence's account, is seldom presented without its cultural and even sociological implications as Lawrence perceives them, and these support his vivid descriptive gifts with an informal intellectual dimension that, even when, as in *Sea and Sardinia,* he is writing with extreme casualness, gives them a permanent seriousness. Or, if the implications are not directly cultural and sociological, they are psychological, as in that most intense evocation of all the places that he drew, the Sicilian landscape in the story "Sun" in which, through the sustained pressure of an almost ferocious sensuosity, ritualistic rebirth is nearly accomplished; and accomplished through the power of place.

Aaron's Rod was a novel with political overtones: wandering through Italy, Aaron is also looking for a spiritual leader to whom he can submit his wounded individuality and be healed. Place becomes the political arena, and as, now, the Lawrencean wanderings themselves are flung out over wider areas in the world, travel and the search for spiritual rest are explicitly equated, in the work as in the life. The Australian novel *Kangaroo,* which follows on the Sicilian period, is a novel of ideas that debates political alternatives for its Lawrencean hero, Lovat Somers. On the raw edge of the world, at once sordid and primitive, corrupt in its abrupt modernity and at the same time inspiring in its continuity with a past forever unawakened, Australia is both exhilarating and terrifying to its hero, as Lawrence makes it to us. The actualization of the dark spirit of this continent on the underside of the world is as solid as the psychological and political judgments are ambiguous, and the spiritually reductive terrors of the one together with the elusive emotional and intellectual demands of the other give Somers no opportunity for genuine choice. He abandons both Australia and the socialist-fascist alternative, and, like Lawrence, leaves for America, where he hopes to find a less disturbing place and a more plausible choice. "One walks away to another place," Lawrence had written to Aldous Huxley seven or eight years earlier, "and life begins anew." And he had added —ominously, prophetically—"But it is a midge's life."

In the New Mexico-Mexico period that follows, the landscape and the cultures and the place-spirit all change, but the pattern of the work remains constant. In his third travel book, *Mornings in Mexico,* Lawrence gives us again his most explicit understanding of the full quality of the new world that absorbs him. In the fiction, place as such becomes more powerful than it has ever been as the arbiter of human fortunes. "St. Mawr" is the story of two Englishwomen, a mother and a daughter, who come to New Mexico to discover a life that will free them from the frustrating triviality of their social past, and in the end the daughter submits to the wild landscape itself, beyond humanity.

> There's something else for me, mother. There's something else even that loves me and wants me. I can't tell you what it is. It's a spirit. And it's here, on this ranch. It's here, in this landscape. It's more real to me than men are, and it soothes me, and it holds me up. I don't know what it is, definitely. It's something wild, that will hurt me sometimes and will wear me down sometimes. I know it. But it's something big, bigger than men, bigger than people, bigger than religion.

It's something to do with wild America. And it's something to do with me. It's a mission, if you like. I am imbecile enough for that!—But it's my mission to keep myself for the spirit that is wild, and has waited so long here: even waited for such as me. Now I've come! Now I'm here. Now I am where I want to be: with the spirit that wants me.—And that's how it is.

In the cruelly beautiful novelette "The Princess," a frozen New England virgin makes a ritual journey, half-fearful, half-wishful, over New Mexican mountains, the symbolic barriers, to her destruction. In "The Woman Who Rode Away," which is a fable rather than a story and the center of which is, literally now, a ritual of sacrifice, a woman yields up her consciousness with her life to the consciousness and the life of the Indians whose religion is continuous with the spirit of the place to which she has come. In each, place triumphs.

The Plumed Serpent, the most ambitious work of this period, alters this pattern in some degree. Nowhere in the length and breadth of this work does Lawrence's prose communicate more fully or more glamorously the physical character of his setting, in all its rich singularity, than in this long novel, yet in the end, in part at least, the human will is more powerful than the spirit of the place. Once more the story concerns a European woman in search of her soul. Lawrence himself is still involved in the political ideas of the great leader that had occupied him in two previous novels. In the atmosphere of Mexican political life, these ideas find a more plausible embodiment than they have previously had, and the attempt of Lawrence's two leaders to replace the imposed Christian god and the Christian saints with the primitive Aztec gods, and to work this effort into the fabric of a larger political program, hardly seems fantastic. But for the European woman, Kate Leslie, as finally for Lawrence, the solution is no solution at all. For that place and for those people who are native to it, some such challenge to the corruptions of Western civilization may be inevitable and even right; but it will solve nothing for the woman from Ireland, even less for the searching miner's son from Nottinghamshire. The future of Kate Leslie is not clear, either in place or time. For Lawrence, the future is clearly not in politics; he well settle for "tenderness," for the individual human relationship, for that whole lovely freedom in self-responsible conduct that was included in his sense of the word *insouciance,* a word he came to love above most others. And so—"It is time to go."

The circle nearly closes. It is time to go to Nottinghamshire. Two books come out of this otherwise ill-fated return. The first, *The Virgin and the Gypsy,* a kind of trial-run for the other, *Lady Chatterley's Lover,* sweeps out the old England with a flood, and gives the virgin life on the crest of it. It is a simple and unfinished story published posthumously, and it is not very interesting apart from the final novel, in which the whole judgment on England is at last delivered. The judgment is not very different from, only more maddened than the judgment that was delivered in such an earlier novel as *Women in Love* or in such an elegy upon a dead culture as the story "England, My England." We are back at the primary, coupled poles as, in *Lady Chatterley's Lover,* they are presented together again, coupled, the fulfilling and the destroying place; and the organization of place-value is now so close and so taut that we remember this novel as we remember a picture: in the background black machinery looms cruelly against a dark sky; in the foreground, hemmed in but brilliantly fresh, stands a green wood; in a clearing of the wood, two naked human beings dance.

There was no place in England where Lawrence could dance, no place there, in fact, where he could breathe. No patterned circle closes upon him! The last writing was done in Italy, at the Villa Mirenda, a farmhouse outside Florence. There were not many places where even a simple insouciance was possible, but this was one where it was.

Class makes a gulf, across which all the best human flow is lost. It is not exactly the triumph of the middle classes that has made the deadness, but the triumph of the middle-class *thing.* . . . the middle class is broad and shallow and passionless. Quite passionless. At the best they substitute affection, which is the great middle-class positive emotion. . . . Yet I find, here in Italy, for example, that I live in a certain silent contact with the peasants who work the land of this villa. I am not intimate with them . . . and they are not working for me; I am not their *padrone.* Yet it

is they, really, who form my *ambiente* . . . I don't expect
them to make any millennium here on earth, neither now
nor in the future. But I want to live near them, because
their life still flows.

And his did. There at the Mirenda, Frieda Lawrence recalls,
Lawrence would go every morning into the nearby woods, settle
himself next to a spring where San Eusebio once meditated,
look at the flowers and the birds at his feet, and remember
that other place, England, while he wrote.

At the very end, he took this world of places that he had
known into another world where the implications of "place"
become more general than those immediately of this world. *The
Escaped Cock* is a fable of the resurrection; it is set in a hot
Mediterranean country; the spirit becomes flesh, is connected
with the beauties and pressures of place, as of society and of
sex. Yet it is a fable—in the major sense, set in a place out of
this world. *Etruscan Places,* which may be called the last of the
travel books, is a re-creation in Lawrence's terms of an ideal
society, colorful and brave and creative and, above all, in-
souciant. Stimulated by the wonderfully vivid paintings in
tombs such as those at Tarquinia, Lawrence created in his
Etruscan "place" the most living of all the societies that he
had drawn. And the Etruscans, Lawrence discovered, put a little
bronze ship of death on the tomb of their dead, symbol of the
vessel that would carry them on further travels. And now
mines disappear, machines disappear, science disappears, England disappears: only wind and sea and sails remain. Only that
which is finally natural, only one last place . . .

> Now it is autumn and the falling fruit
> and the long journey towards oblivion.
>
> The apples falling like great drops of dew
> to bruise themselves an exit from themselves.
>
> And it is time to go, to bid farewell
> to one's own self, and find an exit
> from the fallen self.
>
> Have you built your ship of death, O have you?
> O build your ship of death, for you will need it.

How curious! And how to explain it, Lawrence's restlessness, if one had the temerity! In the last year of his life, he wrote to the Richard Aldingtons in the old, perpetual vein:

> . . . in the late autumn, let's really go somewhere. Would you go to Egypt if we went? We might find some way of doing it cheap—& there *are* quite nice modest pensions in Cairo. Let's go to Egypt in November, en quatre—& go sometimes & see the Dobrees, & go up the Nile and look at the desert and perhaps get shot in Khartoum like General Gordon.— Frieda of course, womanlike, pines for more islands— Majorca & Minorca—but I'm not keen on islands. The other thing is the Mediterranean shore of Spain. I'd like to go to Madrid to the Prado. But I *don't* want to stay in the Mirenda this winter. . . . Have you got lots of flowers, beans & carrots. We have phlox in a tiny fenced garden, & salad & a few turnips & red currants.

And only a month or two before his death he wrote to the Huxleys from that last villa, less than a *pied à terre,* "Beau Soleil" at Bandol,

> I am thankful for this unredeemedly modern and small Beau Soleil, taken for 6 months and no more, and am thankful to God to escape anything like a permanency. "Better fifty years of Europe than a cycle of Cathay." Well, I've had nearly fifty years of Europe, so I should rather try the cycle of Cathay.

The question forces itself: what, up to the bitter black end, impelled him? But no answer comes; it lies in the still undefined history and character of our times.

There were superficial motives, of course. First, and for a long time, Lawrence moved about because he was continually looking for a place where he might conceivably establish that ideal community, Rananim, as it was to be called, for which he yearned over many years, that pre-Jeffersonian community of congenial and creative and co-operative persons (many were called but few chose) who would make their own society, outside the destructive pressures of society at large. Second, Lawrence moved because of his health—first south, then north; to the desert, then up into the mountains—always hoping for a climate in which his bleeding lungs would heal, even while he defied medical opinion and chose the place where he thought that his spirit might find rest.

> I've been in bed this last week with bronchial haemorrhages —due, radically, to chagrin—though I was born bronchial —born in chagrin, too. But I'm better—shaky—shaky—and we're going to Austria tomorrow, D. V.—whoever D. may be —to the mountains.

> . . . Well here we are—got through on Thursday night in the wagon-lit—not too tired and no bad consequences. I feel already much better. What with cool air, *a cool bed,* cool mountain water—it's like a new life. I never *would* have got well, down there in that heat in Tuscany. . . . It is such a mercy to be able to breathe and move. I take little walks to the country—and we sit by the river—the Drave—in the little town, under the clipped trees, very 18th-century German—Werther period. The river comes from the ice, and is very full and swift and pale and silent. It rather fascinates me . . .

And third, he moved about because he had an inexhaustible belief that somewhere a place would present itself that was in every way better than any other place he had known. In his writing, this place is finally discovered to be outside society but it is conceived in all of the most glowing colors of the natural world. Yet the last sentence of his last letter dies with his breath: "This place no good." It was time to move again.

He found no place where he could stay for long. But how much more beautiful and exciting and desirable, because of his vividly hopeful explorations of it, is this place where all the rest of us still are!

Raymond Williams

THE SOCIAL THINKING OF D. H. LAWRENCE

It is easy to be aware of Lawrence's great effect on our thinking about social values, but it is difficult, for a number of reasons, to give any exact account of his actual contribution. It is not only that the public projection of him is very different from his actual work, and that this has led to important misunderstandings (that he believed that "sex solves everything"; that he was "a precursor of the Fascist emphasis on blood"). These, in the end, are matters of ignorance, and ignorance, though always formidable, can always be faced. The major difficulties are, I think, two in number. First, there is the fact that Lawrence's position, in the question of social values, is an amalgam of original and derived ideas. Yet because of the intensity with which he took up and worked over what he had learned from others, this is, in practice, very difficult to sort out. Secondly, Lawrence's main original contribution is as a novelist, yet his general writing, in essays and letters, which for obvious reasons expresses most clearly his social ideas, cannot really be separated or judged apart from the novels. For example, his vital study of relationships, which is the basis of his original contribution to our social thinking, is naturally conducted in the novels and stories, and has constantly to be turned to for evidence, even though it is very difficult, for

Raymond Williams, a native of Wales, is a graduate (M.A.) of Trinity College, Cambridge. Since 1946 he has been Senior Staff Tutor, Oxford University Delegacy for Extra-Mural Studies. He is a member of the editorial board of *Essays in Criticism;* his publications include *Reading and Criticism* (1950), *Drama From Ibsen to Eliot* (1952), and *Drama in Performance* (1954). The present essay is taken from his book *Culture and Society, 1780–1950,* copyrighted, 1958, by Raymond Williams, and reprinted by permission of Columbia University Press and Mr. Williams.

technical reasons, to use it just as evidence. Again, he has certain clear positives, which appear in a central position in his general arguments, yet which again depend on what he learned, and shows, in the writing of the novels. We can quote him, for example, on vitality, or on spontaneity, or on relationship, but to realize these as the matters of substance which for him they were, we can only go as readers to this or that novel.

The thinker of whom one is most often reminded, as one goes through Lawrence's social writings, is Carlyle. There is more than a casual resemblance between the two men in a number of ways, and anyone who has read Carlyle will see the continuity of such writing as this in Lawrence:

> The Pisgah-top of spiritual oneness looks down upon a hopeless squalor of industrialism, the huge cemetery of human hopes. This is our Promised Land. . . . The aeroplane descends and lays her eggshells of empty tin-cans on the top of Everest, in the Ultima Thule, and all over the North Pole; not to speak of tractors waddling across the inviolate Sahara and over the jags of Arabia Petraea, laying the same addled eggs of our civilization, tin cans, in every camp-nest. . . .
>
> . . . It is the joy for ever, the agony for ever, and above all, the fight for ever. For all the universe is alive, and whirling in the same fight, the same joy and anguish. The vast demon of life has made himself habits which, except in the whitest heat of desire and rage, he will never break. And these habits are the laws of our scientific universe. But all the laws of physics, dynamics, kinetics, statics, all are but the settled habits of a vast living incomprehensibility, and they can all be broken, superseded, in a moment of great extremity.

The bitter sweep of this fleering of industrialism; this vibrant repetitive hymn to the "vast incomprehensibility": these, across eighty years, belong uniquely to Lawrence and Carlyle, and the resemblance, which is not only imitation, is remarkable. Lawrence takes over the major criticism of industrialism from the nineteenth-century tradition on point after point, but in tone he remains more like Carlyle than any other writer in the tradition, then or since. There is in each the same mixture of argument, satire, name-calling, and sudden wild bitterness.

The case is reasoned and yet breaks again and again into a blind passion of rejection, of which the tenor is not merely negative but annihilating—a threshing after power, which is to be known, ultimately, only in that force of mystery at the edge of which the human articulation breaks down. The impact of each man on the generation which succeeded him is remarkably similar in quality: an impact not so much of doctrines as of an inclusive compelling, general revelation. [Since writing this paragraph, I have read Dr. Leavis' censure (in *D. H. Lawrence, Novelist*) of a comparison of Lawrence with Carlyle. He traces the comparison to Desmond MacCarthy, and predicts that it will "recur." Well, here it is, but not, so far as I am concerned, from that source. As my comparison stands, I see no reason for withdrawal.]

The points which Lawrence took over from the nineteenth-century tradition can be briefly illustrated. There is, first, the general condemnation of industrialism as an attitude of mind: "The industrial problem arises from the base forcing of all human energy into a competition of mere acquisition." Then, when narrowed to competitive acquisitiveness, human purpose is seen as debased to "sheer mechanical materialism":

> When pure mechanization or materialism sets in, the soul is automatically pivoted, and the most diverse of creatures fall into a common mechanical unison. This we see in America. It is not a homogeneous, spontaneous coherence so much as a disintegrated amorphousness which lends itself to perfect mechanical unison.

Mechanical, disintegrated, amorphous: these are the continuing key words to describe the effect of the industrial priorities on individuals and on the whole society. It is this condition of mind, rather than industry as such, which is seen as having led to the ugliness of an industrial society, on which Lawrence is always emphatic:

> The real tragedy of England, as I see it, is the tragedy of ugliness. The country is so lovely: the man-made England is so vile. . . . It was ugliness which betrayed the spirit of man, in the 19th century. The great crime which the moneyed classes and promoters of industry committed in the palmy

Victorian days was the condemning of the workers to ugliness, ugliness, ugliness: meanness and formless and ugly surroundings, ugly ideals, ugly religion, ugly hope, ugly love, ugly clothes, ugly furniture, ugly houses, ugly relationship between workers and employers. The human soul needs actual beauty even more than bread.

Or again:

The blackened brick dwellings, the black slate roofs glistening their sharp edges, the mud black with coal-dust, the pavements wet and black. It was as if dismalness had soaked through and through everything. The utter negation of natural beauty, the utter negation of the gladness of life, the utter absence of the instinct for shapely beauty which every bird and beast has, the utter death of the human intuitive faculty was appalling.

Lawrence is here carrying on a known judgment, yet with his own quick perception and in his own distinctive accent. This kind of observation has to be made again and again, in every generation, not only because the atmosphere of industrialism tends to breed habituation, but also because (in ironic tribute to the strength of the tradition of protest) it is common to shift the ugliness and evil of industrialism out of the present, back into the "bad old days." The reminder that the thing is still here has repeatedly to be issued. Lawrence is little concerned, historically, with the origins of industrialism. For him, in this century, it is a received fact, and at the center of it is the "forcing of all human energy into a competition of mere acquisition"—the common element in all the diverse interpretations of which the tradition is composed.

i

Lawrence's starting point is, then, familiar ground. The inherited ideas were there to clarify his first sense of crisis. When we think of Lawrence, we concentrate, understandably, on the adult life, in all its restless dedication. That he was the son of a miner adds, commonly, a certain pathetic or sentimental interest; we relate the adult life back to it, in a personal way. But the real importance of Lawrence's origins is not and cannot be a matter of retrospect from the adult life. It is, rather, that his first social responses were those, not of a man observing the processes of industrialism, but of one caught in them at an exposed point, and destined in the normal course to be enlisted in their regiments. That he escaped enlistment is now so well known to us that it is difficult to realize the thing as it happened, in its living sequence. It is only by hard fighting, and further by the fortune of fighting on a favorable front, that anyone born into the industrial working class escapes his function of replacement. Lawrence could not be certain, at the time when his fundamental social responses were forming, that he could so escape. That he was exceptionally gifted exacerbated the problem, although later it was to help towards solving it. Yet the problem of adjustment to the disciplines of industrialism, not merely in day-to-day matters, but in the required basic adjustments of feeling, is common and general. In remembering the occasional "victories"—the escapes from the required adjustment—we forget the innumerable and persistent defeats. Lawrence did not forget, because he was not outside the process, meeting those who had escaped, and forming his estimate of the problem from this very limited evidence. For him, rather, the *whole* process had been lived, and he was the more conscious of the general failure, and thus of the general character of the system:

> In my generation, the boys I went to school with, colliers now, have all been beaten down, what with the din-din-dinning of Board Schools, books, cinemas, clergymen, the whole national and human consciousness hammering on the fact of material prosperity above all things.

Lawrence could not have written this, with such a phrase as "all been beaten down," if the pressures had not been so intensely and personally felt. In the early stages of the imposition of the industrial system, an observer could see adult men and women, grown to another way of life, being "beaten down" into the new functions and the new feelings. But once industrialism was established, an *observer* could hardly see this. Tension would be apparent to him only in those who had escaped, or half-escaped. The rest, "the masses," would normally appear to him fully formed—the "beating down" had happened, and he had not seen it. It thus became possible for men in such a position to believe, and with a show of reason to argue, that the residual majority, the "masses," had essentially got the way of life they wanted, or even the way of life they deserved—the way "best fitted" for them. Only an occasional generous spirit could construct, from his own experience, the vision of an alternative possibility; even this, because it had to be vision, was always in danger of simplification or sentimentality. The outstanding value of Lawrence's development is that he was in a position to know the living process as a matter of common rather than of special experience. He had, further, the personal power of understanding and expressing this. While the thing was being lived, however, and while the pressures were not theoretic but actual, the inherited criticism of the industrial system was obviously of the greatest importance to him. It served to clarify and to generalize what had otherwise been a confused and personal issue. It is not too much to say that he built his whole intellectual life on the foundation of this tradition.

A man can live only one life, and the greater part of Lawrence's strength was taken up by an effort which in terms of ideas achieved perhaps less than had already been reached by different paths. Lawrence was so involved with the business of getting free of the industrial system that he never came seriously to the problem of changing it, although he knew that since the problem was common an individual solution was only a cry in the wind. It would be absurd to blame him on these grounds. It is not so much that he was an artist, and thus supposedly condemned by romantic theory to individual solutions. In fact, as we know, Lawrence spent a good deal of time trying to generalize about the necessary common change; he was deeply committed, all his life, to the idea of re-forming society. But his main energy went, and had to go, to the business of personal liberation from the system. Because he understood the issue in its actual depth, he knew that this liberation was not merely a matter of escaping a routine industrial job, or of getting an education, or of moving into the middle class. These things, on Lawrence's terms, were more of an evasion than what he actually came to do. Mitigation of the physical discomforts, of the actual injustices, or of the sense of lost opportunity, was no kind of liberation from the "base

forcing of all human energy into a competition of mere acquisition." His business was the recovery of other purposes
to which the human energy might be directed. What he lived was
the break-out, not theoretically, nor in any Utopian construction, but as it was possible to him, in immediate terms, in opposition alike to the "base forcing" and to his own weakness.
What he achieved in his life was an antithesis to the powerful
industrial thesis which had been proposed for him. But this, in
certain of its aspects, was never more than a mere rejection,
a habit of evasion: the industrial system was so strong, and he
had been so fiercely exposed to it, that at times there was little
that he or any man could do but run. This aspect, however, is
comparatively superficial. The weakness of the exclusively
biographical treatment of Lawrence, with its emphasis on the
restless wanderings and the approach to any way of life but
his own, lies in the fact that these things were only contingencies,
whereas the dedication, and the value, were in the "endless
venture into consciousness," which was his work as man and
writer.

ii

Lawrence is often dramatized as the familiar romantic figure
who "rejects the claims of society." In fact, he knew too much
about society, and knew it too directly, to be deceived for long
by anything so foolish. He saw this version of individualism
as a veneer on the consequences of industrialism.

> We have frustrated that instinct of community which would
> make us unite in pride and dignity in the bigger gesture of
> the citizen, not the cottager.

The "instinct of community" was vital in his thinking: deeper
and stronger, he argued, than even the sexual instinct. He
attacked the industrial society of England, not because it
offered community to the individual, but because it frustrated
it. In this, again, he is wholly in line with the tradition. If in
his own life he "rejected the claims of society," it was not
because he did not understand the importance of community,
but because, in industrial England, he could find none. Almost
certainly he underestimated the degree of community that
might have been available to him: the compulsion to get away

was so fierce, and he was personally very weak and exposed. But he was rejecting, not the claims of society, but the claims of industrial society. He was not a vagrant, to live by dodging; but an exile, committed to a different social principle. The vagrant wants the system to stay as it is, so long as he can go on dodging it while still being maintained by it. The exile, on the contrary, wants to see the system changed, so that he can come home. This latter is, in the end, Lawrence's position.

Lawrence started, then, from the criticism of industrial society which made sense of his own social experience, and which gave title to his refusal to be "basely forced." But alongside this ratifying principle of denial he had the rich experience of childhood in a working-class family, in which most of his positives lay. What such a childhood gave was certainly not tranquility or security; it did not even, in the ordinary sense, give happiness. But it gave what to Lawrence was more important than these things: the sense of close quick relationship, which came to matter more than anything else. This was the positive result of the life of the family in a small house, where there were no such devices of separation of children and parents as the sending-away to school, or the handing-over to servants, or the relegation to nursery or playroom. Comment on this life (usually by those who have not experienced it) tends to emphasize the noisier factors: the fact that rows are always in the open; that there is no privacy in crisis; that want breaks through the small margin of material security and leads to mutual blame and anger. It is not that Lawrence, like any child, did not suffer from these things. It is rather that, in such a life, the suffering and the giving of comfort, the common want and the common remedy, the open row and the open making-up, are all part of a continuous life which, in good and bad, makes for a whole attachment. Lawrence learned from this experience that sense of the continuous flow and recoil of sympathy which was always, in his writing, the essential process of living. His idea of close spontaneous living rests on this foundation, and he had no temptation to idealize it into the pursuit of happiness: things were too close to him for anything so abstract. Further, there is an important sense in which the working-class family is an evident and mutual economic unit, within which both rights and responsibilities are immediately contained. The material processes of satisfying human needs are not separated from personal relationships. Lawrence knew from this not only that the processes must be accepted (he was firm on this through all his subsequent life, to the surprise of friends for whom these things had normally been the function of servants), but also that a common life has to be made on the basis of a correspondence between work relationships and personal relationships: something, again, which was available only, if at all, as an abstraction, to those whose first model of society, in the family, had been hierarchical, separative and inclusive of the element of paid substitute labor—Carlyle's "cashnexus." The intellectual critiques of industrialism as a system were therefore reinforced and prepared for by all he knew of primary relationships. It is no accident that the early chapters of *Sons and Lovers* are at once a marvelous re-creation of this close, active, contained family life, and also in general terms an indictment of the pressures of industrialism. Almost all that he learned in this way was by contrasts, and this element of contrast was reinforced by the accident that he lived on a kind of frontier, within sight both of industrial and of agricultural England. In the family and out of it, in the Breach and at Haggs Farm, he learned on his own senses the crisis of industrial England. When the family was broken by the death of his mother, and when the small world of the family had to be replaced by the world of wages and hiring, it was like a personal death, and from then on he was an exile in spirit and later in fact.

The bridge across which he escaped was, in the widest sense, intellectual. He could read his way out in spirit, and he could write his way out in fact. It has recently been most valuably emphasized by F. R. Leavis that the provincial culture which was available to him was very much more rich and exciting than the usual accounts infer. The chapel, the literary society attached to it, the group of adolescents with whom he could read and talk: these were not the drab, earnest institutions of the observers' clichés, but active, serious, and, above all, wholehearted in energy. What they lacked in variety and in contact with different ways of living was to a large extent balanced by just that earnestness which is so much larger and finer a thing than the fear of it which has converted the word into a gesture of derision. Lawrence's formal education, it must be remembered, was also by no means negligible.

iii

This then, in summary, is the background of Lawrence's inherited ideas and social experience. It remains to examine his consequent thinking about community, at the center of his discussion of social values. This depends on what was his major "venture into consciousness": the attempt to realize that range of living, human energy which the existing system had narrowed and crippled. He put one of his basic beliefs in this way:

> You can have life two ways. Either everything is created from the mind, downwards; or else everything proceeds from the creative quick, outwards into exfoliation and blossom. . . . The actual living quick itself is alone the creative reality.

Lawrence's exploration was into this "creative reality," not as an idea, but in its actual processes: "The quick of self is *there*. You needn't try to get behind it. As leave try to get behind the sun." This "quick of self," in any living being, is the basis of individuality:

> A man's self is a law unto itself, not unto *himself*, mind you. . . . The living self has one purpose only: to come into its own fullness of being. . . . But this coming into full, spontaneous being is the most difficult thing of all. . . . The only thing man has to trust to in coming to himself is his desire and his impulse. But both desire and impulse tend to fall into mechanical automatism: to fall from spontaneous reality into dead or material reality. . . . All education must tend against this fall; and all our efforts in all our life must be to preserve the soul free and spontaneous . . . the life-activity must never be degraded into a fixed activity. There can be no ideal goal for human life. . . . There is no pulling open the buds to see what the blossom will be. Leaves must unroll, buds swell and open, and *then* the blossom. And even after that, when the flower dies and the leaves fall,

> *still* we shall not know. . . . We know the flower of today, but the flower of tomorrow is all beyond us.

Lawrence wrote nothing more important than this, although he wrote it differently, elsewhere, using different terms and methods. The danger is that we recognize this too quickly as "Lawrencean" ("that gorgeous befeathered snail of an *ego* and a personality" which Lawrence and his writing could be at their worst), and accept it or pass it by without real attention. For it is quite easy to grasp as an abstraction, but very difficult in any more substantial way. In all Lawrence's writing of this kind one is reminded of Coleridge, whose terms were essentially so different and yet whose emphasis was so very much the same: an emphasis, felt toward in metaphor, on the preservation of the "spontaneous life-activity" against those rigidities of category and abstraction, of which the industrial system was so powerful a particular embodiment. This sense of life is not obscurantism, as it is sometimes represented to be. It is a particular wisdom, a particular kind of reverence, which at once denies not only the "base forcing of all human energy into a competition of mere acquisition," but also the dominative redirection of this energy into new fixed categories. I believe that it sets a standard, in our attitudes to ourselves and to other human beings, which can in experience be practically known and recognized, and by which all social proposals must submit themselves to be judged. It can be seen as a positive in thinkers as diverse as Burke and Cobbett, as Morris and Lawrence. It is unlikely to reach an agreed end in our thinking, but it is difficult to know where else to begin. We have only the melancholy evidence of powerful and clashing movements that begin elsewhere. When this is so, every renewed affirmation counts.

For Lawrence, the affirmation led on to an interesting declaration of faith in democracy, but this was something rather different from the democracy of, say, a Utilitarian:

> So, we know the first great purpose of Democracy: that each man shall be spontaneously himself—each man himself, each woman herself, without any question of equality or inequality entering in at all; and that no man shall try to determine the being of any other man, or of any other woman.

At first sight, this looks like, not democracy, but a kind of romantic anarchism. Yet it is more than this, essentially, even though it remains very much a first term. Our question to those who would reject it must rest on the phrase "no man shall try to determine the being of any other man." We must ask, and require the answer, of anyone with a social philosophy, whether this principle is accepted or denied. Some of the most generous social movements have failed because, at heart, they have denied this. And it is much the same, in effect, whether such determination of human beings is given title by the abstractions of production or service, of the glory of the race or good citizenship. For "to try to determine the being of any other man" is indeed, as Lawrence emphasized, an arrogant and base forcing.

iv

To Lawrence, the weakness of modern social movements was that they all seemed to depend on the assumption of a "fixed activity" for man, the "life activity" forced into fixed ideals. He found this

> horribly true of modern democracy—socialism, conservatism, bolshevism, liberalism, republicanism, communism: all alike. The one principle that governs all the *isms* is the same: the principle of the idealized unit, the possessor of property. Man has his highest fulfilment as a possessor of property: so they all say, really.

And from this he concludes:

> All discussion and idealizing of the possession of property, whether individual or group or State possession, amounts now to no more than a fatal betrayal of the spontaneous self. . . . Property is only there to be used, not to be possessed . . . possession is a kind of illness of the spirit. . . . When men are no longer obsessed with the desire to possess property, or with the parallel desire to prevent another man's possessing it, then, and only then, shall we be glad to turn it over to the State. Our way of State-ownership is merely a farcical exchange of words, not of ways.

In this, Lawrence is very close to the socialism of a man like

Morris, and there can be little doubt that he and Morris would have felt alike about much that has subsequently passed for socialism.

v

Lawrence's attitude to the question of equality springs from the same sources in feeling. He writes:

Society means people living together. People *must* live together. And to live together, they must have some Standard, some *Material* Standard. This is where the Average comes in. And this is where Socialism and Modern Democracy come in. For Democracy and Socialism rest upon the Equality of Man, which is the Average. And this is sound enough, so long as the Average represents the real basic material needs of mankind: basic material needs: we insist and insist again. For Society, or Democracy, or any Political State or Community exists not for the sake of the individual, nor should ever exist for the sake of the individual, but simply to establish the Average, in order to make living together possible: that is, to make proper facilities for every man's clothing, feeding, housing himself, working, sleeping, mating, playing, according to his necessity as a common unit, an average. Everything beyond that common necessity depends on himself alone.

This idea of equality is "sound enough." Yet when it is not a question of material needs but of whole human beings,

we cannot say that all men are equal. We cannot say A = B. Nor can we say that men are unequal. We may not declare that A = B + C. . . . One man is neither equal nor unequal to another man. When I stand in the presence of another man, and I am my own pure self, am I aware of the presence of an equal, or of an inferior, or of a superior? I am not. When I stand with another man, who is himself, and when I am truly myself, then I am only aware of a Presence, and of the strange reality of Otherness. There is me, and there is *another being.* . . . There is no comparing or estimating. There is only this strange recognition of *present otherness.* I may be glad, angry, or sad, because of the presence of the

the other. But still no comparison enters in. Comparison enters only when one of us departs from his own integral being, and enters the material mechanical world. Then equality and inequality starts at once.

This seems to me to be the best thing that has been written about equality in our period. It gives no title to any defense of material inequality, which in fact is what is usually defended. But it removes from the idea of equality that element of mechanical abstraction which has often been felt in it. The emphasis on relationship, on the recognition and acceptance of "present otherness," could perhaps only have come from a man who had made Lawrence's particular "venture into consciousness." We should remember the emphasis when Lawrence, under the tensions of his exile, falls at times into an attitude like that of the later Carlyle, with an emphasis on the recognition of "superior" beings and of the need to bow down and submit to them. This "following after power," in Carlyle's phrase, is always a failure of the kind of relationship which Lawrence has here described: the impatient frustrated relapse into the attempt to "determine another man's being." Lawrence can show us, more clearly than anyone, where in this he himself went wrong.

I have referred to the tensions of exile, and this aspect of Lawrence's work should receive the final stress. In his basic attitudes he is so much within the tradition we have been following, has indeed so much in common with a socialist like Morris, that it is at first difficult to understand why his influence should have appeared to lead in other directions. One reason, as has been mentioned, is that he has been vulgarized into a romantic rebel, a type of the "free individual." There is, of course, just enough in his life and work to make this vulgarization plausible. Yet it cannot really be sustained. There is something quite central to Lawrence in his famous declaration: "Thank God I am not free, any more than a rooted tree is free." And again:

Men are free when they belong to a living, organic, believing community, active in fulfilling some unfulfilled, perhaps unrealized purpose.

But this in practice was the cry of an exile: of a man who wanted to commit himself, yet who rejected the terms of the available commitments. Lawrence's rejection had to be so intense, if he was to get clear at all, that he was led into a weakness which found its rationalization. He kept wanting to see a change in society, but he could conclude:

> Every attempt at preordaining a new material world only adds another last straw to the load that already has broken so many backs. If we are to keep our backs unbroken, we must deposit all property on the ground, and learn to walk without it. We must stand aside. And when many men stand aside, they stand in a new world; a new world of man has come to pass.

This is the end of the rainbow: the sequel to that Rananim which had been one more in the series of attempts to evade the issues: an idealized substitute community, whether Pantisocracy, New Harmony, or the Guild of St. George. Lawrence's point is that the change must come first in feeling, but almost everything to which he had borne witness might have shown how much "in the head" this conclusion was. He knew all about the processes of "beating down." He knew, none better, how the consciousness and the environment were linked, and what it cost even an exceptional man to make his ragged breathless escape. There is something false, in the end, in the way he tries to separate the material issues and the issues in feeling, for he had had the opportunity of knowing, and indeed had learned, how closely intermeshed these issues were. It is not a question of the old debate on which conditions are primary. It is that in actuality the pressures, and the responses creating new pressures, form into a whole process, which "is *there*. You needn't try to get behind it. As leave try to get behind the sun."

vi

Lawrence came to rationalize and to generalize his own necessary exile, and to give it the appearance of freedom. His separation of the material issues from the issues in consciousness was an analogy of his own temporary condition. There is something, in the strict sense, suburban about this. The attempt to separate material needs and the ways in which they are to be met, from human purpose and the development of being and relationship, is the suburban separation of "work" and "life" which has been the most common response of all to the difficulties of industrialism. It is not that the issues in consciousness ought to be set aside while the material ends are pursued. It is that because the process is whole, so must change be whole: whole in conception, common in effort. The "living, organic, believing community" will not be created by standing aside, although the effort towards it in consciousness is at least as important as the material effort. The tragedy of Lawrence, the working-class boy, is that he did not live to come home. It is a tragedy, moreover, common enough in its incidence to exempt him from the impertinences of personal blame.

The venture into consciousness remains as a sufficient life's work. Toward the end, when he had revisited the mining country where the pressures of industrialism were most explicit and most evident, he shaped, as a creative response, the sense of immediate relationship which informs *Lady Chatterley's Lover,* and which he had earlier explored in *The Rainbow, Women in Love* and "St. Mawr." This is only the climax of his exploration into those elements of human energy which were denied by the "base forcing," and which might yet overthrow it. It is profoundly important to realize that Lawrence's exploration of sexual experience is made, always, in this context. To isolate this exploration, as it was tempting for some of his readers to do, is not only to misunderstand Lawrence but to expose him to the scandal from which, in his lifetime, he scandalously suffered. "This which we are must cease to be, that we may come to pass in another being": this, throughout, is the emphasis. And, just as the recovery of the human spirit from the base forcing of industrialism must lie in recovery of "the creative reality, the actual living quick itself," so does this recovery depend on the ways in which this reality can be most immediately apprehended: "the source of all life and knowledge is in man and woman, and the source of all living is in the interchange and meeting and mingling of these two." It is not that sexual experience is "the answer" to industrialism, or to its ways of thinking and feeling. On the contrary, Lawrence argues, the poisons of the "base forcing" have extended themselves into this. His clearest general exposition of this comes in the essay on Galsworthy, where he derides the proposition of "Pa-assion," and its related promiscuity, as alternatives to the emphasis on money or property which follows from men being "only materially and socially conscious." The idea of sex as a reserve area of feeling, or as a means of Byronic revolt from the conventions of money and property (a Forsyte turning into an anti-Forsyte), is wholly repugnant to Lawrence. People who act in this way are "like all the rest of the modern middle-class rebels, not in rebellion at all; they are merely social beings behaving in an anti-social manner." The real meaning of sex, Lawrence argues, is that it "involves the whole of a human being." The alternative to the "base forcing" into the competition for money and property is not sexual adventure, nor the available sexual emphasis, but again a return to the "quick of self," from which whole relationships, including whole sexual relationships, may grow. The final emphasis, which all Lawrence's convincing explorations into the "quick of self" both illumine and realize, is his criticism of industrial civilization:

> If only our civilization had taught us . . . how to keep the fire of sex clear and alive, flickering or glowing or blazing in all its varying degrees of strength and communication, we might, all of us, have lived all our lives in love, which means we should be kindled and full of zest in all kinds of ways and for all kinds of things.

Or again, as an adequate summary of the whole "venture into consciousness":

> Our civilization . . . has almost destroyed the natural flow of common sympathy between men and men, and men and women. And it is this that I want to restore into life.

Richard Foster

CRITICISM AS RAGE: D. H. LAWRENCE

THE essential function of art is moral. Not aesthetic, not decorative, not pastime or recreation." This principle, stated in *Studies in Classic American Literature,* is perhaps the only general idea that D. H. Lawrence and T. S. Eliot could have approached agreement on. Eliot, spokesman for tradition and the disciplined sensibility, is certainly the leading critical spirit of our time; while Lawrence, prophet of rebellion and "the blood," is virtually unheard as a critic. Perhaps the band of dedicated apologists Lawrence has always had would say that this is because the times are now not right for the reception of a mind like Lawrence's. But this wouldn't help much, because the times are never right for men of his temperament. For he participates in an odd kind of subtradition of his own made up of intellectual renegades, of violently creative minds, of brilliant and angry men whom the ordering techniques of the historian never quite succeed in assimilating into the homogeneous textures of their "periods."

One thinks of Dante, of Milton, of Swift, of Voltaire, perhaps of Thoreau, and even of Dr. Johnson; and in our time, certainly of Gide, of Shaw, of Pound. It isn't sufficient simply to label such men "iconoclasts," for they are makers as well as breakers. They are indeed "originals," and they are that long after they have become part of cultural history; but they are toughly men of intellect also, and so one does not think of Shelley with these. They possess compulsively responsive moral

---

Richard Foster, educated at Oberlin, Michigan, and Syracuse (Ph.D.), teaches at the University of Minnesota, and has written for various professional journals, including the *Yale Review, Prairie Schooner, College English, Accent,* and *Hudson Review;* he has just completed the manuscript of a book, "Modern Critics and Romantic Sensibility."

natures that must be expressed: thus the sharp and special "insights" they seem to have while most of their contemporaries, small and great, go on confirming the historical process as history in its slow wisdom comes to see that process. Such men never achieve revolutions—*make* history—though they make disciples as readily as they make enemies. They are too selfish and inconsistent to lead causes. They are never specialists, always instinctively amateurs. And their prejudices are queer, pronounced, grotesque, sometimes verging upon the insane.

But these men have more perfectly "whole" sensibilities than their contemporaries, for almost nothing relating to the human condition in their times seems to escape them. Their wholeness consists in this personal moral confrontation of the whole range of possible and actual human experience; and if they survive history at all, they survive "alive" in this sense. I think this is the way Lawrence will survive—his wholeness as a man surviving more importantly and permanently than his novels or his poetry, or than himself as a fact and cause of literary history as such. The wholeness can be felt in the continuity (and this is a matter of *style* in the deepest and broadest sense, as well as of "ideas") of fiction and poetry with reminiscence and essay, of reminiscence and essay with criticism, and of the criticism—because it is also *art*—back round again with the fiction and poetry.

His criticism, which especially interests me because, with my time, I feel a need for a "return" to something like *moral* criticism, provides the sharpest and most direct expression of his moral nature. And by criticism I mean not only the essays and reviews and prefaces, but also the letters; and of course by implication all the confirmations of the criticism in his fiction and poetry. Literature was to Lawrence a vast expressive record of the intellectual and emotional—and so, to him, moral—errors of mankind. Perhaps the place to begin with Lawrence as critic, then, is with the essential Lawrence—those raw, uncut, and unspoiled responses to literature that take the form of sudden and fierce moral assaults upon it.

Classic figures, old or modern, were not sacred to Lawrence because of their status: Blake was to him one of those "ghastly, obscene knowers"; Richardson "with his calico purity and his underclothing excitement sweeps all before him"; *The Scarlet Letter* was a "masterpiece, but in duplicity and half-false excitement"; and *The Marble Faun* "one of the most bloodless books ever written." He called Dostoievsky "a lily-mouthed missionary rumbling with ventral howls of derision and dementia," Chekhov a "second-rate writer and a willy wet-leg," and Proust "too much water-jelly." Many of Lawrence's nearer contemporaries received the same kind of sudden vitriol. Wells's work showed "a peevish, ashy indifference to *everything*, except himself, himself as the center of the universe"; Galsworthy's novels, read together, "just nauseated me up to the nose"; Huxley was only "half a man" as a writer, "a sort of precious adolescent"; and Thomas Mann "is old—and we are so young . . . the man is sick, body and soul."

Such are the characteristic moments of frank rage, many of them yielded to in the privacy of personal letters. And some of these same writers, Huxley for example, occupied more favorable positions in the longer run of Lawrence's judgment. For there were a number of writers that, though he regarded them as gravely flawed in some way or other, Lawrence valued for some actual if unfulfilled capacity for feeling or seeing. They constitute an odd Limbo, when one begins naming them over— Melville, Whitman, Emerson, Shelley, George Gissing, Frederick Rolfe alias Baron Corvo, whose *Hadrian the Seventh* he called "a clear and definite book of our epoch, not to be swept aside," and so on. Lawrence's strong literary enthusiasms were few. He seconded the greatness that tradition had conferred upon Shakespeare, Homer, and the Greek tragedians, but he wrote nothing about them. Synge was apparently the only modern dramatist he cared for at all. There was Giovanni Verga, of course— a major and lasting literary love. And the one poet—perhaps the one writer in whatever medium—for whom Lawrence seems to have had an entirely unalloyed admiration was Robert Burns. He loved Burns "as a brother" because Burns despised "society," affirmed life, and accepted the flesh. Lawrence admired Burns so much, in fact, that he once considered writing a novel about him.

This partial and hasty catalogue of his literary opinions illustrates no more, of course, than that Lawrence as a critic was subjective, capricious, dogmatic. It fails to show two very important things. One is that, as I have said, his criticism is also art. Not art in the sense of highly wrought and "formed," for Lawrence's expression, whether in letters or essays, is characteristically fragmented, repetitious, *dis*ordered. But art rather in the sense of effect: it is, as Lawrence would say of good art, overwhelmingly *alive*. His criticism has a breathless immediacy about it, an intensity of caring, a violent energy due in part to Lawrence's marvelously articulate rage, and in part also to his marvelously articulate humor. For humor, sometimes felt to be lacking in his fiction, is abundant in the criticism, though its function is vituperative, to articulate the rage.

But conviction about the art of Lawrence's criticism may be allowed to accrue by itself as we pursue a second matter: the fact that, spontaneous and subjective as his critical performance may seem, Lawrence knew quite consciously—that is to say, theoretically and philosophically—what he expected of art, and he knew how to use those expectations as principles, even as the basis and threshold for a general *method* of criticism peculiarly his own. Lawrence's principle was that the function of literature is moral. But, he wrote in *Studies in Classic American Literature,* it is a "passionate, implicit morality, not didactic"; it "changes the blood" before it changes the mind. Lawrence does not, then, intend to mean that poetry is a "meter-making argument." He means that the arts are enactments, not sermons; they are experienced discoveries of moral "facts" or "laws" inherent in the very substance of our living. If we can imagine a liberated Emerson whose Truth is *in* nature—not "beyond" at all, but wholly inter-inanimate with it—then we have imagined an approximate image of Lawrence's principle. Since Lawrence believed, for example, that sexual love was an enactment not only of biological and psychological but of moral and religious truth as well, a novel imitating the progress of sexual love in a man and woman could not but be, therefore, an actualization of moral and religious ideas.

These are the things Lawrence meant when he said, in *Assorted Articles,* that "art is a form of religion, minus the Ten Commandments business, which is sociological, . . . a form of supremely delicate awareness and atonement—meaning at-oneness . . ."; and in "Morality and the Novel" that "the business of the novel is to reveal the relation between man and his circumambient universe, at the living moment"; and in "Why the Novel Matters" that "if you're a parson, you talk about souls in heaven. If you're a novelist, you know that paradise is in the palm of your hand, and on the end of your nose, because both are alive. . . ." Lawrence, of course, believed his own work as a novelist to be a dedication of art to the moral experience of man. As early as 1913 he wrote in a letter of England's need for a "readjustment between men and women, and a making free and healthy of this sex. . . ." "Oh, Lord," he cried, "and if I don't 'subdue my art to a metaphysic,' as someone very beautifully said of Hardy, I do write because I want folk—English folk—to alter, and have more sense."

Lawrence necessarily had a view of criticism which prescribed that critics be "alive" in much the same sense as artists. This was a difficult affair, for it required in the critic both an intense moralism of purpose and a total freedom and openness of sensibility. Lawrence condemned all forms of academic and methodological criticism and frankly proposed an impressionistic substitute, but clearly only for those who had the moral wisdom to use it in truth and reverence. He wrote in his essay on Galsworthy that the critic must be not only "emotionally alive in every fibre," but also "intellectually capable and skillful in essential logic, and then morally very honest." It was this last quality that Lawrence seemed to feel most strongly about in modern criticism (he called critics "canaille" when he was angry at their moral blindness). "To my way of thinking," he once said in a review, "the critic, like a good beadle, should rap the public on the knuckles and make it attend during divine service. And any good book is divine service." There could be no more satisfactory image than this of Lawrence's own activity as critic, unless it were to be that of Lawrence as messianic scourge whipping out of the temple various perpetrators of literary fraud and sacrilege.

The arts, as Lawrence said of the novel, "can help us live, as nothing else can." But he believed that art first had to destroy, to wreck the forms and monuments of dead beliefs so that new life could take root in cleared ground. He valued writers as disparate as the Futurist poets, Huxley, and Baron Corvo for their destructive force. He respected "hate, a passionate, honourable hate," when he saw it in writers like Swift, Gogol, and

Mark Twain. Even Galsworthy, who so suffocated Lawrence with his "faked feelings," was worth something as a destroyer, as a satirist of the bourgeois "social being." "Satire," wrote Lawrence in the Galsworthy essay, "exists for the very purpose of killing the social being, showing him what an inferior he is and, with all his parade of social honesty, how subtly and corruptly debased." But Lawrence distinguished between the literature of repudiation, which in destroying the old makes a place for new life, and the literature of negation, which in accepting defeat makes room only for death. He could approve Dos Passos' *Manhattan Transfer* as an honest but unreconciled vision of a whole civilization going into a dark nowhere, and Hemingway's *In Our Time* where the self of the stories rejects everything outside it only in order to preserve its own identity and integrity. But he could not approve Arnold Bennett ("I hate Bennett's resignation. Tragedy ought really to be a great kick at misery") and Conrad ("I can't forgive Conrad for being so sad and for giving in") because they seemed to be reconciled to negation as its own finality, because they had lost the moral passion of life.

If Lawrence saw in his own work the most nearly perfect realization of a life-affirming literature, opposite to the literature of negation and complement to the literature of repudiation, he certainly saw it nowhere else. Perhaps Verga, with his sense of the "spirit of place" and his unaffected primitivism, was the next closest, among the moderns, to Lawrence's ideal. But everywhere else Lawrence turned as a critic he was met by attitudes and philosophies and programs that had about them the charnel smell of death. All that was ideologically and psychologically most noisome to him was related directly or indirectly to what I will call the "bourgeois spirit." To Lawrence the bourgeois spirit was the life-killing force of the modern mass-mentality that transformed living men into empty and corpse-like "social beings." In 1927 he wrote to Donald Carswell, ". . . You can't know Robert Burns unless you hate . . . all the estimable bourgeois and upper classes as he really did— the narrow-gutted pigeons." This tells us a great deal about Lawrence's affection for Burns, about the themes of *Lady Chatterley's Lover,* about the Melvilles in the story "Things," about Kate's difficult choice at the end of *The Plumed Serpent.*

But it is also a key sentence for the understanding of Lawrence's moral rage at almost everything by other writers that he read.

As Lawrence saw it, literature under the influence of the bourgeois spirit, instead of expressing "the relationship between man and his circumambient universe," expressed him instead in a relationship of mechanically prescribed responsibility to the organized mass of other man, called "society." All forms of society-worship, from Galsworthy's middle-class conscience to Shaw's polemic socialism to Tolstoy's and Dostoievsky's evangelical Christianity to Whitman's metaphysical impulse to merge his identity with that of others, were to Lawrence disease symptoms of the bourgeois spirit, and were thus heresies against the life-force and the sacredness of man alive. For though Hardy instinctively recognized, as Lawrence put it in his "Study of Thomas Hardy," "a great background, vital and vivid, which matters more than the people that move upon it," he compulsively defeated his "aristocrats" of the blood, his great individuals in quest of fulfillment, by forcing upon them some defeating attachment to community and convention. Hardy shows the weakness of modern tragedy, "where transgression against the social code is made to bring destruction, as though the social code worked our irrevocable fate."

The abstract social reason merges into another dimension of the bourgeois spirit—sentimental humanitarianism. Lawrence once jeered at the social pity of Wells, Middleton Murry, and J. M. Barrie for "all other unfortunates" as "elderly bunk." "It's courage we want, fresh air, not suffused sentiments." But he found little courage in 1914 in the War Number of *Poetry:* "Your people have such little pressure," he wrote to Miss Monroe. "Their safety valves go off at a high scream when the pressure is still so low. Have you no people with any force in them?" Things were even worse when in 1923 he reviewed *A Second Contemporary Verse Anthology:* "The spirit of verse prefers now a 'composition salad' of fruits of sensation, in a cooked mayonnaise of sympathy." He quotes: " 'For after all, the thing to do/Is just to put your heart in song—' " and comments, "Or in pickle." And he dismisses his friend Amy Lowell, who once gave him a typewriter, as "sounds sweetly familiar, linked in a new crochet pattern. . . . 'Christ, what are patterns for?' But why invoke deity? Ask the *Ladies' Home Journal.*"

But Lawrence saw the most serious ravages of the humanitarian pathos in realistic and naturalistic fiction, which had destroyed the idea of the hero and taught its readers to identify instead with pathetic and helpless little Emma Bovary. The trouble with realism, Lawrence wrote in a preface to Verga's *Mastro-Don Gesualdo,* was that serious writers could now do no more than pour their own perhaps "deep and bitter tragic consciousness into the little skins" of trivial people, mere husks and nothings like the Bovarys, until the "seams of pity" show. Even with Verga one must discount, he says, as one must with Balzac, Hawthorne, Dickens, and Charlotte Brontë, "about twenty per cent of the tragedy." Lawrence seems to have regarded humanitarian sympathy, whether in life or art, as a kind of moral false coin passed between social beings who fear the *real* experience of living.

"Spunk is what one wants," Lawrence once wrote to Murry, "not introspective sentiment. This last is your vice. You rot your own manhood at the roots with it." As the social reason begets humanitarian sympathy, humanitarian sympathy begets self-sympathy—a state where the self abandons the divine business of living and turns a fascinated mental eye inward upon the actions and reactions of its own consciousness. *Self*-consciousness was to Lawrence the last station of the bourgeois spirit's progress toward death. In men it brought about the kind of softness he believed was overcoming Murry, and the complete psychic degeneration he saw in Poe. In art it had produced a set of perversions ranging from the ludicrous to the ghastly. The modern serious novel, as portrayed in the essay "Surgery for the Novel—Or a Bomb," was "self-consciousness picked into such fine bits that the bits are most of them invisible, and you have to go by smell." It is dying "in a very long-drawn-out fourteen-volume death-agony, and absorbedly, childishly interested in the phenomenon. 'Did I feel a twinge in my little toe, or didn't I?' asks every character of Mr. Joyce or of Miss Richardson or of M. Proust." And as the step children of T. S. Eliot, we can but listen when Lawrence warns us, "One has to be self-conscious at seventeen . . . but if we are going it strong at thirty-seven, then it is a sign of arrested development. . . . And if it is still continuing at forty-seven, it is obviously senile precocity."

It was this quest for self-consciousness that had brought about the mentalization of sex, the subtle perversion of genuine passional instincts into nasty conceptualizations—what in "Pornography and Obscenity" Lawrence called "the dirty little secret"—until writers and their readers alike had come to despise the body's health with the dirtiness of their own minds. Richardson, George Eliot, Hawthorne, Charlotte Brontë, Goethe (one of the "grand orthodox perverts"), Tolstoy, Dostoievsky, Strindberg—these were some of the older writers Lawrence accused of playing with mentalized sex, and then either rarifying it into bloodless ideality or scourging it as ineluctable sin. But the moderns, scorning the perfumery and prudery in which sex had been traditionally veiled by art, plunged straight into it like pigs into a wallow. It was still sex mentalized, but now in a worse form of perversion—that of parading the "dirty little secret" out in the open. It was sensationalism—Joyce ("What a clumsy *olla putrida*") was one of Lawrence's "serious" examples—and thus a viler kind of sacrilege against life. "The tragedy is," he wrote of *Fantazius Mallare,* a now forgotten book by Ben Hecht, "when you've got sex in your head, instead of down where it belongs. . . ." It was perhaps just such books that caused his own to be misunderstood. "Anybody who calls . . . *Lady Chatterley's Lover* a dirty sexual novel is a liar," he wrote to his agent, Curtis Brown. "It's not even a sexual novel: it's phallic. Sex is a thing that exists in the head, its reactions are cerebral, and its processes mental. Whereas the phallic reality is warm and spontaneous."

Lawrence seems to have believed that self-consciousness had desiccated not only the life-content of literature but its life-form as well. He hated, for example, any and all conscious rules for metrical scansion, and he found the poetry of Poe, one of the most relentless of mentalizers, hopelessly "mechanical." He also deplored ideas of the "art" of the novel as strangling its natural life in the bonds of willed artistic precision, and particularly condemned the French for their creed of artistic "self-effacement," which he traced directly to an inverted form of the sin of "self-consciousness." Part of the reason he could not stomach Thomas Mann was that he saw him as compensating for a sick vision of life by seeking to perfect the statement of his disgust— a trick of perversely conscious and mental "art" learned from Flaubert and the "Paris smarties." "Theorise, theorise all you like," he advised painters in the essay "Making Pictures," "but when you start to paint, shut your theoretic eyes and go for it with instinct and intuition." Rhyme, he told Catherine Carswell, must be "accidental," and rhythm in poetry, he wrote to Edward Marsh, "all depends on the *pause*—the natural pause, the natural *lingering* of the voice according to the feeling—it is the hidden *emotional* pattern that makes poetry, not the obvious form." As for the novel, he wrote to J. B. Pinker, "all rules of construction hold good only for novels which are copies of other novels. A book which is not a copy of other books has its own construction."

Lawrence's artistic faith, like that of the great Romantics, clearly centered on the idea of "organic" or "expressive" form —a faith, alas, that can cover a multitude of incompetencies. We know that Lawrence "rewrote" his novels and poems, some of them several times; but there is reason to believe that the rewriting was more than anything else a matter of further out- pourings from the "passional self." And we also know from some early letters to Edward Garnett that on occasion he felt in himself a lack ("Trim and garnish my stuff I can- not. . . ." "I have always got such a lot of non-essential stuff in my work") of craftsmanship in the "French" sense. But he believed in the long run in the principle of expressive freedom and in the special *instinctual* skills, as he said, "much finer than the skill of the craftsman," that such a freedom requires. And such a principle of form, whether or not it served to excuse Lawrence's insufficiencies as a craftsman, was of course wholly consistent with his demand that art be a spontaneous discovery of life-truths untrammeled by limiting and dead conventions, a dynamic and revealing "divine service" in honor of life.

With these ideas, and in his critical use of them, "principles," before us, something yet remains to be said of what is perhaps most interesting about Lawrence as a critic—his *method*. For he did have a method, though it was really half unconscious, or more accurately, instinctive. His instinctive judgments of art by the standard of his personal moral vision, which of course he believed to be objectively "true," become at least a kind of quasi-method when we put them into alignment with two of Lawrence's fundamental assumptions. The first assumption, amply illustrated in all that has been said so far, is that nearly every modern writer, great and small, has been so infected by what has been called here the "bourgeois spirit" that he is unable to tell false from true, good from bad, living from dead. The second assumption is suggested by Lawrence in the first chapter of *Studies in Classic American Literature:* "Never trust the artist. Trust the tale. The proper function of the critic is to save the tale from the artist who created it." Lawrence's method may be described, then, as a kind of literary psycho-interpretation in which the critic goes beneath the surface excrescences of a writer's distorted psyche in order to illuminate the life-truths inevitably present in the subconscious levels of his work. Lawrence the critic thus discovers in literary works the "real" truths that their creators were themselves unaware of.

But it must not be concluded that Lawrence was merely an eccentric subjectivist who perversely misunderstood everybody else's work in terms of his own. He knew perfectly well, for example, when he wrote his essay on the Grand Inquisitor what Dostoievsky's intentions had been; he was only pointing out that Dostoievsky in a sense misunderstood his own materials, that there were inherently truer truths in them than in Dostoievsky's intentions, and that these truths come forward of their own power if we are alive as we read. When Lawrence said in the introduction to his book of paintings that "even to Milton, the true hero of *Paradise Lost* must be Satan," he didn't mean at all what Shelley appears to have meant; he was only saying, really, that Satan is too much alive for the willed moral abstractions of Milton's theology to contain dramatically. Perhaps no one has shown as well as Lawrence how and why Satan and the Grand Inquisitor are so powerful, how and why they seem to break loose from the intentions of their creators and set up such an overwhelming counterforce of meaning and feeling of their own.

Studies in Classic American Literature, one of the few great works of modern literary criticism, I believe, is the same sort of psycho-interpretation applied to a whole culture through its literature as seen in extended historical perspective. Historical consciousness is functional in nearly all of the criticism, and though it is stamped always with Lawrence's own personality, it is far more dynamically and dramatically operative—a *felt* presence of history—than in, say, Eliot's essays. In the *Studies* Lawrence reads American literature as an instinctive projection of America's sloughing-off the humanistic European conscious-ness and dying into the *self*-annihilation of the democratic consciousness, the whole process seen as promising a Phoenix rebirth of "It"—the life of the blood renewed, and the true individuality of the fulfilled "deepest self" refound. Lawrence seems sometimes to have believed that he was on the threshold of some kind of latter day, and so all this sounds a little bizarre in the saying. But the energy with which he applied his unusual convictions to our literature yields illuminations that can be matched nowhere else in criticism.

As is his habit, Lawrence works dialectically—sometimes with contrasting authors, sometimes with conflicting impulses within individual authors. He pairs Franklin and Crèvecoeur, for example, as representative respectively of two basic aspects of the dying American psyche: Franklin, with his apothegmatic directives on self-reliance, is the dry little architect of the prac-tical mental machinery of "Americanizing and mechanizing . . . for the purpose of overthrowing the past"; and Crèvecoeur, who blinked at the bloody Indians in order to thrill the English romantics with "a new world . . . of the Noble Savage and Pristine Nature and Paradisal Simplicity and all that gorgeous-ness that flows out of the unsullied fount of the ink bottle," becomes the emotional prototype of the American by mental-izing "the blood" into characteristic sentimentality.

Cooper's "white" novels comprise both of these archetypes: sex is just sentiment, and living human beings get "pinned down, . . . transfixed by the idea or ideal of equality and democracy, on which they turn loudly and importantly, like propellers propelling." But there is a counterimpulse in Cooper's Leatherstocking novels, an impulse which is prophetic of the coming Natural Man: "Natty was Fenimore's great Wish. . . . Fenimore, in his imagination, wanted to be Natty Bumppo, who, I am sure, belched after he had eaten his dinner." In Cooper, then, there is both the "sloughing-off of old consciousness" and the forming of a new one.

Poe shows only one of these—that of the dying consciousness, projected through a fascinatedly morbid mental dissection of diseased love. But Lawrence seems to see Hawthorne's *The Scarlet Letter* as a kind of sociological counterpart to Poe's more purely psychological "Ligeia." He sees Hawthorne's novel as an unconscious but "colossal" satire on male-female relationships in America; it is "one of the greatest allegories in all literature," an allegory—unwitting, of course—of how the honest fact of sexual passion turns to "sin" through "self-watching, self-consciousness."

Dana and Melville, who came so close to the life-force in their dealings with the sea, were also led astray by "self-consciousness." As Tolstoy and Hardy and Verga ultimately failed with the soil-male principle, Dana fails with the sea-female principle. He wants to "know" the sea: "Dana sits and Hamletizes by the Pacific—chief actor in the play of his own existence." Similarly, Moby Dick is the "deepest blood-being of the white race . . . hunted by the maniacal fanaticism of our white mental consciousness."

But Lawrence sees Whitman, finally, as the great unconscious prophet of a new life for the race. Though Whitman's merging is a kind of death-agony of the old, specifically because it confuses love with salvation in a societal "charity," it is also an unconscious recognition of a new morality that smashes the old moral idea that "the soul of man is something 'superior' and 'above' the flesh." After Whitman's death-rhapsodies we have only to await the Phoenix-fires.

This is, of course, only the barest sort of summary. The book is a major critical work rich with historical, sociological, psychological, and mythic perceptions. It is sensitively aware of symbolism: just as an example, Lawrence is critically at home with the polar symbolism of dark and light ladies in American fiction some years before Professor Mathiesson and others were to make it critical coin of the realm. It is also notable, I think, that he is discussing American "classics" almost before we knew we had such things, at least of the sort he interests himself in: the book was published in 1923, and some of the chapters were written much in advance of Professor Weaver's inauguration of the Melville industry, which led a spate of discoveries and rediscoveries of a number of important writers from the American past.

But while the book is historically significant, it is also a permanent contribution to criticism and an extraordinarily vital piece of literature. It is written with enormous verve and color, and the management of the whole is rhythmic, contrapuntal, climactic. And it is an antidotal book—destructive, purgative, creative. The chapters on Poe, Hawthorne, Melville, and Whitman ought to be prescribed counterreading to the overwhelming quantity of academic, formalistic, and mythographic commentary we have on these writers—if only because Lawrence will be satisfied with none of them on *moral* grounds. And his lively chapters on such more dimly historical figures as Franklin, Crèvecoeur, Cooper, and Dana, refresh them amazingly. One can only regret that he wrote nothing on Thoreau, and that he did not live to tackle Faulkner, as he almost certainly would have. The occasional essays, the prefaces, and the "Study of Thomas Hardy" are full of the same sort of wrathfully brilliant insights vividly and wittily expressed. The essay on "Art and Morality" alone, for example—better, I think, than the more familiar "Pornography and Obscenity"—is indispensable as a profound and superbly written study in the sociology of modern taste.

It is perhaps a commonplace about Lawrence that one is either for him, like F. R. Leavis, or against him, like T. S. Eliot. But no one can mistake the fact that everywhere in his work mind and conscience are in strenuous encounter with the blank neutrality of existence. It is Lawrence's fierce integrity that makes him so necessary to us now—necessary perhaps especially as a critic, because in our time critics characteristically choose or are taught to be less than he is: a man alive who illuminates literature in an infinity of directions with his powerful vision of its moral relationship to all our human experience.

Herbert Lindenberger

LAWRENCE AND THE ROMANTIC TRADITION

In the genealogy of the novel, we have often been told
of late, there have been two persistent traditions. The first
of these might be called the novel of social relations. Its prime
concern is not the individual in isolation, but in a given social
situation. Its climaxes take the form of dramatic interchanges
between people, and if its affinities lie with any other genre,
it is surely with drama. Such traditional designations as "comic"
and "tragic" are often applicable to it, and in addition, through
its preoccupation with the intricacies of social behavior, it frequently has recourse to the ironic mode. In the hands of certain
of its masters, such as Jane Austen or Flaubert, it invites such
a term as "classic form." It is pre-eminently this type of novel
which Mr. Trilling had in mind when, in his essay "Manners,
Morals, and the Novel," he spoke of the central role that money,
snobbery, and the seemingly trivial details of daily living have
played in the history of fiction.

On the other side there is another tradition, too discontinuous
perhaps to be designated by a single name, though some, like
William York Tindall, call it the symbolist novel, and others,
like Richard Chase, writing within the context of American
literature, the romance. It is a form concerned less with the
individual's connection with other people than his relation to
larger forces and, for that matter, to himself. Its climaxes are
usually the protagonist's moments of intuition and revelation or,

Herbert Lindenberger, educated at Antioch, Northwestern, and the University of Washington (Ph.D.), Fulbright Fellow in Austria, 1952–53,
teaches Comparative Literature and German at the University of California, Riverside, and contributes to the leading professional journals;
he spent the year of 1958–59 in Europe researching for a book on
Romanticism.

if these climaxes take the form of interchanges, they are not so often interchanges between man and man as between man and nature. Its affinities are with poetry rather than drama (it is significant that many of its great practitioners—the Brontës, Melville, Hardy, Lawrence—were also serious poets). We often have good reason to complain of its wildness, its lack of discipline and, more specifically, its failure to deal on a concrete level with human motivation. On those rare occasions that we apply the term "classic form," as in the case of *The Return of the Native,* we feel uneasy that the form has perhaps been imposed artificially on the material. This is a type of novel often hortatory or persuasive in tone, since it attempts to give expression to a world view. As such it is seldom a self-contained entity, and we often complain of our inability to grasp the meaning of a particular work without knowing more of the author's works and interests. It is an introspective, self-conscious form, attempting to depict inward processes of growth and disintegration—in nature and in the individual. It is usually uneasy with plot, which is a convention taken over from the opposing tradition. Indeed, plot sometimes seems little more than a necessary evil, at best a peg onto which to hang reflections and intuitions that might otherwise stream into the impalpable. Often this newer tradition creates its plot through the image of the journey, sometimes an actual journey which its characters take, on other occasions a more general journey through life. It is a form obviously resulting from the thematic interests and literary methods which we have come to associate with the Romantic Movement.

One detects a fashion in recent years to assimilate Lawrence within the tradition of the social novel. Thus, when Arnold Kettle in his *Introduction to the English Novel* (London, 1953) interprets *The Rainbow* principally as "a revelation of the nature of personal relationships in twentieth-century England" (Vol. II, *124*), or when Dr. Leavis in his distinguished book on Lawrence stresses the social tensions in his writings, one suspects that Lawrence's new-found classical status is dependent on those aspects of his work that tie him to the dominant, obviously more respectable tradition in English fiction. Perhaps it is time to look once more at that other side of Lawrence, that side which, in the often stormy correspondence with Edward Garnett during the composition of *The Rainbow* and *Women in Love,* so firmly declared its revolt against the limitations imposed by the novel of social relations. At the start of the correspondence Lawrence was still unable to define the direction he was going: he knew only that the new work (at first conceived as a single novel) was "quite unlike *Sons and Lovers,* not a bit visualized," that he was moving away from the concrete, visually apprehensible social milieu of his previous novel. Somewhat later, when Garnett made specific criticisms of the manuscript, for instance, finding the character of the heroine "incoherent," Lawrence replied, "But if this, the second half, also disappoints you, I will, when I come to the end, leave this book altogether. Then I should propose to write a story with a plot, and to abandon the exhaustive method entirely." This "exhaustive method" he attempted to describe in some detail a half-year later, in what, through the example set in his resulting creative achievement, must remain one of the classic statements in the history of novel criticism:

. . . but somehow—that which is physic—non-human, in humanity, is more interesting to me than the old-fashioned human element—which causes one to conceive a character in a certain moral scheme and make him consistent. The certain moral scheme is what I object to. In Turgenev, and in Tolstoi, and in Dostoievsky, the moral scheme into which all the characters fit—and it is nearly the same scheme—is, whatever the extraordinariness of the characters themselves, dull, old dead. . . . You mustn't look in my novel for the old stable *ego* of character. There is another *ego,* according to whose action the individual is unrecognizable, and passes through, as it were, allotropic states which it needs a deeper sense than any we've been used to exercise, to discover are states of the same single radically unchanged element. . . . Again I say, don't look for the development of the novel to follow the lines of certain characters: the characters fall into the form of some other rhythmic form, as when one draws a fiddle-bow across a fine tray delicately sanded, the sand takes lines unknown.

(*Letters,* ed. Huxley, London, 1932, *177–99, passim.*)

The significance lies not in whether Lawrence was able to follow through with his program—to take it to its logical conclusion he would have had no characters, no social context at all—but in his search for an alternative to a narrow conception of the novel too easily taken for granted by his correspondent and all his contemporaries.

In his criticism of other writers Lawrence not only maintained this sense of an antithesis between two kinds of novel, but his sympathies were overwhelmingly with the nonsocial tradition, with any manifestations he could find of "that other rhythmic form" into which an author's characters might fall. In his "Study of Thomas Hardy," that strange dialogue with himself which he carried on while working on his two greatest novels, he wrote of *The Return of the Native:*

> What is the real stuff of tragedy in the book? It is the Heath. It is the primitive, primal earth, where the instinctive life heaves up. . . . This is a constant revelation in Hardy's novels: that there exists a great background, vital and vivid, which matters more than the people who move upon it.
>
> (*Phoenix,* London, 1936, *415* and *419*)

And the same phrase was echoed years later when, in a review of Grazia Deledda's *The Mother,* he wrote approvingly, "But the interest of the book lies, not in plot of characterization, but in the presentation of sheer instinctive life" (*Phoenix,* p. 265). It is no accident, moreover, that Lawrence's most searching and fruitful efforts as a critic were devoted to the American writers of the early and mid-nineteenth century. Quite in contrast to English and French fiction, the dominant strain in the Americans, with their attempt to express an all-encompassing vision in their work, was something to which Lawrence must have felt an instinctive kinship; and if his lively arguments with them are more solidly imprinted in our memory than his points of agreement, we must think of these arguments as essentially family quarrels. Throughout his criticism he always reminds us where his affinities lie: Flaubert, Thomas Mann, the Russians (his attitude toward the latter of course wavered), all served on various occasions as whipping boys; and Forster's *Passage to India* was dismissed with the remark, "Life is more interesting in its undercurrents than in its obvious; and E. M.

does see people, people and nothing but people: *ad nauseum"* (*Letters, 605–6*). To complain that Lawrence did not really understand these writers is like complaining of Charlotte Brontë's famous attack on Jane Austen: the aims and sensibilities of the writers in the two traditions are so fundamentally opposed that the statements they make about each other, while true on one level, are ultimately beside the point. The ironic vision is inevitably anathema to a novelist of the romantic tradition; and it seems only natural that Lawrence and Joyce, the two major, and complementary, novelists of their time, were unable, as many of their respective critics still are today, to reach a sympathetic understanding of each other's work.

ii

We can perhaps see those qualities which distinguish Lawrence's art from the social novel in a clearer light if we set his work momentarily next to an earlier masterpiece—itself neither fiction nor prose—with which it has some rather fundamental affinities. I am thinking of Wordsworth's *Prelude,* and its affinities to Lawrence's novels, especially *The Rainbow* and *Women in Love,* seem to me a matter both of the types of human experience with which they are concerned and of the modes of literary organization which they bring to bear on this experience. Most fundamental perhaps is the fact that both writers find a central purpose and motivation in their attempt to seek out the sources and manifestations of power in human life and the physical universe. When we come upon such a passage in *The Prelude* as the following:

> And after I had seen
> That spectacle, for many days, my brain
> Work'd with a dim and undetermin'd sense
> Of unknown modes of being; in my thoughts
> There was a darkness, call it solitude,
> Or blank desertion, no familiar shapes
> Of hourly objects, images of trees,
> Of sea or sky, no colours of green fields;
> But huge and mighty Forms that do not live
> Like living men mov'd slowly through the mind

By day and were the trouble of my dreams.
(i, *417–27* [1805])

and this one from *Women in Love:*

> Ursula set off to Willey Green, towards the mill. She came
> to Willey Water. It was almost full again, after its period of
> emptiness. Then she turned off through the woods. The night
> had fallen, it was dark. But she forgot to be afraid, she who
> had such great sources of fear. Among the trees, far from
> any human beings, there was a sort of magic peace. The more
> one could find a pure loneliness, with no taint of people,
> the better one felt. She was in reality terrified, horrified in
> her apprehension of people.
>
> She started, noticing something on her right hand, between
> the tree trunks. It was like a great presence, watching her,
> dodging her. She started violently. It was only the moon, risen
> through the thin trees. But it seemed so mysterious, with its
> white and deathly smile. And there was no avoiding it.
> Night or day, one could not escape the sinister face,
> triumphant and radiant like this moon, with a high smile.
> She hurried on, cowering from the white planet. She would
> just see the pond at the mill before she went home . . . ,
>
> (Chapter xix)

we are aware of a continuing tradition, stretching over a century, which attempts to render that mysterious life existing far
below the level of everyday, social experience. The dark gods
with which Lawrence grappled in their many guises share this
life with Wordsworth's "underpresences," "underpowers," "un-
dersoul," "underconsciousness"—all of these being words
which Wordsworth himself coined in *The Prelude* to express
something for which he could find no adequate existing names.

Moreover, in their attempt to find verbal expression for this
mysterious life, both writers appear to be giving an explanatory
"account" of their experiences or their characters, often em-
ploying what we would normally call abstract language to do
so. Dr. Leavis once wrote of *Tintern Abbey:* "Wordsworth
produces the mood, feeling or experience and at the same time
appears to be giving an explanation of it" (*Revaluation,* London, 1936, *159*). In the process of the telling us *about* the

"unknown modes of being" in the above passage, Wordsworth has, in effect, re-enacted the structure of the experience itself. Something of the same occurs in Lawrence. Writing at a time when abstractions and rhetoric were coming to be shunned, when the type of dramatic objectivity which we associate with Flaubert had become dogma for poet and novelist alike, Lawrence is not afraid to approach the seemingly undefinable experience from the outside, as when he depicts Ursula's spiritual exhaustion after her frenzied vision of the horses at the end of *The Rainbow:*

> As she sat there, spent, time and the flux of change passed away from her, she lay as if unconscious upon the bed of the stream, like a stone, unconscious, unchanging, unchangeable, whilst everything rolled by in transience, leaving her there, a stone at rest on the bed of the stream, inalterable and passive, sunk to the bottom of all change.
>
> (Chapter XVI)

The risk of course is overwriting, and, when removed from the full flow of the narrative, such a phrase as "time and the flux of change" or the attempt at incantation in "unconscious, unchanging, unchangeable," may seem to fall flat, yet in the course of "explaining" Ursula's sensations he has also succeeded in rendering the feeling of exhaustion. Lawrence's ambitious and not always successful attempts to portray sexual experience must be seen as part of the same attempt to explain directly and at the same time to render the nature of the experience dramatically.

But a still more basic affinity exists in the fact that both writers depend on certain central images and symbols as a prime way of asserting meaning. In *The Prelude,* with its obviously poetic organization, such recurrent images as the wind and the water function as a sort of symbolic "ground" through which the poet is able to probe into the deeper layers of human experience. Thus, in the following famous passage, though it starts out on the level of naturalistic description, Wordsworth gradually leads us into the area of visionary experience:

> There was a Boy, ye knew him well, ye Cliffs
> And Islands of Winander! many a time

At evening, when the stars had just begun
To move along the edges of the hills,
Rising or setting, would he stand alone
Beneath the trees, or by the glimmering Lake,
And there, with fingers interwoven, both hands
Press'd closely, palm to palm, and to his mouth
Uplifted, he, as through an instrument,
Blew mimic hootings to the silent owls
That they might answer him.—And they would shout
Across the watery Vale, and shout again,
Responsive to his call, with quivering peals,
And long halloos, and screams, and echoes loud
Redoubled and redoubled; concourse wild
Of mirth and jocund din! And when it chanced
That pauses of deep silence mock'd his skill,
Then sometimes, in that silence, while he hung
Listening, a gentle shock of mild surprize
Has carried far into his heart the voice
Of mountain torrents; or the visible scene
Would enter unawares into his mind
With all its solemn imagery, its rocks,
Its woods, and that uncertain Heaven, receiv'd
Into the bosom of the steady Lake.

(v, 389–413 [1805])

The water and, in fact, the whole natural scene are sensuously present for us, yet in the process of presenting them Wordsworth has also made us feel a deeper reality behind them. In something of the same way, the scene in which Birkin throws stones at the image of the moon in the pond not only serves as an indication of the progress of his relationship with Ursula, but also makes a larger symbolic statement about the nature of energy and will that goes far beyond the purely social context of the novel:

> He stood staring at the water. Then he stooped and picked up a stone, which he threw sharply at the pond. Ursula was aware of the bright moon leaping and swaying, all distorted, in her eyes. It seemed to shoot out arms of fire like a cuttlefish, like luminous polyp, palpitating strongly before her.
> And his shadow on the border of the pond, was watching

for a few moments, then he stooped and groped on the ground. Then again there was a burst of sound, and a burst of brilliant light, the moon had exploded on the water, and was flying asunder in flakes of white and dangerous fire. Rapidly, like white birds, the fires all broken rose across the pond, fleeing in clamorous confusion, battling with the flock of dark waves that were forcing their way in. The furthest waves of light, fleeing out, seemed to be clamouring against the shore for escape, the waves of darkness came in heavily, running under towards the centre. But at the centre, the heart of all, was still a vivid, incandescent quivering of a white moon not quite destroyed, a white body of fire writhing and striving and not even now broken open, not yet violated. It seemed to be drawing itself together with strange, violent pangs, in blind effort. It was getting stronger, it was re-asserting itself, the inviolable moon. And the rays were hastening in in thin lines of light, to return to the strengthened moon, that shook upon the water in triumphant reassumption.

(Chapter XIX)

For both Wordsworth and Lawrence the objects and processes of the natural world—it is noteworthy that both in *The Prelude* and *Women in Love* water serves as a dominant symbol—are basic modes of perception *through* which each writer moves to encompass the other aspects of his theme. The mist that surrounded Wordsworth as he climbed Mount Snowden and the loud torrents that he heard on reaching the top are an essential part of the process by which the meaning of the imagination was revealed to him. In the same way, the lifeless world of snow and ice in which Gerald Crich meets his death is Lawrence's way of apprehending and evaluating the *ethos* which his character represents.

There is still another, closely related affinity between Wordsworth and Lawrence which lies in the larger forms of literary organization which they employ. In their over-all structure the major novels of Lawrence, like *The Prelude,* attempt to portray processes of spiritual growth and exploration. What Lawrence once said of Hardy's novels as a whole, "The tale is about becoming complete, or about the failure to become complete" (*Phoenix, 410*), is obviously applicable to his own work. *Sons and Lovers* and *The Rainbow* are directly in the tradition of the novel of apprenticeship (of which *The Prelude* is a sort of indirect ancestor), and in his later work, when he is no longer concerned specifically with the growth of the child, he symbolizes growth and change through the image of the journey—Lou Carrington's search for fulfillment in the mountains of New Mexico, Kate Leslie's journey into the world of the re-awakened Aztec gods, and, conversely, Gerald Crich's search for spiritual and physical extinction in the Tyrolean snows. At numerous points in *The Prelude* Wordsworth refers to the course of the whole poem as a journey, but he also crowds the work with examples of actual, shorter journeys, like the ascent of Snowden, which serve as physical symbols of the spiritual experiences he is representing.

Fundamental also to both writers are the individual moments of intuition and revelation which one might call the basic structural units of their work. *The Prelude* is not so much a single tightly organized narrative as a succession of intense moments of visionary experience—like the episode of the stolen boat or the crossing of the Simplon Pass, what Wordsworth in another passage calls "spots of time"—often somewhat loosely related to one another, yet relevant to the poem's larger theme. Lawrence's work is full of comparable moments: one thinks of Birkin soothing his naked body in the woods of Breadalby after Hermione hit him with a paperweight, or of Anna Lensky being taken out to help her stepfather feed the animals while her mother was in childbirth. It might be said that the real plot of Lawrence's novels—and this is especially true of *The Rainbow* and *Women in Love*—cannot be traced so much through the character's external actions and fortunes as through the succession of concentrated moments of inward experience that they undergo. These moments are by no means always of an uplifting sort, but (analogous perhaps to Wordsworth's evocation of the teeming crowds of London in Book VII of *The Prelude*) are often markedly negative in nature, like Ursula's vision of the horses, or the demonic emptiness that finally overcomes the "man who loved islands." It is striking, moreover, that both Wordsworth and Lawrence have given us memorable portraits of human endurance in the face of the disintegrating forces of nature—Wordsworth in *The Ruined Cottage,* in the story of Margaret, who with elemental stubbornness endured the cold and damp of her disintegrating hut until she died, "last human tenant of these ruined walls"; Lawrence, in the story of the trader's wife in "St. Mawr" who though eventually abandoning the fight put up a gallant resistance to the "vast and unrelenting will of the lower life" in her ranch high in the New Mexico mountains.

The Lawrencean moments of revelation are not limited to man's experiences in nature, but are also basic to his relations with other human beings. Similarly to Wordsworth's encounters with solitaries like the discharged soldier in *The Prelude* or the leech-gatherer, the meetings between Lawrence's characters do not, as is usual in narrative, work principally to further the dramatic action, or to reveal new information about the characters, but rather they should be seen as a sort of communion (if I may borrow a term used by Mark Spilka in his study, *The Love Ethic of D. H. Lawrence*), a ritualized demonstration of the vitality and mystery latent in human relationships.

Perhaps the most memorable of these rituals is the moonlit scene in *The Rainbow* in which Will and Anna are shown gathering the sheaves of grain, both of them losing their separate identity as they enter upon a deeper, more elemental rhythm. The process they undergo is something of what Lawrence meant in the statement to Garnett quoted earlier: "There is another *ego,* according to whose action the individual is unrecognizable, and passes through, as it were, allotropic states." This ritual in *The Rainbow* is strongly reminiscent of another great scene of harvest. I am thinking of that scene in *Anna Karenina* in which the landowner Levin joins his peasants in the task of mowing hay: at first he is hard put to keep up with them and finds himself too fatigued to go on, but gradually he lets himself lose track of his conscious thoughts and soon he has entered upon the rhythm of the others. Neither of these scenes, however, resolves itself in the total dissolution of human personality, for each culminates in communion, in a ritualized meeting of people. In Tolstoy the climax is a temporary merging of social classes, as Levin sits down to share some bread and home-brew offered him by an aged peasant; in Lawrence it is the recognition of human love. For Lawrence such moments of communion— whether specifically of a sexual nature or in the achievement of understanding between sharply diverse personalities, as in the story "The Blind Man"—are the highest goals toward which his characters can strive. It is here, perhaps, that the gulf which separates Lawrence from Joyce reveals itself most clearly—for *Ulysses almost* culminates in a moment of communion between its two heroes, but the ritual is ultimately stifled and subjected to parody.

iii

In isolating a romantic tradition in fiction to contrast with that of the novel of society, I have perhaps implied that the two traditions are mutually exclusive. Actually every extended narrative is bound, to some degree, to deal with characters within a specific social context. Even *Moby Dick* is not concerned merely with ultimates, but also with personal relationships aboard the *Pequod*. In *Anna Karenina,* dealing as it does with Levin's self-development on one side, and with the heroine's relations to society on the other, we find the two traditions operating alternately by means of double plot. It could be said, moreover, that Lawrence in his best work was able to fuse the two traditions, and it may well be that his contribution to the history of the novel will be seen in his success in instilling the dominant strain of English fiction with the essentially poetic materials of the romantic tradition. His first two novels, *The White Peacock* and *The Trespasser,* are still distinctly outside the social realm, and Lawrence indicates a sense of their limitations in a letter describing the early stages of his third book: *"Paul Morel* will be a novel—not a florid prose poem, or a decorated idyll running to seed in realism: but a restrained, somewhat impersonal novel" (*Letters, 5*). But the resulting *Sons and Lovers* was not so far removed from the romantic tradition as Lawrence seems to have planned: despite the conventional novelistic framework and its wealth of naturalistic detail and vivid character analysis, its inner structure is determined by a succession of moments of high tension, or "waves," to borrow a term used by Seymour Betsky in his interpretation of this novel (in *The Achievement of D. H. Lawrence,* Norman, Oklahoma, 1953). The fusion of plot frame and inner structure in *Sons and Lovers* is not altogether complete, and it is in the following period, in *The Rainbow* and *Women in Love,* that Lawrence was first able to weld elements of the two traditions successfully. His success in *The Rainbow* is due to his letting the novelistic elements remain in the background, using the conventions of the family novel and the apprenticeship novel, which shape the two halves of the book, to provide the necessary continuity for Lawrence's more pressing interests—processes of growth and change, the search for fulfillment, and, inextricably connected with these, man's relationship to the natural world. In *Women in Love,* the two traditions are more evenly balanced and, in fact, are so intricately blended that each element serves as a sort of comment on and extension of the other throughout the book. Thus, the "instinctive life" that emanates from the famous rabbit implicitly defines the character and relationship of the two characters who seek to confine it. The accidental drowning at the water-party, with all its wider poetic reverberations, is the natural culmination of all we have learned about life at Shortlands up to that point in the book.

In none of his later work, except for some of the tales, was Lawrence able to keep the two traditions so successfully in harmony with one another as in these two major novels. In "The Captain's Doll," "The Princess," and "St. Mawr" he creates a balance of forces similar to that of *Women in Love,* though on a smaller scale: the first half of each of these tales is predominantly social comedy, to a large degree even ironic, while the final portions, with their evocations of the vitality inherent in their Austrian and New World mountain settings, work to enrich and extend the meanings of the social situations with which Lawrence had begun. In "The Man Who Loved Islands" the very absence of social setting gives the work a profoundly social meaning. But the balance is lost in the later novels. In *Aaron's Rod* the hero's search for fulfillment never really gets off to a proper start. In *The Lost Girl,* though its early chapters of provincial life show Lawrence's extraordinary talent as social novelist in the Arnold Bennett tradition, the means by which the heroine seeks to transcend her narrow environment are implausible and incapable of carrying the necessary symbolic weight. *Kangaroo* succeeds as an evocation of the spirit of Australian place, and also as political reflection—but the very emptiness which it evokes so well betrays its failure to find adequate social embodiment for its essentially social theme. *The Plumed Serpent,* except for its opening chapters, is insufficiently rooted in any concrete social milieu, and its attempt to evoke a lost pagan world, for all its rhetorical splendor, ultimately has a hollow ring. *Lady Chatterley's Lover* seems successful more as a novel of social than of sexual relations; despite the high prophetic purpose evident from the first line, the elements belonging to the romantic tradition, except for the fierce negative vision of the desecration of the Midlands landscape, lack the drive and symbolic power that they had in earlier works. Only in *The Escaped Cock,* perhaps because of its brevity and its distancing in time, was Lawrence successful in creating a work almost totally without the traditional novelistic elements and fully on the level of pastoral idyll.

And yet one feels uneasy assigning degrees of "success" so neatly to individual works; for Lawrence ultimately defies what we today call "critical analysis"—a mode of criticism dedicated to the demonstration of the unity of form and meaning within a work, a mode that originated as a defense of certain modern poets (not including Lawrence) and as a response to the Metaphysical and Symbolist tradition in poetry and the type of novel typified by Flaubert and Henry James. Lawrence is of course not wholly alien to these traditions, and it is much to Dr. Leavis' credit that he has been able to demonstrate where the modern "classical" (though not the specifically Flaubertian) virtues are to be found in Lawrence—his discussion, for instance of "The Captain's Doll" has drawn attention to a work largely immune to the prejudices of modern criticism—as well as to point out the traditional human pieties at the center of his work. But for a larger understanding of Lawrence as novelist one must also take into account certain factors distinctly inimical to the critical canons of the present day. For one thing, it is difficult to approach any one of his works (except perhaps for the tales) as an independent, self-sustained entity in the way we can, say, *Madame Bovary* or *Tom Jones:* even a work like *Women in Love* would give the reader who is unfamiliar with anything else by or about Lawrence little sense of its meaning or stature. One could speak of a sort of overflow principle in his work ("overflow" was what Wordsworth called those passages which he could not accommodate in his poems) whereby the interests, attitudes, methods, and also the mannerisms of one novel flow not only into other novels, but also into the travel books, poems, letters, and essays. One must not expect consistency of tone from him, for Lawrence alternately exhorts, asserts, elegizes, celebrates: that mode of presentation which we dignify as "objective" and "dramatic" can only be found intermittently in his work. Nor can we expect economy in the classical sense (except again for some of the tales): to portray the types of experience that most deeply concern him he must often resort to a highly adjectival, repetitive style, and with the inevitable risk of stridency and overstatement (traits which are far less forgivable to modern taste than laxness and lack of statement).

An adequate critical approach, then, must take into account the *kind* of writer Lawrence was and, like all good criticism past or present, must be grounded not on abstract standards but on principles which have been defined as an honest response to the impact of the writing itself. One suspects that our understanding of Lawrence will gain in perspective through some of the recent studies that have sought to re-examine the nature of nineteenth-century literature and its relation to that of the present. I refer to such works as Robert Langbaum's *The Poetry of Experience,* John Bayley's *The Romantic Survival,* and Frank Kermode's *The Romantic Image,* all of which, though concerned specifically with poetry, attempt to demonstrate the continuity, both rhetorical and thematic, between the Romantics and the writers of the early twentieth century. Perhaps even more directly relevant to Lawrence is John Holloway's *The Victorian Sage* which, through close analysis of rhetorical methods and aims, describes a distinctive type of writing exemplified in a line of artist-moralists extending from Carlyle to Hardy. Thus far only Raymond Williams, who in his chapter on Lawrence in *Culture and Society* juxtaposes passages from the expository writings of Lawrence and Carlyle, has begun to relate Lawrence to the writers of the preceding century. Lawrence is surely a direct descendant of the tradition

Mr. Holloway has described, and if we have been hesitant to link him to his romantic and Victorian forebears, this is not only an obvious consequence of our lack of interest in this tradition, but also a tribute to Lawrence's distinctly contemporary relevance.

A. Alvarez

D. H. LAWRENCE: THE SINGLE STATE OF MAN

Art itself doesn't interest me, only the spiritual content.
D. H. LAWRENCE, Letter to Eunice Tietjens, 1917.

THE only native English poet of any importance to survive the First World War was D. H. Lawrence.[1] Yet his verse is very little read. As a minor adjunct to the novels it has come in, on occasions, for a little offhand comment. More often it is used as a go-between, joining the prose to the biography. Anthologists have printed a few poems grudgingly, out of piety, and even the critic who introduced the best English selection, in the Penguin Poets, seemed to feel that the poems succeed despite themselves, because they were written by Lawrence.

I had better state my position straightaway: I think the poems very fine indeed, with a fineness of perception and development that was always Lawrence's, and an originality that makes them as important as any poetry of our time. For their excellence comes from something that is rare at best, and now, in the 1950's well-nigh lost: a complete truth to feeling. Lawrence is the foremost emotional realist of the century. He wrote too much verse, like Hardy and Whitman, the two poets who influenced him most. But even his badness is the badness of genius; and there are quite enough good poems to make up for it. As for the influences and the styles he brushed with,

A. Alvarez, a native of London, who received his B.A. at Oxford and his M.A. at Princeton (1956), has taught in the Creative Writing Program at Princeton, has been editor of *The Journal of Education* and a frequent contributor to British and American magazines. His essay is reprinted from *Stewards of Excellence,* by A. Alvarez, with permission of Charles Scribner's Sons. Copyright, 1958, by A. Alvarez. (British title: *The Shaping Spirit,* published by Chatto and Windus, London, 1958.)

Georgian and imagist, I will have nothing to say of them here. They have no part in his best work.

Lawrence's poetry is usually hustled out of court by way of its "carelessness." I believe it was Eliot who first said that Lawrence wrote only sketches for poems, nothing ever quite finished. In one way there is some truth to this: he was not interested in surface polish; his verse is informal in the conventional sense. Indeed, the tighter the form the more the poet struggles, as in "Love Storm":

> Many roses in the wind
> Are tapping at the window-sash.
> A hawk is in the sky; his wings
> Slowly begin to plash.

It is the last word that jars. I see what he means, but the need to rhyme is like a wedge driven between the object and the word. The thing is forced and uneasy, even a little journalistic. Again and again, when Lawrence uses strict metrical forms, the poetry fails because of them, or succeeds despite them. At times he can manage complicated stanzas, but only because they allow him to get away from close correspondence of rhyme; they give him space to move around. The fainter the chime, the more remote the echo, the more convinced the poetry seems; close and perfect rhyme is invariably a constriction to him. For an essential part of Lawrence's genius was his fluency; and I mean something more literal than the ease with which he wrote: rather, the sense of direction in all the flowing change and variation in his work. This fluency has its own forms without its own conventions. It is not plottable: ear-count, finger-count, and what might be called the logic of received form have nothing to do with it. What matters is the disturbance. "It doesn't depend on the ear, particularly," he once wrote, "but on the sensitive soul." It is something that can never be laid out into a system, for it comes instead from the poet's rigorous but open alertness. And so there is care, even discipline, but no formal perfection and finish. In an introductory note to *Fire and Other Poems* Frieda Lawrence wrote: "He just wrote down his verse as it came to him. But later, when he thought of putting them into a book to be printed, he would work them over with great care and infinite patience." And she has remarked that in a way he worked harder at his poetry than at the novels. When the prose would not go right he threw it away and began afresh. But the poems he worked over again and again. As proof there are the early drafts of "Bavarian Gentians" and "The Ship of Death," which are now printed as an appendix to the *Collected Poems*. Still, his diligence had nothing to do with mere technical efficiency. Lawrence's controlling standard was delicacy: a constant, fluid awareness, nearer the checks of intimate talk than those of regular prosody. His poetry is not the outcome of rules and formal craftsmanship, but of a purer, more native and immediate artistic sensibility. It is poetry because it could not be otherwise.

He was well aware of what he was about. He put his case in the introduction to *New Poems:*

> To break the lovely form of metrical verse, and dish up the fragments as a new substance, called *vers libre,* this is what most of the free-versifiers accomplish. They do not know that free verse has its own *nature,* that it is neither star nor pearl, but instantaneous like plasm. . . . It has no finish. It has no satisfying stability, satisfying for those who like the immutable. None of this. It is the instant; the quick.

If Lawrence is trying to get the weight of formalism off his back, it is not for laziness. "The instant; the quick" is as difficult to catch, to fix in exact language, as the most measured and stable formulations of experience. For this sort of impulse is in opposition to poetic conventions. The writer can never rely on a code of poetic manners to do part of the work for him. At the same time, of course, Lawrence knew his own powers and limitations well enough to realize that "art" in some way deflected him from the real poetry. "Art for my sake," he said. Perhaps this is what he meant in the introduction to the *Collected Poems:*

> The first poems I ever wrote, if poems they were, was when I was nineteen: now twenty-three years ago. I remember perfectly the Sunday afternoon when I perpetrated those first two pieces: "To Guelder Roses" and "To Campions"; in springtime, of course, and, as I say, in my twentieth year.

Any young lady might have written them and been pleased with them; as I was pleased with them. But it was after that, when I was twenty, that my real demon would now and then get hold of me and shake more real poems out of me, making me uneasy. I never "liked" my real poems as I liked "To Guelder Roses". . . . Some of the earliest poems are a good deal rewritten. They were struggling to say something which it takes a man twenty years to be able to say. . . . A young man is afraid of his demon and puts his hand over the demon's mouth sometimes and speaks for him. And the things the young man says are very rarely poetry. So I have tried to let the demon say his say, and to remove the passages where the young man intruded. So that, in the first volume, many poems are changed, some entirely rewritten, recast. But usually this is only because the poem started out to be something which it didn't quite achieve, because the young man interfered with his demon.

This is at the opposite pole to Eliot's defense of Pound's hard work. For Eliot, the continued business of versifying was a way of keeping the bed aired until such time as the Muse should decide to visit. Lawrence's work was in coming to terms with his demon, so that the utterance would be unhindered. For it was the utterance, what he had to say, which was poetic; not the analyzable form and technique. So for all his trouble, he never innovated in Pound's or Eliot's way. His discoveries were a matter of personal judgment and response. In the poems the speed and stress varies with the immediate, inward pressure. This is why the words "loose" and "careless" so clearly do not describe Lawrence's verse.

To have an example down on the page, there is "End of Another Home Holiday." To my mind, it is the best of the early rhyming poems. The demon has his say without awkwardness, but there is just enough of the earlier contrivance to show what Lawrence had left behind:

When shall I see the half-moon sink again
Behind the black sycamore at the end of the garden?
When will the scent of the dim white phlox
Creep up the wall to me, and in at my open window?

Why is it, the long, slow stroke of the midnight bell
    (Will it never finish the twelve?)
Falls again and again on my heart with heavy reproach?

The moon-mist is over the village, out of the mist speaks
    the bell,
And all the little roofs of the village bow low, pitiful, be-
    seeching, resigned.
—Speak, you my home! What is it I don't do well?

Ah home, suddenly I love you
As I hear the sharp clean trot of a pony down the road,
Succeeding sharp little sounds dropping into silence
Clear upon the long-drawn hoarseness of a train across the
    valley.

    .   .   .   .

The light has gone out from under my mother's door.
    That she should love me so!—
    She, so lonely, greying now!
    And I leaving her,
    Bent on my pursuits!

       Love is the great Asker.
       The sun and the rain do not ask the secret
       Of the time when the grain struggles down in the dark.
       The moon walks her lonely way without anguish,
       Because no-one grieves over her departure.

Forever, ever by my shoulder pitiful love will linger,
Crouching as the little houses crouch under the mist when
    I turn.
Forever, out of the mist, the church lifts up a reproachful
    finger,
Pointing my eyes in wretched defiance where love hides her
    face to mourn.

       Oh! but the rain creeps down to wet the grain
       That struggles alone in the dark,
       And asking nothing, patiently steals back again!
       The moons sets forth o' nights
       To walk the lonely, dusky heights
       Serenely, with steps unswerving;

Pursued by no sigh of bereavement,
No tears of love unnerving
Her constant tread:
While ever at my side,
Frail and sad, with grey, bowed head,
The beggar-woman, the yearning-eyed
Inexorable love goes lagging.

The wild young heifer, glancing distraught,
With a strange new knocking of life at her side
    Runs seeking a loneliness.
The little grain draws down the earth, to hide.
Nay, even the slumberous egg, as it labours under the shell
    Patiently to divide and self-divide,
Asks to be hidden, and wishes nothing to tell.

But when I draw the scanty cloak of silence over my eyes
Piteous love comes peering under the hood;
Touches the clasp with trembling fingers, and tries
To put her ear to the painful sob of my blood;
While her tears soak through to my breast,
    Where they burn and cauterise.

.   .   .   .

The moon lies back and reddens.
In the valley a corncrake calls
    Monotonously,
With a plaintive, unalterable voice, that deadens
    My confident activity;
With a hoarse, insistent request that falls
    Unweariedly, unweariedly,
Asking something more of me,
    Yet more of me.

I have put the poem there in full because, like all of Lawrence's
verse, it needs its whole length to express its complexity. It
seems to me a difficult poem. Yet there is nothing immediately
incomprehensible about it, none of those tough intellectual obstacles that stop you short in Eliot's work. There is a curious
intermixing of people and scene and nature. But beyond that
the difficulty is in the state of mind: the pull between love and
guilt, the tension between man and child.

It is all in the first four lines. They have a kind of awakened rhythm which cuts below the expectations of formality to the "sensitive soul." As Lawrence said of a line by Whitman, "It makes me prick my innermost ear." Only in the first ten-syllabled line will finger-count pay. After that the poem moves off on its own way. There is more in question than nostalgia; the speed of the lines varies with the flexibility of the talking voice. Part troubled, part meditative, the nostalgia is quick-ened instead of being expanded into a mood. If my comments are vague and assertive, I can only add another assertion: they have to be. Everything depends on the reader's direct response to the rhythm. In that is all the disturbance which the rest of the poem defines.

Perhaps "define" is the wrong word; "draw out" might be closer. For what follows is done without a hint of abstraction. What is there to be defined is a complex of feelings, nothing that can be tidily separated out into formulae. All that is pos-sible, and all the poet attempts, is to reach through intelligence some balance in the conflict.

Why is it, the long, slow stroke of the midnight bell
    (Will it never finish the twelve?)
Falls again and again on my heart with a heavy reproach?

There are three forces: the young man, literary and fond of word-painting; then, undercutting him, uneasy impatience; and finally, guilt. Mercifully, there is no need to go through the poem line by line to show how these two feelings take over all the details of the scene, so that it becomes a sort of living presence for the poet to face. The result is that he can move from his village to his mother, from natural to artistic creation, without the least strain.

The poet is peculiarly unembarrassed and open about his feelings. He values his independence, but he doesn't assert it: the hint of self-absorption in "Bent on my pursuits" has the same touch of irony about it as, for example,

But when I draw the scanty cloak of silence over my eyes
Piteous love comes peering under the hood;

And his central theme, "Love is the great Asker," is both ac-knowledgment *and* criticism: the demands of love touch the vital part of him, "Where they burn and cauterise"; yet even while they expose what is shallow and selfish in him, they expose themselves by their own nagging insistence.

The theme is love, but there is nothing in the poem of a "Definition of Love," with all that implies of dapper logic and clear-cut distinctions. Lawrence's logic is more intimate. It is carried forward by a rigorous worrying, probing down to the quick of the feelings. Although the personal conflict is set off by the cycle of nature, no parallels are drawn. The forces work in harmony rather than in contradistinction. Despite all the talk of the sun and the moon, the grain and the heifer, and even that "slumberous egg," the focus stays personal. In phrases like

> No tears of love *unnerving*
> Her constant tread

you see how the same difficult, intimate preoccupation runs under the whole thing. So without any of Marvell's syllogizing there is still a completeness to the poem; in the end, something has been settled. It is done by what Eliot called a "logic of sensibility" (though, in fact, he probably meant something quite different). The toughness, instead of being in the logic, is in the truth to feeling, the constant exertion of the poet's intelligence to get close to what he really feels, not to accept on the way any easy formulation or avoidance.

This is why a set meter would have been impossible—as it was impossible in Coleridge's "Dejection." Each line has its own force and rhythm, and they flow together, varying with the shifts in feeling. This is true of almost all Lawrence's poems; the inner pressure and disturbance gives to every one its own inherent form. Each starts afresh and appeals directly to the attention of "the sensitive soul." The controlling factor is in the intelligence. His poems are not effusions; they don't run off with him. Instead, the intelligence works away at the emotions, giving to each poem a finished quality, an economy in all the repetitions. It is a matter of the fullness with which the subject is presented.

This intelligent honesty and pertinacity of Lawrence's verse has had very little attention. The poems which have come in for most notice, the *Birds, Beasts and Flowers,* are usually thought of as little more than vivid little pieces of description,

like the so-called "lyric" passages in his novels. In fact, the
nature poems are quite as personal as any of his others. In
them he doesn't merely describe, nor does he go at his subjects
with a preconceived idea and try to twist them into meanings
they would not naturally take. They are neither all subject nor
all poet. It is a matter of a vital and complex relationship between the two, difficult, fluent, inward, and wholly unabstract.
He even avoids the final abstraction of formal perfection. For
that gives to experience a kind of ghostly Platonic idealness:
in the end, everything is so perfectly accounted for that the
poetic world is complete and isolated. In the relationship
Lawrence tries to catch, everything is in flux; it is a flow between two creatures, with nothing fixed. The artist has constantly to improvise at the full pitch of his intelligence. And according to Lawrence, who judged intelligence by its delicacy
and awareness, not by its command of rationalization, the
greater the intelligence the nearer the result came to poetry.
The foreword to *Pansies* says:

> It has always seemed to me that a real thought, a single
> thought, not an argument, can only exist easily in verse, or
> in some poetic form. There is a didactic element about prose
> thoughts which makes them repellent, slightly bullying.

The same sort of intelligence is at work in the novels, but
the actual method is rather different. Again, the didactic sections
hardly matter—though in some of the later novels they take
up more space than they are worth. The whole method is to set
the characters in motion, so there is a curious fusion of feeling
and action, each dependent on the other, deepening the other,
and yet resisting any single interpretation. Hence the word
"symbolism" that is often tacked on to his method; I prefer
Dr. Leavis' term, "dramatic poem." Of course, Lawrence himself is there in all his novels; but at the remove of fiction. There
is no need to make an exact identification, for the author has
given himself enough room to dramatize and judge with a free
hand. The poems are more intimate, and their personal statements are outright. He said of the *Collected Poems:* "I have
tried to establish a chronological order, because many of the
poems are so personal that, in their fragmentary fashion, they
make up a biography of an emotional and inner life." There

precisely is the difference: the theme of both the novels and the poems is fulfillment, the spiritual maturity achieved between man and woman. But in the novels the fulfillment is acted out; the forces, like the morality, are "passionate, implicit." By contrast, the poems present nakedly the inner flow that runs below the actions, the forces before they are externalized in drama. It is as though they presented not the body that acts but the blood itself, the lifeline of experience and feeling that feeds and supports the novels.

Here, for example, is a passage from a novel which develops much the same theme as "End of Another Home Holiday":

No man was beyond woman. But in his one quality of ultimate maker and breaker, he was womanless. Harriet denied this, bitterly. She wanted to share, to join in, not to be left out lonely. He looked at her in distress, and did not answer. It is a knot that can never be untied; it can only, like a navel string, be broken or cut.

For the moment, however, he said nothing. But Somers knew from his dreams what she was feeling: his dreams of a woman, a woman he loved, something like Harriet, something like his mother, and yet unlike either, a woman sullen and obstinate against him, repudiating him. Bitter the woman was grieved beyond words, grieved till her face was swollen and puffy and almost mad or imbecile, because she had loved him so much, and now she must see him betray her love. That was how the dream woman put it: he had betrayed her great love, and she must go down desolate into an everlasting hell, denied, and denying him absolutely in return, a sullen, awful soul. The face reminded him of Harriet, and of his mother, and of his sister, and of girls he had known when he was younger—strange glimpses of all of them, each glimpse excluding the last. And at the same time in the terrible face some of the look of that bloated face of a madwoman which hung over Jane Eyre in the night in Mr. Rochester's house.

The Somers of the dream was terribly upset. He cried tears from his very bowels, and laid his hand on the woman's arm saying:

"But I love you. Don't you *believe* in me? Don't you *be-*

lieve in me?" But the woman, she seemed almost old now—
only shed a few bitter tears, bitter as vitriol, from her distorted face, and bitterly, hideously turned away, dragging
her arm from the touch of his fingers; turned, as it seemed
to the dream-Somers, away to the sullen and dreary, everlasting hell of repudiation.

He woke at this, and listened to the thunder of the sea
with horror. With horror. Two women in his life he had loved
down to the quick of life and death: his mother and Harriet.
And the woman in the dream was so awfully his mother,
risen from the dead, and at the same time Harriet, as it were,
departing from this life, that he stared at the night-paleness
between the window-curtains in horror.

"They neither of them believed in me," he said to himself.
Still in the spell of the dream, he put it into the past tense,
though Harriet lay sleeping in the next bed. He could not get
over it.

This is from *Kangaroo,* where Somers is no less Lawrence than
the much younger man who wrote the poem. And the same
demon is at work in both, the same crucifixion between guilt
and love, between independent male activity and unanswerable
emotional ties; and, in the end, the same sense of inevitable
betrayal. Yet although the dream allows Lawrence to use a kind
of emotional shorthand and a bare directness of presentation,
the novel and the poem only converge from opposite directions.
In the verse the feelings *are happening* to the poet in all their
conflict. In the novel they are embodied in action. They are
given sides and the complexity is left to flower in the spaces
between.

The whole of Lawrence's power and originality as a poet
depends on the way he keeps close to his feelings. This is why
he had to rid himself of conventional forms. The poems take
even their shape from the feelings. And so it is a long way
off the mark to think of them as jotted-down talk. The span of
the lines is not that of the talking voice. The tone is: that is, it
is direct and without self-consciousness. But the poems, for
instance, use more repetitions than talk. Yet this is a matter of
fullness, not of rhetorical elaboration. It is part of the purpose-
fulness with which the poems explore the emotions in their

entirely. And with the same sureness he can let them go; when he is writing from no more than an impulse or an irritation, short and transient, the poetry is equally brief and to the point —*Pansies,* for example; but when the feelings are profound and sustained, so is the verse form: as in, say, "Bavarian Gentians," one of his masterpieces. The dependence of the form on the subject means that the poems find it very hard to rarify themselves into mere words and device.

The lines themselves help to the accuracy and delicacy of the expression. They are a means of emphasis rather than a pause for breath, as in "Snake":

> He drank enough
> And lifted his head, dreamily, as one who has drunken,
> And flickered his tongue like a forked night on the air,
>   so black,
> Seeming to lick his lips,
> And looked around like a god, unseeing, into the
>   air. . . .

Again, it is a question of movement, or rather of two movements, one playing against the other. There are actions, the ordinary, recognizable sanity of things happening in a human, or almost human way; these get the short matter-of-fact lines: "He drank enough," "Seeming to lick his lips." And then, in subtle contrast, is the running, disturbed movement of the longer lines in which the poet catches up the factual description into his own excitement. The known merges with the unknown: "as one who had drunken" becomes "like a forked night on the air," and ends "like a god." And so, within the framework of a description, the interchange between these two creatures takes on the dignity of a strange visitation. He is unloosing, in fact, the reserves of power of two earlier lines in the poem:

> Someone was before me at my water-trough,
> And I, like a second comer, waiting.

For all the implications, there is nothing "otherworldly" about this. The stuff of Lawrence's poetry, the "lifeline," are those essential experiences in which he registers his full humanity. His poems are the inner flow of a man in the act of becoming aware—aware not only of his feelings and their cause, but of their full implications. By the flexibility of his verse forms he can catch this flow in all its immediacy, and with peculiarly little fuss. For fuss has no part in what he has to say. Lawrence is not a mystic; his poetry has to do with recognitions, not with revelations. It should be read not against the cant of "dark gods" and the stridency of *The Plumed Serpent,* but against the sanity of the "creed" with which he answered Benjamin Franklin:

> That I am I.
> That my soul is a dark forest.
> That my known self will never be more than a little clearing in the forest.
> That gods, strange gods, come forth from the forest into the clearing of my known self, and then go back.
> That I must have the courage to let them come and go.
> That I will never let mankind put anything over me, but that I will always try to recognize and submit to the gods in me and the gods in other men and women.

There is only reverence, attention, awareness, and an unprejudiced independent intelligence at the bottom of this; no otherworldliness, nothing in the least of overblown pretension. It is the imaginative strength with which Lawrence voiced the fullness of his humanity that has got him the name of mystic and prophet, as it did for Blake. Lawrence does not have second sight, he has only a piercingly clear first sight. His genius is in rendering that, rather than waiting until his perceptions have gathered about them a decent abstraction, as the warm-blooded body of a whale is enclosed in protective blubber. Lawrence's mysticism is merely his firsthandness, his distance from convention.

Earlier, I remarked that the controlling force in the verse is neither any formal metrical guide nor a set of preordained principles; it is the working intelligence. On this his most genuine and effective poetry relies. The intelligence is primarily in the honesty with which he acknowledged his feelings and recognizes his motives with neither shuffling nor abstraction. But it is there too in the wit, the endless liveliness of his verse:

How beastly the bourgeois is
especially the male of the species—

Presentable, eminently presentable—
shall I make you a present of him?

Or

It is a fearful thing to fall into the hands of the living
    God
But it is a much more fearful thing to fall out of
    them . . .

Or

You tell me I am wrong.
Who are you, who is anybody to tell me I am wrong?
I am not wrong.

The closeness of this last to "For Godsake hold your tongue, and let me love" seems to me to be apparent enough. Yet Lawrence's verse, for all its wit and swing, has never been resurrected in the craze for Donne. The reason is simply that the twentieth-century Metaphysical style has been used as an excuse for obliqueness. The canons of irony invoked to display its excellence are merely ways of avoiding commitment, a technical sleight of mind by which the poet can seem to take many sides while settling, in fact, for none. Lawrence, clearly, does not suffer from this—neither, I believe, did Donne. The wit of both is not a sparkle on top of indifference; it is a manifestation of intelligence:

Imagine that any mind ever *thought* a red geranium!
As if the redness of a red geranium could be anything
        but a sensual experience
and as if sensual experience could take place before
        there were any senses.
We know that even God could not imagine the redness
        of a red geranium
nor the smell of mignonette
when geraniums were not, and mignonette neither.
And even when they were, even God would have to
        have a nose to smell at the mignonette.

You can't imagine the Holy Ghost sniffing at cherry-
pie heliotrope.
Or the Most High, during the coal age, cudgelling his
mighty brains
even if he had any brains: straining his mighty mind
to think, among the moss and mud of lizards and
mastodons
to think out, in the abstract, when all was twilit green
and muddy:
"Now there shall be tum-tiddly-um, and tum-tiddly-
um,
hey presto! scarlet geranium!"

We know it couldn't be done.
But imagine, among the mud and the mastodons
god sighing and yearning with tremendous creative
yearning, in that dark green mess
oh, for some other beauty, some other beauty
that blossomed at last, red geranium, and mignonette.

It is hard to know whether to emphasize more the ease and
originality of the piece, or its tact. There is neither a jot of
pretentiousness in the poem, nor of vulgarity, though the opportunity for both certainly offered. Lawrence uses his wit not
in the modern fashion, to save his face, but to strengthen the
seriousness of what he has to say. There is no disproportion
between the colloquial liveliness of the opening and the equally
alive tenderness of the close. The wit is not a flourish; it is one
of the poetic means; it preserves the seriousness from sentimentality and overstatement, as the seriousness keeps the wit
from flippancy.

Lawrence wrote too many poems. Their standard is not
uniformly high; some of them are frankly bad. In this count I
am leaving out *Pansies* and *Nettles*. Though some of these are
good, they were intended primarily as squibs; and even if they
have a serious enough edge to their satire, few are particularly
memorable as poetry. Nor is he to be held responsible for the
faults of his early verse; they are the faults of a poet who is
still trying to find his own voice. The bad poems are those which
have a complete originality, yet still fail. For example, the
sequence "Wedlock" in the transitional volume *Look! We Have*

Come Through! Like his best poems, they go down to the pith of the feelings and present that in its singleness. But they fail because they are too naked. It is as though the feelings were overwhelming beyond speech, yet still the poet insisted on nothing less than their full force, muffled by no sort of poetic device. In "Burnt Norton" Eliot justifies a long series of images which suggest an intense experience without stating it by the comment: ". . . human kind/Cannot bear very much reality." In these poems, Lawrence is insisting on nothing short of the emotional reality, and the poetry cannot quite bear it. They are not private as the *Pisan Cantos* are private; they have no references which remain in the poet's keeping. They are private in the other sense: they make the reader feel he is listening in where he shouldn't be. It is for this reason that *Look!,* although it contains some excellent poems, is more successful as a series than in any one piece. Lawrence himself said, "They are intended as an essential story, or history, or confession," and Amy Lowell thought they made up "a greater novel even than *Sons and Lovers."* That is an overstatement which was worth making. The impact of the book seems to me as direct and painful as anything since Clare. Yet it would be hard to localize this power in any one poem. If some of the pieces fail because of their nakedness, it is because they are approaching the vanishing point of poetry, where expression itself is some sort of intrusion. It took genius and great courage even to fail in that way. When Lawrence's poems are bad they are victims of that peculiar honesty which, at other times, made for their strength.

Lawrence was honest about the emotions without being absorbed in them for their own sakes. He is not taken up in himself. The lifeline of his poems is something more active, harder and more delicate. "But it's no good," he wrote to Murry, "Either you go on wheeling a wheelbarrow and lecturing at Cambridge and going softer and softer inside, or you make a hard fight with yourself, pull yourself up, harden yourself, throw your feelings down the drain and face the world as a fighter.—You won't though." Lawrence's poems are about that "hard fight." He never relished his feelings, nor played with them in front of the mirror; hence he never simplified them. But he always kept extraordinarily close to them; and so he never fell into oversubtlety, the intellectual counterpart of emotional looseness. The language of the poems, lucid, witty, vivid, often a bit slangy, preserved the balance. It made any kind of overstatement or evasion very hard.

The question why Lawrence's poetry has had so little recognition, despite its originality, delicacy, wit, and above all its honesty and intelligence, is answered in that word "carelessness." Our modern poetry began with a vigorous attack on outworn conventions of feeling and expression. But the emphasis has gradually gone so much on the craft and technicality of writing that the original wholeness and freshness is again lost. One sort of academic nullity has been replaced by another: the English "gentleman-of-letters" conceit, which prevailed at least until the end of the Georgians, has gone under. In its place is a Germanic *Ponderismuskeit,* a deadening technical thoroughness. Lawrence's demon is as out of place in that as it was in the old port-and-tweed tradition.

I used to think that one of the troubles with the poetry we have now was that, despite the stress Eliot has laid on the intelligence, no one seemed capable of thinking. I was wrong—not about the inability to think, but in expecting it at all; or at least in expecting thinking to be carried on with something of the precision of the seventeenth century. Of course, no one is trained in the syllogism; nowadays that sort of logical clarity is impossible, or it is forced. In place of the old patterns the modern poet has to rely far more heavily on his own native intelligence, on his ability to feel accurately, without conceit or indulgence; to feel, that is, when he has "thrown his feelings down the drain." He is left then not with a vague blur of emotions or a precise, empty dialectic, but with the essential thread that runs beneath the confusion, with "the instant; the quick." This, I believe, is the real material of poetry, material which could not take any other form. This inner logic is quite as difficult as its older formal counterpart. It depends on getting close to the real feelings and presenting them without formulae and without avoidance, in all their newness, disturbance, and ugliness. If a poet does that he will not find himself writing in Lawrence's style; but, like Lawrence, he may speak out in his own voice, single and undisguised.[2]

NOTES

[1] Robert Graves, whose poetry I admire, does not seem to me to have survived the war. For all his debonairness he has remained essentially a war poet. That is, he has created a drawing-room art out of anything but drawing-room feelings. His moments of savagery and tenderness appear like crevasses in a snowfield, unexpected and disconcerting. Lawrence himself summed it up in *Aaron's Rod:* "In this officer, of course, there was a lightness and an appearance of bright diffidence and humour. But underneath it was all the same as in the common men of all combatant nations: the hot, seared burn of unbearable experience, which did not heal nor cool, and whose irritation was not to be relieved. The experience gradually cooled on top: but only with a surface crust. The soul did not heal, did not recover."

[2] Since writing this chapter it has occurred to me that the clue to the technical originality of Lawrence's mature verse may be that it has a different metrical norm from most other English poetry. Its point of departure is not the iambic pentameter; instead, it is the terser movement of his narrative *prose.* I can see no other way of explaining the extraordinarily wide and subtle variation of rhythmical period within the span of a single line of free verse.

Harold Bloom

LAWRENCE, BLACKMUR, ELIOT,
AND THE TORTOISE

Art was too long for Lawrence; life too close.
R. P. BLACKMUR

As a judicial critic, R. P. Blackmur approximates the Arnold of our day. He *ranks* poets. His essay "Lord Tennyson's Scissors: 1912–1950" creates a new scriptural canon out of modern poetry in English. Class I: Yeats, Pound, and Eliot. Plenty of other classes, but all their members standing below Pound and Eliot. In a rather sad class, the violent school, lumped in with Lindsay, Jeffers, Roy Campbell, Sandburg, etc., are D. H. Lawrence and Hart Crane. Lawrence and Crane "were outside the tradition they enriched. They stood at the edge of the precipice which yawns to those who lift too hard at their bootstraps." [1]

Presumably, Blackmur bases this judgment upon two of his own more influential essays: "D. H. Lawrence and Expressive Form" and "New Thresholds New Anatomies: Notes on a Text of Hart Crane." [2] Both essays will be sizable relics when most specimens of currently fashionable analysis are lost. But because they attempt so little *description* and so much value judgment they will be relics at best. By their documentation we will remember what illusions were prevalent at a particular moment in the history of taste.

Blackmur is a critic of the rhetorical school of I. A. Richards. The school is middle-aged to old; it is in the autumn of its body.

Harold Bloom, who was educated at Cornell, Yale, and Cambridge University, has published articles on Blake and Wordsworth. He has been teaching in the English Department at Yale since 1955. Two of his books, *Shelley's Mythmaking* and *Romantic Dialectic*, were published in 1959.

Soon it will be dead. "Lord Tennyson's Scissors" is only an episode in the school's dying. But, as criticisms die so grudgingly, the essay is worth clinical attention.

Northrop Frye has recently said that all selective approaches to tradition invariably have some ultracritical joker concealed in them. A few sentences from Frye's *Anatomy of Criticism* are enough to place Blackmur's pseudo-dialectics as false rhetoric:

> The dialectic axis of criticism, then, has as one pole the total acceptance of the data of literature, and as the other the total acceptance of the potential values of those data. This is the real level of culture and of liberal education, the fertilizing of life by learning, in which the systematic progress of scholarship flows into a systematic progress of taste and understanding. On this level there is no itch to make weighty judgments, and none of the ill effects which follow the debauchery of judiciousness, and have made the word critic a synonym for an educated shrew. Comparative estimates of value are really inferences, most valid when silent ones, from critical practice, not expressed principles guiding its practice.[3]

What I propose to do here is to examine Blackmur's "debauchery of judiciousness" in his criticism of Lawrence, and to suggest where it is inadequate to the poetry.

Poetry is the embodiment of a more than rational energy. This truth, basic to Coleridge and Blake, and to Lawrence as their romantic heir, is inimical to Blackmur's "rationally constructed imagination," which he posits throughout his criticism. Eliot's, we are to gather, is a rational imagination, Lawrence's is not. Eliot is orderly; the lines beginning "Lady of silences" in *Ash-Wednesday* convey a sense of controlled hysteria. Lawrence is merely hysterical: the concluding lines of "Tortoise Shout" are a "ritual frenzy." The great mystics, and Eliot as their poetic follower, saw their ultimate vision "within the terms of an orderly insight." But Lawrence did not. Result: "In them, reason was stretched to include disorder and achieved mystery. In Lawrence, the reader is left to supply the reason and the form; for Lawrence only expresses the substance."[4]

The underlying dialectic here is a social one; Blackmur respects a codified vision, an institutionalized insight, more than the imaginative Word of an individual Romantic poet, be he Blake or Lawrence or Crane. In fairness to Blackmur one remembers his insistence that critics are *not* the fathers of a new church, as well as his quiet rejoinder to Eliot's *After Strange Gods:* "The hysteria of institutions is more dreadful than that of individuals." [5] But why should the order of institutions be more valid for poetry than the order of a gifted individual? And why must order in poetry be "rational," in Blackmur's minimal sense of the word? Lawrence's poetry, like Blake's, is animate with mental energy: it does not lack *mind.* For it is precisely in a quality of mind, in imaginative invention, that Lawrence's poetry excels. Compared to it, the religious poetry of Eliot suggests everywhere an absence of mind, a poverty of invention, a reliance upon the ritual frenzy of others.

Blackmur, who is so patient an exegete of verse he admires, will not even grant that Lawrence's poetry is *worth* descriptive criticism:

> You cannot talk about the art of his poetry because it exists only at the minimum level of self-expression, as in the later, more important poems, or because, as in the earlier accentual rhymed pieces written while he was getting under way, its art is mostly attested by its badness.[6]

Neither half of this confident judgment is true, but Blackmur has a thesis about Lawrence's poetry that he wants very much to prove. The poetry does not matter if the essay can be turned well to its despite. For Lawrence, according to this critic who denies his fatherhood in a new faith, is guilty of the "fallacy of expressive form." Blackmur's proof-of-guilt is to quote Lawrence external to his poetry, analyze the quotation, and then to quote without comment some fragments of Lawrence's verse ripped from context. But the fact is that Lawrence was a bad critic of his own poetry. Lawrence may have believed in "expressive form"; his poetry largely does not.

Blackmur quotes the final lines of "Medlars and Sorb Apples":

> Orphic farewell, and farewell, and farewell
> And the *ego sum* of Dionysos
> The *sono io* of perfect drunkenness.
> Intoxication of final loneliness.

Here, for Blackmur, "the hysteria is increased and the observation becomes vision, and leaves, perhaps, the confines of poetry." We can begin by restoring the context, so as to get at an accurate description of these "hysterical" lines. For the tone of "Medlars and Sorb Apples" is very quiet, and those final lines which Blackmur would incant as "ritual frenzy" are slow with irony, if that word is still available in the discussion of poetry. The Orphic farewell is a leave-taking of a bride left in the earth, and no frenzy accompanies it here.

"Medlars and Sorb Apples" might be called a natural emblem poem, as are most of the *Birds, Beasts and Flowers* sequence; one of the signatures of all things. In the "brown morbidity" of the medlar, as it falls through its stages of decay, Lawrence tastes the "delicious rottenness" of Orphism, the worship of the "Dionysos of the Underworld," god of isolation and of poetry. For the retorts of medlars and sorb apples distill the exquisite odor of the autumnal leave-taking of the year, essence of the parting in Hades of Orpheus and Eurydice. The intoxication of this odor, mingled with Marsala, provides that gasp of further isolation which imaginatively completes the loneliness of the individual soul. The poem is an invocation of this ultimate loneliness as the best state of the soul. The four final lines are addressed directly to medlar and sorb apples as an Orphic farewell, but different in kind from the Eurydice-parting, because of Lawrence's identification of Orpheus with Dionysius. This Orphic farewell is a creative vivification, a declaration of Dionysiac being, a perfect lonely, intoxicated finality of the isolated self of the poet. What smells of death in the autumnal fruit is life to him. Spring will mean inevitable division, crucifixion into sex, a genuine Orphic farewell to solipsistic wholeness. The poem is resolved finally as two overlapping cycles, both ironically treated.

"Tortoise Shout" is Blackmur's prime example of "the hysteria of expression" in Lawrence, where "every notation and association, every symbolic suggestion" possible is brought to bear upon "the shrieking plasm of the self." In contrast, Eliot's Rose Garden with Virgin is our rational restorative to invocatory control.

Eliot's passage is a simple, quite mechanical catalogue of

clean Catholic contradictions, very good for playing a bead-game but not much as imaginative meaning. The Virgin is calm and distressed, torn and most whole, exhausted and life-giving, etc. To Blackmur, these ritualistic paradoxes inform "nearly the same theme" as "Tortoise Shout." Unless *Ash-Wednesday* takes all meaning as its province, I am at a loss to know what Blackmur thinks he means. He invites us to "examine the eighteen pages of the poems about tortoises" with him, but as he does not do any examining, we ought perhaps to read them for ourselves.

The Tortoise poems, a continuous sequence, communicate a homely and humorous, if despairing, love for the tortoise, in itself and as emblematic of man and all created nature involved in sexual division and strife. The Tortoise-Christ identifications have throughout them a grim unpretentious joy, which Blackmur, on defensive grounds, takes as hysteria.

"Baby Tortoise," the first poem, celebrates the infant creature as Ulyssean atom, invincible and indomitable. The best parallel is Whitman, in his praise of animals who do not whine about their condition. "No one ever heard you complain." The baby tortoise is a life-bearer, a Titan against the inertia of the lifeless. But he is a Titan circumscribed by a demiurge like Blake's Urizen; this is the burden of the next poem, "Tortoise Shell," which seems to me closer to Blake than anything else by Lawrence or by Yeats. Blake's Urizen, the Old Man of the Compasses, draws horizons (as his name and its derivation indicate). The Nobodaddy who made the Tortoise in its fallen condition circumscribes with the cross:

> The Cross, the Cross
> Goes deeper in than we know,
> Deeper into life;
> Right into the marrow
> And through the bone.

On the back of the baby tortoise Lawrence reads the terrible geometry of subjection to "the mystic mathematics of the city of heaven." Under all the eternal dome of mathematical law the tortoise is subjected to natural bondage; he exhibits the long cleavage of division. An arbitrary division, a Urizenic patterning, has been made, and the tortoise must bear it eternally.

Lawrence's earlier tone of celebration is necessarily modulated into a Blakean and humanistic bitterness:

> The Lord wrote it all down on the little slate
> Of the baby tortoise.
> Outward and visible indication of the plan within,
> The complex, manifold involvedness of an individual
> 　　　creature
> Plotted out.

Against this natural binding the tortoise opposes his stoic individuality, his slow intensity. In "Tortoise Family Connections" his more-than-human independence is established, both as against Christ:

> He does not even trouble to answer: "Woman, what
> 　　　have I to do with thee?"
> He wearily looks the other way

and against Adam:

> To be a tortoise!
> Think of it, in a garden of inert clods
> A brisk, brindled little tortoise, all to himself—
> Adam!

The gentle homeliness that follows, in "Lui Et Elle" and "Tortoise Gallantry," is punctuated by a purely male bitterness, in preparation for the great and climactic poem of the series, "Tortoise Shout."

This last poem is central in romantic tradition, deriving ultimately as much from Wordsworth as from Whitman. Parallel to it is Melville's enigmatic and powerful "After The Pleasure Party":

> For, Nature, in no shallow surge
> Against thee either sex may urge,
> Why hast thou made us but in halves—
> Co-relatives? This makes us slaves.
> If these co-relatives never meet
> Self-hood itself seems incomplete.
> And such the dicing of blind fate
> Few matching halves here meet and mate.
> What Cosmic jest or Anarch blunder

> The human integral close asunder
> And shied the factious through life's gate?

Lawrence also is not concerned with asking the question for the answer's sake:

> Why were we crucified into sex?
> Why were we not left rounded off, and finished in
>   ourselves,
> As we began,
> As he certainly began, so perfectly alone?

The subject of "Tortoise Shout" is initially the waking of the tortoise into the agony of a fall into sexual division, a waking into life as the heretofore silent creature screams faintly in its arousal. The scream may be just audible, or it may sound "on the plasm direct." In the single scream Lawrence places all cries that are "half music, half horror," in an instructive ordering. The cry of the newborn, the sound of the veil being rent, the "screaming in Pentecost, receiving the ghost." The ultimate identity, achieved in an empathy dependent upon Wordsworthian recollection, is between the tortoise-cry in orgasm, and Christ's Passion on the Cross, the connecting reference being dependent upon the poem "Tortoise Shell."

The violence of expression here, obscene blasphemy to the orthodox, has its parallels in Nietzsche and in Yeats when they treat the Passion. Lawrence structures this deliberate violence quite carefully. First, a close account of the tortoise in coition, emphasizing the aspects of the act beyond the tortoise's single control. Then a startling catalogue (the form from Whitman, the mode from Wordsworth) of memories of boyhood and youth, before the major incantation assigned by Blackmur to the realm of the hysterical.

The passage of reminiscence works by positing a series of similitudes which are finally seen as a composite identity. The cries of trapped animals, of animals in passion, of animals wounded, animals newborn, are all resolved on the human plane as the infant's birth-pang, the mother singing to herself, the young collier finding his mature voice. For all of these represent:

> The first elements of foreign speech
> On wild dark lips.

The voice of the solitary consciousness is in each case modified, usually by pain, into the speech of what is divided, of what is made to know its own separateness. Here, as in Wordsworth's great *Ode,* the awareness of separateness is equated to the first intimations of mortality.

The last protesting cry of the male tortoise "at extremity" is "more than all these" in that it is more desperate, "less than all these" in that it is faintest. It is a cry of final defeat:

> Tiny from under the very edge of the farthest far-off
> horizon of life.

One sees why Lawrence has chosen the tortoise; the horizon of separateness-in-sexual-division could not be extended further and still be manageable in a poem of this kind. From this extreme Lawrence carries us to the other pole of human similitude, Christ or Osiris being divided, undergoing ultimate dismemberment:

> The cross,
> The wheel on which our silence first is broken,
> Sex, which breaks up our integrity, our single inviolability, our deep silence,
> Tearing a cry from us.
>
> Sex, which breaks us into voice, sets us calling across
> the deeps, calling, calling for the complement,
> Singing, and calling, and singing again, being answered, having found.
>
> Torn, to become whole again, after long seeking for
> what is lost,
> The same cry from the tortoise as from Christ, the
> Osiris-cry of abandonment,
> That which is whole, torn asunder,
> That which is in part, finding its whole again throughout the universe.

Much of the meaning in this is conveyed through rhythmical mastery; the scattering and reuniting of the self is incanted successively, now widening, now narrowing.

The cross here is the mechanical and mathematical body, the fallen residue of Blake's Human Form Divine. It is also the circumscribed tortoise body, as adumbrated in "Tortoise Shell." As such, the cross is a demonic image, symbolizing enforced division (into male and female, or *in* the self, or self kept from another self) and torture (tearing on the wheel, crucifixion). The tortoise, torn asunder in coming together, and perpetually caught in that cyclic paradox, utters the same cry as the perpetually sacrificed Osiris in his vegetative cycle. Christ's cry of forsakenness, to Lawrence, is one with these, as the divine nature is torn apart in the Passion. The sexual reduction in this last similitude is imaginatively unfortunate, but as interpretation does not issue from Lawrence alone.

Blackmur, defending Eliot as a dogmatic critic and poet, has written that "conviction in the end is opinion and personality, which however greatly valuable cannot satisfy those who wrongly expect more." [7] The remark is sound, but Blackmur has been inconsistent in its application.

Lawrence, as a Romantic poet, was compelled by the conventions of his mode to present the conceptual aspect of his imagery as self-generated. I have borrowed most of this sentence from Frye's *Anatomy of Criticism,* where it refers to Blake, Shelley, Goethe, and Victor Hugo.[8] What Frye calls a mode of literature, mythopoeia, is to Blackmur "that great race of English writers whose work totters precisely where it towers, collapses exactly in its strength: work written out of a tortured Protestant sensibility." [9] We are back in a social dialectic external to criticism being applied to criticism. Writers who are Protestant, romantic, radical, exemplify "the deracinated, unsupported imagination, the mind for which, since it lacked rational structure sufficient to its burdens, experience was too much." This dialectic is out of Hulme, Pound, and Eliot, and at last we are weary of it. Under its influence Blackmur has tried to salvage Wallace Stevens as a late Augustan, while Allen Tate has asserted that Yeats' romanticism will be invented by his critics. That the imagination needs support can perhaps be argued; that a structure properly conservative, classical and Catholic enough is its necessary support is simply a social polemic, and irrelevant to the criticism of poetry.

Lawrence himself, if we allow ourselves to quote him out of context, can be left to answer his judicious critic:

> What thing better are you, what worse?
> What have you to do with the mysteries
> Of this ancient place, of my ancient curse?
> What place have you in my histories? [10]

NOTES

[1] R. P. Blackmur, *Language as Gesture* (London: George Allen & Unwin, 1954) p. 433.

[2] *Ibid.*, pp. 286, 301.

[3] Northrop Frye, *Anatomy of Criticism* (Princeton: Princeton University Press, 1957) p. 25.

[4] Blackmur, *op. cit.*, p. 299.

[5] *Ibid.*, p. 379n.

[6] *Ibid.*, p. 288.

[7] *Ibid.*, p. 179.

[8] Frye, *op. cit.*, p. 65.

[9] Blackmur, *op. cit.*, p. 286.

[10] *The Complete Poems of D. H. Lawrence*, 3 Vols. (London: Heinemann, 1957), "Under The Oak," Vol. 1, p. 117.

Christopher Hassall

BLACK FLOWERS: A NEW LIGHT ON
THE POETICS OF D. H. LAWRENCE

IN March, 1927, Lawrence visited the tombs of ancient Etruria, and soon afterwards wrote the fourth and last of
his travel books, *Etruscan Places*. An exhaustive work on the
subject by George Dennis was already in existence. It contained descriptions of no less than fifty sites which Lawrence
never had the opportunity to examine. *Etruscan Places* deals
with only four burial sites, and although more than a year after
his first visit Lawrence was still contemplating a second journey
to the ruins, he never went again. Richard Aldington has explained that by 1928 Lawrence was too sick to sustain the fatigue of another Etruscan tour, and that he considered it idle
to compete with Dennis, whose explorations had already covered the field. No doubt these were reasons enough for *Etruscan
Places* to remain a fragment, if you regard it solely as a travel
book, but I believe there was another reason. On the plane
where archaeological facts may be found to serve a symbolic
purpose, the book was complete. On that plane its theme was
no longer the relics of ancient Etruria but something quite different—the principles underlying Lawrence's conception of
poetry. In his travels over the globe (and in March, 1927, he
had just got back from Mexico), he had searched in vain for a
community which was managing to remain immune from the

Christopher Hassall, English poet educated at Oxford, is a Fellow of
the Royal Society of Literature and a Hawthornden Prize winner whose
verse dramas have been performed at the Canterbury and Edinburgh
Festivals and in Westminster Abbey; he has written several biographies,
including *Edward Marsh* (1959), and has starred as a reader of verse
at the Stratford-upon-Avon Poetry Festival and, in 1958, at the Edinburgh Festival, where he read, among other poets, D. H. Lawrence.

evils of industrial civilization. He never found it on the face of the earth, flourishing in the present. Instead I believe he discovered it at last in the remote past, no more than hinted at in the tombs of Etruria, but it was enough. There were the unmistakable clues. Among the fragmentary relics of death he found the wholeness of life he had been seeking—"the natural flowering of life" as he called it—and by exercise of the sympathetic imagination he lifted it into the present in the descriptive pages of his book. For this reason alone *Etruscan Places* would be especially important. It is the record of an act of spiritual excavation. Among the treasures he exhumed there was something of his essential being. The Etruscans provided him with a group of symbols. Read in this light, and with the guidance of his one critical essay on the subject, his last travel book becomes his most revealing statement on the name and nature of poetry, although poetry is never specifically mentioned, and poems themselves are disguised as what he calls "black flowers." From among the archaeological facts and his deductions there emerges a prose poem on a theme of literary criticism.

Some eight years earlier he had written a short critical essay to which I suggest this secondary theme of his travel book should be regarded as sequel. In an introduction to the American edition of *New Poems,* published in 1920, Lawrence said his remarks had best be considered as applying retrospectively to his previous volume *Look! We Have Come Through!;* but for what his views were worth here they were, better late than never. *Look! We Have Come Through!,* it will be remembered, was a poetical journal of the fluctuating relationship with his wife, roughly covering the five years 1912 to 1917. Technically, it showed that he was rejecting the earlier influences on his work—notably the verse of Hardy—and was feeling his way toward a less formalized, freer style, adapted to his purpose from Whitman. To the first of his writings largely in this Whitmanesque style which Lawrence was in the process of making his own, the *New Poems* essay is in effect the proper introduction, and it may now be taken as a critical prelude to all the verse which he wrote subsequently—his finest single volume *Birds, Beasts and Flowers* of 1923, *Nettles, Pansies,* and of course the posthumous *Last Poems* which are of especial interest in connection with *Etruscan Places.*

In the preface to *New Poems,* Lawrence describes how all traditional verse, as he sees it, is made out of moments of certitude and repose after reflection. It either harks back in contemplation of the past or reaches forward in aspiration to the future. "It is in the realm of all that is perfect," he says, and "the finality and the perfection are conveyed in exquisite form, the perfect symmetry, the rhythm which returns upon itself like a dance where the hands link and loosen and link for the supreme moment of the end." He pictures the traditional poet seated at a gateway looking east or west, looking, that is, into the past or the future. We hear what the poet has to say and "our hearts surge with response," but while we are "in the midst of life" (within the gateway, standing in the present time) either the poet does not choose to speak or we deny him our attention.

And yet here, in the immediate present, there could be poetry of a more urgent kind than that of the past or future. Here is no certitude, "no rhythm which returns upon itself, no serpent of eternity with its tail in its mouth." Rather is it "direct utterance from the instant, whole man." Here is no perfection, no consummation, for the strands are loose and flying. This "pure present," he contends, is a realm we have so far never conquered. "The seething poetry of the incarnate Now is supreme, beyond even the everlasting gems of the before and after." And he acknowledges Whitman as his great precursor, telling how "his heart beats with the urgent, insurgent Now. . . . He is so near the quick." And in the course of all this Lawrence tries to convey his meaning by way of a poetic image representing the characteristic poem of the gateway. "The perfect rose is only a running flame, emerging and flowing off, and never in any sense at rest, static, finished." Not satisfied he tries again—"A water-lily heaves herself from the flood, looks round, gleams, and is gone." It is this lily and that very rose which are united in *Etruscan Places* in the mysterious and potent symbol of "black flowers." This is his last and most successful emblem for the poetry "whose very permanency lies in its wind-like transit."

On an early page of "Cerveteri," the first of his Etruscan localities, Lawrence starts developing his dominating theme that the beauty of Etruscan things lies in their quality of evanescence. They were expendable. Even the houses and temples were delicately built of wood, so that whole cities "vanished as completely as flowers. Only the tombs, the bulbs, were underground." The images of the lily and the rose in the preface to *New Poems* are already as it were entering the sphere of ancient Etruria, and one suspects that, in the writer's subconscious, things archaeological and ideas on poetical theory are beginning to fuse. Barely four pages later it is with quite a shock that we stumble upon the seed of what is perhaps the finest of his *Last Poems:*

> Through the inner doorway is the last chamber, small and dark and culminative. Facing the door goes the stone bed on which was laid, presumably, the Lucumo and the sacred treasures of the dead, the little bronze ship of death that should bear him over to the other world, the vases of jewels for his arraying, the vases of small dishes. The little bronze statuettes and tools, the weapons, the armour: all the amazing impedimenta of the important dead.

The Lucumo was the chief man or prophet of the settlement. As a latter-day Lucumo Lawrence must have seen himself in his last days, building his own Etruscan ship of death. "Have you built your ship of death, oh have you?" begins the third draft of the familiar poem, and in the second draft we read:

> But for myself, but for my soul, dear soul
> let me build a little ship with oars and food
> and little dishes, and all accoutrements
> dainty and ready for the departing soul.

From the Etruscans Lawrence learned that attitude of acceptance of death which ennobles these last poems. "And death, to the Etruscan, was a pleasant continuance of life, with jewels and wine and flutes playing for the dance." And he goes on to talk yet again of their temples "small, dainty, fragile, and evanescent as flowers." Soon follows the paragraph which, by inference and on the plane of symbolism, concerns what he has called "the poetry of before and after," the poetry of solidity and of certitude beyond or behind the gateway.

> Why has mankind had such a craving to be imposed upon?
> Why this lust for imposing creeds, imposing deeds, imposing

buildings, imposing language, imposing works of art? The
thing becomes an imposition and a weariness at last. Give us
things that are alive and flexible, which won't last too long
and become an obstruction and a weariness. Even Michel-
angelo becomes at last a lump and a burden and a bore. It
is so hard to see past him.

He next explains how in the end "that which lives lives by
sensitiveness," and he borrows the symbol peculiar to Whitman in *Leaves of Grass:* "It is the grass of the field, most
frail of all things, that supports all life all the time. But for
the green grass, no empire would rise, no man would eat
bread. . . . The Etruscan element is like the grass of the
field and the sprouting of corn, in Italy: it will always be so."
The extended passage has about it an air of mounting excitement as the writer's wanderings bring him to the museum of
Tarquinia and the collection of pottery: hundreds of imitation
Greek vases, and also the cruder kind, of native Etruscan design,
either plain black or decorated with scratches, called black bucchero ware. Finding the two types of vase side by side he comes
upon the ideal analogy for the contrast between the poetry on
either side of the gateway, in the past or in the future, and that
which lies within the portals. The reference to Keats is particularly apt and illuminating.

> If one looks for the Greek form of elegance and convention,
> those elegant "still-unravished brides of quietness," one is
> disappointed. But get over the strange desire we have for ele-
> gant convention, and the vases and dishes of the Etruscans,
> especially many of the black bucchero ware, begin to open
> out like strange flowers, black flowers, with all the softness
> and the rebellion of life against convention, or red-and-black
> flowers painted with amusing free, bold designs. It is there
> nearly always in Etruscan things, the naturalness verging on
> the commonplace, but usually missing it, and often achieving
> an originality so free and bold, and so fresh, that we, who
> love convention and things 'reduced to a norm,' call it a
> bastard art, and commonplace.

The passage is not so much instinct with the excitement of
discovery (though that is a part of it) as with the joy and relief of
justification. The "naturalness verging on the commonplace but

usually missing it"—he might have been writing directly of his own verse. And from this point on he writes with a welling up of imaginative sympathy, as if he were himself in every respect, except only that of historical time, a citizen of Tarquinia, a latter-day Etruscan. "You cannot think of art," he says, looking at the damaged frescoes, "but only of life itself, as if this were the very life of the Etruscans, dancing in their coloured wraps with massive yet exuberant naked limbs, ruddy from the air and the sea-light, dancing and fluting along through the little olive trees, out in the fresh day."

Lawrence's form of verse was a natural development out of his view of life itself. What Whitman did for him was to demonstrate how to body forth ideas and feelings in a manner that was strictly true to them and did them the minimum of damage in the process; for the expression of a thought in words can be an act of violence which distorts. "To break the lovely form of metrical verse," Lawrence wrote in the *New Poems* preface, "and to dish up the fragments as a new substance, called *vers libre,* this is what most of the free-versifiers accomplish. They do not know that free verse has its own *nature,* that it is neither star nor pearl, but instantaneous like plasm." In *Etruscan Places* it is some pages after my last quotation that Lawrence arrives at a definition of the characteristic Etruscan quality—"the natural flowering of life." To that ancient people, he says, the whole universe, the whole cosmos, was one, a living thing made up of living parts, "a single aliveness with a single soul" from which it was man's aim in life to draw more and more vitality. The augur of the temple, at one with the sky, was in peculiarly intimate contact with external nature. "If the augur could see the birds flying *in his heart,* then he would know which way destiny too was flying for him," for if you live by the cosmos, then you naturally look in the cosmos for your clue. Lawrence is still talking of augury when he goes on: "All it depends on is the amount of *true,* sincere, religious concentration you can bring to bear on your object. An act of pure attention, if you are capable of it, will bring its own answer." The priest of augury has here become the archetypal poet of the gateway whose works are "neither star nor pearl but instantaneous like plasm." And the passage ends, "The soul stirs, and makes an act of pure attention, and that is a discovery." Existing in that spontaneous mode of life, which is its own "natural flowering," the augur performs an act of divination or the poet makes a "discovery"—his poem. Pure attention has brought a poem into being just as God created the red geranium and mignonette in the poem of that name among the last things to come from Lawrence's pen. With that free verse which is not arbitrary but of its very nature free, being a part of the natural flowering of life—as it was in the mature work of Lawrence the neo-Etruscan—the soul stirs, and makes an act of pure attention, devoting to the "object" all it can of "true, sincere, religious concentration" which brings its own answer, the discovery, the poem. A terrible discipline of sincerity has been substituted for the craftsman's discipline of form. Each poem obeys its own natural law.

A year after his visit to the tombs, Lawrence recalled the passage we have just been considering while writing a preface to a book called *Chariot of the Sun* by Harry Crosby. "The essential quality of poetry," he wrote, "is that it makes a new effort of attention, and 'discovers' a new world within the known world." About the same time, in the autumn of 1928, he wrote his essay called *Hymns in a Man's Life*. The central passage describes the sense of wonder which he called the *natural* religious sense. "When all comes to all, the most precious element in life is wonder." For this too he found the seed in his travel book of a year before. "The ancients saw, consciously, as children now see unconsciously, the everlasting wonder in things."

When in his travel book he turns to Etruscan painting, it is the same quality of "life" itself rather than what we academically regard as "art" which attracts his notice. The subtlety in such work lies "in the wonderfully suggestive *edge* of the figures. It is not outlined. It is not what we call 'drawing.' It is the flowing contour where the body suddenly leaves off upon the atmosphere." It is this "suggestive edge" of his own verses, which at first gives the appearance of a rough sketch, and instead of exhibiting formal shape suggests a state of flux, a flowing contour where the body "suddenly leaves off upon the atmosphere," which is characteristic of Lawrence. As against this method there is the classical art which, as Lawrence argues, debased the Etruscan spirit into "a desire to resist nature, to produce a mental cunning and a mechanical force that would outwit Nature and chain her down completely." So much for the element of artifice in the traditional poet's craft! In elaborating his conscious craft, and mistrusting or ignoring the evidence of his senses, the modern artist has rendered himself capable only of an act of *impure* attention. "We haven't exactly plucked our eyes out, but we've plucked out three-fourths of their vision."

And what, in the last analysis, is the forfeit we post-Etruscans have paid? Lawrence gives his answer in "Volterra," the last of his Etruscan places. "One wearies of the aesthetic quality —a quality which takes the edge off everything, and makes it seem 'boiled down.' A great deal of Greek beauty has this boiled down effect. *It is too much cooked in the artistic consciousness"* (italics mine). The bowls of black bucchero ware were shaped into beauty and usefulness by fingers and thumbs alive with the natural flowering of life, and they came and went as evanescent as flowers, black flowers, like the divinations of the augur whose soul had stirred. This is the nature of their beauty, to have come and to have gone. But with a poem there *is* a difference, so Lawrence maintains. "What lives lives by sensitiveness" and its "very permanency lies in its wind-like transit."

He never went back to the tombs of Etruria. He was ill, and Dennis had indeed gone before him, but he had already found far more than ever he had sought. "The Etruscans are not a theory or a thesis. If they are anything, they are an experience." There was nothing more they could teach him. He discovered that he was one of them. He had come home. So much that he had thought and felt beforehand now seemed radiantly justified, even the hitherto somewhat nebulous ideas underlying his practice as a poet. Everything fell into place. He knew and understood himself. Without first accepting Lawrence as a guide among the tombs of the dead we cannot properly experience the life in his later poems, those black flowers which he left behind after building his ship of death and sailing away into the Etruscan past.

Karl Shapiro

THE UNEMPLOYED MAGICIAN

ONCE in his life, at a time of his own choosing, each poet is allowed to have an interview with the god of letters. He is a real god, I think, and maybe much more than that. He can answer all questions about poetry, especially the ones poets and philosophers have never been able to settle; I suspect that he can answer every other question as well. The poet, unfortunately, cannot return with the answers; as he shakes hands and says good-bye to the god, the visitor is automatically brainwashed. All recollection of the god's wisdom is obliterated and the poet returns home to write—criticism.

Recently I held my meeting with this deity. I am not sure I really remember our talk, but I have a small facility in reconstructing dreams, and I am under the impression that I can recount the most important questions and answers that passed between us.

The god was sitting behind his desk, polite and prepared to listen to questions he had answered thousands of times before. I had a slight temptation to ask *better* questions than others had, but I dropped this pose the moment I saw him slip into his desk a book of mine I had never seen. The cover said *Poems* by Karl Shapiro, 1913 (the date I was born) and it had the *other* date. The sight of this book sobered me somewhat, and the god tried to put me at ease by remarking that poets were usually a little startled by his appearance. I said, on the contrary, his was a rather familiar appearance.

Karl Shapiro, Pulitzer Prize poet, Professor of English at the University of Nebraska, former editor of *Poetry* and now editor of the *Prairie Schooner,* is the author of various volumes of poetry, including *Person, Place and Thing* (1942), *V-Letter* (1944), and *Poems of a Jew* (1958), and of a volume of lectures, *Beyond Criticism* (1953). His essay originally appeared in *Poetry* for December, 1957.

Yes, said the god, I appear to the poets as they think I look. But beyond that my opinions are my own.

I then confided that he bore a remarkable resemblance to T. S. Eliot and, although there was no conceivable connection, to Sigmund Freud. I now noticed that he was holding the perennial cigar that Freud never put down, and which was his emblem. He moved the box in my direction but I declined.

I am not large enough to smoke cigars, I said.

You are taller than Freud, the god replied beneficently. And he added: I have noticed that you are frequently concerned with the appearances of poets. I put this down to your interest in descriptive verse.

That is not quite it, Sir, I answered. Do you mind if I call you *Sir?* I always call critics Sir. (He bowed his head in approval.) I am really interested in the motility of poets; how the poet gets across the street. So many of them don't.

A poet, said the god cryptically, should never be in a position in which he has anything to lose.

But, I said, I am not talking about drunkenness or bawdry, and I am not thinking about rearing a stable of healthy poets.

The deity chuckled.

That is just as well. As soon as a man publishes something, people begin to say he drinks too much. You must know by now that it is not the alcohol but the poetry that kills alcoholic poets. Alcohol is the poetry of the people, as the newspaper is the wisdom of the people. Poetry is a killer. Still (I thought he shrugged) it is a way of life.

More than a way of life, I ventured. It is an affliction.

For those who want it, smiled the god. It is a choice, after all.

I decided not to say poets are born not made, but the god anticipated me by remarking, Anyone, of course, can be a poet.

I gasped painfully and reached for a cigar.

It is the commitment you are not allowed to break. It is the tattoo in your flesh that will never rub out.

But if what you say is true, I asked, why are there so few poets, and so few good ones?

Statistics is not my strong point, he answered; but the world can tolerate only so many poets at any one time. Frequently the world gathers the first handful of poets it sees and lets genius waste away. To the world, you know, one poet serves as well as another. It is enough for them that a man has chosen to be a poet. Good or bad, he is a poet.

I can't believe that the world has so little regard for literary standards.

Then you are deluding yourself, said the god quietly. But do not be mistaken. The world needs poets and creates a place for them. Your nice sense of discrimination has nothing to do with their need.

Nice! Doesn't it matter if people think Anne Morrow Lindberg is as good a poet as Shakespeare?

It is unimportant if they do. Bad poetry is as immortal as good. Would you have all men created equal in sensibility and capacity and hope? What a gray world that would be. But the world does give way to the judgments of poets about poetry sooner or later and for better or for worse. The judgments of poets, I might add, are anything but reliable.

Are the judgments of critics any better? (My tone was a little rude, for his remarks had begun to ruffle me.)

You poets are always putting words in my mouth, the god replied. Why should I judge poetry? It is judged soon enough by men.

But is it judged well?

That is not my affair. Your works of art seek judgment and they find it. I abstain entirely. Why are you troubled about the squabbles of critics? Really, it shouldn't concern you any more than it concerns me. Try to remember that to the world the existence of a poet is the same thing as poetry itself.

I don't understand.

Look at it this way. To the world you are a man set apart because of your occupation, or rather vocation, if you insist on calling it that. You have a responsibility to maintain separateness. It is a simple matter of distance by elevation. Place any man on a stage, a platform, or a soapbox, and he is immediately transformed. The angle of declension is what matters. But let this man lose his distance and he is finished. Among savages a magician who loses his hold over the tribe is killed. So with you poets.

Are you putting poets in the same class as politicians and witch doctors?

I did not mean to offend you, said the god; the only difference is the difference of time. A politician is interested in holding you in his spell only until you go to the polls, whereas the poet asks you to elect him for at least a thousand years. Thus the quality of the poetic article is more durable, *aere perennis,* and harder to sell.

You make it sound rather commercial.

Since you have used the word, yes. But the commercialism of poets exceeds the limits of mere words. In short, I have never known a poet who did not want everything. Partly for that reason he *is* a poet. From the child in his crib you withdraw bit by bit the world he thinks he possesses, until the limits are fixed and he can define what is his and what is not. To the poet there is no line, no boundary between subject and object, sleep and waking, intoxication and sobriety. I am exaggerating but you see my point.

That may be so, I said, but it tells me nothing about what the poet gives the world.

What does he give the world? the god asked innocently.

But I came to ask you that. I can only give you the contradictory answers of the past.

The god thought a moment and then said, I am willing to tell you, on two conditions. One, that you follow me through an illogical cross-examination and, two, that you prepare yourself for an unpleasant result.

I will take it on, I said; hemlock and all.

Very well then, he began. Let us confine ourselves to the poetry of your own time, as that is the most alive to you and is the poetry that concerns you most. Who would you say are the best poets of your own language in your own time?

Well, to take the best known, I would say, Eliot, Pound, Stevens, Yeats, Auden . . .

That is enough for the moment, interrupted the god. Now if you will pardon this parlor trick, if you were allowed to take one book of poems with you to a desert island, which one would you take?

Why, I answered, I think I would take the poems of—D. H. Lawrence.

But you didn't even mention Lawrence. Why?

I mean that I enjoy Lawrence more than the others, but the others are by objective standards better poets.

What objective standards are you referring to?

The old standards, I said: originality, suitable intensity, applicability, ability to transport, re-readability, contemporaneity.

Those are nice big terms to hide behind, said the god. Is that what you tell your students?

To tell you the truth, Sir, I am reluctant to tell them what I really think. It would not fit in with the curriculum.

A normal state of affairs, answered the god. But to come back to the point: doesn't your desert island poet fit the terms you give?

To a degree, but he is too outspoken. Lawrence misses the mystery of language-making in his passion for his own ideas.

I take it then that Lawrence's *ideas* are very close to yours and would keep you good company on your desert island?

No, Sir. I can't swallow a single idea of his.

What! You would carry with you a poet whose ideas you dismiss and whose language lacks great astistry?

I feel (I stammered) that Lawrence in his sincerity, fool that he was, broke through the façade of artistry and literary affectation and stood at the doorway of poetry itself.

Not a very good metaphor, said the god. You are trying to say you don't know what you mean.

I don't know, yet I believe what I say.

You are accusing Eliot, Pound, Stevens, and Yeats of literary affectation. Are they all affected in the same way or do they have different affectations?

The affectation is pretty much the same. Literary affectation always comes when poets have stopped listening to their own voice and try to invent the speech of their contemporaries. Then they become parodists, humorists. . . .

One moment, said the god. Do you label this affectation parody and humor?

Parody, I answered, is the literary style of our age. Joyce, Pound, Eliot, whatever else they may be, are all masters of imitation. Or to put it bluntly, copying.

And Stevens also?

Stevens, I said, beautiful beautiful Stevens is a magnificent poet who is really devoid of imagination. He dreams that imagination will come to him, but it does not come. So he becomes a parodist of the imagination.

Perhaps, the god answered, but surely the parodistic—as you say—Eliot and Pound are men of fine imagination.

They are men of fixed ideas, men of programs. They call poetry the dance of ideas. Ideas can't dance.

And these you say are your best poets? Tell me, in what is Yeats a parodist?

Heavens! Yeats is the parodist of belief. Surely you can't deny it. Yeats lived the mask of Yeats for seventy years.

Do you grant the sincerity of Eliot?

Absolutely.

But Eliot, the god said, pleads with us to accept his poetry whether we accept his beliefs or not.

That is the noose in which they all hang, I said.

Yet you accept Lawrence on the grounds of sincerity, although you have no use for his ideas. At the same time you disagree with Eliot's formula for appreciating poetry while keeping the beliefs to one side. And you call Yeats insincere while you profess to admire his craft. Please explain this tangle of contradictions.

I have already admitted, I replied, that I am stopped by a mystery. I am very much concerned about the beliefs of poets. My final opinion of their poetry is colored by what I think of their beliefs. I realize that this is an old-fashioned way to read the poets. As for Lawrence—Lawrence's style is at least true to himself. With the others, the style, the life, and all the rest of it are secondary to some fixed idea. Pound's crooked thinking gives him a crooked style. I don't deny that he is a great inventor, the best we have. Lawrence is wrong but honest. But this conclusion leaves me nowhere.

I have noticed that you haven't mentioned William Carlos Williams. Surely you cannot call this poet dishonest or insincere or parodistic.

No; I might try to sneak in a copy of Williams to my desert island. And yet . . .

And yet?

Williams, I said, lets me down in another way. He is *too* sincere.

What! So sincerity can be a vice also?

I mean that Williams' refusal to be anything *but* true to the language, as he calls it with a capital L, becomes just another fixed idea.

If I follow your logic then, the god said, you are accusing Williams of insincere sincerity.

Let's call it stylistic obsession, I said; that's the vice we are talking about. It permits poets to be fools without damaging their reputations.

In other words, my friend, you would have poets be true to themselves, you would have them avoid mannerisms, and you would have them entertain ideas with which you agree. At that rate you would have no poetry left to read except your own. But very well, I will accept your terminology in order to get on. You object to the best modern poets, as you call them, on the grounds of stylistic obsessions. You believe they have forced themselves to become insincere in one way or another. Their brilliant artifice you dismiss in favor of the bare prophetic verses of Lawrence. You agree, I think, that Lawrence's beliefs about man and the modern world are savage and atavistic and perhaps childish?

I do.

How then do you account for the greater appeal of Lawrence to your poetic sensibilities than of Eliot or Williams?

I cannot account for it.

Do you think you might possibly agree secretly with Lawrence's harangues about the revival of the blood religions and the lower Consciousness?

That is unthinkable, I said.

Would you say that Lawrence had greater writing skill than, say, James Joyce?

I credit them both with great writing genius, but Joyce, that master manufacturer of literary cuckoo clocks—he is the absolute opposite of Lawrence.

Is it the literal nature of Lawrence's verses that appeals to you?

Certainly that is fascinating. But I must remind you, Sir, that I do not class Lawrence as a poet with the others at all.

Then he is something of a prophet or a mystic in your mind?

Something like that, I said.

And since you repudiate his ideas, would you call him a false prophet?

Yes, I suppose so.

Permit me, the god then said, to recite four lines of the song of a cannibal minstrel who is boasting about his chief. This was overheard by an American traveler to the Ivory Coast. Before a huge assemblage the minstrel shouted at the top of his voice:

> My chief Fire Helmet has thirty-nine wives,
> Their necks are like giraffes,
> Their breasts are always full of milk,
> And they are always pregnant!

Do these lines have the literal quality you admire in Lawrence?

They do have the ring of truth, I said, and they make a crude kind of poetry.

Yet, the god went on, the traveler says this is only a spontaneous boasting-song, and he adds that the chief is really impotent.

All the same, I said, it presents a worthy truth, one which the cannibal chief fervently desires, I presume.

The god laughed.

Is it a truth because of the worthiness of the possibility?

Yes, I said stubbornly, I mean worthy in that sense. The truth of so much modern poetry does not seem worthy to me and I reject it.

You are correct in your judgment of the cannibal verses, said the god, except for one thing. They are not poetry.

Why not poetry?

Because there is no poetry or art among savages.

But, my dear Sir, what about the masks, the costumes, the sand paintings, the cave drawings, the epics in verse, the music and all the rest of it?

All of which are so beloved by your twentieth-century writers? Yet, I repeat, they are not poetry, not art.

Now you are quibbling. What are they then?

I hesitate to say the word, said the god. Have you ever heard the singing of primitive people?

I once listened to some Polynesians singing something to the tune of "Show Me the Way To Go Home." They said it was a hymn.

That will serve, the god answered. Did they seem to take pleasure in the singing?

Now that you mention it, I have never seen such expressions of exquisite pain on anyone's faces.

Would you call this a condition of transport?

I would rather reserve the word for higher moments, I answered.

And there you have the basis of the chief error in what you call literary criticism, said the god.

I am completely in the dark.

Let us approach the subject from another angle. What do your chief psychologists have to say about the sources of art?

If you mean Freud and Jung and those people, I replied, they say nothing. They both confess that the secret of art is forever a closed book.

That is one interpretation, the god said. But doesn't that strike you as peculiar, coming from men whose specialty is the revealment of secrets?

Yes, I said, I have wondered about it sometimes.

Have you also wondered why both Freud and Jung display poor literary taste when they are trying to explain the cause of a work of art? Not always but on occasion, as when Jung falls back on Rider Haggard's *She* and Freud on Wilhelm Jensen's *Gradiva*, both very inferior works of art?

I have not read these novels, but I accept your opinion.

And can you supply any reason why both Freud and Jung should avoid the issue so important to them concerning the cause and source of works of literature?

I cannot think of any. It is completely unreasonable that they should leave us in the dark.

Would you entertain the possibility that they are hiding something they are afraid to bring to light? the god asked.

Failing any other explanation, I would. But Freud is as much a pioneer as Columbus and has told us the most unpleasant things about ourselves we have ever heard. As for Jung, he has had the courage to revive the despised science of alchemy and apply it to a study of the unconscious mind.

Would you say these two scientists are reverent toward the arts or otherwise?

Most reverent, I said, in the nineteenth-century German fashion.

Do you think their scientific opinions about culture and art are colored by this reverence?

Very likely, but I still do not see what you are driving at.

One moment, said the god. I want you to tell me what you think of these lines of Freud's. You recall Freud's expression "the omnipotence of thought"? It is a disturbance in which one's thought produces an hallucination of reality. That is, if you are alone and happen to be thinking about your mother who is 3,000 miles away, and the door opens and your mother walks in, you are inclined to connect your thinking about her with the actual arrival. Now listen to this:

Only in one field has the omnipotence of thought been retained in our own civilization, namely in art. In art alone it still happens that man, consumed by his wishes, produces something similar to the gratification of these wishes, and this playing, thanks to artistic illusion, calls forth effects as if it were something real. We rightly speak of the magic of art and compare the artist with the magician. But this comparison is perhaps more important than it claims to be. Art, which certainly did not begin as art for art's sake, originally served tendencies which today have for the greater part ceased to exist. Among these we may suspect various magic intentions.

I am beginning to see your point, I said suspiciously. But this means that poetry would be stripped of its civilizing power entirely. I have read that passage several times before and it never appeared to me in that light before.

What about Freud's idea of the sexual basis of neurosis and of everyday acts—do you think they were accepted with open arms?

Not at all, I answered; and in fact I believe that these ideas have already been re-repressed.

Yes, said the god, it seems to be the nature of the mind to sidestep the truth—for instance the truth that poetry is not art and does not civilize. But now we have said the magic word, we can proceed to your main question: what the poet gives the world.

I'm sorry; I am not ready. What is the magic word?

Magic, said the god. Magic itself.

Is this the disappointment you promised me?

Yes. I asked you to consider a singular fact, namely, that when any critic or esthetician or philosopher discusses poetry, he stops on the word *magic* and runs away with his tail between his legs. Their usual dodge is to translate *magic* into *prayer*. These writers say poetry is prayer; poetry is the Logos; poetry is a form of medicine; poetry is incantation. They will say anythink except that poetry is savage magic.

(I tried to think of some who did but could only call to mind a cynical writing of Peacock's.)

Peacock, said the god (who was reading my mind), wrote that cynical essay that stung his friend Shelley into writing the awful squeal called *The Defence of Poetry*. Yet Peacock knew that the poet is a semibarbarian in a civilized community. For this reason you do not teach him at school. Whereas your students fairly wallow in Shelley. Nor do you learn what Macaulay said: that as civilization advances, poetry almost necessarily declines, that as the philosophizing tendency progresses, generalization takes the place of particularization, and men make better theories and worse poems; that the Greeks fell into convulsions when they heard Homer, as did the Welsh and Germans when they heard their bards; and that, briefly, poetry works best in a dark age, among rude folk, and that the man who aspires to be a great poet in a civilized age must tear to pieces the web of his mind and become as a little child. Here, I think, you have an apt description of the modern poet with his psychoses, his treasons against society, and his egomania.

It seems to me, I said, that you side with the League for Sanity in Writing and other defenders of mediocrity.

On the contrary. At the moment I side with both Plato and Freud, not to mention Macaulay. We were saying that poetry does not exist among savages but that it is something else. Men have finally discovered that the cave paintings of extreme antiquity, those splendid depictions in the darkest recesses of the grottoes, were not meant to be admired or to delight the weary hunter (as Jackson Pollock delights the weary financier); they were meant to produce an effect upon the animal hunted. Nor were they what you call or miscall religious symbols; they were machines of control, a crude method for dominating nature.

Is poetry a crude method for dominating nature?

It is worth considering, the god answered. Soothsaying, bone-pointing, love philters, poison brews, Black Masses, are all quite at home in poetry and practically nowhere else! Poetry is physical. It is when it begins to talk about the ideal that it goes to pot. Good poetry is a love potion. I grant its higher forms of stimulation, yet it never gives up the lower. In your time poets have taken refuge in the dream; that is the modern cloak of respectability. Some of you are dishonest enough to claim that poetry is after all *only* an art, only a game. But it is a game in deadliest earnest to anyone who takes it as it is meant.

How is it meant?

It is meant to transform what it touches; it is meant to transform the reader. There is no need to deny it. The poet exists in that ancient state of mind in which everything is living and animate and subject to his spell. Naming is magic; naming, which some call metaphor, is a cage. A literal translation of Genesis says that the Lord brought to the human being each thing to see what he would *cry out* to it, and all that the human being cried out to each living thing, such was its name. This crying out of names is the power of poetry.

You make us medicine men. Druggists!

Precisely. Poems are patent remedies, many of them fakes, some of them poisons. But a surprising number have effected cures. Generally, of course, poets are trying to cure themselves.

Of what?

That depends on the case, he answered. The most common ailment is Love. Age is another. Disbelief is another, and so on. In your time the most common ailment is Reason. Poets have tried to cure themselves of consciousness and they even pride themselves on a certain degree of derangement. Hence their silly masks, as if the uniform of the violent ward will summon the Muse out of time and space.

Well, I said, we don't have much choice with the so-called rational element warring on men of the imagination.

Pure fiction, answered the god. The forms of modern poetic madness are quite boring. Someone once asked Jung what he thought of the Dadaists. He answered: they are too idiotic to be a decent form of insanity. In other words, my friend, your modern poets have been looking for the panacea when they should have been out picking herbs.

But you yourself have said that the community, the tribe, looks to us for inspiration.

That is true, he replied. Wizards are the most ancient class of men. Wizardry belongs to all times. Music, dancing, acting all have their origin in magic. This wizardry is sometimes frightening: it has driven people to mass hysteria, flagellation, and even suicide. People are aware of this. They expect you to build a bridge from the unconscious to the conscious. They want to come under your power. But they have withdrawn their faith from you.

What would they have, these people you mention?

They would have you perform the primary acts of language and leave off apologetics and sociology. They will permit incomprehensibility but not sleight-of-hand. They expect detachment and even secrecy, but they do not allow failure. Every sign, every mark of punctuation in every language is believed by them to be magical. Writing is taboo to most men, you know; they fear it and they put their trust in you. Man has not detached himself from writing magic. The people reject the word even in your so-called literate civilization. How long did it take for them to turn all your books back into pictures? Are you familiar with the final page of that endless story called *The Golden Bough?* Frazer says, "The dreams of magic may one day be the waking realities of science." What do you take that to mean?

It sounds like fuzzy sentimentality to me, I said. Frazer fell in love with his subject and hated to see it come to an end.

No, he meant that even science tends to drift back to the magical view, not that magic may one day compete with science.

That they will someday have a common ground?

Not really. Because magic is personal as science cannot be. It works well or badly according to the personality of the magician and his power over the audience. Poetry is discontinuous. You cannot take it out of context. Historians like to think of literary progress and literary criteria. They do not exist.

Good heavens! One might as well be a beachcomber if nothing is left of our work but personal will and idiosyncrasy.

All the same, the god went on, the criteria are imaginary and are invented after the fact. There is no universal poetry. Until a poet recognizes this simple fact he will not write his best verses. He will only mouth abstractions.

Then I see no reason to be a poet, I said, today or any other time.

If there is a reason, said the god playfully, I do not think it could have been stated before your time.

What on earth do you mean?

I mean the twentieth century. Literary philosophy you think is ancient and honorable. You teach the opinions of Plato and Aristotle, thinking you are beginning at the beginning when you are beginning at the end.

I am lost again. Plato and Aristotle are at the end of what?

When Plato wrote about poetry, the god said, he wrote as a man who had emerged from the darkness of time and had no wish to return man to the shadows. Hence his expulsion of poets from the perfect city. His reason won out over his admiration of the poet; he knew that poetry and civilization don't mix. Don't forget that the Athenians associated their play-going with Dionysian worship and did not allow the plays to be enacted except during festivals of the god. Plato and his famous student both searched for ways to justify the arts to man, knowing they could not erase them completely.

Do you mean they would have liked to?

Unquestionably. But what I wanted to say was that it is not until your time that man has been in a position to know what art is. Your time, because your contemporaries have rediscovered the jungle of art, the natural undergrowth of it. A century ago and all the centuries before, a man who hung an African mask on his living-room wall would have been sent to Bedlam. Today it is considered the mark of the gentleman.

What you call poetry (he went on) is a modern thing. What reason had Plato, himself one of the greatest writers and also an initiate in the mystery religions, to condemn the poet? Because he recognized in the poet a disguise of the old savagery. The poet is an interloper in civilization. Poetry falls between religion and science and has nowhere to go and nothing to do.

You are only trying to provoke me. You can't make me believe you agree with Voltaire that Shakespeare was a magical savage.

I happen to dislike Voltaire, said the god, but there you have it. Does not Voltaire represent what *you* call civilization?

Shakespeare, I said, is the touchstone of all poetry. Was he a magical savage?

He was the last of the natural poets, said the god. After him it is all increasingly artificial. John Donne is the first of the self-conscious moderns. In his time poetry flees from the stage as from the plague. Milton writes the last epic. The novel is invented; psychology begins in earnest. And poetry is left on the shelf. Am I not right? You must admit that for the past three hundred years poetry has done nothing but engage in a running battle with science. In your own time poets have even come out in the open and have done everything in their power to sabotage civilization.

But if we don't fight against pure consciousness we shall all be snuffed out like so many candles.

It will be your own doing if you are. Poetry has been interfering with the growing light of consciousness but it has only succeeded in drawing the curtains over its own windows. Your jealousy of science is matched only by your dishonest appropriation of religion and your unconvincing revival of antiquated metaphysics. Your interest in Lawrence, of course, reflects this desperation. Lawrence would have no science, no religion, except his own. I grant that times are hard for poets today. That is no reason for poets to run amuck. The trouble with you is that you pretend to be unemployed when you are really too peevish to sit down at your desks. You are so busy trying to impress society, so busy setting yourselves up as referees in the game of value judgments, so busy aping philosophers, so busy jabbing pins into scientists, that your whole lifetime output of verse is thinner than a seed catalogue.

Some of us are voluminous, I muttered.

Voluminous about what? Economic systems, astrological systems, anthropological systems, metaphysical systems, historical cycles, theology. . . .

But in this age, I spluttered, this beastly, standardized, reason-ridden, overpopulated, shallow . . .

My friend, said the god, it is not that your age is devoid of poetry or the need for it but that your poets have turned their backs on their own times. The poetry of your age is all war poetry; it has warred on your world. It is dying of peace. Are you historians? What business have you with dates and diagrams? Why must you change the Past, calling it a sacred cow, making it a Tradition? What business have you with the future of man, much less with my future?

You would leave us without human rights, without judgment. We have a social responsibility as well as the next man.

So much and no more, he answered. Your social responsibility will not make your poetry better or worse. And please do not think because you are a poet that your political opinions are better than those of a taxi driver.

Nor moral nor esthetic opinions? I asked weakly.

You force me to say that the moral opinions of poets are of little or no value. As for your esthetic opinions, even those are suspect.

I fail to see that we are good for anything. What is our magic for? What good are our myths if they exist only on paper for antiquarians to read?

Myths, said the god, with a snort. That is the prettiest piece of jargon you poets have come up with. After you lost the battle with consciousness, you sidled up to religion, and when you couldn't compete with religion you invented Myth. Myth would put you back on the map.

But myth is everything to us, I shouted. The beliefs and legends of every age are re-formed in our poems to give them new life and to give life its meaning for those who would live only as human animals. It is metaphysic in its purest form. It is the very protoplasm of poetry!

You sound like Shelley, the god said. (He made a move as if to stand up.)

Wait. You promised to tell me what the poet gives to the world. I don't see that you have.

It was clever of you poets, I must say, to switch your affections from the church to the university. Now you are playing second fiddle to sociologists you are practically respectable. Next you will be asking for a laboratory to work in. Instead of taking a walk you will go on a field trip. Myth, mythic form, spatial form, the Tradition, theories of the imagination, and all your hundred thousand Isms are so much bogus philosophy. You have succeeded in fooling yourselves and a few English professors and no one else. But you no longer deserve the name of poet. You pride yourselves on your little aberrations and your upset stomachs. When one of you dies of social life you shout Down with the Industrial Revolution. You look upon a healthy man as a leper. Neurosis, you sing, Mother of the Muses.

What does the poet give the world? I asked again, ignoring his insults.

The god looked at me over his spectacles.

One thing and one thing only. The present. Others give the past. Still others give the future. The poet gives this moment and that is all. Poetry is humanizing, not civilizing. It allows men to survive in the only world they know—the world of themselves. Not outside the law but in spite of it. Why is the law-breaker or the man of passion a hero? Because in him the drama of the human predicament comes to life. Why is Odysseus a hero? Because he is both loyal and treacherous. Why is Oedipus a hero? Because he committed instinctively the most terrible crime against nature. Why is Hamlet a hero? Because he is weak in his nobility. Every schoolboy knows Milton's sympathy for Satan, that prince of exiles upon whom you model yourself. But the perfect man or the perfect devil puts you to sleep. He has no reality, no presence.

Then the poet is humanity's apologist?

Please don't use words like that. The poet is not trying to prove anything. Beware of the poet who tries to bring you over to his side; he is a confidence man and power hungry. The next time you read a poet whose opinions disturb you, ask yourself whether he is on the side of his characters or on the side of the law—any law. If he is on the side of the law then you may call him an apologist and begin to doubt him as a poet.

I began to quote Hopkins: Wert Thou my enemy, O thou my friend.

Precisely. Or as Yeats put it: poetry is made out of the quarrel with oneself.

It is curious to hear you quote Yeats while I quote Hopkins.

But I like poetry, answered the god, I take it where I can find it. Religious poets may use flattery; unfortunately the most effective hymns are nearly always literary trash. The art that leads to consequences is bad art. Art comes back to the artist. *He* is the standard.

Surely you aren't saying that the artist considers himself a god?

Ah, you are close to a marvelous truth. Don't you think it splendid that almost nothing is known of Shakespeare and that scholars still wonder if there ever was such a person?

It is splendid. I hope and pray that no one will ever be able to solve the mystery.

Yes, said the god. It is a great tribute to him that he did not care to leave the world strewn with his laundry bills, love letters, and canceled checks. In your country, I understand, there are libraries devoted to such collections.

Then you are saying that the greatest poet not only did not consider himself a god but hardly even a man worthy of leaving his signature?

The artist who considers himself a god is either a madman or a criminal or both. The true poet is the village practitioner. The Greeks pictured the seer as blind; that was a way of putting it. In the end, the true poet is awed by what he sees and by what he has done. But he does not thank himself. He disappears, sometimes name and all, and sometimes his works. Do you know the highest compliment that can be paid the poet?

No, I asked eagerly, what is it?

For a man to travel thousands of miles to a strange land, to stand in a certain spot and say: So this is where Thomas Hardy got his hair cut.

I started to protest but it was too late. Someone came forward with a blackboard eraser which he held over my head. I shook hands with the god, who smiled and winked to the attendant. As the door closed quickly behind me I managed one more glimpse over my shoulder. The man in the chair—I still can't believe it—was D. H. Lawrence.

DATE DUE